LIFE / LINES

Theorizing Women's Autobiography

EDITED BY

BELLA BRODZKI

AND

CELESTE SCHENCK

Cornell University Press

ITHACA AND LONDON

Copyright © 1988 by Cornell University

"Non-Autobiographies of 'Privileged' Women: England and America," copyright © 1988 by Carolyn G. Heilbrun.

Mary Jean Green, "Structures of Liberation: Female Experience and Autobiographical Form in Quebec," first appeared in *Yale French Studies* 65 (1983). "The Other Voice: Autobiographies of Women Writers," by Mary G. Mason, is reprinted by permission of Princeton University Press from James Olney, ed., *Autobiography: Essays Theoretical and Critical,* copyright © 1980 by Princeton University Press. "Writing Fictions: Women's Autobiography in France," is reprinted from Nancy K. Miller, *Subject to Change: Reading Feminist Writing,* copyright © 1988 Columbia University Press. We gratefully acknowledge permission to reprint these essays. Photographs of Charlotte Salomon's paintings that accompany Mary Felstiner's essay are published courtesy of the Joods Historisch Museum, Amsterdam.

First published 1988 by Cornell University Press.

International Standard Book Number (cloth) 0–8014–2208–6
International Standard Book Number (paper) 0–8014–9520–2
Library of Congress Catalog Number 88-47718
Printed in the United States of America

*Librarians: Library of Congress cataloging information
appears on the last page of the book.*

*The paper in this book is acid-free and meets the guidelines for
permanence and durability of the Committee on Production Guidelines
for Book Longevity of the Council on Library Resources.*

FOR OUR STUDENTS
at Barnard College, Smith College,
Sarah Lawrence College

Contents

Foreword

GERMAINE BRÉE

Life/lines: the metaphor is ambiguous and invites us to ponder its relation to the subtitle. Lifelines, ropes thrown to ships or persons floundering in deep waters nearby; lifelines, ropes that link the deep-sea diver to the mother-ship; lifelines, more metaphorically, essential routes of communication between mutually dependent communities; but again, and differently, lifelines, those lines in the palm of the hand that in palmistry, dictionaries tell us, supposedly reveal facts about a person's life to the person who can decode the meaning.

Used here in relation to women's autobiographies, *Life/Lines* is more than a metaphor; it defines a critical space or scene and suggests a purpose. In the passage from life to writing, what strategies have women who "writ [their] own lives" adopted, when confronting their world, to free themselves from the images of role personae and desire encoded in the language? How have they moved beyond silence to speech, engendering through writing alternative motives and myths? And reached that authenticity in the weaving of a text which puts its mark on "literary" writing?

How can a collection of theoretical essays on a specifically designated topic "women's autobiography" justify the polyvalent metaphor? Academic women in Western countries are quite obviously an elite, but an elite just as prone as others to remain bound by its own cultural paradigms even as it challenges them. What all the definitions of lifelines have in common is the emphasis on interdependence and communication, a common code, that is, the lifeline available or, in the case of the palmist, the need to probe into the future (I am not, of course, putting forth a plea for palmistry). Of late, all our academic disciplines have been reexamining the theoretical assumptions on which their activities rest. Not least among these disciplines are the "social sciences" or, covering a broader range, what we sometimes call the "human sciences" or, indeed, the humanities. It so happened that the vigorous, irresistible expansion of women's studies coincided in chronological time with that reassessment, was at its very crux, and sometimes spoke unknowingly in two languages: the language of the social sciences, of "scientific," "objective" research based on factual data, questionnaires, and statistics; and the languages of linguistic analysis and psychoanalysis, sometimes conjoined, sometimes at odds, which raised questions concerning the inscription of the subject in speech and writing. Autobiographies, newly prominent as "texts," became central in wide-ranging critical and theoretical debate on the status of self, the nature of self-representation, of language. The serenely "male" approach to those questions has by now been disrupted by the careful attention with which autobiographies by women are being approached, the same methods yielding more complex perspectives.

Though those engaged in the social sciences became increasingly aware of the limitations of their methodology, and those in the humanities, of the complex interplay of social structure and social content in the multiple network of relations through which the "I" must compose a "self," a sometimes acrimonious polemic divided the two modes of investigation. It was, and sometimes still is, particularly articulate among feminist scholars. Essentially concerning women and more dramatically than in regard to men, the text defining the social status of women and the more elusive text of individual women in which language, desire, and situation play their games seemed irreconcilable. In the first "modern" form of this text, Western feminists understandably thought in terms of duality, of confrontation and exclusivities: male versus female; heterosexual versus homosexual; independence versus the constraints of family; passive acquiescence to society's dictates versus revolt and militant activism.

In the meantime, so complex and wide-ranging has become our apprehension of the feminine presence and action in the world, past and present, that we are no longer as prone to think in absolutes. At the outset it was, no doubt, essential in our Western world to speak in terms of pure "gender"—her/story, his/story—but as became clear, doing so boxed Western women into the basic habits of thought of a culture in which they did not entirely share. It closed the way—difficult to be sure—to their recognition and elaboration of a language absent from the normative male language, yet operative within the social group through which women could speak their difference and sameness as individuals within shifting cultural configurations. In this context, approaches to the specific question of the feminine subject would of necessity be vitiated if they did not take into account the radical change toward language that informs all fields of inquiry today, without some sense of which "consciousness-raising" initiatives, necessary as they are, can only be strictly limited. Thence came the explosion of abstract theorization, inspired in part by European philosophies, to which more directly committed feminist activists so strenuously objected. Here again, a critical reappraisal has been taking place.

This anthology proposes to reexamine in a careful assemblage of texts some of the assumptions of feminist theory concerning women's autobiographies, clarifying and questioning extant systems of valuation of the autobiographical text. The provenance of the texts differs widely in time, geographical location, and social positioning. The contributors and the editors who selected the texts they present are all among those who have given women's studies academic credibility. They bring together the two main trends in an effort to open up a rich perspective where "difference" and plurality do not erupt in the either/or dichotomies of uncritical argumentation and common logic.

We are more fully aware today of the difficult dialectic and imbalance between the descriptive and the conceptualized which define the dynamics of the mind, and the realm of writing itself. And it is writing that provides a space within which the "self" may best appear in its complexity, conscious and unconscious of its "difference" and similarities with respect to the characteristics of a given culture. The texts examined in *Life/Lines* are rich in the wide diversity of routes by which women, in vastly different circumstances, have asserted their place as active subjects challenging the oppressive representation and actions of powerful hierarchies, not only in regard to their individual situation but in terms of a social group. True, there are the limitations and self-delusions, the inevitable strategies and complicities out of which particular individuals make their way to open up that culture which has bent their language and mental perspectives to new shapes.

Life/Lines addresses these issues at a moment of particular significance for women's studies, which, like comparative studies to which they are closely bound, oscillate between the lure of infinite dilution and the temptation of rigorous compartmentalization. The issue, as conceived by its two editors, is to explore the many "lines" women have devised to speak of themselves for themselves and for their readers, going beyond the constraints of traditional boundaries. It eschews the temptation to elude questions of the specificity of the self, of its "presence" in the writing, its informing strategies. These are inseparable from our further understanding of the genre and its creative potential. Theories then become modes of clarification open to revision, dynamic elements in shaping our awareness of the significance and richness of the genre.

Acknowledgments

Life/Lines has been a collaboration in every sense of that critical word. We particularly thank Bernhard Kendler of Cornell University Press for vital encouragement in the very earliest stages of this project and for substantial editorial advice at every single step of its preparation. In final form, *Life/Lines* owes much to the provocative, intelligent, and, as it turned out, usefully contradictory reports of the press's two anonymous readers. Very special thanks go to our contributors for helping us realize our editorial conception by speaking to *and* against its metaphors and categories in their own individual essays.

Marilyn Yalom and the Center for Research on Women at Stanford University provided an important forum for gender and autobiography at their 1986 conference and subsequently gave us much encouragement and help with the collection. Arnold Krupat provided generous and incisive criticism on two chapters. Jill Harris did more than type, proofread, and index the manuscript with professional skill; she also provided significant editorial assistance. Faculty secretary Janet Held and research assistant Pia Barone at Sarah Lawrence College, and English Department secretary Connie Budelis, research assistant Deborah DeRosa, and Office Services at Barnard College provided expert and timely clerical aid.

We also gratefully acknowledge the support of family and friends who threw us lifelines on both crucial and unexpected occasions during the book's evolution.

B.B. AND C.M.S.

Life/Lines

Introduction

BELLA BRODZKI AND
CELESTE SCHENCK

To the uncritical eye, autobiography presents as untroubled a reflection of identity as the surface of a mirror can provide. The corresponding assumption has been that autobiography is a transparency through which we perceive the life, unmediated and undistorted. In fact, the debate between art and life has raged in all areas of literary discourse, especially of late in criticism of autobiography, in which genre the relationship between literature and life has turned out to be most problematic. The (masculine) tradition of autobiography beginning with Augustine had taken as its first premise the mirroring capacity of the autobiographer: *his* universality, *his* representativeness, *his* role as spokesman for the community. But only a critical ideology that reifies a unified, transcendent self can expect to see in the mirror of autobiography a self whose depths can be plumbed, whose heart can be discovered, and whose essence can be definitively known. No mirror of *her* era, the female autobiographer takes as a given that selfhood is mediated; her invisibility results from her lack of a tradition, her marginality in male-dominated culture, her fragmentation—social and political as well as psychic. At both extremes of subjectivity and publicity, the female autobiographer has lacked the sense of radical individuality, duplicitous but useful, that empowered Augustine and Henry Adams to write their representative lives large. A feminist reconstruction of women's autobiography, against the backdrop of twentieth-century philosophical questioning of the self, can begin to use autobiography for the fertile ground it is.[1] Autobiography localizes the very program of much feminist theory—

1. Ostensibly lacking cultural overlay, the genre was relegated until recently to inferior critical status, and criticism of autobiography has accordingly remained preoccupied with generic definitions. James Olney's groundbreaking critical and editorial work on the genre

I

problematic status of self

the reclaiming of the female subject—even as it foregrounds the central
issue of contemporary critical thought—the problematic status of the
self.

Autobiography as Mirror

The classic stance of the male autobiographer is summed up by a
famous characterization of Henry Adams as a "representative of the
time, a mirror of his era." The purpose of this book is to demonstrate
that such an implicit attitude toward the masculine representative self is
reflective as well of a generic exclusivity in the critical treatment of
autobiography, rendering this model inadequate for a theory of wom-
en's autobiography. We propose instead a theoretical and comparative
approach to women's autobiographical writing which aims both at
modifying inherited critical definitions and at enlarging the canon. By
denying women writers a place in the historical development of autobiography, critical work in the field, for all its insistence on mirroring
universals, has presented a distorted reflection of the history of the
autobiographical genre.

The masculine autobiography, from the definitive spiritual autobiography of Saint Augustine to Roland Barthes's fragmented "family
romance," *Roland Barthes par Roland Barthes,* assumes the conflation of
masculinity and humanity, canonizing the masculine representative self
of both writer and reader. In Augustine's *Confessions,* the autobiographer explicitly identifies with the male divinity, albeit a bit ambiva-
lently, in order to claim for himself as a convert the highest place accorded a man on the human-to-divine continuum; the certainty with
which the narrator speaks results from his position in the text as the
literary analogue to God. An *imitatio Christi,* the *Confessions* both cru-
cifies and redeems the autobiographer. In contradistinction, a sister spiritual autobiographer, Margery Kempe, in *The Book of Margery Kempe,*
might claim a number of relationships with the deity, but historical
circumstance (and theology) would never allow her to posit a relation of
analogue.

The very authority of masculine autobiography derives from the as-

---

began in 1966. His history of criticism of autobiography forms the first chapter of the collection he edited, *Autobiography: Essays Theoretical and Critical* (Princeton: Princeton University
Press, 1980). Domna Stanton rehearses the approaches of French theory to the autobiographical mode in her "Autogynography: Is the Subject Different?" the introductory chapter of *The
Female Autograph* (New York: New York Literary Forum, 1984), citing the feminist work on
the genre to that date.

sumption held by both author and reader that the life being written/read is an exemplary one. "But many people who know me, and others who do not know me but have heard of me or read my books," writes Augustine, "wish to hear what I am now, at this moment, as I set down my confessions."[2] Jean-Jacques Rousseau romanticizes Augustine's project, but in a secular key claims no less than uniqueness for his life narration of human fallibility, which, in its induplicability, remains both generic and universal. The paradigmatic act of confession, for Rousseau, implies that he already has an audience:

> I have resolved on an enterprise which has no precedent and which, once complete, will have no imitator. . . . I am made unlike anyone I have ever met: I will even venture to say that I am like no one in the whole world. I may be no better, but at least I am different. Whether Nature did well or ill in breaking the mold in which she formed me, is a question which can only be resolved after the reading of my book. . . . So let the numberless legion of my fellow men gather round me, and hear my confessions. Let them groan at my depravities and blush at my misdeeds. But let each one of them reveal his heart at the foot of Thy throne with equal sincerity, and may any man who dares, say "I was a better man than he."[3]

Perhaps Henry Adams, more than any other autobiographer, felt himself to be the fulcrum of historical and cultural forces, an elect representative of his unique place in his family's and the nation's history. His own brother felt him to be "capable of teaching the people and becoming a light to the nations."[4] Even as a boy of twelve, on the famous visit to Washington, he could afford to be singularly unimpressed with the White House: "The boy half thought he owned it, and took for granted that he should some day live in it. He felt no sensation whatever before Presidents. A President was a matter of course in every respectable family; he had two in his own."[5] A man whose birth entitled him to such cavalier dismissal of presidential prestige was undoubtedly secure in his own. Adams's sense of himself as a spokesman comes through in *The Education*—narrated in an ostensibly objective third-person voice— even as he seems to undercut the whole notion of a man's suitedness to his times in his pessimistic, iconoclastic, even apocalyptic reading of contemporary American history. Not unlike Augustine, Adams

2. Augustine, *Confessions*, trans. R. S. Pine-Coffin (New York: Penguin, 1961), p. 209.

3. Jean-Jacques Rousseau, *The Confessions*, trans. J. M. Cohen (New York: Penguin, 1953), p. 17.

4. Ernest Samuels, *The Young Henry Adams* (Cambridge: Harvard University Press, 1948), p. 58.

5. Henry Adams, *The Education of Henry Adams: An Autobiography* (Boston: Houghton Mifflin, 1918), p. 46, hereafter cited in the text.

believed that by discovering the meaning of his own life, he could offer a model of order to the world.[6] Not unlike Rousseau, he exposed his own shortcomings, deplored the failure of his education, and mourned the passing of a more innocent age. Not unlike Whitman, whose *Song of Myself* is poetic autobiography in the fully American grain, he placed himself at the center of his own cosmology. In the face of progress, technology, and an array of contradictory and confusing historical forces, Adams determined that "if he was to reduce all these forces to a common value, common value could have no measure but that of their attraction on his own mind" (p. 383). With Augustine, Rousseau, and Whitman, Adams affirms the Western, transcendent, and masculine norm of autobiographical selfhood.

Even when autobiography spills over into other genres, it still advertises the male representative self. Whitman's *Song of Myself* claims the same centrality to American experience as another of Adams's models, the more orthodox *Autobiography of Benjamin Franklin.* Whitman reigns over the sphere of nature as Franklin rules over that of culture, each defining as distinctly American what he singularly represents. *Song of Myself* begins with an assumption that Whitman speaks for every American:

> I celebrate myself,
> And what I assume you shall assume,
> For every atom belonging to me as good belongs to you.[7]

The providential voice of Whitman's originary "I," imperious but benign, threatens to displace even Rousseau's grand self-claims, founding in the process of articulation, writes Albert Stone, a "democratic" tradition of American autobiography which pretends to mirror "the social, historical and aesthetic varieties of our national experience."[8] Norman Mailer's performance in the aptly titled *Advertisements for Myself* is a pastiche of a life history which weds self-celebration and American literary history in a series of imaginary prefaces to Mailer's own work. The generic autobiographical subject is still presidentially minded in this passage from Mailer's "First Advertisement":

> Like many another vain, empty, and bullying body of our time, I have been running for President these last ten years in the privacy of my mind,

6. Robert Sayre, *The Examined Self* (Princeton: Princeton University Press, 1964), p. 91.

7. Walt Whitman, *Complete Poetry and Collected Prose,* ed. Justin Kaplan (New York: Library of the Americas, 1982), p. 27.

8. Albert E. Stone, *The American Autobiography: A Collection of Critical Essays* (Englewood Cliffs, N.J.: Prentice-Hall, 1981), p. 2.

and it occurs to me that I am less close now than when I began. Defeat has left my nature divided, my sense of timing is eccentric, and I contain within myself the bitter exhaustions of an old man, and the cocky arguments of a bright boy. So I am everything but my proper age of thirty-six, and anger has brought me to the edge of the brutal. In sitting down to write a sermon for this collection, I find arrogance in much of my mood. It cannot be helped. The sour truth is that I am imprisoned with a perception which will settle for nothing less than making a revolution in the consciousness of our time.[9]

All these representative masculine autobiographies rest upon the Western ideal of an essential and inviolable self, which, like its fictional equivalent, character, unifies and propels the narrative. Paul Jay, in a recent, judiciously Derridean reading of self-reflexive literary forms, gives an incisive history of (masculine) autobiographical form. He begins with Augustine's reflection and reification of "a particular philosophical (or theological) conception of the subject" and then traces the undermining of this ideology in twentieth-century works "whose preoccupations are more philosophical than biographical and whose subjects are represented in fragmented discursive forms that seek by their fragmentation to mirror what modern criticism has come to call . . . 'the divided self.'"[10] According to Jay, not until Roland Barthes does the male autobiographer in quest of self-representation patently acknowledge the distortion as well as the allure of the mirror. Jay traces this deconstructive turn in the fortunes of the masculine autobiography in texts from Carlyle to Wordsworth to Eliot, reading Barthes's text as a first deliberate undoing of time, continuity, coherence, and selfhood.

In spite of the symmetry of its title, *Roland Barthes par Roland Barthes* presents the autobiographical relation between author and subject, text and life, as purely textual, noncoincident, and open-ended. This relation, neither existential nor mimetic, constituted only by the act of nomination, is posited through the very practice of writing. Indeed, the "subject" of his autobiography is not the self but writing itself. "I do not say: 'I am going to describe myself,' but: 'I am writing a text, and I call it R.B.'"[11] In a text that is euphorically self-aware, joyfully contradictory, and full of digressive intensity, what is absent is any pretense toward discovering, capturing, or restoring an ego, because "the subject is merely an effect of language" (p. 79). This ego, whose domain is dis-

9. Norman Mailer, *Advertisements for Myself* (New York: G. P. Putnam's Sons, 1959), p. 17.

10. Paul Jay, *Being in the Text* (Ithaca: Cornell University Press, 1984), pp. 27, 37.

11. Roland Barthes, *Roland Barthes par Roland Barthes,* trans. Richard Howard (New York: Hill and Wang, 1977), p. 56, hereafter cited in the text.

course and desire, does not seek to render interior experience in representable terms, because "in the field of the subject, there is no referent" (p. 56). This book of the self is therefore provisional, undecidable, and dispersive. Barthes's radical aesthetics has as its only ideological commitment the proliferation of polygamous meanings. When Barthes says, "I myself am my own symbol, I am the story which happens to me: freewheeling in language, I have nothing to compare myself to" (p. 56), Rousseau, of course, ironically reverberates. Here, however, the highest law is not sincerity or authenticity or truth but consciousness deriving a remarkably ungendered sensual pleasure from the exercise of its own intelligence.

We are not far from our female subject at this confluence of recent theoretical interest in autobiography and radical autobiographical practice. What Barthes's project arguably offers to a feminist reading of autobiography is a model of nonrepresentative, dispersed, displaced subjectivity. Barthes's subversive inside attack on the autobiographical genre and the self that putatively supports it, his eroticizing of the mode in an unmasculine but otherwise unspecified way, can be said to have something in common with the strategies of some women autobiographers dating as far back as the fifteenth century. Yet his experimental practice still caps "the great tradition" of Jay's book—a lineage astonishingly devoid, even in the hands of a self-conscious critic, of female autobiographers, critics, even readers. "The variety of textual strategies" Jay attributes to Barthes and his (masculine) predecessors "testifies both to the writer's resiliency in the face of such a confrontation and to language's uncanny ability to lure *him* again and again into its web."[12] The omission of women from deconstructive treatments of autobiography has delayed critical dialogue on the genre between feminist criticism and deconstruction. For example, Candace Lang's review of autobiographical theory, provocatively deconstructing the work of traditional critics James Olney and William Spengemann, does not consider the case of women's autobiography, does not even take up the crucial issue of gender in its deconstructive polemic against the romanticization of the subject.[13] What feminist criticism could add to Lang's already extended perspective is that women are equally implicated in and adept at the "process of collaboration between an individual consciousness and that Other which permeates it" (Lang, p. 16). If female subjectivity

12. Jay, p. 183, emphasis added.
13. Candace Lang, "Autobiography in the Aftermath of Romanticism," *Diacritics* 12 (Winter 1982): 2–16, a review of Olney's collection and William Spengemann, *The Forms of Autobiography: Episodes in the History of a Literary Genre* (New Haven: Yale University Press, 1980). Domna Stanton's anthology is the notable exception.

could be restored without romanticization, then feminist criticism might benefit from engagement with deconstructive practice, and deconstruction conversely, might be challenged anew to address the imperative of gender. Gender as a cultural construction cannot be evaded by any critical perspective if a *female* autobiographical subject is to be recuperatively canvassed at this historical moment.

Framing the Subject

The archetypal female prop of the mirror has been used variously in relation to woman, and almost always *against* her. For example, it has historically served to imprison femininity: for a woman to be reassured of her "looks" is to know she will be looked at. But beyond a woman's (always mediated) subjective relationship to her hand mirror is a range of ways in which she herself serves as mirror. Virginia Woolf has noted that women are "looking glasses" themselves, "reflecting the figure of man at twice its natural size."[14] Sandra Gilbert and Susan Gubar in their analysis of "Snow White" argue that women have been fixed in the distorting mirror of the male-inscribed literary work, the "glass coffin of the male-authored text."[15] And as recent feminist theoreticians of film phrase it, women have been framed by the male gaze. We propose a feminist reappropriation of the mirror, a framing actively understood, anticipated by the French psychoanalyst Luce Irigaray. Irigaray uses the (image of the) speculum, the gynecological instrument that seeks both to reflect and to penetrate feminine interiority, as the structuring device for her deconstruction of Western philosophical discourse since Plato.[16] After Irigaray, the question remains: how have *women* articulated their own experience, shaped their own texts artistically, met their own reflections in the problematic mirror of autobiography?

We begin with readings of two female autobiographies, central in their different ways to what might be termed a female autobiographical tradition. Margaret Cavendish seems at a first reading to be virtually framed by the conditions of her femininity, social class, and marital status. She is the ultimate centerfold, embedded—when her text is pub-

14. Virginia Woolf, *A Room of One's Own* (1929; rpt., New York: Harcourt, Brace and World, 1957), p. 35.

15. Sandra M. Gilbert and Susan Gubar, *The Madwoman in the Attic: The Woman Writer and the Nineteenth-Century Literary Imagination* (New Haven: Yale University Press, 1979), pp. 36–44.

16. *Speculum of the Other Woman*, trans. Gillian C. Gill (Ithaca: Cornell University Press, 1985). A book-length study of women, mirrors, and identity, by Jenijoy La Belle is *Herself Beheld* (Ithaca: Cornell University Press, 1988).

lished—within the pages of her husband's biography. Cavendish's claims are above all "modest" (her word). She insists that her breeding was accomplished in full accordance with her birth and the nature of her sex: "virtuously, modestly, civilly, honourably, and on honest principles."[17] She also distinguishes between her lord's self-re-creation by means of his pen and her own scribbling, between his wit and her words. This "delineation of identity by alterity," as Mary G. Mason defines it in the first essay of this volume, this self-definition in relation to significant others, is the most pervasive characteristic of the female autobiography.

But Cavendish's modestly framed text has a compelling subtext—as she herself puts it, "but however that little wit I have, it delights me to scribble it out, and disperse it about" (p. 206). And this disseminative exuberance defies socially constructed definitions of appropriate female behavior. The criticisms she defends herself against, when inventoried, amount to a profile of Renaissance femininity: how much she talks, how much she eats, how fast she walks, how often she dances, travels, writes, how flamboyantly she dresses, how much she reads. Shot through with qualifications—protestations as to her modesty, insistence upon her dependence on her husband—her autobiography is nonetheless an exploration of self-inscription and subjectivity.

> For I think it no crime to wish myself the exactest of Nature's works, my thred of life the longest, my chain of destinie the strongest, my mind the peaceablest; my life the pleasantest, my death the easiest, and the greatest saint in Heaven. Also to do my endeavour, so far as honour and honesty doth allow of, to be the highest on Fortune's Wheele, and to hold the wheele, from turning if I can; . . . But I fear my ambition inclines to vain-glory, for I am very ambitious; yet, 'tis neither for beauty, wit, titles, wealth, or power, but as they are steps to raise me to fame's tower, which is to live by fame's remembrance on after-ages. (P. 211)

As Domna Stanton glosses the much-quoted peroration of Cavendish's autobiography, subjectivity predates relation: "The 'I' asserted that she

17. Margaret Cavendish, duchess of Newcastle, *The True Relation of My Birth and Breeding*, in *The Life of William Cavendish (Duke of Newcastle)*, ed. C. H. Fine (London: George Routledge and Sons, n.d.), p. 188, hereafter cited in the text. Cavendish's autobigraphical project has an unlikely counterpart in John Stuart Mill's *Autobiography*, another renowned male "mirror of [its] era," which overtly refuses the totalizing representativeness of our other male examples above. A classic autobiography, Mill's book nonetheless contains inset chapters and a final chapter devoted to his dead wife, Harriet Taylor, whom he credits not only with opening his eyes to the injustice of sexual inequality but also with having virtually formulated his theory of the subjection of women.

'writ her own life' 'for [her] own sake,' out of the need to differentiate
the self from others, only to show that its constitution and individuation
predicated reference and relatedness to others."[18] Cavendish's autobiography is the discourse of a detailed, rich, textured, female self,
which fears immolation under her social identification as My Lord's
second wife: "I might easily have been mistaken," she concludes poignantly, "especially if I should dye and My Lord marry again" (p. 213).
Happy as she is to be the real duke of Newcastle's wife, she refuses
designation as his property. Within the text, she shuttles between objective representation of her husband and the Renaissance prescription for
ideal femininity. By inhabiting the space between these two poles, she
manages to refuse inscription into either. Her deft evasions and purpo-
sive self-contradictions serve to detail a vivid and protean personality, to
render a self that is impossible to fix or to name. She understands that
identity is dangerous when stabilized. Cavendish succeeds in being remembered, the express goal of her text, precisely because she finds a
way to make displacement work for her. Reading women's autobiographies back into "the great tradition," shouldn't we view Margaret Cavendish's rhetorical strategy as a precursor of Roland Barthes's?

Gertrude Stein, at the other end of the female tradition in autobiography, also poses as a biographer in order to write her own autobiography; her goal, too, is to be remembered. But Stein specifies, in a way
Cavendish cannot, that she wants to be immortalized as a genius. Like
Cavendish, Stein knows what modern theorists have come to tell us
about autobiography: that for women it is relational; that for modernists
it is defamiliarized; that for theorists it is impossible to capture the self
otherwise than in pieces, fragments, refractions. *The Autobiography of
Alice B. Toklas* is a mediated text as well, but in this case, Stein's verbal
self-portrait is framed in the autobiographical narrative of her devoted
secretary-lover, in a transgressive generic practice foregrounded by the
title page. Stein contrives to write her own autobiography and call
herself a genius by putting words into Toklas's mouth. "I may say,"
says Alice at the outset,

> that only three times in my life have I met a genius and each time a bell
> within me rang and I was not mistaken, and I may say in each case it was
> before there was any general recognition of the quality of genius within
> them. The three geniuses of whom I wish to speak are Gertrude Stein,
> Pablo Picasso and Alfred Whitehead. I have met many important people, I
> have met several great people but I have only known three first class

18. Stanton, p. 16, hereafter cited in the text.

geniuses and in each case on sight within me something rang. . . . In this way my new full life began.[19]

This opening portrait of Stein is the first of many in the text, all paradigmatic of Stein's theory that selves cannot be interiorly known but only represented visually and textually.

Stein's ventriloquism gives her access to the same space filled by Cavendish's apologetic voice some four hundred years earlier. This strategy of impersonation allows her to be neither Alice B. Toklas nor a self (with essence and duration) herself. As effectively as Cavendish, Stein inhabits a textual/sexual space between the covers of her book in a way that deliberately prevents inscription into anything like traditional selfhood. What, in fact, does Stein, as self-portraitist, actually frame? To begin with, her radical textual practice defines itself in the very terms of modern art: subjectivity cannot be totalized and regularized; it does not move fluidly through time; the surface of the thing can be approached in successive images, or still lifes, which are more disjunctive than synergistic.[20] Along with the avant-garde of her day, what Stein frames, in fact, is a *refusal* to frame identity, conventionally and mimetically understood. "After all," she writes, "the human being essentially is not paintable" (p. 119). But all its protestations to the contrary, *The Autobiography* retains what might be viewed as a conventional autobiographical strategy, the display of ego and the remarkably "unfeminine" assumption of authorial power and voice. Gertrude and Alice emerge here both as indiscernible, interwoven stylistic effects *and* as distinct personalities.

But even more important, the reader of autobiography is invited to consider how the radicalism of Stein's achievement, some fifty years before Barthes's own, alters the configuration of the autobiographical canon. He still, after all, writes on himself, however he construes that chameleon-like and uncapturable substance; she, in what might be viewed as the farthest reach to date of autobiography as genre, pushes self-portraiture to an undreamt-of place by writing of herself in another

19. Gertrude Stein, *The Autobiography of Alice B. Toklas* (New York: Vintage, 1933), p. 5, hereafter cited in the text.

20. A number of feminist critics have linked Stein's practice to that of the avant-garde, and some have even suggested her practice anticipates that of deconstruction. See James Breslin, "Gertrude Stein and the Problems of Autobiography," in *Women's Autobiography: Essays in Criticism,* ed. Estelle C. Jelinek (Bloomington: Indiana University Press, 1980), pp. 149–62; Marianne DeKoven, *A Different Language: Gertrude Stein's Experimental Writing* (Madison: University of Wisconsin Press, 1983); and Shari Benstock, "Beyond the Reaches of Feminist Criticism: A Letter from Paris," *Tulsa Studies in Women's Literature* 3 (Spring/Fall 1984): 5–27.

woman's voice. More deliberately even than Cavendish, a woman auto-biographer once again uses displacement strategically. *The Autobiogra-phy*, finally, is too conspicuously absent in Paul Jay's history of deconstructive challenges to the mode. Is it only because she is a woman that she is deprived of her rightful place in a "tradition" of ruptures in autobiographical practice? Is it only because Gertrude Stein is a woman that Michael Sprinker does not use her as a point of reference in "The End of Autobiography"?[21]

We close with Stein because her text is the ultimate female auto-biography—with a difference. It is, of course, radically relational in its ironic confusion of the textual identities of Toklas and Stein. Noëlle Batt points out that the title itself is a paradox, an impossibility, "une coexis-tence abusive": readers expecting a traditional autobiography feel com-pelled to choose between the biography of Toklas and the autobiogra-phy of Stein.[22] Reading, in fact, requires no such choice: the blurred boundaries between Stein and Toklas as the autobiography constitutes them creates a textual third place from which "she" speaks. Where Cavendish made necessity into a virtue, Stein aligns narrative practice with a modernist suspicion of identity. The pretext (we are told coyly on the last page) and pretense, however seriously one wants to take them, are that Gertrude took things in hand when Alice—"a pretty good housekeeper and a pretty good gardener and a pretty good needle-woman and a pretty good secretary and a pretty good editor and a pretty good vet for dogs"—found it hard to find time to be "a pretty good author" of "My Life With The Great" as well (p. 252). This elaboration of domestic politics governs autobiographical practice here as thoroughly as it directed Cavendish's inset autobiography. Both au-thors—in different periods, with different motivations, with some of the same results—find a way to challenge inscription into conventional feminine identity and autobiographical representative selfhood while exploiting the textual ambiguity of their partnership with significant others. Being *between two covers* with somebody else ultimately replaces singularity with alterity in a way that is dramatically female,[23] provides a mode of resisting reification and essentialism, and most important, allows for more radical experimentation in autobiographical form than recent critics, notably Jay and Sprinker, have been willing to attribute to women writers. The local examples of Cavendish and Stein—neither is

21. Michael Sprinker, "The End of Autobiography," in *Autobiography*, pp. 321–42.
22. Noëlle Batt, "Le Cas particulier de l'autobiographie d'Alice Toklas: *The Autobiography of Alice B. Toklas* by Gertrude Stein," *Recherches Anglaises et Américaines* 15 (1982): 128.
23. See Mary G. Mason on relationality and Doris Sommer on metonymy, this volume.

"a mirror of [her] era"—among the many documented in this collection, call for a reframing of autobiographical theory as produced by the Western, masculine canon.

Life/Lines

Criticism of women's autobiography over the last five years reflects important shifts in feminist argument and commitment. This book was conceived as a complement to Estelle Jelinek's groundbreaking *Women's Autobiography* and Domna Stanton's recently reissued *The Female Autograph*.[24] With Jelinek and Stanton, we share an interest in addressing the problematic status of women's life writing, but each anthology reveals a different agenda, corresponding to a feminist discussion that has evolved since the late seventies over the nature of the female self. Jelinek's book is the first to postulate the existence of a distinct female tradition in autobiography. "The cross-section of the criticism being written today," which she collected in 1980, amounted largely to Anglo-American criticism on English or American autobiographies (p. ix). The essays in her collection survey the terrain of that undiscovered country, but they do so without providing the metacommentary that would prepare for a theory of women's autobiography. Stanton's *The Female Autograph* investigates, some five years later, women's nontraditional literature in a pluralistic, comparative, and highly theoretical manner. Her strategy is to "undermine the generic boundaries that have plagued studies of autobiography, often confining them to lists of unconvincing criteria for distinguishing various modes of self-inscription" by assembling a "collage of pieces" from different fields, modes, cultures and eras (p. vii). Her retrospective assessment of her own collection, however, is that "issues of class, race and sexual orientation have only been sporadically addressed" (p. xi). We concur with Stanton's sense of the lack of strong theoretical scholarship on women's autobiography and the need for revising "existing discursive and ideological boundaries" and take seriously her call for a "more probing analysis of (possible) differences of female autographic writing" and for "a heuristic search" for a tradition of women's autobiography. But we intend, for starters, to restore the *bio* Stanton excised from autobiography. We strongly believe that the duplicitous and complicitous relationship of "life" and "art" in

24. For a theorizing of the female subject see Nancy K. Miller, "Arachnologies," in *The Poetics of Gender,* ed. Nancy K. Miller (New York: Columbia University Press, 1986), pp. 271–95; and Teresa de Lauretis, *Alice Doesn't: Feminism, Semiotics, Cinema* (Bloomington: Indiana University Press, 1984).

autobiographical modes is precisely the point. To elide it in the name of eliminating the "facile assumption of referentiality" is dangerously to ignore the crucial referentiality of class, race, and sexual orientation; it is to beg serious political questions. What we suggest is no naive replacement of the text with life, a confusion that has tended to trouble both feminist criticism and criticism of autobiography more generally. The dialectic can be retained along with strong theoretical discourse. Our title, *Life/Lines: Theorizing Women's Autobiography,* aims at safeguarding that tension.

Revisionist in intention, our book gathers a range of widely varying feminist critical perspectives on texts medieval to modern. That is, we have invited theory ranging from ethnographic to psychoanalytic, from Marxist to formal, from generic to cultural and historicist, as well as the rich proliferation of French critical approaches. Additionally, our book strives to name the "ghostly absence" on the library shelf of criticism on women's autobiography, which Stanton calls a form of "collective repression" (p. 6). We view our book, paired with hers, as a form of collective restoration, and we hope collections that follow ours will be able to represent an even greater ethnic diversity than we have been able to offer here: Asian women's autobiographies, despite our strenuous efforts to include them, remain underrepresented in our collection. The first section, "Positioning the Female Autobiographical Subject," addresses the problem of the female subject from perspectives as widely varied as English medieval and Renaissance (Mason), nineteenth- and twentieth-century French (Miller), "privileged" English and American (Heilbrun), and lesbian (Martin). "Colonized Subjects and Subversive Discourses" takes its examples from the collective forms of Latin-American testimonials (Sommer), Native American women's stories as distorted by ethnographers (Carr), a turn-of-the-century Egyptian feminist (Ahmed), Afro-American life narratives (McKay), and Quebecois "récits retrospectifs en prose" (Green). Part III, "Double Messages: Maternal Legacies/Mythographies," addresses Margaret Oliphant's revisions of reproductive imagery in her autobiographical self-conception (Reimer), the generative maternal intertext in Audre Lorde's "biomythography" (Raynaud), the ambiguous maternal legacy of language in Nathalie Sarraute and Christa Wolf (Brodzki), and mother lack in multicultural autobiographical accounts sited in Algeria and Mauritius (Lionnet). The last section, "De-Limiting Genre: Other Autobiographical Acts," reaches for new critical configurations: the chiasmus between women's poetry and autobiography and its implications for genre theory (Schenck), displacement of autobiography by epistolary traditions at the turn of the eighteenth century in Germany (Goodman), reconstruction of the multigeneric autobiography of a Jewish woman in occupied France (Felstiner), and cinematic representation of women's subjectivity (Portuges). The volume as a whole aims at generating new metaphors for the self-projection of the woman autobiographer.

At this felicitous juncture of feminism, psychoanalysis, and modern critical theory, the case of autobiography raises the essential problem in contemporary feminist theory and praxis: the imperative situating of the female subject in spite of the postmodernist campaign against the sovereign self.[25] Thus the critical and political stance of *Life/Lines* is to maintain female specificity and articulate female subjectivity without either falling back into the essentialism that has plagued both American feminist criticism and *écriture féminine* in France or retreating into a pure textuality that consigns woman—in a new mode to be sure—to an unrecoverable absence. Modern theory, of course, warns of the dangers of positing selfhood, indeed eulogizes and then celebrates the death of the author.[26] But a feminist agenda cannot include further or repeated marginalization of female selfhood without betraying its own political program. Instead, the feminist enterprise should, as we see it, take its cue from contemporary theory and not promote a simplistic identification with the protagonist of the autobiographical text; at the same time, however, it should provide the emotional satisfaction historically missing for the female reader, that assurance and consolation that she does indeed exist in the world which a femininity defined in purely textual terms cannot provide.[27]

Life/Lines thus aims at preserving the tension between life and literature, between politics and theory, between selfhood and textuality, which autobiography authorizes us to enjoy. Editorial practice, we have found, can enforce this difficult but necessary mediating position: we have thus included pieces diverse enough, both ethnically and politically, that it becomes impossible to generalize about female experience, and we have also chosen both essays that attempt to define female specificity as an identifiable feature in a text and essays that problematize

25. See also Jelinek, *The Tradition of Women's Autobiography: From Antiquity to the Present* (Boston: Twayne, 1986). Since the conception of this volume, we have learned of two forthcoming books: Sidonie Smith, *A Poetics of Women's Autobiography: Marginality and the Fictions of Self-Representation* (Bloomington: Indiana University Press, 1987); and *The Private Self: Women's Autobiographical Writings*, ed. Shari Benstock (Chapel Hill: University of North Carolina Press, 1988).

26. Barthes, "The Death of the Author," *Image, Music, Text*, trans. Stephen Heath (New York: Hill and Wang, 1977); Michel Foucault, "What Is an Author?" *Language, Counter-Memory, Practice: Selected Essays and Interviews*, ed. Donald Bouchard (Ithaca: Cornell University Press, 1977).

27. For an elaboration of this view in relation to novels and novel readers, see Rachel Brownstein, *Becoming a Heroine: Reading about Women in Novels* (New York: Penguin, 1984).

female identity (for example, by politicizing it) as well. In fact, the intersection of levels of theoretical discourse even within individual essays suggests new responsibilities for feminist reading: gender is no longer the only situating category of interest to some of the book's contributors. Besides opening up the autobiographical canon by including noncanonical life writing, we have chosen essays representing varying theoretical perspectives to avoid privileging an increasingly hegemonic French critical practice. Rather than impose a single theoretical line, we have tried to promote political and theoretical dialogue among the contributors. "One sings, the other [exuberantly, defiantly] doesn't." As we see it, this vigilant stance can help us to push beyond the mere overturning of binary oppositions, the implications of which are as crucial for male as for female readers and critics of autobiography. The establishment of a separatist female tradition, even feminist critics have warned, carries the danger of reverse reification. Autobiography can thus provide male and female readers with fertile ground for re-seeding, along newly drawn feminist lines, contemporary ideas about selfhood.

This collection is meant to stand as testimony: to become a feminist reader of autobiography is to become a new kind of subject.

PART I

POSITIONING THE FEMALE AUTOBIOGRAPHICAL SUBJECT

I

The Other Voice:
Autobiographies of Women Writers

MARY G. MASON

"Why hath this lady writ her own life?" The question posed by Margaret Cavendish, duchess of Newcastle, near the end of the *True Relation of My Birth, Breeding and Life* (first published 1656) is no doubt a rhetorical one, set up to be knocked down by the response that would follow. But for Margaret Cavendish it was also a question that existed in a real realm of controversy outside the rhetorical mode, for looking forward it anticipated "carping tongues" and "malicious censurers" who would ask it "scornfully" after the *True Relation* had been published, and looking back it echoed a question that Dame Julian of Norwich, the first Englishwoman to protest that she *would* speak out about herself, felt compelled to bring up nearly three centuries earlier: "But because I am a woman, ought I therefore to believe that I should not tell you of the goodness of God, when I saw at the same time that it is his will that it be known?"[1] Behind Julian's account is God's desire that his goodness in his dealings with her be known; behind the duchess's account there lies quite a different desire. In both instances, however, it is "because I am a woman" that the two writers feel it necessary to defend—whether mildly or otherwise—their excursions into autobiographical writing.

"Why hath this lady writ her own life? since none cares to know whose daughter she was or whose wife she is, or how she was bred, or what fortunes she had, or how she lived, or what humour or disposition she was of." Having thus granted speech to the scurrilous tongues, the

1. Julian of Norwich, *Showings,* trans. Edmund Colledge and James Walsh (New York: Paulist Press, 1978), chap. 6 ("short text"), p. 135. This edition of the "Showing of God's Love" or the "Sixteen Revelations of Divine Love" includes both the "short text," written shortly after Julian experienced the revelations, and the "long text," written some twenty years later; it supersedes all previous editions and will hereafter be cited in the text.

duchess proceeds to give as good as she foresaw getting and in so doing reveals some highly pertinent facts about women's lives and the writing of women's lives that are applicable not only to the fourteenth through the seventeenth centuries but to our century as well.

> I answer that it is true, that 'tis to no purpose to the readers, but it is to the authoress, because I write it for my sake, not theirs. Neither did I intend this piece for to delight, but to divulge; not to please the fancy, but to tell the truth, lest afterages should mistake, in not knowing I was daughter to one Master Lucas of St. Johns, near Colchester, in Essex, second wife to the Lord Marquis of Newcastle; for my Lord having had two wives, I might easily have been mistaken, especially if I should die and my Lord marry again.[2]

That she was more or less willing to be defined by her relationship to her father and her husband/lord is a matter of considerable moment in the life and the life writing of the duchess of Newcastle; that she undertook that life writing "for my own sake," "to divulge," and "to tell the truth" so that posterity should not mistake her for the first duchess, for a possible third duchess, or for any other duchess at all is of very different but equal moment. And it is to be remarked too that in her response Margaret Cavendish succeeds in shifting the emphasis of the question from "why hath this *lady* writ her own life" to "why hath *this* lady writ her own life"—which transforms the issue from a sterile battle of the sexes into a creative exploration of particular past experience and unique present being.

Strict generic classification might refuse to consider either Julian's *Revelations* or Margaret Cavendish's *True Relation* to be autobiography on the grounds that there is relatively little self-disclosure or narrative content in Julian's account of God's dealings with her and that the *True Relation* is compromised as "genuine" autobiography both by its brevity (some twenty-four pages) and by the circumstances of its composition and publication (originally shuffled together with a motley of sketches in verse and prose—*Natures Pictures Drawn by Francies Pencil*—it was left out of the 1671 edition of that collection). Nevertheless, these two early women writers established patterns of relationship and of self-identity that were to be followed by later women whose works were incontesta-

---

2. *A True Relation of My Birth, Breeding and Life,* appended to *The Life of William Cavendish, Duke of Newcastle,* ed. C. H. Firth, 2d ed. (London: George Routledge and Sons, n.d.). p. 178. Citations in the text are to this edition of the *True Relation*. The "carping tongues" and "malicious censurers" are in an "epistle" on p. 154. *A True Relation* first appeared in 1656 as part of *Natures Pictures Drawn by Francies Pencil to the Life* and was republished as appendix to *The Life of William Cavendish* in 1667.

bly autobiographies; moreover they were joined by two other women, each of whom "writ her own life"—again one in the fourteenth/fifteenth and one in the seventeenth century—to fill out, as it were, a quaternity of possible patterns according to which women would compose their lives and their autobiographies in succeeding centuries. And though it is not generally recognized, one of these writers—Margery Kempe—produced (ca. 1432) what is actually the first full autobiography in English by anyone, male or female— *The Book of Margery Kempe,* "a schort tretys and a comfortabyl for synful wrecchys," in which she narrates her astonishing life as a demonstration of "þe hy & vnspecabyl mercy of ower souereyn Sauyowr Cryst Ihesu."[3]

The fourth of these early prototypes, Anne Bradstreet, wrote her very brief spiritual autobiography (only five pages long) about the same time Margaret Cavendish published her *True Relation,* intending it not as surety of identity for posterity nor as a comforting treatise for "synful wrecchys" but as a legacy "to my dear children," who she hoped might "gain some spiritual advantage by my experience." Though she did not bring nearly as many children into the world as did Margery Kempe (eight to the other's fourteen), it is nevertheless highly characteristic that Anne Bradstreet should address her autobiographical exercise to her children and that their spiritual welfare should have been foremost in her thoughts.

In these four works—Julian's *Revelations* or *Showings, The Book of Margery Kempe,* Margaret Cavendish's *True Relation,* and Anne Bradstreet's spiritual account "To My Dear Children"—we can discover not only important beginnings in the history of women's autobiography in English as a distinct mode of interior disclosure but also something like a set of paradigms for life writing by women right down to our time. And while there are some obvious disadvantages inherent in distinguishing literary works by gender, in the specific instance of autobiography, where a life is so intimately joined to the act of writing, one can achieve certain important insights into the possibilities and necessities of self-writing if one first isolates according to gender and then brings female and male autobiographical types back into proximity in order that they may throw light (at times by sheer contrast) on one another. Nowhere in women's autobiographies do we find the patterns established by the two prototypical male autobiographers, Augustine and Rousseau; and conversely, male writers never take up the archetypal models of Julian, Margery Kempe, Margaret Cavendish, and Anne Bradstreet. The dra-

3. *The Book of Margery Kempe,* ed. Sanford Brown Meech (London: Oxford University Press, 1940), p. 1. Citations in the text are to this edition of *The Book of Margery Kempe.*

matic structure of conversion that we find in Augustine's *Confessions*, where the self is presented as the stage for a battle of opposing forces and where a climactic victory for one force—spirit defeating flesh—completes the drama of the self, simply does not accord with the deepest realities of women's experience and so is inappropriate as a model for women's life writing. Likewise, the egoistic secular archetype that Rousseau handed down to his romantic brethren in his *Confessions*, shifting the dramatic presentation to an unfolding self-discovery where characters and events are little more than aspects of the author's evolving consciousness, finds no echo in women's writing about their lives. On the contrary, judging by our four models, the self-discovery of female identity seems to acknowledge the real presence and recognition of another consciousness, and the disclosure of female self is linked to the identification of some "other." This recognition of another consciousness—and I emphasize recognition of rather than deference to—this grounding of identity through relation to the chosen other, seems (if we may judge by our four representative cases) to enable women to write openly about themselves.

Both Julian and Margery Kempe, writing in the mystical tradition of personal dialogue with a divine being who is creator, father, and lover, discover and reveal themselves in discovering and revealing the other. Speaking in the first person, with a singleness of vision that allows for no distractions or ambivalences, Julian establishes an absolute identification with the suffering Christ on the cross; yet, while such a total identification might seem to suggest a loss of self, the fact is that Julian is in no way obliterated as a person, for her account is shot through with evidence of a vivid, unique, and even radical consciousness. Margery Kempe, by way of contrast, speaks in the third person (she figures throughout her narrative as "*pis* creatur") to a Christ who, when he is not her infant ("for *pu* art to me a very modir," he once tells her [p. 91]) is her manly bridegroom. Unlike Julian's single-visioned *Revelations*, *The Book of Margery Kempe* displays a dual sense of vocation: the wife-mother, pilgrim-mystic roles, which were continuous throughout Margery Kempe's life, represent a rather more common pattern of women's perception of themselves as maintaining two equally demanding identities, worldly and otherworldly, both of which, however, are ultimately determined by their relation to the divine.

Like Julian's, Anne Bradstreet's brief retrospection is possessed of a singleness of focus, but because her spiritual autobiography comes out of the Puritan tradition and the early days of the New England colonies, its intense focus falls not on a personal figure but on a spiritual community. When we place Anne Bradstreet's prose autobiography alongside her autobiographical poetry, we can observe in both a unique harmonizing of the divine, the secular, and the personal, a unifying of a public and a private consciousness.

Margaret Cavendish, author of the first important secular autobiography by a woman, limns her own portrait in a double image, herself and her husband, the duke of Newcastle. (Here, incidentally, the history of women's life writing parallels the history of men's life writing, secular autobiography being in both cases a latter-day development out of or away from religious self-examination.) The focus of the *True Relation* might better be called duo than dual, and while Margaret Cavendish does not exactly subordinate herself to her husband's image, she obviously identifies herself most sharply when she is identifying him too. The full-length biography of her husband was written some ten years after the duchess produced her own short autobiography, and at about the same time she was writing the life of her husband she was also composing a utopian fantasy, *The Blazing World,* in which she once again splits and reunifies the self-image, appearing both as duchess of Newcastle and as empress of the Blazing World—as both herself and another. As we shall see, this duo pattern is a fairly common one in women's autobiographies (indeed in Margaret Cavendish's time two other well-known women, Lucy Hutchinson and Lady Anne Fanshawe, wrote their memoirs and actually appended them to their husbands' biographies).

The duchess of Newcastle was insistently and prolifically literary, which might seem to set her *True Relation* off from the three spiritual autobiographies; likewise, those three spiritual and didactic documents might not appear amenable to consideration as works of literature. However, as with Margaret Cavendish, the assertion of self in Julian, Margery Kempe, and Anne Bradstreet is accompanied by a strong sense of themselves as authors. Julian's literary intentions were obviously not primary, but even she shows consciousness of being an author, and the book she produced has gradually assumed its rightful place in the great lyrical-mystical tradition of English literature. Margery Kempe, though she was illiterate and was therefore obliged to dictate her story to others, nevertheless took her role as author very seriously indeed—so seriously that the composing and transcribing and the recomposing and retranscribing of her book became a major obsession. But in the end she found the satisfaction of that obsessive need to be both creative and curative: "And sche was many tyme seke whyl þ is tretys was in writyng, and, as sone as sche wolde gon a-bowte þe writyng of þis tretys, sche was heil & hoole sodeynly in a maner" (p. 219). Like Julian, Margery Kempe made a contribution not only to the development of autobiography in

English but to other literary modes as well: the eclectic structure of her *Book* draws on a number of literary conventions of the time—voyage and pilgrimage literature, lives of saints, fables—and in its strung-along plot of dramatized episodes, it moves toward fiction and the picaresque novel.

Margaret Cavendish leaves the reader in no doubt about her sense of a literary calling. In the *True Relation* she tells us that she was conscious of her vocation in childhood, and was even then "addicted . . . to write with the pen [rather] than to work with the needle" (p. 172). This long-standing addiction to "scribbling" (as she herself called it) eventually made the duchess one of the first "literary ladies" of England: she published thirteen books in her lifetime, and as she makes very clear in the epistle prefatory to the *True Relation,* she will not have it that any hand other than her own was involved in the production of these volumes. Moreover, besides being a very early secular autobiography, her *Life* also foreshadowed later developments both in the novel of education and in social novels. Anne Bradstreet, though she was vastly different from Margaret Cavendish both as a woman and as an author, nevertheless echoes her contemporary in the prologue to "The Four Elements" when she declares her fondness for the "poet's pen" and writes, "I am obnoxious to each carping tongue / Who says my hand a needle better fits."[4] In its distilling of a spiritual story to its essence, the little autobiography that came from that pen can be seen as a paradigm of the Puritan "way of the soul," and of course Anne Bradstreet's contribution to the American poetic tradition requires no demonstration. It was important for each of the four autobiographic exemplars to consider herself in one way or another an author, or else her days would have been consigned to work with the needle, and her story, with its self-discovery and self-expression achieved through "other" reference, would have gone untold.

Although we know little about the facts of her life, since the *Revelations* are of spiritual truths and not factual details, Dame Julian of Norwich was probably from a well-bred family and educated at the convent of Carrow by Benedictine nuns, who would have taught her some reading and writing . . . and some needlework. The scholarly and literary allusions in her *Revelations* tell us that as a recluse she acquired much learning and a broad knowledge of classical spiritual writings. Julian received a religious vocation early in her life, and she prayed for an

---

4. *The Works of Anne Bradstreet,* ed. Jeanine Hensley (Cambridge: Harvard University Press, 1967). p. 16. All references to Anne Bradstreet's writing in the text will be this edition. "Carping tongue(s)" is also, interestingly enough, Margaret Cavendish's phrase in much the same context.

illness that would both confirm and deepen her vocation; that illness, the gift and sign of her grace, she experienced on 13 May 1373 during her thirty-first year. After surviving this crisis and confirmation of illness, she was granted a vision of Christ and the Crucifix that lasted for a period of five hours with fifteen "showings" or lessons of divine love, followed by a sixteenth "showing" one night later. On her recovery she became an anchoress, spending over twenty years of her life in an anchorage adjoining Saint Julian's Church in Conesford, Norwich.[5] Apparently she recorded her experience soon after her illness with the help of a scribe (this is the version that has been known to us for some time as *A Shewing of God's Love*), but in 1393, after twenty more years of meditation and revelation, she set down a fuller account of her experience in the version commonly known as *Sixteen Revelations of Divine Love*.

A Shewing of God's Love, which I take to be the better text for consideration as an autobiography, has nothing of the climactic structure of a conversion story (being thus set off from the Augustinian masculine model) but concentrates instead on the illumination of one moment—the vision of Christ and the crucifix—gradually undestood by way of the sixteen revelations following it. Although the account shares the traditional movement of the "ascent toward God" of mystical writings, it is primarily a narrative that is told on the one hand with amazing detachment and objectivity but on the other hand with an intense personal identification with the figures of God and Christ who converse with Julian directly and answer the questions troubling her. There are three distinct autobiographical sections to Julian's narrative: the first, a description of herself before the illness; the second, a description of the illness; and the last (five hours after the "shewings"), an account of her reaction to her recovery. Always aware of the possibility of self-delusion, Julian took care to record the physical changes and effects of her illness with a dry precision approaching clinical detachment. The reactions of others present are noted: her mother, for example, Julian says, "held up her hand in front of my face to close my eyes, for she thought that I was already dead or had that moment died" (p. 142). Her narrative also recalls the physical sensations that she experienced with approaching death—"After that I felt as if the upper part of my body were beginning to die. My hands fell down on either side, and I was so weak that my head lolled to one side" (p. 128). Later a series of moods follows

5. A comprehensive source for biographical materials on Julian is to be found in a group of commemorative essays edited by Frank Dale Sayer, *Julian and Her Norwich* (Norwich: Celebration Committee folio, 1973).

as a state of deathly resignation gives way to joy and awe at the miracle of the vision and recovery, followed in turn, after the showings, by a period of doubt and despair—"And I was as barren and dry as if the consolation which I had received before were trifling" (p. 162)—but this too is eventually resolved into the final method of "rest and peace."

This personal narrative of illness, vision, and recovery employs a traditional "homely" imagery[6] that, in addition to serving the ends of narrative, is also possessed of a poetic resonance vastly expanding the significance of Julian's story and, especially in moments of epiphany, charging it with dramatic intensity. Following her initial vision of Christ, the first "shewing" reveals Julian's special place in God's love and in the plan of his creation.

> And in this he showed me something small, no bigger than a hazelnut, lying in the palm of my hand, and I perceived that it was as round as any ball. I looked at it and thought: What can this be? And I was given this general answer: It is everything which is made. I was amazed that it could last, for I thought it was so little that it could suddenly fall into nothing. And I was answered in my understanding: It lasts and always will, because God loves it. (P. 130)

Identifying not only with the insignificance and frailty of the hazelnut but also with its particularity and durability as part of God's creation, Julian sees in herself something of the mystery and grace of the Virgin Mary, who is "a simple, humble maiden, young in years," but who for all her humility and insignificance will become, as the queen of heaven, "greater, more worthy and more fulfilled, than everything else which God has created and which is inferior to her" (p. 131). The hazelnut, symbol of the strength of the meek and insignificant, becomes a guiding metaphor for this narrative of a woman—Julian or the Virgin—who is in herself less than the least but in God's love greater than the greatest.[7]

The most intense moment of Julian's narrative follows this poetic disclosure when, after a vision of Christ's "blessed face . . . caked with dry blood" (p. 136), there is a sudden revelation of the unity and harmony of all things contained in the smallness of a hazelnut: "And after this I saw God in a point,[8] that is, in my understanding, and by this vision I saw that he is present in all things. . . . I marvelled at this vision with a

---

6. On the use of traditional imagery, cf. Karl Stone, *Middle English Prose Style: Margery Kempe and Julian of Norwich* (The Hague: Mouton, 1970).

7. For the concept of a guiding metaphor, see James Olney, *Metaphors of Self: The Meaning of Autobiography* (Princeton: Princeton University Press, 1972).

8. This is the literal reading; the phrase is rendered "in an instant of time" in the Colledge/Walsh edition.

gentle fear, and I thought: What is sin?" (p. 137). This sense of unity—the medieval view that God is a circle whose center is everywhere and whose circumference is nowhere—is at the very heart of all religious perception, and it informs as well the entire tradition of revelatory English lyric poetry from the Anglo-Saxon "Dream of the Rood" right down to the latter-day romantic model that transfers the role of the religious mystic to the poet. The fact that in Julian it is rather the other way around—that is to say, the role of the poet is assumed by the religious mystic—does nothing to alter the essential similarity. Although she still had moments of doubt and despair to pass through before returning to the serenity of achieved understanding, the ultimate impression Julian leaves her reader with is the sense of peace that comes with her unitary vision: "And so our good Lord answered to all the questions and doubts which I could raise, saying most comfortingly in this fashion: I will make all things well. . . . you will see that yourself, that all things will be well" (p. 151).

As commentators have lately pointed out, there are certain revolutionary elements in Julian's work that we are in a peculiar position to appreciate perhaps only as a result of recent events—elements that in some ways make her achievement seem closer to our time than to the fourteenth century. When coupled with the profoundly traditional nature of Julian's mystical writing, however, the real effect of this "modernness" is to give to her individual achievement the feeling of timelessness that invests any archetype or archetypal work. During the twenty years of meditation and study between the first and second versions of her experience, Julian gradually arrived at an understanding of the nature of God that, because it was determined by her understanding as a woman, seems startling contemporary to the reader today. Through use of what might be called feminine imagery in the closing chapters of the second version of her book, Julian develops a concept of the feminine principle of the Godhead that attributes the feminine to the Third Person of the Trinity, the Holy Spirit. This was indeed an ancient theological concept, but it was probably unknown to Julian in the fourteenth century, and it is almost completely lost to us in the twentieth century. Although she uses some maternal imagery that was conventional in her day—the imagery, for instance, of Christ's love for mankind as a mother's for her child—Julian is doing something strikingly original and going far beyond the conventional or the received when she says, "God almighty is our loving Father, and God all wisdom is our loving Mother, with the love and goodness of the Holy Spirit, which is all one God, one Lord" (p. 293), or again when she declares simply, "As truly as God is our Father, so truly is God our Mother" (p. 296). This conjunction restores the feminine Sophia to her rightful place of honor and glory. She is not only mother, daughter, and bride of the Deity but an equal One with the other Two of the Trinity: "And so I saw that God rejoices that he is our Father, and God rejoices that he is our Mother, and God rejoices that he is our true spouse, and that our soul is his beloved wife" (p. 279). Of course God is father, but he is mother too, and this—though Julian sensed it and expressed it clearly enough—is what was forgotten for so long. In reformulating this little-known concept, Julian adds to her earlier conclusion that "all things will be well" a new understanding of just *how* things will be well.[9] "All will be well and all will be well, and every kind of thing will be well" (p. 225) when we recognize the diverse unity and plenitude of God's creation, when we perceive the breadth and variety of human consciousness, realized here in Julian herself, and when we acknowledge the needful balance of man and woman in the understanding of God's nature. Embracing another in mystical revelation thus does not obliterate Julian's consciousness as a person or as a woman, nor does it lead to any poverty of personality; on the contrary, it intensifies and deepens her uniquely feminine understanding of the importance, indeed the needfulness, of both man and woman in God's creation as in his/her being.

If Julian figures among women autobiographers as the recluse who chooses a life of contemplative withdrawal, Margery Kempe offers us a potrait of the pilgrim engaging in the world continuously, actively, even aggressively. Although *The Book of Margery Kempe* has considerably less stylistic merit than Julian's *Showings,* it nevertheless represents an important, alternative mode of self-conception and self-narration of a life possessed of a dual vocation. In 1413 when Margery Kempe went to Julian (by that time a well-known anchoress) for spiritual counsel, she was a woman forty years old and twenty years married but now sworn to live chaste with her spouse. She had borne fourteen children, had tried her hand at home brewing and a milling business, and had experienced a spiritual conversion that gave her a special religious vocation (rather unnerving in some of its manifestations) that was to mark her out as most eccentric in manner, hence suspect to many she encountered, and that created the dilemma of conflicting roles that eventually defined her life. Although they could hardly have been more dissimilar as personalities, the two women seem to have gotten on well enough

9. A recent study of this aspect of Julian's teaching points out that although she does not attribute motherhood to the Holy Spirit specifically, her description of what the Holy Spirit *does* fits in with the hypothesis that this person of the Godhead might properly be called God the Mother. See Sister Mary Paul, *All Shall Be Well: Julian of Norwich and the Compassion of God* (Oxford: SLG Press, Convent of the Incarnation, 1976).

together, as we can gather from Margery Kempe's account of the meeting. Presumably Julian found some comforting words to offer about the authenticity of Kempe's vocation; she may also have advised the younger woman to record her experiences in writing (as the Norwich White Friar, Master Allan, had already suggested she do), so the uniqueness and peculiarity of those experiences should not be lost to the world.

Kempe's special brand of religious enthusiasm, although generally recognized as authentic by church divines somewhat removed from direct contact with it, led local English officials to a suspicion of Lollardy—to a suspicion, that is, that she was one of those followers of John Wycliffe who went about the English countryside preaching against the establishment of church and state. The religious vocation she enjoyed and others suffered was expressed in extreme emotionalism; in particular, she was possessed of the "gift of tears," a spiritual boon that manifested itself in hysterical weeping and in copious whoops and shouting (this latter gift of shouting was given to Kempe in Jerusalem while she was on her pilgrimage to the Holy Land)—all a consequence of a compelling identification with the Passion. Her demonstrations of faith were extreme and bizarre: in church, for instance, she insisted on praying while lying prostrate in front of the altar, a position, as one commentator has noted drily, "inconvenient to parishioners"; and she was uniformly aggressive in her advice to cleric and lay person alike, whether on civic or spiritual matters. While such characteristics are not unusual in saints' lives, they were nevertheless disturbing to the simple countrymen around her, who had little experience of the ways of saints. They were also often disturbing to her fellow pilgrims, who had not been granted all the gifts that afflicted Margery Kempe.

Kempe's third-person ("þis creatur") narrative proceeds more or less chronologically (the chronology is sometimes a bit shaky because she dictated from memory to two different amanuenses on two separate occasions) through a series of dramatized scenes and episodes, interspersed with revelatory conversations between herself and Christ, who appears to the creature "in lyknesse of a man, most semly, most bewtyuows, & most amyable" (p. 8). Kempe's exercise of the traditional third person is a minor stroke of genius, for it confers some sense of objective reality on scenes that might otherwise have little enough of the realistic about them—for example, her vision of her mystical marriage to the godhead in Rome in the company of Mary, the Twelve Apostles, Saint Katherine, Saint Margaret, and many others of the saintly fold. Another kind of episode also benefits from the quasi objectivity of the third-person perspective: these are the "court scenes" depicting interviews with clerics and officials. Although they are thoroughly traditional and evoke similar episodes in the lives of, for example, Catherine of Siena and Saint Thomas More, they were nevertheless drawn directly from Kempe's own experience. Her account of one such episode, in which the archbishop of York hinted at heresies and accused her of Lollardy, reads thus: "Sche [the creature], answering þerto, seyde, 'I preche not ser, I come in no pulpytt. I vse but comownycacyon & good wordys, & þat wil I do whil I leue'" (p. 126). Exasperated by Margery's persistence, her fearlessness, and her superiority in disputation, the archbishop finally responded with a lament that was itself almost archetypal. Driven beyond the limits of his tolerance, he asked, "Wher schal I haue a man þat myth ledyn þis woman fro me?" The archbishop was doubtless not the first (nor would he be the last) figure of the establishment whose immediate heart's desire was to find a man—stable, reliable, and ungifted in religious ways—that might lead this woman away from him.

In one of her revelations, God informs his "dowtyr" Margery, "I haue ordeynd þe to be a merowr amongys hem [the people of the world] for to han gret sorwe þat þei xulde takyn exampil by þe" (p. 186). Indeed Kempe's *Book* does mirror her as a religious model of sorrowing human compassion, but it also mirrors—and from a specifically feminine point of view—the entire medieval world in which her remarkable presence moved and had its being. More than five hundred years later, we as readers are introduced to townspeople, pilgrims, foreigners, Englishmen abroad, clerics both hostile and friendly, magistrates, nobility, the poor and sick whom Kempe served. And in closer focus her *Book* brings to life a whole array of individual characters: the divine figures of God, Christ, Mary, and a host of saints; Margery Kempe's family, husband, son, and daughter-in-law; a number of spiritual confessors, among them Master Allan, who was responsible for encouraging her religious enthusiasm; figures of historical or social prominence such as Philip Repington, bishop of Lincoln, Thomas Arundel, archbishop of Canterbury, the duke of Bedford, the mayor of Leicester; and finally a number of individualized commoners such as the lascivious steward who tried to rape Kempe at Leicester and the protecting jailer who saved her, or the broken-backed Richard who lent her money in Rome. This is the very stuff of the novel, a form yet to be born, and Kempe's progress through it seems modeled on the structure of picaresque fiction before the model itself existed.

The "fiction" of Margery Kempe's *Book* is framed by the author's story of personal conversion, and while it follows a stylized, conventional pattern—a first conversion after sickness, a period of penance and temptation ending in a second conversion or illumination, a five-year period of initiation culminating in a mystical marriage in Rome—it also bears Kempe's individual and individualized imprint, whether it be in her particularized portrait of her husband, who was more supportive than other husbands faced with a "holy" wife, or in her fear of being deluded and her consequent meticulous concern for accuracy. As Hope Emily Allen says in her prefatory note to *The Book of Margery Kempe,* "I have found no equivalent production anywhere," and she goes on to say that she finds Margery Kempe's originality in this, the first full-length autobiography in English, similar to the originality of "other creators of literary types" (p. lvii).

The ultimate frame for both her conversion tale and her picaresque progress is the story of the book's composition given in the proem. In creating her book Kempe was creating her proper image, in creating her text she was re-creating her exemplary life—hence her obsession with getting it right. According to the account in the proem, Margery Kempe had been urged early in her life to write down her experiences, but she refused, perhaps fearing the difficulties other women had encountered when they claimed personal revelation. Then, when she felt the time was right, she became frustrated by the inadequacy of her scribe (an Englishman who had lived in the Lowlands and whose language and pen were both poor), so she set out after a better scribe in the person of a priest—"a priest whech þis creatur had gret affeccyon to" (p. 4)—who, however, at first demonstrated a mighty reluctance to transcribe the story of "þis creatur" inclined to hysteria. Nevertheless, having exhausted the full range of excuses available to him, the reluctant priest finally surrendered to Kempe's insistence, and having gone so far as to agree to be her amanuensis he went the rest of the way to become her staunchest supporter.

Various miraculous events associated with the priest's transcription of Kempe's story are recounted in the proem by way of "authenticating" the sanctity of that story, and one wonders if the priest was not perhaps responsible for introducing this traditional device of hagiographic literature. Be that as it may, however, the chief manipulator of *The Book of Margery Kempe* is Margery Kempe herself, as we can clearly perceive in the originality of the book's form and in the individuality of the voice that speaks through it. Whether she was primarily trying to promote herself as a saint or merely felt that her story was interesting enough to be told, Kempe was doing what every autobiographer does—tracing a perceived pattern in her life story, thus realizing for her readers a portrait of the individual that she was. Margery Kempe was a determined woman, in no way more than in this very determination to get her story told and to get it told right, which always involved the delicate balance of those dual elements that composed her tale as they composed her personality: wife and pilgrim, mother and mystic, superior debater but equally superior weeper, earthly bride of John Kempe and mystical bride of Jesus Christ, mother not only of fourteen children but "very modir" of the Savior as well. Hers was a woman's story well worth the telling, and tell it she would and did.

Margaret Cavendish, otherwise a very different woman from Margery Kempe, could hardly be said to have been less determined about telling her story than her predecessor in literary self-portraiture; nor was the woman Virginia Woolf called "the hare-brained, fantastical Margaret of Newcastle" (*A Room of One's Own*) much behind the tear-gifted mystic/pilgrim of Lynn in the ways of eccentricity. But turn eccentricity to another light and it becomes indistinguishable from the great Western ideal of individualism, and as any reader can testify, the most notable quality of the duchess of Newcastle's writing is the sense of a strong individual, a sharply distinctive personality overwhelmingly present in every line. "For I think it no crime," the duchess says, "to wish myself the exactest of Nature's works, my thread of life the longest, my chain of destiny the strongest . . . also to do my endeavour, so far as honour and honesty doth allow of, to be the highest on Fortune's wheel and to hold the wheel from turning, if I can" (p. 176). And the duchess set about making herself, if not "the exactest," at least one of the most singular of Nature's works, outfitting herself in such a bizarre manner that crowds gathered around to amuse themselves with the sight of her whenever she ventured forth in her coach. But such attention was not unwelcome to the duchess, for as she said of the strange garments that caught the world's eye, "I am so vain (if it be vanity) as to endeavour to be worshipped, rather than not to be regarded" (p. 177). The crowds that came to laugh may not have stayed to worship, as the duchess fondly imagined, but merely in regarding her they already fulfilled a large part of her desire.

Yet, for all her singularity, for all her strong individuality and distinctiveness of personality, for all her fantasticalness, Margaret Cavendish required a substitute figure, or other—an alter ego really—with and through whom she might identify herself. This need makes itself felt particularly in the telling of her life story. Margaret Cavendish found in the duke of Newcastle both her husband and her lord, but remarkably enough, she succeeds in making this of him without ever dimming the bright light of her own personality. "And though I desire to appear to the best advantage, whilst I live in the view of the world," she writes immediately after the passage on the prodigality in her dress that took the world's fancy, "yet I could most willingly exclude myself, so as never to see the face of any creature but my Lord as long as I live, inclosing myself like an anchorite, wearing a frieze gown, tied with a cord about my waist" (pp. 1787–78). Julian also did this—that was her life story, though her Lord was quite a different one—and while we may doubt that the duchess would have been as successful as she imagines in imitation of Julian, we shall never know for certain because neither the duke nor her life ever demanded that she essay the existence of an anchoress. Receiving her revelations and showings, Julian relates to a superior figure: she looks *up* to Christ and the crucifix. On the other hand, in her biography of her husband and in her *True Relation,* Margaret Cavendish's gaze is directed neither up nor down but dead level: he is the warrior of an epic, but his wife is beside him—in all ways equal to him—as a poet. Your deeds, she says to the duke in an epistle prefatory to his biography, "have been of war and fighting, mine of contemplating and writing" (p. xxxviii). And it is revealing that in *The Blazing World* the duchess all but drops the duke from the picture—but doing so she finds it necessary to come up with another alter ego, the empress of the Blazing World herself, who is not only empress but philosopher, warrior, and goddess, a more than sufficient replacement for the discarded husband and lord and a satisfactory stand-in for the duchess's own imagined self.

A True Relation of My Birth, Breeding and Life, written when the young Margaret Cavendish was in exile with her husband in Antwerp (they waited out the period of the Commonwealth abroad), is a very loosely structured narrative that tends to rattle on, but it is not chaotic or irrational as some critics have claimed. The first of the two main parts of the narrative composes an exterior portrait of the sitter, describing her "birth, breeding and actions"; the second gives "something of my humour, particular practice and disposition." It composes an interior portrait, including the sitter's temperament and her moral character. The fitting conclusion to this narrative is the duchess's "apology" for writing her own life, which argues, as we have noted, that she has a right to tell her story, a right to be ambitious and to try to control her fate, and above all a right to make her identity known as Margaret Lucas Cavendish, all three of the nominal elements being of equal significance in the identity.

This assertiveness at the end brings us a considerable distance from the hesitancy of the girl at the beginning, for although the narrative seems to proceed aimlessly, the truth is that all the details are made to contribute to the portrait of an emerging young woman. Margaret Lucas, daughter, sister, and lady-in-waiting (and more or less submissive in all three roles) becomes Margaret Cavendish, marchioness, wife of a marquis in exile (her husband was made a duke after their return to England), and a woman on her way to becoming a confident and prolific author in half a dozen different modes. The story she tells is of a comfortable and pleasant adolescence interrupted by fate in the form of the "unnatural wars" that came "like a whirlwind" destroying the Lucas family who had been "feasting each other like Job's children" (p. 160); exiled from her home by fortune, she found her husband, he too a victim of fate, and because he respected her as a person and gave her his affection with an "unalterable decree of his promise," she honored and loved him—though "it was not amorous love," she explains, for "I never was infected therewith, it is a disease, or a passion, or both, I only know by relation, not by experience" (p. 162). He who "was her only tutor" became likewise her lord, and at this point in her life Margaret Cavendish could do little but accept her "self" as a mere shadow of the duke. According to the young woman composing her portrait in a double image, even in writing he was greatly her superior, for he wrote "what wit dictates to him," while she could lay claim to nothing more than "scribbling." Her express fear was that in her "scribbling" her pen could not keep up with her "fancies," and indeed she had some reason to fear, for the syntax of individual sentences frequently gives way altogether before the heated rush of all the swarming, ill-assorted, and half-formed thoughts besetting her brain.[10] Even so, and already at this young age, she was not without literary ambition or untouched by "that last infirmity of noble mind." On the contrary, she writes, "I fear my ambition inclines to vain-glory, for I am very ambitious; yet 'tis neither for beauty, wit, titles, wealth, or power, but as they are steps to raise me to Fame's tower, which is to live by remembrance in after-ages" (p. 177). This passage is followed shortly by the duchess's claim that she could easily renounce the world for her lord, and the *True Relation* then concludes with her own very strong uxorial self-identification, humble as yet as an author but confidently assertive as a marchioness.

The Life of William Cavendish, written almost twenty years after the

10. For example, in a passage at the end of the epistle that stands before *A True Relation*, the duchess characteristically combines undaunted self-confidence with touching frankness about her limitations: "I desire all my readers and acquaintance to believe, though my words run stumbling out of my mouth, and my pen draws roughly on my paper, yet my thoughts move regular in my brain. . . . For I must tell my readers, that nature, which is the best and curiousest worker, hath paved my brain smoother than custom hath oiled my tongue, or variety hath polished my senses, or art hath beaten the paper whereon I write" (p. 154). Cf. the duchess's anger at the reason for the limitations of women's knowledge and skill, which she credits to their lack of education. In a famous epistle, written in 1655 to the universities of Oxford and Cambridge, explaining her views on the neglect and "despisements" of "the masculine sex to the female," she writes, "So we [women] are become like worms that only live in the dull earth of ignorance, winding ourselves sometimes out by the help of some refreshing rain of good education, which seldom is given us." See *Philosophical and Physical Opinions* (London: William Wilson, 1663).

True Relation and ostensibly to glorify her husband as a loyal subject and successful general, is clearly the work not of a novice but of a writer certain that she has arrived both as author and as woman, who conveys that certainty in her relationship to her subject and in the assurance of her manner. While the duchess no doubt sincerely wished to promote her husband's career with her book, she was equally intent on answering her own critics and skeptics and on establishing herself in fame right alongside her duke. "But the great God, That hath hitherto blessed both your Grace and me," she says to the duke in a prefatory address, "will, I question not, preserve both our fames to after ages, for which, we shall be bound most humbly to acknowledge His great mercy" (p. xxxviii)— and also, no doubt, his great justice, for separate and equal "fames to after ages" for the duke and duchess were no more than the simple due of each of them. Alterity but equality—this might be the motto of *The Life of William Cavendish,* for it nicely describes the marital relationship the biography defines and also the identity the duchess herself achieves in both the biography and the earlier autobiography.

Social convention and the responsibility of her rank would scarcely permit the duchess to write an autobiography as long as her husband's biography or as long as she might have felt she deserved, but she got around those inconveniences of social decorum and etiquette by composing an extended fantasy self-portrait in *The Blazing World.* In this work she manages to appropriate to herself, through identification with the empress, those various roles of author, warrior, scholar, and leader earlier assigned to the duke. The heroine of this story escapes abduction and rape to become the empress of a hidden kingdom where she presides over a symposium of learned men, becomes founder of a church specifically designed for women, and leads a successful military campaign. In the latter role of warrior-goddess she appears "in her garments of light, like an angel or some Deity." At the suggestion of her wise men—and very wise they prove to be, too—the empress summons up the soul of the duchess of Newcastle to act as her scribe, and the two of them strike it off very well indeed as the duchess becomes the empress's Platonic other self and her fondest companion. The two of them share a number of adventures, including an aerial flight to London and to Welbeck where the duke, who is practicing horsemanship and fencing, proves gallant and charming but not really up to the problem posed by the two Platonically united women. In the end, with the duke pretty much forgotten, the duchess is so enamored of the order and peace and harmony of the realm over which the empress presides that she feels she must have one herself and so sets about creating a world of her own, equally well ordered, harmonious, and delightful.

What Margaret Cavendish is about in *The Blazing World* is made clear in the prologue, in which she tries to come to terms with that ambition that had frustrated her as a woman but had given her a vocation as a writer:

> Though I cannot be Henry the Fifth, or Charles the Second, yet I endeavor to be Margaret the First; and although I have neither power, time nor occasion to conquer the world as Alexander and Caesar did; yet rather than not to be Mistress of one, since Fortune and the Fates would give me none, I have made a World of my own; for which no body, I hope will blame me, since it is in every one's power to do the like.

This fantasy world, created by the duchess to replace the real world that she had "neither power, time nor occasion to conquer," has about it much of the "female gothic" (as Ellen Moers describes the mode) wherein imaginary heroines have all the adventures and the fulfillments denied their creators in life.[11] As she implies in "Some Few Notes of the Authoress," tacked on at the end of her biography of the duke, Margaret Cavendish was not willing to be "a spectator rather than an actor," but since the world offered her no stage on which she might act, she had to imagine into existence another world, a blazing world and "a Peaceable World" as she calls it,[12] of which, more than spectator or actor, she was the empress and ultimately the "onlie begetter." Her husband might be an epic warrior, the world might refuse to permit Margaret Cavendish such ambition, but in the end she creates or re-creates even her husband and his epic deeds and through creation of him and his world she also creates herself and her own world—or World, to give it the uppercase grandeur she herself confers on it. The focus and the image of Margaret Cavendish's self-creation and self-projection would perhaps have been double in any time—other women have chosen to split or double their self-images in a similar way in later centuries—but they were more certain to be so in the seventeenth century, which may in part account for one's feeling that the duchess of Newcastle is the real archetype of the double-focus writer: that is, she was the one who established the pattern according to which many subsequent women would imagine their lives and literary careers and would structure their autobiographies.

Anne Bradstreet, born in Cavalier England some ten years before Margaret Cavendish, ended her life in the far-off American colonies,

---

11. Ellen Moers, *Literary Women: The Great Writers* (New York: Doubleday, 1976), pp. 122–40.

12. *The Description of the New World Called the Blazing World* (London: Printed by A. Maxwell, 1666), p. 14.

and upon her first coming to that strange land she felt almost as much an exile from her true home as Margaret Lucas had felt when forced to leave England fore the Continent. "After a short time," Anne Bradstreet tells her children in the little account of her spiritual life, "I changed my condition and was married, and came into this country, where I found a new world and new manners, at which my heart rose" (p. 241). In contrast to the duchess of Newcastle, however, who determined "to be the highest on Fortune's wheel and to hold the wheel from turning, if I can," Anne Bradstreet soon subdued her heart and her will to what she saw as God's providence and accepted the complex fate of being an American and a member of the Puritan community as her destiny, for she never supposed it was in her power to turn Fortune's wheel as she chose or to prevent its turning if she would: "But after I was convinced that it was the way of God, I submitted to it and joined to the church at Boston." Although this submission did not put an end to all of her sorrows, she felt that all tribulation, like all good fortune, was from the hand of God, who "never suffered me long to sit loose from Him, but by one affliction or other hath made me look home, and search what was amiss" (pp. 241–42). After the full secularized *True Relation* of the duchess of Newcastle, Anne Bradstreet's brief and eloquent account represents a return to the tradition of religious autobiography but with this great difference: the author realizes her own deepest self-image not through identification with Christ as the crucified savior or the resurrected bridegroom but through identification with an entire spiritual community as a collective order. This is to be profoundly in the world and of it, but a world newly transformed, and transformed through and through, by the power of providential destiny, so that its people are become God's Chosen People. If it was exile, then, to leave England for the colonies, it was exile to something closely approximating the Promised Land.

Addressing her life story "To My Dear Children," Anne Bradstreet draws circles of identity around herself—the inner circle of her immediate family through whom she achieves her most intimate identity; the intermediate circle of the Puritan communities of Cambridge, Ipswich, and Andover; and the outer circle of the Massachusetts Bay Colony—which returns us, in a sense, to the inner circle, for her father, Thomas Dudley, was governor of the colony, and her husband, Simon Bradstreet, was both an important leader in the community and a representative of the colony in the mother country (and later, after his wife's death, he too became governor of the colony). This reconciliation—indeed merger—of an individual and a collective consciousness doubtless came naturally to Anne Bradstreet not only because of her family's involvement in community and colony governance but also because of her thoroughly traditional Renaissance understanding of cosmic order. According to this understanding, the world in which we play out our moral destinies is the center of a divine plan harmonized by a series of natural, civil, theological, and human correspondences—in effect, "the great chain of being" of poets and philosophers of the sixteenth and seventeenth centuries. Anne Bradstreet's quaternity of poems about natural and human quaternities (dedicated, significantly, to her father)— "The Four Elements," "Of the Four Humours," "Of the Four Ages," "The Four Seasons"—demonstrate well enough her natural, unquestioning acceptance of these divine/human/natural correspondences establishing cosmic order all up and down the chain. For such a cosmos, God is the provider, and his is the providence that determines every event of greatest or least apparent significance; in that cosmos God can at any time choose to intervene, selecting some group of people—a family, a community, a colony—to be his Chosen People, elected to execute His divine plan in a new world.

Anne Bradstreet's identification with the secular and religious community of the Massachusetts Bay Colony was made personal through her father and then through her husband. Her much loved and admired—in fact, almost worshiped—father represented for her not only a parent but also a governor, magistrate, and spiritual model: in a very real sense, he *was* the community for her, and as he embodied her public and private consciousness, the colony came to be her extended family. In the elegy written on her father's death in 1653 ("To the Memory of My Dear and Ever Honoured Father Thomas Dudley, Esq."), she says that his God shall be "God, the second masculine embodiment of her secular and divine community, Anne Bradstreet of me and mine" (p. 202), and in the conclusion of the poem she imagines his spiritual destiny and her own as one, foreseeing their ultimate reunion in heaven, "Where we with joy each other's face shall see, / And parted more by death shall never be."

With Simon Bradstreet, the second masculine embodiment of her secular and divine community, Anne Bradstreet enjoyed a relationship that was equally intimate and powerful, though of course different in kind from the relationship with her father. "If ever two were one, then surely we," she declares in the first line of the poem "To My Dear and Loving Husband" (p. 225), and this two-in-oneness, this virtual sharing of a single individual consciousness, seems an exact expression of her singular good fortune in discovering her private passion perfectly at one with her public duty: both were figured for her in her husband, and with him she developed a private community of eight children, who came to represent a most intimate collective consciousness in her life. In her poem "In Reference to Her Children" (p. 232), she tells the personal history of her sons and daughters—"eight birds hatched in one nest"—most of whom have grown up and left the family community. Her tender but unsentimental acceptance of their departure, which leaves her free to further develop her own gifts, shows her sure sense of her own identity even as her private community dissolves.

The task of writing her spiritual autobiography (apparently undertaken at the suggestion of her son Simon) was the fulfillment of a sacred duty to her family, both immediate and extended, who in the early stages of infancy and colony might "gain some spiritual advantage" from her experience, her example, and her encouragement. "I will begin," she says, "with God's dealing with me from my childhood to this day" (p. 240). She then divides her life into four periods: childhood development of conscience; a youthful period of folly; a conversion after smallpox; and a final acceptance of her spiritual destiny after arrival in the New World. The events recorded from her life are few, and they were all selected because they bear ultimate reference to her experience in community—community of family, community of Puritans, community of God. Included are her first "correction" by God when he "smote" her with smallpox, her marriage, her arrival in New England, her joining of the church or "community," the long-awaited arrival of her first child, and finally, an event of the future, the hope that each of her children would come to a new spiritual birth: "I now travail in birth again of you till Christ be formed in you" (p. 241).

Looking back over her spiritual progress, Anne Bradstreet acknowledges the efficacious "chastening" administered by God through sickness, weakness, and weariness, and she confesses to spiritual doubts—not, however, doubts about the existence of God, which is revealed "in the wondrous works that I see, the vast frame of the heaven and earth" (p. 243), but doubts about the exclusive rightness of the Puritan way. "Why may not the Popish religion be the right [one]?" is a question, she says, that "hath sometimes stuck with me" (p. 244), and a startling question it is for a Puritan to admit to in her spiritual record; but it bears witness to her scrupulous honesty and even more to her generous embrace of a wider spiritual reality and more various spiritual possibilities than the confining doctrine of her community would allow for. Even so, Anne Bradstreet says, she overcame her doubts, rejected the Popish religion for its "vain fooleries . . . , lying miracles and cruel persecutions of the saints," and in effect submitted her more tolerant religious conscience to the straiter and stricter conscience of the community.

Having come through all afflictions and overcome all doubts,

Bradstreet concludes her spiritual record with a prayer to the God she has chosen and who has chosen her: "Now to the King, immortal, eternal, and invisible, the only wise God, be honour, and glory for ever and ever, Amen." Or at least one supposes this would be the conclusion—after all, where can you go from "Amen"?—but in fact there is yet to come a brief personal address to her children, the beginning and end of Anne Bradstreet's life story: "This was written in much sickness and weakness, and is very weakly and imperfectly done, but if you can pick any benefit out of it, it is the mark which I aimed at" (p. 245). This brings us back to the beginning and to that most intimate, inner circle of identity that was Anne Bradstreet's family, for her spiritual autobiography commences which the address to "My dear children" immediately following a little dedicatory poem:

> This book by any yet unread,
> I leave for you when I am dead,
> That being gone, here you may find
> What was your living mother's mind.
> Make use of what I leave in love,
> And God shall bless you from above.

What is surprising about Bradstreet's story is that a woman born and educated in Cavalier England with the natural gifts and inclination to be a poet could confine herself to such an exacting Puritan community and still create the mature and distinct poetry of her later life. For Anne Bradstreet, it was the merging of her private consciousness with her collective consciousness that freed her to achieve her own unique identity as a poet. Her autobiography illustrates this merging and unifying process from the inner circle of husband, family, and community to the outer circle of God's providential creation. Her poetry witnesses her individual voice.

Julian's intensity of focus on a single divine figure and a corresponding intensity of being, realized through relationship to that figure; Margery Kempe's dual vocation in this world and in another and her dual focus on these two separate, secular/religious worlds; Margaret Cavendish's pairing of her image with another, equal image and her doubling of the self-image whether in husband or in fantasy creation; and Anne Bradstreet's harmonious merger and identification with a collective consciousness and a corporate other—these are the four great originals, the lived and recorded patterns of relationship to others that allowed these women, each in her own characteristic way, to discover and delineate a self and to tell the story of that self even as it was being uncovered and coming into existence. Later women, while participating to a degree in one or another of these early archetypes, naturally varied the patterns of their *Lives* as the various experiences of their lives required them to do—mixing two or three patterns of their own. One element, however, that seems more or less constant in women's life writing—and not in men's—is the sort of evolution and delineation of an identity by way of alterity that we have traced in the four paradigms. Relation to another autonomous being (Margaret Cavendish), relation to one single, transcendent other (Julian), relation to two others (Margery Kempe), relation to a multiple collectivity, a many-in-one (Anne Bradstreet)—these are four distinct possibilities, and while there are no doubt more, the number of possibilities is certainly not infinite.

The patterns most frequently adopted (and adapted) by later women has unquestionably been the solution recorded in the life and writing of Margaret Cavendish—the pairing of one's own image with another, equal image. A modern parallel to her story is to be found in the two-volume autobiography of Beatrice Webb, another woman with a strong sense of identity. Her first volume, *My Apprenticeship,* is dedicated to Sidney Webb, Beatrice Webb's marital other; the second volume, *The Partnership,* opens with a chapter titled "The Other," which, unsurprisingly, is a minibiography of her husband/partner. Likewise, Elizabeth Barrett (Browning as she was to become) as a young girl wrote brief autobiographical accounts that reveal—as with the duchess of Newcastle—an early vocation as a writer.[13] In her autobiographical *Sonnets from the Portuguese,* she tells the story of her identification with Robert Browning, her husband, a poet less known than she was when they married. In the present century, Simone de Beauvoir's public/private relationship to Jean-Paul Sartre has often been at the center of the self-defining efforts of her autobiographical volumes without at all diminishing the strong sense of her identity. In recent American autobiography, Lillian Hellman reveals most about herself in her trilogy when she creates portraits of other people in her life, and though she depicts more than one other, these others come as it were in succession rather than collectively. A variant on this pattern of alterity-equality is to be found in stories where the other is neither a partner nor an equal, neither a spouse nor a creation of the writer but is instead an over-

13. "Two Autobiographical Essays by Elizabeth Barrett," in *Browning Institute Studies,* ed. William S. Peterson (New York, 1974), 2:119–34. The first essay, "My Own Character," was written when Elizabeth Barrett was twelve (1818); the second, "Glimpses into My Life and Literary Character," when she was fourteen (1820). That these two essays should have been published in *Browning Institute Studies* is not without a certain poignant significance.

whelming model or ideal that has to be confronted in order that the author's identity be realized—such is the relationship, for eample, of H.D. (Hilda Doolittle) to Freud in her autobiographical *Tribute to Freud* where the author figures as analysand rather than wife. Margaret Cavendish's second way of doubling the self-image not in biography/autobiography but in fantasy (*The Blazing World*) has found favor with women novelists who have either projected that image so that they might enjoy in fiction what they never could in life (*Jane Eyre,* for example, to which Charlotte Brontë, incidentally, gave the subtitle "autobiography" only a few years after that word had first been used by an author as title for a book) or have projected male images (father, brothers, lovers, husbands, clergymen) so that they might resolve feelings of hostility or unwilling compliance in themselves toward such masculine figures.[14]

Although it is unusual to find the singleness of Julian's mystical vision in later writers, there is something of this in Emily Brontë's "Imagination" or "sterner power," as she calls the divine presence in one of her poems, and Heathcliff, Brontë's fictional other, is virtually a demonic version of Julian's personal God. Christina Rossetti, one of the few important literary women of the nineteenth century to write autobiography undisguised (*Time Flies: A Reading Diary,* which doubles as an Anglican devotional text), conveys both in religious verse and in love poetry a feeling of single-mindedness reminiscent of Julian's. In our time, Simone Weil, radical activist and religious contemplative, has displayed a Julianesque intensity and scrupulosity in many essays devoted to autobiographical self-examination; with her vision focused on both this world and a world beyond, she also continues the attempt of Margery Kempe to discover herself in worlds usually opposed but here joined by the being of the autobiographer. For echoes of Margery's accounts of peregrinations and pilgrimages in this world, we should look to the writing of women travelers—the narrratives of Harriet Martineau, for example, and the itineraries with commentaries by Anna Brassey (*A Voyage in the Sunbeam,* 1880), Lady Duff Gordon (*Letters from Egypt,* 1865), and Lady Anne Blunt (*A Pilgrimage to Nejd,* 1881), the granddaughter of Lord Byron, who set off on horseback with her husband, Wilfred Scawen Blunt, into the interior of Arabia (and there discovered and translated some important Arabic poetry, published as *The Seven Golden Odes*) but later left Blunt to continue her pilgrimage as her own writer and her own woman.

14. Cf. Elaine Showaltzer, *A Literature of Their Own: British Women Novelists from Brontë to Lessing* (Princeton: Princeton University Press, 1977), esp. pp. 133–52.

Few subsequent women writers have found themselves in a personal/public community like Anne Bradstreet's—or indeed in a family like hers—and when considerable strain is not evident in the attempt to harmonize private vision with communal duties, it is most often because the attempt has not been made in such a total, inclusive context as was Bradstreet's (*The Autobiography of Saint Thérèse of Lisieux,* 1911, gives testimony from nineteenth-century France of the heroism it took for a young woman to preserve a sense of self that balanced the opposed claims of a religious community with those of a possessive family). Angela Davis may think of identifying with "the people" in her *Autobiography,* but that group is more a political abstraction than a living reality, and she must relate to a personal other (George Jackson is clearly more to her than an emblem of a black revolutionary hero) through letters written to him in prison. Although Dorothy Day's *The Long Loneliness* bears witness to a harmony of public and private life, Day has chosen not to become a writer but to record her story through her life as she lives it.

The four models discussed here by no means exhaust the possibilities. For some women writers, it is not a man or men or a community but a woman or women who provide the other of identity: Margaret Mead, though thrice married, is most self-revealing in *Blackberry Winter* when she writes about her daughter and about her own role as daughter; in *Memories of a Catholic Girlhood,* a portrait of the adolescent Mary McCarthy emerges from daguerreotypes of the grandmother, the aunt, and the deceased mother; and Nikki Giovanni's *Gemini* outlines a similar pattern with the grandmother, the mother, and a friend (Claudia) all helping the author define herself as a black woman poet. On the other hand, there is a kind of unattached "otherness" about Gertrude Stein's *Autobiography of Alice B. Toklas* and *Everybody's Autobiography* or about Isak Dinesen's *Out of Africa.* And as one might well expect, there have been failures and negative results consequent upon attempts at self-identification through relation to another: between *Snapshots of a Daughter-in-Law* (1963) and *Diving into the Wreck* (1973) Adrienne Rich saw the failure inherent in a conventional identification with her husband (this she attempts in *Snapshots*) and abandoned it in the latter volume as a way of arriving at a valid image of herself. Ellen Moers has noted the revealing similarity in the titles of Sylvia Plath's *Bell Jar,* Anaïs Nin's *Under a Glass Bell,* and Violette Leduc's *L'Asphyxie,* translated as *In The Prison of Her Skin,*[15] all of them suggesting psychological enclosure, imprisonment, and suffocation. And the autobiography of imprisonment, repre-

15. Moers, *Literary Women,* p. 297.

sented in women's writings from Charlotte Perkins Gilman's autobiography to the story of Sylvia Plath, tells the grim tale of a woman's
claustrophobia when she cannot get out of the prison of the self or of her
nightmare when she is kept from coming into her own self through the
proximate existence of another or others.

"Why hath this lady writ her own life?" Dame Julian had reasons that
the duchess of Newcastle could scarcely know, and Margery Kempe's
motives were not at all Anne Bradstreet's. Yet, for all the surface dis-
similarities, for all the diversity of motive and manner among the four,
there is something that ties these life stories together and draws them
into proximity with autobiographical excursions by later women writers while setting them apart from autobiographies written by men in
any place and any time. It is inconceivable that a man should have—
could have—written a book like *The Book of Margery Kempe* or the
Showings of Julian of Norwich (although the mystic comes closest to
expressing the human spirit without the confinement of gender), un-
imaginable that Simon Bradstreet could have produced such an address
as his wife's "To My Dear Children" or that William Cavendish would
have been capable of writing *A True Relation* bearing any resemblance at
all to Margaret Lucas Cavendish's *True Relation*. It will be well to recall
here a point made earlier: that the question should bear the emphasis,
"why hath *this* lady writ her own life"—and together with that question should go its corollary, "*How* hath this lady writ her own life?"
Four different women have told four different stories in four different
ways and yet have told this essential story—essential to each of them as
an individual, essential to women in general, and essential to the history
of autobiography—so that we recognize them, each and all, as distinctively, radically the story of a woman. And this recognition should help
us to the conclusion that since the history of autobiography is largely a
history of the Western obsession with self and at the same time the felt
desire to somehow escape that obsession, our four models, who record
and dramatize self-realization and self-transcendence through the recognition of another, represent an important addition to that history. Along
with later women who followed, varied, or diverged from the original
patterns in writing out their lives, these four pioneers have had a special
role to play in the development of the genre of autobiography.

2

Writing Fictions:
Women's Autobiography in France

NANCY K. MILLER

Were I a writer and dead, how I would love it if my life, through
the pains of some friendly and detached biographer, were to reduce
itself to a few details, a few preferences, a few inflections, let us say
to "biographemes."

Roland Barthes, *Sade, Fourier, Loyola*

Is there, for me, no other haven than this commonplace room?
Must I stay forever before this impenetrable mirror where I come
up against myself, face to face?

Colette, *The Vagabond*

The oft-cited and apparently transparent epigraph to Colette's *Break
of Day*—"Do you imagine in reading my books that I am drawing my
portrait? Patience: it's only my model"[1]—challenges the reader's competence in distinguishing life from art, nature from imitation, autobiography from fiction. Although this inaugural gesture, anticipating
both our misreading and our improper labeling of the text, will prove to
be more than a simple inveighing against the fallacy of reference, let us,
for the moment, proceed as docile and linear readers. The novel opens
with a letter, and the author's first words ostensibly authenticate the
document: "This note, signed 'Sidonie Colette, née Landoy,' was written by my mother to one of my husbands, the second. A year later she

A different version of this essay first appeared in *Women and Language in Literature and Society,*
ed. Sally McConnell-Ginet, Ruth Borker, and Nelly Furman (New York: Praeger, 1980). It is
reprinted here from a revised version that appears in my *Subject to Change: Reading Feminist
Writing* (New York: Columbia University Press, 1988).

1. See, for example, Elaine Marks in her critical study *Colette* (New Brunswick, N.J.:
Rutgers University Press, 1960), p. 213; translation is hers. All future references to *Break of
Day,* however, will be drawn from the Enid McLeod translation (New York: Farrar, Straus
and Cudahy, 1961). All translations from the French here will be mine unless otherwise
indicated.

died at the age of seventy-seven" (p. 5). The invitation thus extended to
seal the identity gap between the "I" of narration and Sidonie Gabrielle
Colette is reissued in the second chapter. Defending herself against "one
of my husband's" claims that she could write nothing but love stories,
the narrator (a novelist) reviews the history of her fictional heroines and
the genealogy of her *name:*

> In them I called myself Renée Néré or else, prophetically, I introduced a
> Léa. So it came about that both legally and familiarly as well as in my
> books, I now have only one name, which is my own. Did it take only
> thirty years of my life to reach that point, or rather to get back to it? I shall
> end by thinking that it wasn't too high a price to pay.[2]

Who is speaking? And in whose name? The liminary warning operates
like a free-floating anxiety, already there at the very threshold of the text
to prevent the foreclosure of identification. The "I" of narration may,
like Colette, have "only one name" but her project is no less ambiguous
for that symmetry.[3] To bypass the ambiguity would be to assume, for
example, that the fiction of *Break of Day* is a page from Colette's autobiography, and hence to perform a "masculine" reading:

> Why do men—writers or so-called writers—still show surprise that a wom-
> an should so easily reveal to the public love-secrets and amorous lies and
> half-truths? *By divulging these, she manages to hide other important and obscure
> secrets which she herself does not understand very well. . . .* Man, my friend, you
> willingly make fun of women's writings because they can't help being
> autobiographical. On whom then were you relying to paint women for
> you . . . ? On yourself? (P. 62, my emphasis)

"Colette" would have her critics not confuse "the illuminated zone" of
the feminine sector, love's brilliant disasters, with the darker, shadowy
text of the female self, "the true intimate life of a woman" (pp. 62–63).
But that intimacy, that maskless self, has to do with "preference," and
here, we are told, she will "keep silent" (p. 45).

Shall we take "Colette" at her word then? That what we have are delib-

---

2. *Break of Day*, p. 19. Christiane Makward has pointed out the importance of this evolution in her analysis of patronyms and their relationship both to women's writing and to the
representation of femininity: "Not only is the father's name feminized and stripped of its
function (to signify descendance) but it takes the place of a first name. 'Colette' is no longer a
first name, a patronym or a pseudonym but *the name* that a free woman took fifty years to make
for herself." "Le Nom du père: Ecritures féminines d'un siècle à l'autre" (paper delivered at the
Third Annual Colloquium in Nineteenth-Century French Studies, Oct. 1977, Columbus,
Ohio).

3. Elaine Marks comments, citing the same passage: if the narrator is "no longer wearing
an obvious mask . . . she is, however, wearing the mask of 'Colette.'" And this "Colette"
only exposes a self protected by inverted commas. *Colette*, pp. 212–13.

erate *fictions* of self-representation, "rearranged fragments of . . . emotional life" as she calls them (p. 45), and not autobiography after all? Philippe Lejeune, whose *Autobiographie en France* constitutes the first attempt to define and classify autobiography in the French tradition as a genre, would have it so. He excludes Colette from his repertory, citing her own reluctance to talk about herself: but more to the point, the absence of what he poses as a necessary condition of autobiography: the "autobiographical pact."[4] This pact is a declaration of autobiographical intention, an explicit project of sincere truth telling; a promise to the *reader* that the textual and referential "I" are one. For Lejeune, however confessional a text may seem, without that covenant of good faith, we remain in the realm of fiction.

It seems, perhaps, perverse that despite the caveat implicit in "Colette's" jibe at the male reader expecting to find autobiography seeping through the pages of women's literature, we so reluctantly accept her exclusion from the French autobiographical canon.[5] This resistance comes not so much from doubts about the legitimacy of Lejeune's criteria (as they do or do not apply to Colette) as from a hesitation about embracing wholeheartedly any theoretical model *indifferent* to a problematics of genre as inflected by gender. With this hesitation in mind, let us consider instances of those female autobiographers included by Lejeune—George Sand, Daniel Stern (Marie d'Agoult), and Simone de Beauvoir. Taking his criteria as a point of departure, and moving dialectically between the points of textual production and reception, of authorship and readership, we will return in closing—with some stops along the way—to Colette. Thus by virtue of her undecidable relation to the androcentric paradigm Colette will serve as the fiction, the pretext really, which allows us to play with the theory.

Lejeune's definition of autobiography as the "retrospective narrative in prose that someone makes of his own existence, when he places the main emphasis on his individual life, in particular on the history of his personality" (p. 14), provides a point of departure from which to ask the question: is there a specificity to a female retrospective; how and where will it make itself felt? To the extent that autobiography, as Diane Johnson has put it, "requires some strategy of self-dramatization" and "contains, as in fiction, a crisis and a denouement,"[6] what conventions,

---

4. Philippe Lejeune, *L'Autobiographie en France* (Paris: Armand Colin, 1971), pp. 72–73.

5. It is a nice paradox that Colette is always read biographically and at the same time excluded from the corpus of autobiographical writing. Perhaps this is a useful way to think about the place of women's writing.

6. Diane Johnson, "Ghosts," *New York Review of Books* 24 (3 Feb. 1977): 19. In Lejeune's terms, autobiographical writing itself is an act of "staging": "L'écriture y est mise en scène" (p. 73). In a way, the theatricality of female subjectivity is central to feminist writing, thematically autobiographical or not.

we might then ask, govern the production of a female self as *theater?* How does a woman writer perform on the stage of her text?

Historically, the French autobiographer, male or female, has had to come to terms with the exhibitionist performer that is Jean-Jacques Rousseau.[7] Both George Sand and her contemporary Daniel Stern take a certain distance from the *Confessions* because of the inclusive quality of his rememorations. Sand, for example, asks in the "pact" to *L'Histoire de ma vie:* "Who can forgive him for having confessed Mme de Warens while confessing himself?"[8] Daniel Stern takes up the same point in her *Mémoires,* rejecting Rousseau's promiscuous gesture and concluding that for herself, "I felt neither the right nor the desire in recalling my own memories, to mix in, inappropriately, those of others."[9] And both issue warnings that the reader hoping for scandalous revelations will be disappointed; their truth, if not their memory, will be selective. Now the problem of selectivity is of course not a problem for women only. Every autobiographer must deal with it. Chateaubriand, for one, writes in the preface to *Mémoires d'outre-tombe* that he will "include no name other than his own in everything that concerns his private life."[10] To some extent, then, this reticence about naming names is a matter of historical context: the nineteenth-century backlash to the tell-all stance of Rousseau—especially in the area of the sexual connection, the erogenous zones of the self. But not entirely. The decision to go public is particularly charged for the woman writer.

In the preface to her second volume of memoirs, Simone de Beauvoir too goes back to Rousseau: "It may be objected that such an inquiry concerns no one but myself. Not so; if any individual—a Pepys or a Rousseau, an exceptional or a run-of-the-mill character—reveals himself honestly, everyone, more or less, becomes involved. It is impossible for him to shed light on his own life without at some point illuminating the lives of others.[11] But then, following this relative indifference to the contiguity of other lives, a familiar caveat:

7. For Lejeune, French autobiography officially begins with Rousseau, and he dates the genre from around 1760. As for the response to Rousseau, Lejeune writes: "Rousseau is the only one to say aloud what everyone thinks in private. All the autobiographical pacts that follow are written against Rousseau's disastrous frankness" (p. 82).

8. George Sand, *Histoire de ma vie,* in *Oeuvres autobiographiques* (Paris: Gallimard, 1970), 2:13. Béatrice Didier, in "Femme/Identité/Ecriture: A propos de *L'Histoire de ma vie* de George Sand," begins her article with an excerpt from Sand's correspondence: "I confess that I am neither humble enough to write confessions like Jean-Jacques nor impertinent enough to praise myself like the literary lights of the century. Furthermore, I don't believe that private life falls within the purview of the critics." *La Revue des Sciences Humaines: Ecriture, Féminité, Féminisme* 168 (1977): 561–76.

9. Daniel Stern, Avant-Propos to *Mémoires* [1833–54] (Paris: Calmann-Lévy, 1927), p. 11.

10. René de Chateaubriand, *Mémoires d'outre-tombe* (Paris: Flammarion, 1948), 1:547.

11. Simone de Beauvoir, *The Prime of Life,* trans. Peter Green (New York: Harper, 1976), p. 10, hereafter cited in the text.

At the same time I must warn [my readers] that I have no intention of telling them everything. I described my childhood and adolescence without any omissions. . . . I cannot treat the years of my maturity in the same detached way—nor do I enjoy a similar freedom when discussing them. I have no intention of filling these pages with spiteful gossip about myself and my friends; I lack the instincts of the scandal monger. There are many things which I firmly intend to *leave in obscurity*. (P. 10; my emphasis)

And she adds (in the next sentence): "On the other hand, my life has been closely linked with that of Jean-Paul Sartre. As he intends to write his own life story, I shall not attempt to perform the task for him." It is fair, I think, to assume that while for all autobiographers already figures of public fiction there is a strong sense of responsibility about speaking out, because, being known, they expect their words to have an impact within a clearly defined readers' circle, the female autobiographers know that they are being read as *women;* women, in the case of Sand, Stern, and Beauvoir (and this is no less true for Colette), known for (or even through) their liaisons with famous men. The concern with notoriety, then, functions as an additional grid or constraint placed upon the truth. Rather, upon"the shaping of the past" as truth.[12]

Daniel Stern articulates with the greatest insistence the role played by the fact of femininity in the autobiographical venture, and the *gender* of sincerity. She asks a friend in 1850, years before actually writing the first volume of her memoirs: "How do you think a work of this sort written by a woman, by a mother, should be composed? . . . I would favor a grave confession, narrow in scope, disengaged from detail, rather moral and intellectual than real. But I am told that that would be without charm."[13] And thirteen years later, in a diary entry (but by this time, it would seem, she has already begun writing): "No, my friend, I won't write my *Mémoires*. . . . My instinctive repugnance has conquered. . . . I had conceived of a daring book. Feminine confessions as sincere as and consequently more daring (because of public opinion) than those of Jean-Jacques. Once I thought this book was going to come about: *L'Histoire de ma vie* was announced. *I* cannot do it."[14] The book does get written, however, and in the preface to *Mes souvenirs,* Stern traces the logic of her hesitations: "I was a woman, and as such, not bound to a

---

12. The expression, somewhat out of context here, is from Roy Pascal, *Design and Truth in Autobiography* (Cambridge: Harvard University Press, 1960), p. 5.

13. Letter to Hortense Allard, cited by Jacques Vier, in *La Comtesse d'Agoult et son temps* (Paris: Armand Colin, 1961), 4:250.

14. Cited by Vier, 4:255. Thus Stern distances herself from Sand's *Histoire de ma vie* as well as Rousseau's *Confessions*. Stern comments on Sand's work—based on an incomplete reading: "It seems to me that [the work] is true or not true enough, and that is not how I would conceive of Confessions," letter to Hortense Allard, dated 1855, cited by Vier, 4:307 n. 727.

virile sincerity," but when a woman's life is not governed "by the common rule . . . she becomes responsible, more responsible than a man, in the eyes of all. When this woman, because of some chance or talent, comes out of obscurity she instantly contracts virile duties."[15]

Thus an exceptional woman, by virtue of that exceptionality, becomes subject to a double constraint: masculine responsibilities and feminine sensitivity. For whatever is wrong in the world, Stern contends, "woman has felt it more completely in her whole being." If a woman is an instrument more sensitive than a man in picking up the "discordances" of society, however, she must nevertheless be more discreet than a man in rendering those vibrations: "My persuasion being . . . that a woman's pen was more constrained than another's by choice within the truth" (*Mémoires*, p. 11).

Although, as Georges Gusdorf has written in his well-known essay on autobiography, "the man who tells his story . . . is involved not in an objective and disinterested occupation but in a work of personal justification," and although such self-justification in the eyes of the world may well constitute "the most secret intention"[16] of any autobiographical undertaking, for Stern (as is true in varying degrees of intensity for Sand and Beauvoir) the self being justified is indelibly marked by what Beauvoir calls "*féminitude:* a culturally determined status of difference and oppression."[17] Thus Stern would show (and surely this is the not-so-very-hidden agenda for Sand and Beauvoir) that while a woman may fly in the face of tradition, that is, of traditional expectations for women, particularly in regard to the institution of marriage, she is no less a *human being* of merit; that while on the face of it she is an outlaw, the real fault lies with society and its laws. To justify an unorthodox life by writing about it, however, is to *reinscribe* the original violation, to reviolate masculine turf: hence Stern's defensiveness about the range of her pen. The drama of the self (to return to the histrionic metaphor proposed earlier) is staged in a public theater, and it is *thesis* drama. The autobiographies of these women, to invoke another literary genre, are a defense and illustration, at once a treatise on overcoming received notions of femininity and a poetics calling for another, freer text. These autobiographies, then, belong to that type of women's writing Elaine Showalter has described as "feminist": "*protest* against [the] standards of art and its views of social roles," and "*advocacy* of minority rights and values, including a demand for autonomy."[18] The subject of women's

15. Daniel Stern, Preface to *Mes Souvenirs* (Paris: Calmann-Lévy, 1980), pp. vii–ix.

16. Georges Gusdorf, "Conditions et limites de l'autobiographie," in *Formen des Selbstdarstellung* (Berlin: Duncker and Humbolt, 1956), p. 115.

17. Simone de Beauvoir, "interroge Jean-Paul Sartre," *L'Arc* (1975), 12.

18. Elaine Showalter, *A Literature of Their Own* (Princeton: Princeton University Press, 1977), p. 13.

autobiography here is a self both occulted and overexposed by the fact of her femininity as a social reality.

It should come as no surprise that for women determined to go beyond the strictures of convention, conventionally female moments are not assigned privileged status. One does not find even metaphorical traces of what Hélène Cixous calls for in her "feminine future," "the gestation drive—just like the desire to write: a desire to live self from within, a desire for the swollen belly, for language, for blood."[19] Autobiology is not the subtext of autobiography. It is not, however, entirely repressed. George Sand, for example, who gives birth nine months after her marriage, embraces her pregnancy with pleasure and female solidarity: "I spent the winter of 1822–23 at Nohant, rather ill, but absorbed by the feeling of maternal love that was revealing itself to me through the sweetest dreams and the liveliest aspirations. The transformation that comes about at that moment in the life and thoughts of a woman is, in general, complete and sudden. It was so for me as for the great majority" (2:32). Forced by her doctor to remain in bed, perfectly still for six weeks, Sand comments: "The order . . . was severe, but what wouldn't I have done to maintain the hope of being a mother?" (2:35). And the account of childbirth itself, if abbreviated and discreet, is no less positive: "My son Maurice came into the world June 30, 1823, without mishap and very hardy. It was the most beautiful moment of my life, that moment when after an hour of deep sleep which followed upon the terrible pains of that paroxysm, I saw, on waking up, that tiny being asleep on my pillow. I had dreamed of him so much ahead of time, and I was so weak, I wasn't sure I wasn't still dreaming" (2:37).

Colette, in that slim volume of reminiscences called *The Evening Star* also gives pregnancy a few pages of retrospective attention. Taken by surprise at age forty, Colette is, in the beginning, less sanguine and more anxious than (the younger and at that point in her life more conventional) Sand: "I was simply afraid that at my age I would not know how to give a child the proper love and care, devotion and understanding. Love—so I believed—had already hurt me a great deal by monopolizing me for the past twenty years."[20] This concern results in secrecy about her condition, which, when finally revealed to a male

---

19. Hélène Cixous, "The Laugh of the Medusa," trans. Keith Cohen and Paula Cohen, *Signs* 1 (Summer 1976): 891.

20. Colette, *The Evening Star (L'Etoile Vesper)*, trans. David LeVay (Indianapolis: Bobbs-Merrill, 1973), p.132. LeVay's translation, however, is so unfaithful to Colette in spirit and style that I have actually quoted those passages from this volume of recollections as anthologized by Robert Phelps in *Earthly Paradise* (New York: Farrar, Straus, Giroux, 1966) (in this case p. 199); his translator, Herma Briffault, does honor to Colette's text. For those who might wish to consult the passages cited in context, I also provide the page references to the complete translation.

friend, leads him to say: "You're behaving as a man would, you're having masculine pregnancy!"[21] The "masculine" pregnancy, however, temporarily gives way to a slightly ironized but no less "feminine" text:

> Insidiously, unhurriedly, the beatitude of pregnant females spread through me. I was no longer subject to any discomfort, any unease. This purring contentment, this euphoria—how give a name either scientific or familiar to this state of preservation?—must certainly have penetrated me, since I have not forgotten it and am recalling it now, when life can never again bring me plentitude. . . . One gets tired of keeping to oneself all the unsaid things—in the present case my feeling of pride, of banal magnificence, as I ripened my fruit. (P. 200; pp. 132–33)

Despite the euphoria, Colette continued to write: "The 'masculine pregnancy' did not lose all its rights; I was working on the last part of *The Shackle*. The child and the novel were both rushing me, and the *Vie Parisienne,* which was serializing my unfinished novel, was catching up with me. The baby showed signs that it would win the race, and I screwed on the cap of my fountain pen" (p. 203; p. 135). The account of childbirth itself is characterized less by benign irony and humorous reticence than by a brutal distancing from the female lot: "What followed . . . doesn't matter and I will give it no place here. What followed was the prolonged scream that issues from all women in childbed. . . . What followed was a restorative sleep and selfish appetite" (p. 203; p. 136). But the anaphora already perceptible in this passage ("What followed"/ *la suite*) continues to structure insistently the narrative of this *hapax,* this unique moment in the writer's life, connecting an undifferentiating and hence (for Colette) negative female bond to a singular and bittersweet experience, her postpartum response to her daughter: "But what followed was also, once, an effort to crawl toward me made by my bundled up little larva that had been laid down for a moment on my bed. What animal perfection! The little creature guessed, she sensed the presence of my forbidden milk, and blindly struggled toward that blocked source. Never did I cry more brokenheartedly. Dreadful it is to ask in vain, but small is that hurt when compared with the pain of not giving" (pp. 203–4; p. 136). Colette accords a few more paragraphs to her passage into motherhood, but she quickly returns to the "competition between the book and the birth," the saving grace—for her writing—of her "jot of virility" (pp. 205–6; p. 137), to conclude with speculation about her own mother's probable reaction to this improbable maternity: "When I was a young girl, if I ever happened to occupy myself with some needlework, Sido always shook her soothsayer's head and com-

---

21. Phelps, p. 169; LeVay, p. 132, hereafter cited in the text, Phelps preceding LeVay.

mented, 'You will never look like anything but a boy who is sewing!' She would now have said, 'You will never be anything but a writer who gave birth to a child,' for she would not have failed to see the accidental character of my maternity" (pp. 205–6; p. 137).

A writer who gave birth to a child, this *hierarchization* of roles has everything to do with the shape of the autobiographies under consideration here: mothers by accident of nature, writers by design. While marriage (and for Beauvoir the decision not to marry) and childbearing (and again for Beauvoir the decision not to bear children) indeed punctuate the female retrospective, they are not self-evidently *signifying* moments. They shape lives rather in counterpoint to the valorized trajectory: the transcendence of the feminine condition through writing. If there is, to return to the language of theatricality invoked earlier, crisis and drama and denouement in the staging of the autobiographical self, it takes place around the act of writing. Although Beauvoir is the only autobiographer of this group to oppose in mutually exclusive categories writing and maternity, her assumption of writing as a vocation and as locus of identity is paradigmatic: "I knew that in order to become a writer I needed a great measure of time and freedom. I had no rooted objection to playing at long odds, but this was not a game: the whole value and direction of my life lay at stake. The risk of compromising it could only have been justified had I regarded a child as no less vital a creative task than a work of art, which I did not" (67). Mothers or not, maternal or not,[22] destiny is not tributary of anatomy in these texts.

Sand, who is the least ambivalent of the three about her maternity, in the autobiographical account of her apprenticeship to writing in Paris tells (with great relish) the following anecdote about writing and children. As a young woman, already a mother (Sand comes to live in her Parisian mansard with her little daughter) she ponders the ways of the world of letters and wonders whether she has what it takes to make it as a writer in Paris. On the recommendation of a friend, she pays a visit to a certain M. de Kératry, the successful author of *Le Dernier des Beaumanoir* (a story in which a woman, thought to be dead, is raped by the priest whose task it is to bury her), and seeks his advice about her

22. The contrast between Sand and Stern is interesting to note. Sand writes, for example, about maternal feelings: "I wasn't deluded by passion. I had for the artist [Chopin] a kind of very intense, very true maternal adoration, but which could not for an instant compete with maternal love [*l'amour des entrailles*], the only chaste feeling that can be passionate." George Sand, *Histoire de ma vie,* 2:433. Stern, for her part, reverses the hierarchy: "Let [women] say and repeat that maternal love surpasses all other forms of love, while they cling to it as a last resort [*un pis-aller*], and because they have been too cowardly, too vain, too demanding, to experience love and to understand friendship, those two exceptional feelings which can only germinate in strong souls." Stern, *Mémoires,* p. 82.

project. The man is terse: "I'm going to be frank with you. A woman shouldn't write." Sand decides to see herself out, but the man suddenly becomes loquacious. He wants to expose his theory on women's inferiority, "on the impossibility for even the most intelligent among them to write a good book." Finally, seeing Sand about to make her exit, he utters his parting shot (that Sand characterizes as an example of Napoleonic wit): "Believe me, don't make books, make babies" (2:150).

The cogito for Sand, Stern, and Beauvoir would seem to be, I write, therefore I am. Writing—for publication—represents entrance into the world of others, and by means of that passage a rebirth: the access through writing to the status of an autonomous subjectivity beyond the limits of feminine propriety established by a Kératry.[23] The meaningful trajectory is thus literary and intellectual.[24] The life of the mind is not, however, cooly cerebral. It is vivid and impassioned. Thus Stern describes her motivation in becoming a writer: "I needed to get outside of myself, to put into my life a new interest, which was not love for a man, but an intellectual relationship with those who felt, thought and suffered as I did, I published therefore . . . " (Mémoires, p. 215). The textualization of a female "I" means escape from the sphere inhabited by those "relative beings" (as Beauvoir has characterized women) who experience the world only through the mediation of men. To write is to come out of the wings, and to appear, however briefly, center stage.

It is in those terms that Beauvoir describes the publication of her first novel: "So through the medium of my book I aroused curiosity, irritation, even sympathy: there were people who actually liked it. Now at last I was fulfilling the promises I had made myself when I was fifteen. . . . For a moment it was sufficient that I had crossed the threshold: She Came to Stay existed for other people, and I had entered public life" (p. 441). One arrives then at this curious but finally not very surprising paradox: these autobiographies are the stories of women who succeeded in becoming more than just women, and by their own negative definition of that condition.

Sand, for example, reflecting on Montaigne's exclusion of women

---

23. "L'Histoire de ma vie is especially and in the end the story of a birth to writing—birth deferred, sometimes occulted, difficult, of which the narrative traverses the entire text. . . . this birth becomes . . . the very object of the book." Didier, pp. 567–68.

24. This emphasis on intellectual pursuits is not restricted, it would seem, to women writers in France. In "Female Identities," Patricia Spacks comments on the autobiographical works of four eighteenth-century English writers, Mrs. Thrale, Mrs. Pilkington, Mrs. Clarke, and Lady Mary Wortley Montagu: "With an almost mythic insistence all four of these women reiterate a theme common in the century's fiction: the female apology, heavily tinged with resentment, for the life of the mind. Men think, therefore exist; women, who—men believed—hardly think at all, have therefore perhaps a questionable hold on their own existences." Patricia Meyer Spacks, Imagining a Self (Cambridge: Harvard University Press, 1976), pp. 78–79.

from the chapter on friendship by virtue of their inferior moral nature, protests and would exempt herself—at least partially—from that category by virtue of her education:

> I could see that an education rendered somewhat different from that of other women by fortuitous circumstances had modified my being. . . . I was not, therefore, entirely a woman like those whom the moralists censure and mock; in my soul I had enthusiasm for the beautiful, thirst for the true, and yet I was indeed a woman like all the others, sickly, highly strung, dominated by my imagination, childishly vulnerable to the tender emotions and anxieties of maternity. (2:126–27)

While Sand in this reflection concludes that "the heart and the mind have a sex" and that "a woman will always be more of an artist and a poet in her life, a man always more in his work" (but objects to an interpretation of that difference as a definition of "moral inferiority"), she no less aspires to transcendence, dreaming of those "male virtues to which women can raise themselves" (2:127). The question one must now ask is whether the story of a woman who sees conventional female self-definition as a text to be rewritten, who refuses the inscription of her body as the ultimate truth of her self, to become, if not a man, an exceptional woman (hence like a man), is a story significantly different from that of a man who becomes an exceptional man (particularly in this instance of figures who became exceptional by virtue of their writing).[25]

The difference of gender *as genre* is there to be read only if one accepts the terms of another sort of "pact": the pact of commitment to decipher what women have said (or, more important, left unsaid) about the pattern of their lives, over and above what any person might say about his, through genre. I say "his" deliberately. Not because men in fact lead genderless lives, but because the fact of their gender is given and received literarily as a mere donnée of personhood, because the canon of the autobiographical text, like the literary canon, self-defined as it is by the notion of a human universal, in general fails to interrogate gender as

---

25. Historically, for example, for women writers in France, artistic activity must seem to be economically motivated in order to be socially justified, to justify the violation of gendered identity. In this sense, Claudine Herrmann argues in *Les Voleuses de langue* that George Sand "sought in every way to convince her readers that she was writing to earn a living." Herrmann invokes Sand's "alibi" in the context of Stendhal's discussion of female authorship in *De l'amour*. Stendhal (who, Hermann comments, audaciously compares women's condition to that of black slaves in nineteenth-century America, and who further observes that "all geniuses born as women are lost to the public good") remarks: "For a woman under the age of fifty to publish a book, is to subject her happiness to the most terrible of lotteries; if she is fortunate enough to have a lover, the first thing that will happen is that she will lose him. I see one exception only: a woman who writes books [*fait des livres*] to feed and raise her family" (31–33).

a meaningful category of reference or interpretation. This is not to say of course that the male autobiographer does not inscribe his *sexuality*. And Rousseau is hardly silent on the matter. But when, for example, Rousseau writes at the beginning of his *Confessions:* "I want to show my fellow men [*mes semblables*] a man in all nature's truth," he conflates in perfect conformity with the linguistic economy of the West maleness and humanity, as do most of the readers of autobiography cited in these pages.[26]

To read for difference, therefore, is to perform a diacritical gesture, to refuse a politics of reading that depends on the fiction of a neutral (neuter) economy of textual production and reception. This refusal of a fiction of degendered reading is a movement of oscillation which locates difference in the negotiation between writer and reader. The difference of which I speak here, however, is located in the "I" of the beholder, in the *reader's* perception. I would propose, then, the notion of gender-marked reading: a practice of the text that would recognize the status of the reader as a differentiated subject, a reading subject named by gender and committed in a dialectics of identification to deciphering the inscription of a female subject. (This move is what in "Arachnologies" I call "overreading.")[27]

Let us now engage a less docile reading of our autobiographers, and especially of Colette. Toward the end of *The Evening Star,* Colette imagines a publisher asking her: "When will you make up your mind to give us your memoirs?" And has herself answer: "Dear Publisher, I will write them neither more, nor better nor less than today" (p. 141). She thus rejects the specifically autobiographical project in its generic specificity. But then she suddenly wonders about an earlier female writer and autobiographer:

> How the devil did George Sand manage? Robust laborer of letters that she was, she was able to finish off one novel and begin another within the hour. She never lost either a lover or a puff of her hookah by it, produced a twenty volume *Histoire de ma vie* into the bargain and I am completely staggered when I think of it. Pell-mell, and with ferocious energy she piled up her work, her passing griefs, her limited felicities. I could never have done so much, and at the moment when she was thinking forward to her full barns I was still lingering to gaze at the green, flowering wheat. (P. 502; p. 141)

26. Jean-Jacques Rousseau, *Les Confessions* (Paris: Garnier-Flammarion, 1968), 1:43.
27. "Arachnologies: The Woman, the Text, and the Critic," in *Subject to Change: Reading Feminist Writing* (New York: Columbia University Press, 1988).

Colette, reading Sand, wonders about that life: the weave of writing, love, happiness, unhappiness. And makes the comparison to her own: she/I. If, as Gusdorf suggests, the "essence of autobiography" is its "anthropological significance" (p. 119), Colette is a good *reader* of autobiography because the text of another's life sends her back to her own (which has been the challenge of autobiography since Augustine). Why Sand, and how does Colette think back to Sand? Having introduced, as we have just seen, the question of memoirs, and having rejected the undertaking, Colette then imagines her image in a publisher's eyes: "God forgive me! They must expect a kind of 'Secret Journal' in the style of the Goncourt brothers!" (p. 141). By ellipsis Colette rejects this negative and implicitly masculine, dirty-secrets model. Instead, thinking about how much time and what sacrifices were involved in the elaboration of her own life's work—"It has taken me a great deal of time to scratch out forty or so books. So many hours that could have been used for travel, for idle strolls, for reading, even for indulging a feminine and healthy coquetry" (p. 502; p. 141)—Colette makes a feminist connection: how did Sand manage?[28]

This structure of kinship through which readers as women perceive bonds relating them to writers as women would seem to be a "natural" feature of the autobiographical text. But is it? Are these autobiographies the place par excellence in which the self inscribed and the self deciphering perform the ultimate face-to-face? I don't think so. Despite the identity between the "I" of authorship and the "I" of narration, and the pacts of sincerity, reading these lives is rather like shaking hands with one's gloves on.[29] Is this decorum a feature of gender? To the extent that autobiography, like any narrative, requires a shaping of the past, a making *sense* of a life, it tends to cast out the parts that don't add up (what we might think of as the flip side of the official *reconstructed* personality). Still, autobiography can incorporate what Roy Pascal has called the "cone of darkness at the center"; indeed, as he comments, "it

28. This is oddly close in language to Woolf's remarks on Colette's writing. In a letter to Ethel Smythe, 25 June 1936, about an article of Colette's on Anna de Noailles, Woolf says: "I'm almost floored by the extreme dexterity, insight and beauty of Colette. How does she do it? No one in England could do a thing like that. If a copy is ever going I should like to have one—to read it again, and see how its [*sic*] done: or guess. And to think I scarcely know her books! Are they all novels? Is it the great French tradition that lifts her so serenely, and yet with such a flare, down, down to what she's saying? I'm green with envy." I am grateful to Brenda Silver for finding this reference for me.

29. I am tempted, though the context is radically different, by the passage in Toni Morrison's *Sula* where we read this contrast between "that version of herself . . . she sought to reach out to and touch with an ungloved hand" and "the naked hand" (p. 121) as a way of talking about degrees of intimate contact.

seems to be required of the autobiographer that he should recognize that there is something unknowable in him" (pp. 184–85). One has the impression reading Stern,[30] Sand, and Beauvoir that the determination to have their lives make sense and thus be susceptible to *universal* reception blinds them, as it were to their own darkness: the "submerged core," "the sexual mystery that would make a drama."[31] It is as though the anxiety of gender identity, of a culturally devalued femininity, veils its inscription in strategies of representation.

But should we give up so easily? We are after all given clues in the autobiographies telling us where to look (or not to look), for what Colette calls the "unsaid things." When Beauvoir, for example, describes the stakes of her fiction writing, how she wanted to be read, she tells us something important about her other self:

> I passionately wanted the public to like my work; therefore like George Eliot, who had become identified in my mind with Maggie Tulliver, I would myself become an imaginary character, endowed with beauty, desirability, and a sort of shimmering transparent loveliness. It was this metamorphosis that my ambition sought. . . . I dreamed of splitting into two selves, and of having a shadowy alter ego that would pierce and haunt people's hearts. It would have been no good if this phantom had had overt connections with a person of flesh and blood; anonymity would have suited me perfectly. (P. 291)

30. I must here, somewhat belatedly, distinguish between *Mes souvenirs* (1806–33) and *Mémoires* (1833–54). Both were published posthumously, in 1880 and 1927, respectively. The later text, which is an account of Stern's love affair with Liszt, is extraordinarily "personal" and moving. However, the volume itself is a construction, a compilation made by the editor, Daniel Ollivier. It includes journal entries (hers and Liszt's), notes, and fragmentary chapters of the unfinished *Mémoires*. (As one might imagine, the journal is the more passionate, disturbed, and disturbing document.) Stern herself seems to have favored this installment of her life's story. In a letter dated 1867, cited by Vier (*La Comtesse,* p., 262), she writes: "I am just finishing the second volume of the *Mémoires:* the story of passion that will not be a masterpiece, but *my* masterpiece" (Stern's italics). As I will argue, if one is reading to discover, uncover, a female self, the corpus must be expanded by breaking down the barriers of genre, rather, the hierarchies of the canon: fiction, autobiography, correspondence, diaries, and so on. Here Vier's remarks on reading the *Mémoires* with the correspondence are very much to the point: "It is Marie whom the *Mémoires* portray; the letters give us glimpses of the countess d'Agoult; the former is fragile and passive, the latter châtelaine and suzeraine; the former belongs completely to the man she loves and admires, the latter knows herself to be an original mind and senses in herself a literary vocation" (1:275).

31. Pauline Kael, reviewing Lillian Hellman's *Julia* with *Pentimento,* the filmic fiction with the autobiography, *New Yorker,* 10 Oct. 1977, pp. 100–101. Not surprisingly, Hellman's conclusion to the volume of her memoirs called *An Unfinished Woman* (New York: Bantam, 1974), points to the dangers lurking in the passion for a coherent self: "I do regret that I have spent too much of my life trying to find what I called 'truth,' trying to find what I called 'sense.' I never knew what I meant by truth, never made the sense I hoped for. All I mean is that I left too much of me unfinished because I wasted too much time. However" (p.244).

Sand points us in the same direction:

> It was inevitably said that *Indiana* was my person and my story. It is
> nothing of the sort. I have presented many types of women, and I think
> that after reading this account of the impressions and reflections of my life,
> it will be clear that I have never portrayed myself [*mise en scène*] as a woman
> [*sous des traits féminins*]. I am too much of a romantic [trop romanesque] to
> have seen the heroine of a novel in my mirror. . . . Even if I had tried to
> make myself beautiful and dramatize my life, I would never have suc-
> ceeded. My *self,* confronting me face-to-face would have dampened my
> enthusiasm. (2:160)

By suggesting, as I am, that a *double* reading—of the autobiography
with the fiction—would provide a more sensitive apparatus for
deciphering a female self, I am not proposing a return to the kind of
biographical "hermeneutics" that characterizes a Larnac (in his 1929
Histoire de la littérature féminine). Like Colette's interpellated male reader
in *Break of Day,* Larnac reads all women's fiction as autobiography: "In
the center of every feminine novel, one discovers the author. . . . Incapable of abstracting a fragment of themselves to constitute a whole,
[women writers] have to put all of themselves into their work."[32] (It is
not, of course, a question of saying, as he does, Indiana is George
Sand—in female drag.)

I am proposing instead an intratextual practice of interpretation
which, in articulation with the gendered overreading I have just proposed, would privilege neither the autobiography nor the fiction but
take the two writings together in their status as text. Germaine Brée has
performed such a reading. In an essay on George Sand entitled "The
Fictions of Autobiography," Brée isolates what she calls the "matrix of
fabulation" and analyzes its function in both the autobiography and the
fiction.[33] The matrix is that structure through which Sand deals with the
problem of origins and identity. Brée decodes the Sandian inscription of
the self, allowing the "fictional fiction" and the "fictions of autobiography" to illuminate each other (p. 446). Because of the historical protocol
and cultural taboos that historically have governed women's writing,
and the problems of imagining public female identities, not to perform

---

32. Jean Larnac, *Histoire de la littérature feminine* (Paris: Kra, 1929), pp. 253–54.

33. Germaine Brée, "The Fictions of Autobiography," *Nineteenth-Century French Studies,* 4
(Summer 1976): 446. Gusdorf himself seems to make a case for a double reading when he
remarks: "There would therefore be two versions, or two instances of autobiography: on the
one hand, the confession strictly speaking, on the other, the entire work of the artist which
takes up the same subject matter in complete freedom and with the protection of incognito" (p.
121).

an expanded reading, in this instance, not to read the fiction *with* the autobiography, is to remain prisoner of a canon that bars women from their own texts.

And Colette?

Let us return briefly now to the epigraph from *Break of Day*. Early in the novel, the narrator gives us a portrait of her mother taking stock at the end of her life. The metaphor used for this putting into perspective of the past is that of a painter before a canvas: "She stands back, and returns, and stands back again, pushing some scandalous detail into place, bringing into the light of day a memory drowned in shadow. By some unhoped-for art she becomes—equitable. Is anyone imagining as he reads me, that I'm portraying myself? *Have patience: this is merely my model*" (pp. 34–35; my emphasis). In context, then, the epigraph seems to narrow its focus. Indeed, it has been taken to mean that the model in question is "the model of the mother" and that this "affilia-tion, recognized and reclaimed," constitutes the deep structure of the novel;[34] painter of her mother, and through her mother, herself. This is no less, however, the portrait of the writer in this same novel as auto-biographer: "No other fear, not even that of ridicule, prevents me from writing these lines which I am willing to risk will be published. Why should I stop my hand from gliding over this paper to which for so many years I've confided what I know about myself, what I've tried to hide, what I've invented and what I've guessed?" (p. 62). Every inscrip-tion of the self is an approximation and a projection; a matter of details, shadows, adjustment, and proportion—an *arrangement* of truths. Still, does the collection of self-portraits make an autobiography? Robert Phelps tried to construct one in a volume called *Earthly Paradise: An Autobiography,* in which he strings together moments in Colette's life through passages from her works in a thematic and roughly chronologi-cal continuum. Lejeune rejects Phelps's construction as just that: one does not ghostwrite an autobiography; the "pact" cannot be concluded by a third party.

How then to conclude?

At the end of an article published two years after *L'Autobiographie en France,* Lejeune renounces his previous attempts to find a definition of autobiography that would be coherent and exhaustive. Having decided that autobiography is as much a *mode of reading* as a mode of writing, he looks instead to a history (as yet to be written) of autobiography that would be the history of the way in which autobiography is read. To be sure, Lejeune is not concerned with female autobiography. But his no-

34. Michel Mercier, *Le Roman féminin* (Paris: Presses Universitaires de France, 1976), p. 46.

tion of a contractual genre dependent upon codes of transmission and reception suits our purposes, because it relocates the problematics of autobiography as genre as an interaction between reader and text.[35]

And Colette?

To read Colette is not, perhaps, in the final analysis (pace Lejeune), to read (generically) a woman's *autobiography*.[36] It is, however, to read the inscription of a female self: a cultural fabrication that names itself as such, and that we can identify through the patient negotiation we ourselves make with the neither/nor of "memoirs mixed with fiction, fictions compounded of fact."[37] Colette's textual "I" is not bound by genre. For Sand, Stern, and Beauvoir, despite their pact, the locus of identification, I would suggest, is no different. The historical truth of a woman writer's life lies in the reader's grasp of her intratext: the body of her writing and not the writing of her body.

35. Philippe Lejeune, "Le Pacte autobiographique," *Poétique* 14 (1973), 137–62; cf. esp. 160–62.

36. Reading this essay over and revising it ten years after I wrote it, I am struck and slightly dismayed by the dogged way I follow through and worry about Lejeune's moves. (Particularly since I know how profoundly irreversible the interest is!) And yet am I today cured of the gesture to revise, to begin by turning to the male model to see how and where it doesn't work? When will there be an end to the double work of revision, I wonder.

37. William Gass, "Three Photos of Colette," *New York Review of Books* 24 (14 April 1977): 12.

3

Non-Autobiographies of "Privileged" Women: England and America

Carolyn G. Heilbrun

I write, not without trepidation, on "a select group of college-edu-cated, middle and upper class, married white women," to borrow the description used by Bell Hooks in her essay "Black Women: Shaping Feminist Theory," published in 1984. Indeed if, as Hooks suggests, the feminist movement has hitherto been seen, myopically, as concerned only with "housewives bored with leisure, with the home, with children, with buying products, who wanted more out of life,"[1] this volume may stand as testimony that the study of female autobiography, like other forms of feminist criticism, cannot overlook, any more than it can be confined to, the lot of "college-eduated, middle and upper class" women.

No one is easier to mock than the "privileged" woman. When there are women starving, unable to care for their children, victims of racism and public indifference, one's voice echoes hollowly while pleading for the "more" desired by women with none of these afflictions. I well remember a black woman at a conference in the early days of feminism announcing that she didn't want to get out of her kitchen, she wanted to get out of "yours." This remark, as metaphoric in her case as it would have been in mine, was, nonetheless, well taken and silenced us all, as it has continued to silence those who plead for the "rescue" of women who are "enslaved," if you can believe it, by riches. Hooks accuses Betty Friedan of making "her plight and the plight of white women like herself, synonymous with a condition affecting all American women." The diversity of this volume, then, testifies to the ratification of that mistake.

1. Bell Hooks, *Feminist Theory: From Margin to Center* (Boston: South End Press, 1984), p. 1.

This is not to say that the rescue operation Friedan initiated was not necessary. If we look at the autobiographies of women in England and America in the twentieth century before Friedan, we discover that voicelessness and oppression are linked among the privileged as well as among those oppressed by race and class. Patriarchal oppression inter-acts with race and class, and male violence, like oppression related to religion or sexual preference, cuts across all races and classes. What I shall be considering here are the particular effects of the patriarchy on "privileged" women, effects which, unlike physical abuse, they do not share with women of other classes and races.

It is always possible to say there is no point in bemoaning the state of privileged women while masses of underprivileged women suffer gross indignities in the United States and elsewhere. Hooks says that Friedan "did not tell readers whether it was more fulfilling to be a maid, a babysitter, a factory worker, a clerk, or a prostitute, than to be a leisure class housewife." The question this question leaves unanswered is whether the "leisure class" woman has no demands to make upon so-ciety which are universal for all women.

Indeed, I would suggest that the special circumstances of these "priv-ileged" women have made them particularly likely sources for the rise of a new feminine consciousness. Who else has the time and money for such thoughts, for the enactment of such daring? And we cannot forget that Freud's theories and discoveries rested in great part upon such women, their complaints, symptoms, and silences—all reinforced by Freud's use of such women to bolster his male-centered theories. Flo-rence Nightingale, born thirty-five years before Freud, and Beatrice Webb, born two years after him, might well have been his patients had they been Austrian Jews and of his generation. Their complaints, those of "privileged" women, whether recorded by Freud, Friedan, or the women themselves, are at the very heart of women's oppression: they include sexual abuse and the miseries of a hunger that is not physical and that can be felt by women of all races and classes.

Elaine Showalter in her book *The Female Malady* first quotes Florence Nightingale: "To have no food for our heads, no food for our hearts, no food for our activity, is that nothing? If we have no food for the body, how do we cry out, how all the world hears of it. . . . But suppose one were to put a paragraph in the 'Times', *Death of Thought from Starvation,* or *Death of Moral Activity from Starvation,* how people would stare, how they would laugh and wonder." Showalter herself then uses the lan-guage of starvation: "Surely the 'hungry look' that Savage saw in the faces of his neurasthenic female patients was a craving for more than food. The nervous women of the *fin de siècle* were ravenous for a fuller life than their society offered them, famished for the freedom to act, and make real choices."[2]

Friedan called these women's anguish "the problem that has no name" because that is exactly what it is. Racism, classism, elitism, hunger—these have a name. Women need to be particularly alert to nameless problems: they are problems recognized less even than most by male language. Perhaps the time has come when we may, without fear of accusations of elitism, classism, racism, again look at the lives of "privileged" women.

For Virginia Woolf, the differences between her class and that of working women were clear. Elizabeth Meese has noticed Woolf's comment in *Three Guineas:* "Meanwhile it would be interesting to know what the true born working man or woman thinks of the playboys and playgirls of the educated class who adopt the working-class cause without sacrificing middle-class capital, or sharing working-class experience." Meese goes on to remark, "Woolf's ability to recognize this unromanticized difference in the lives of working women, as well as her personal courage in speaking out against domination, earned her Tillie Olsen's acknowledged and enduring respect."[3] Unfortunately, it did not win her the respect of most Englishwomen, including current feminists in Britain. There was, for example, no marking of Woolf's centennial in 1982 in England, although the Irish were enthusiastically celebrating Joyce's that same year. Woolf was considered too upper-class, too effete—a traditional view of her dating back at least to Queenie Leavis. This sneering at privileged women, whether or not they recognize their difference in experience from working-class women, has done nothing to aid the cause of feminism. Cora Kaplan, writing of the relation of feminism to the "wider socialist feminist project," fears a privileging of gender "in isolation from other forms of social determination."[4] The problem is that it is only in isolation from other forms of social oppression not special to women that gender oppression can be seen in all its most painful ramifications. Alice Walker, for example, has, in *The Color Purple,* shown that what Christine Froula has discussed as the "daughter's seduction" applies across class and race lines, from the American South to Freud's consulting room.

Nonetheless, to say, as Kaplan does, that "privileged" women "fear

---

2. Elaine Showalter, *The Female Malady: Women, Madness, and English Culture, 1830–1980* (New York: Pantheon, 1985), pp. 128, 144.

3. Elizabeth A. Meese, *Crossing the Double-Cross: The Practice of Feminist Criticism* (Chapel Hill: University of North Carolina Press, 1986), p. 107.

4. Cora Kaplan, "Pandora's Box: Subjectivity, Class and Sexuality in Socialist Feminist Criticism," in *Making a Difference: Feminist Literary Criticism,* ed. Gayle Greene and Coppelia Kahn (New York: Methuen, 1985), pp. 147–48.

above all the loss of social status," were this even true, is merely to de-scribe their unique prison.[5] Virginia Woolf and Dorothy Sayers are always condemned (as Woolf is by Kaplan) for snobbism, for being "elite," inevitably a pejorative word. But as Lee Edwards has remarked, Woolf and Sayers are "speaking of, and to, an elite, an heroic cadre, a class of educated women whose education and intelligence demand that they choose, and that they understand their choice and its consequence."[6]

There is a sharp break between the autobiographies of Victorian-born "privileged" women and those born in the twentieth century; the Vic-torian women found, if not a name for it, at least a general description of their condition. Deborah Epstein Nord has set forth this Victorian di-lemma of female autobiography with rare lucidity. Webb's reputation has suffered because she was responded to not as an individual but "as a failed woman or a counterfeit man."[7] These were the only alternatives. When she came to write her autobiography, only male models of auto-biography were available to her. Nord has observed that "only the women novelists of the nineteenth century, notably Charlotte Brontë and George Eliot, could identify, interpret and resolve, however trag-ically or infelicitously, the conflicts that determined and shaped their own—and other women's—lives. . . . And for most nineteenth-cen-tury women of ambition and achievement, the resolution of struggle and satisfactory discovery of sexual and spiritual identity remained pain-fully elusive and, therefore, virtually impossible to describe."[8] But what was clear about that "identity" was that it turned on the woman's recog-nition of male ambition and talent imprisoned in a female body or a strong sense of female power and sexuality imprisoned in female destiny. In the post-Freudian twentieth century this recognition became so disturbing that it could not even be stated. Woolf would, like her Victorian predecessors, embody it in fiction, but not in autobiography as such.

The reason that "privileged" women have not written autobiogra-phies, have been, in fact, so powerless in the midst of their privilege, is not only, as Jane Miller suggests and as many feminists have thought, because such women have been made "dependent on men and restricted by men's plans for them, [and] also been beguiled by what their particu-lar men could offer them as protection, love and values,"[9] but primarily

5. Ibid., p. 165.

6. Lee, Edwards, *Psyche as Hero: Female Heroism and Fictional Form* (Middletown, Conn.: Wesleyan University Press, 1984), p. 295.

7. Deborah Epstein Nord, *The Apprenticeship of Beatrice Webb* (Amherst: University of Massachusetts Press, 1985), p. 8.

8. Ibid., pp. 58–59.

9. Jane Miller, *Women Writing about Men* (New York: Pantheon, 1986), p. 234.

because, as Woolf wrote in *Three Guineas,* "if all the daughters of educated men were to down tools tomorrow nothing essential either to the life or to the war-making of the community would be embarrassed. Our class is the weakest class in the state. We have no weapon with which to enforce our will."[10] Little wonder that such women have been unable to write autobiographies: the very genre excluded them from practicing that art.

If, like Georges Gusdorf, we speak of autobiography as expressing a "concern peculiar to Western men," it is reasonable to assert that there have been no autobiographies of women until the last decade or so. Gusdorf continues: "The man who takes delight in thus drawing his own image believes himself worthy of a special interest. Each of us tends to think of himself as the center of a living space: I count, my existence is significant to the world, and my death will leave the world incomplete. . . . The author of an autobiography . . . looks at himself as being and delights in being looked at—he calls himself as witness for himself; others he calls as witness for what is irreplaceable in his presence." In earlier times, Gusdorf points out, in those periods and places where "the singularity of each individual life" had not yet evolved, there was no autobiography. Inadvertently, he thus describes women's existence as it continued down to the day before yesterday, certainly until long after the period in which men found their "singularity." Gusdorf goes on: "Throughout most of human history, the individual does not oppose himself to all others; he does not feel himself to exist outside of others, and still less against others. . . . The important unit is never the isolated being." And again: "Each man thus appears as the possessor of a role" and not as an "individual."[11]

It requires no great ingenuity (though it did not occur to Gusdorf) to see that these observations explain the dearth, until very recently, of female autobiography in the Western tradition he was describing. Singularity in women was hardly to be boasted of. Even in the twentieth century, before the current women's movement, women had only what Patricia Spacks has called "selves in hiding." Gusdorf's phrase for the curiosity of the male autobiographer, "the wonder that he feels before the mystery of his own destiny,"[12] has become really possible for privileged women in the West only in the last fifteen years.

Only since 1980 in America have critics even bothered to speak of women's autobiography, and then in less-than-confident tones. Indeed,

10. Virginia Woolf, *Three Guineas* (New York: Harcourt, Brace and World, 1938), p. 16.
11. Georges Gusdorf, "Conditions and Limits of Autobiography," in *Autobiography: Essays Theoretical and Critical,* ed. James Olney (Princeton: Princeton University Press, 1980), pp. 29–30.
12. Ibid., p. 29.

women began creeping into studies of autobiography the way they infiltrated academic departments, and as in academe, there had been an "honorary man," or "token woman" already on the premises: Gertrude Stein. Apart from the obvious qualification that her autobiography was an account within the male norms of destiny, its indirect mode of discourse (it was presented as *The Autobiography of Alice B. Toklas*) doubtless provided a comfortable and "literary" angle from which to approach it. James Olney's collection, *Autobiography: Essays Theoretical and Critical,* published in 1980, included only one essay on the autobiographies of women (reprinted in this volume)—in this case four women from before 1700, whom its author, Mary G. Mason, called "early prototypes."[13] The dialogue of these women was with God; thus they manifested Christian virtue, "an excellent thing in woman."

For women, especially for "privileged" women, oppression is not the determining fact. As Arnold Rampersad has shown, the matter is wholly different with black Americans: "It is doubtful whether any single genre holds sway over a culture as powerfully as does autobiography over Afro-American literary expression." If black autobiographies have not been as individualistic as those of white male Americans, they have all been marked by being part of "a long, historic march toward Canaan."[14] To the black consciousness, Canaan was a definable place or condition. As Roger Rosenblatt put it with brilliant succinctness, "No black American author has ever felt the need to invent a nightmare to make his point."[15]

Canaan and nightmare for white, privileged women, on the other hand, were far from palpable: nor had they been described in words universally recognizable and acknowledged. No social alternative to women's dimly perceived oppression presented itself to their imaginations: how could it? Today, two decades into the women's movement, it has not yet clearly done so. And might one identify in public one's own "nightmares," when that very nightmare had been clearly demarcated for millennia as the wholly desirable, indeed, ideal destiny of woman? Even those women who, in their millions, suffered undefined depressions as wives or, in smaller numbers, suffered all too clearly defined scorn as spinsters, professionals, and revolutionaries dared not express, even to themselves, their desire for a wholly different fate.

For privileged women there was only one plot, though we have lately

13. Mary G. Mason, "The Other Voice: Autobiographies of Women Writers," this volume.
14. Arnold Rampersad, "Biography, Autobiography, and Afro-American Culture," *Yale Review* 73.1 (1983):12, 14.
15. Roger Rosenblatt, "Black Autobiography: Life as the Death Weapon," in *Autobiography,* p. 171.

named it diversely: the erotic plot, the marriage plot, the romance plot, all the plots ending, as Nancy Miller has pointed out, with marriage or death: the euphoric or dysphoric plot. The labels change; the outcome is the same. Henry James's words from *The Portrait of a Lady* suffice for the story of women's lives: "She was intelligent and generous; it was a fine free nature; but what was she going to do with herself? This question was irregular, for with most women one had no occasion to ask it. Most women did with themselves nothing at all; they waited, in attitudes more or less gracefully passive, for a man to come that way and furnish them with a destiny."[16] And as we know, Isabel Archer, for all her intelligence and generosity, is provided with a destiny by a man. What other story could there be?

James Olney in a book published in 1972 took the maleness of auto-biography for granted. "Autobiography," he wrote, "seems to mean the most to us because it brings an increased awareness, though an under-standing of another life in another time and place, of the nature of our own selves and our share in the human condition." Olney is interested, he goes on to tell us, in "why men write autobiographies, and have written them for centuries."[17] It did not occur to him that half the human race did not share, in the way he described it, in "the human condition." For women, their "condition" was female rather than human and hardly described or acknowledged.

Albert Stone, commenting on Rosenblatt's statement about blacks having no need to invent a nightmare, adds, "Black autobiography vividly re-creates links between the singular self, the immediate community, and a wider world of sympathetic readers and fellow human beings."[18] For women there were no such links to be re-created: their only "immediate community" was their family or neighbors, to whom no doubts about their condition could easily be expressed; above all, women had been advised, and had internalized the necessity, of possess-ing not a "singular self" but only a self-denial that must always put others first. There were no sympathetic readers, at least none readily identified, and women were inevitably "other" to those "fellow human beings" whom Olney and everyone else referred to simply as "men."

But if the lack of any community or audience for their scarcely de-fined condition of storylessness hampered women's autobiography, their own internalization of patriarchal standards operated more forcefully still. So, in the words of Spacks, writing of eighteenth-cen-

16. Henry James, *The Portrait of a Lady* (New York: Norton, 1975), p. 64.
17. James Olney, *Metaphors of Self* (Princeton: Princeton University Press, 1972), p. vii.
18. Albert E. Stone, Introduction to *The American Autobiography: A Collection of Critical Essays* (Englewood Cliffs, N.J.: Prentice-Hall, 1981), p. 4.

tury women's autobiographies, a fantasy of feminine strength, even if
that were achieved, "transformed itself mysteriously into one more confession of inadequacy." Spacks continues: "The nature of public and
private selves . . . is for women, in some ways, the reverse of what it is
for men. The face a man turns to the world . . . typically embodies his
strength," while the only acceptable models for women "involve self-
deception and yielding."[19]

By the time Spacks came, four years later, to publish "Selves in Hiding,"
she had extended her observation of women's autobiographical disabil-
ities to our own century.[20] The women whose autobiographies she discusses are Emmeline Pankhurst, Dorothy Day, Emma Goldman, Eleanor
Roosevelt, and Golda Meir, each profoundly radical, responsible for
revolutionary acts and concepts, and possessing a degree of personal
power unusual in men as well as women. But Spacks notes, "although
each author has significant, sometimes dazzling accomplishments to her
credit, the theme of accomplishment rarely dominates the narrative. . . .
Indeed," Spacks continues, "to a striking degree they fail directly to
emphasize their *own* importance, though writing in a genre which implies self-assertion and self-display." The women accept full blame for
any failures in their lives but shrink from claiming either that they sought
the responsibilities they ultimately bore or were in any way ambitious.
Day, for example, has what Spacks calls "a clear sense of self—but
struggles constantly to lose it." All these autobiographies "exploit a
rhetoric of *uncertainty*."[21] And in all of them the pain of the lives is, like
the successes, muted, as though women were certain of nothing but the
necessity of denying both accomplishment and suffering.

All of these modern autobiographies, Spacks observes, "represent a
female variant of the high tradition of spiritual autobiography."[22] One
must be called by God or Christ to service in spiritual causes higher than
one's own poor self might envision and authorized by that spiritual call
to an achievement and accomplishment in no other way excusable in a
female self. So Florence Nightingale, in her desperate desire for an
occupation worthy of her talents and desires, four times heard God
calling her to his service. But if, for men, spiritual autobiographies
resulted in personal satisfaction deriving from their spiritual achievement, this was not the case for women. As Mary Mason writes, "No-

19. Patricia Meyer Spacks, *Imagining a Self* (Cambridge: Harvard University Press, 1976),
p. 59.

20. Patricia Meyer Spacks, "Selves in Hiding," in *Women's Autobiography: Essays in Criticism,*
ed. Estelle C. Jelinek (Bloomington: Indiana University Press, 1980), 112–32.

21. Spacks, "Selves in Hiding," pp. 113–14.

22. Patricia Meyer Spacks, "Stages of Self: Notes on Autobiography and the Life Cycle," in
American Autoibiography, p. 48.

where in women's autobiographies do we find the patterns established by the two prototypical male autobiographers, Augustine and Rousseau; and conversely male writers never take up the archetypal models of Julian, Margery Kempe, Margaret Cavendish, and Anne Bradstreet." On the contrary, "the self-discovery of female identity seems to acknowledge the real presence and recognition of another consciousness, and the disclosure of female self is linked to the identification of some 'other.'"[23] Identity is grounded in relation to the chosen other. Without such relation, women did not feel enabled to write openly about themselves; even with it, they did not feel entitled to credit for their own accomplishment, spiritual or not.

Well into the twentieth century, it continued to be impossible for women to admit into their autobiographical narratives the claim of achievement, the admission of ambition, the recognition that accomplishment was neither luck nor the result of the efforts or generosity of others. Jill Conway, in a study of the accomplished women of the Progressive era in the United States (women born 1855–1865), has remarked upon the narrative flatness with which, in their autobiographies, they have described their exciting lives.[24] Their letters and diaries are usually different, reflecting ambitions and struggles in the public sphere; in their published autobiographies they portray themselves as intuitive, nurturing, passive, but never, in spite of the contrary evidence of their accomplishment, managerial.

The autobiography of Jane Addams, Conway points out, is sentimental and passive: her cause finds *her,* rather than the other way around—not so in her letters, where she takes over the family business and fights for her due. The money for Hull House, in the autobiography, fell in off the street; her letters reveal the truth. Conway finds this same pattern in the autobiographies of Ida Tarbell and Charlotte Perkins Gilman. There is a wholly different voice in the letters from that in the autobiographical narrative. All the autobiographies begin confessionally and, except in the case of Gilman, report the encounters with what would be the life's work as occurring by chance: this portrayal was, in every case, quite untrue. Each woman set out to find her life's work, but the only script for women's life insisted that work discover and pursue them, like the conventional romantic lover. As Conway points out, there is no model for the female who is recounting a political narrative. There are no recognizable career stages in such a life, as there would be for a man,

---

23. Mason, this volume.

24. Jill Kerr Conway, "Convention versus Self-Revelation: Five Types of Autobiography by Women of the Progressive Era" (Paper delivered 13 June 1983, Project on Women and Social Change, Smith College, Northampton, Mass.).

nor have women a tone of voice in which to speak with authority. As Natalie Davis has said, women up to the eighteenth century could speak with authority only of the family and religion. These women had no models on which to form their lives, nor could they themselves become mentors since they did not tell the truth about their lives.

Ida Tarbell, for example, one of the most famous of the muckrakers, author of the history of the Standard Oil Company, reports that the subject just "happened to be there" and, Conway shows, credits the idea of her work to others. This hapenstance is wholly belied by her letters. Where anger is expressed in these autobiographies it is not, Conway believes, used creatively, as by black male authors. The expression of anger has always been a terrible hurdle in women's personal progress. Above all, in the lives of Victorian and post-Victorian women, the public and private life cannot be linked, as in male narratives. These women are therefore unable to write exemplary lives: they do not dare to offer themselves as models, but only as exceptions chosen by destiny or chance.

What these women could least express in their autobiographies, Conway demonstrates, is their love of other women. Jane Addams loved her college classmate and hated her stepmother, but none of this can be expressed. The unspoken law that women who "make it" must not identify themselves as women, or dare to annoy men by their self-identification as women, serves to erase from the record these women's love and support of one another. If we look, more or less at random, at biographies of two women of achievement, we find that Fanny Holtzmann, a remarkably successful woman lawyer in the years between the wars, when most women were lost to domesticity, and Diane Arbus, an extraordinarily original photographer who took her own life in 1971, two years short of fifty, are both reported by their biographers as disassociating themselves from other women, of refusing to be identified as a woman. Holtzmann's biographer, Edward Berkman, quotes her answer to a question about encountering difficulties in a man's world: "I make it my business not to look conspicuous—my office in the Bar Building looks like any other legal office, not like a feminine boudoir. My staff are all men. I find that if I assume equality, clients and other lawyers accept me that way."[25] This is as succinct an account of the attitude of an "honorary man" as can be found. Arbus's biographer, Patricia Bosworth, reports: "Although there were a great many fine women photographers working during the sixties, Diane did not associate herself with them. With the exception of Lisette Model, she never

25. Edward D. Berkman, *The Lady and the Law: The Remarkable Story of Fanny Holtzmann* (Boston: Little, Brown, 1976), p. 361.

sought out woman photographers for either advice or friendship." Arbus was often the only woman in an all-male group of photographers; she would say, "Look, I'm a *photographer,* not a woman photographer."[26] She died bereft of female support.

Conway demonstrates that the only lively sections of the autobiographies she discusses are the accounts of childhood. For girls, childhood is often the happiest and freest time. As Spacks has written: "For women, adulthood—marriage or spinsterhood—implied relative loss of self. Unlike men, therefore, they looked back fondly to the relative freedom and power of childhood and youth."[27] It is not only that in childhood girls were allowed to play with boys with a freedom restrictions on female activity would later prevent, but that accounts of childhood were somehow freed from the terrible anxieties induced by adult female ambition and encounters. One notes, therefore, that in *The Autobiography of Alice B. Toklas,* Stein does not recount her childhood but achieves a narrative of frank, mature accomplishment.

Eudora Welty's recent *One Writer's Beginning,* a charming and popular re-creation of her childhood, on the other hand, beautifully exemplifies this pattern. As a highly skillful writer, long and justly renowned for her ability to evoke pain and conflict in accounts of apparently ordinary events, Welty is able to suggest her parents' anguish; her own suffering is never recalled, nor are any facts mentioned that might spark such a recollection. She writes that "of all my strong emotions, anger is the one least responsible for any of my work. I don't write out of anger." She has earlier dismissed her youthful anger as "all vanity. As an adolescent I was a slammer of drawers and a packer of suitcases. I was responsible for scenes."[28] But these outbursts of anger are mentioned no more.

Welty was clearly, like Charlotte Brönte and George Eliot, a homely child. So was Catherine Drinker Bowen, who has written: "I sometimes wonder why women do not write more about the condition of being born homely. It is something that colors a woman's life, almost from the moment of consciousness. . . . Every girl who lacks beauty knows instinctively that she belongs to an under-privileged group, and that to climb up and out she will have to be cleverer and stronger and more ruthless perhaps than she would choose to be."[29] Bowen goes on to say that many successful (and married) women have told her of this and

26. Patricia Bosworth, *Diane Arbus: A Biography* (New York: Alfred A. Knopf, 1984), p. 208.

27. Spacks, "Stages of Self," p. 48.

28. Eudora Welty, *One Writer's Beginnings* (Cambridge: Harvard University Press, 1984), p. 38.

29. Catherine Drinker Bowen, *Family Portrait* (Boston: Little, Brown, 1970), pp. 127–28.

that many of them grew beautiful in their later years. But like Welty, most women do not write of this, nor do they observe that not having been a natural sex object in youth may have turned out to be a very good thing. Childhood may be a happy time, but even as a writer like Welty recalls it, its anxiety and unhappiness are not analyzed. The desire to remember only the good things is perhaps not unconnected with Freud's ultimate conclusion that memories of childhood sexual assault were merely the fantasies of the women who recounted them: the women patients themselves may have conspired in Freud's desire to absolve parents of the charge of cruelty.

In 1962 Lillian Smith, a revolutionary white novelist of the South, analyzed the reasons why no woman had "as yet written a great autobiography." "Women," Stone quotes her as saying, "dare not tell the truth about themselves, for it might radically change male psychology. So—playing it safe—women have conspired to keep their secrets."[30] Smith was right, but she missed, perhaps, the greatest female fear, which was not the assault of the truth upon male psychology but the degree to which women had internalized the "facts" dictated to them by male psychology. And when Albert E. Stone asserts, in *Autobiographical Occasions and Original Acts,* that there has been a remarkable outpouring of autobiographies by American women since 1962, he fails, perhaps from gallantry, to notice that the outpouring is more remarkable than the quality or courage of originality of the autobiographies. The two women Stone chose as exemplars of female autobiography from this period are Margaret Mead and Anaïs Nin, regrettable examples in many ways. Nin's diaries are, of course, diaries and not "autobiography" at all, nor has she freed herself from male-dictated ideas of femininity, even as she rebels against the value and limits placed on those qualities. As Betty Friedan wrote in 1963 of Mead's autobiography, *Blackberry Winter,* Mead confirmed all the then-dominant Freudian prejudices in her "glorification of the female sexual function. Those who found in her work confirmation of their own unadmitted prejudices and fears ignored not only the complexity of her total work, but the example of her complex life."[31] In a similar way, Helene Deutsch, the prime orchestrator of Freud's theories of female masochism and the dangers of female intellectuality and achievement, wholly ignored her own experience as an achieving, professional woman when laying down the law for members of her sex.

Norman Holland has written that "the basic difference between our

30. Albert E. Stone, *Autobiographical Occasions and Original Acts* (Philadelphia: University of Pennsylvania Press, 1982), p. 194.
31. Betty Friedan, *The Feminine Mystique* (New York: W. W. Norton, 1963), p. 137.

experience of fiction and our experience of nonfiction stems from the difference in the amount of reality-testing each asks from us."[32] Yet here, as with so many other statements from the male establishment, the opposite is true for women. It is likely that the amount of "reality-testing" women applied to nonfiction, that is, women's autobiographies, was much less than that which they applied to fiction by and about women, precisely because the autobiographies confirmed them in their internalized patriarchal attitudes and were therefore "real," while some of the fiction challenged these attitudes and could, therefore, be "reality-tested." Even so "unwomanly" an autobiographer as Simone de Beauvoir is not, Alice Schwarzer observes, a "particularly introspective peron."[33] But even had Beauvoir been able to view herself as engaged in a profound female struggle, rather than as a specially endowed individual who opted out of the usual female destiny, her account would not have changed the general picture. For as Cynthia Pomerleau has observed, "as long as women were willing to operate within the system of female subjugation, to see evidence of their own excellence as exceptional, individual marks of courage or intelligence did not threaten the social fabric and perhaps even reinforced it." Without class consciousness and with few friends among women, Pomerleau goes on to observe that women who recorded their own achievements were quick to express their reservations about other women, and men "were quick to foster this separation." She points to the classic example of Swift, who observed that he "never yet knew a tolerable woman to be fond of her own sex."[34]

And indeed, all earlier biographers of Beatrice Webb and Virginia Woolf remarked on their mutual dislike, ignoring their similarities: this is an automatic response with "privileged" women. Yet their important similarities are notable. Both women had problems with the decision to marry. Both married men of a lower class than themselves: Leonard Woolf was Jewish, Sidney Webb lower middle class. Both women also shared a belief about their right to suicide. Woolf wrote to Beatrice Webb: "I wanted to tell you, but was too shy, how much I was pleased by your views upon the possible justification of suicide. Having made the attempt myself from the best of motives I thought . . . the conven-

32. Norman Holland, "Prose and Minds: A Psychoanalytic Approach to Non-fiction," quoted in Stone, *Autobiographical Occasions*, p. 320.

33. Alice Schwarzer, *After the Second Sex*, trans. Marianne Howarth (New York: Pantheon, 1984), p. 20.

34. Cynthia Pomerleau, "The Emergence of Women's Autobiography in England," in *Women's Autobiography*, pp. 24, 34.

tional accusation of cowardice and sin has always rather rankled. So I was glad of what you said."[35]

Webb's use of the male, or conversion, model in her autobiography concealed many of her hidden desires as well as her own construction of the story of her life. Woolf did not write an autobiography. Indeed, it is unclear whether any privileged woman could have allowed herself to write an honest autobiography during Woolf's lifetime. That happened for the first time not in 1962, Stone's watershed, but considerably later.

The remarkable autobiographical accounts to which I refer have, moreover, been tucked away into other forms, other genres, most of them new. Adrienne Rich, Maxine Kumin, May Sarton, Anne Sexton have achieved the first real autobiographies by "privileged" women, but not directly as part of the genre of autobiography.[36] Only recently, in Adrienne Rich's remarkable essay "Split at the Root," has a woman finally produced a searingly honest autobiography that was not concealed as another genre.

But what remains true of these new forms of female autobiography, as of the nonautobiographies of earlier "privileged" women, is that it was, for both generations, only past youth that women began to write the first uncoded, clearly expressed autobiographies. Virginia Woolf, in fact, was in the last months of her life when she wrote "A Sense of the Past," her first wholly open autobiographical sketch; Quentin Bell had not seen it when he published his biography of her. It is a remarkably honest piece of work and, as frequently occurs with such recollections, it was disbelieved. Ellen Moers, to take but one example, regarded Woolf's memories of childhood sexual assaults as probable fantasy. What is important, however, is that exhausted, living in a country fearful of invasion, Woolf wrote her first outspoken autobiography, and then only for intimate friends in the Memoir Club. She was in her late fifties. The American poet Maxine Kumin did not begin writing poetry "as a woman" until she was middle-aged; her autobiographical prose came even later. In 1975, when she was fifty, she said in an interview: "I didn't really begin to be able to write womanly poems until, let's say, my consciousness was raised by my daughters. . . . I was programmed into one kind of life, which was to say: get a college degree, get married, and have a family. . . . And I came to poetry as a way of saving myself because I was so wretchedly discontented, and I felt so guilty about being discontented."[37]

35. Virginia Woolf, *Letters,* ed. Nigel Nicolson (London: Hogarth Press, 1978), 4:305.
36. Carolyn G. Heilbrun, "Women's Autobiographical Writing: New Prose Forms," *Prose Studies* 8.2 (1985): 20–27.

"I was so wretchedly discontented, and I felt so guilty about being discontented." This is the sentence that best describes those "privileged" women who feel, as Bell Hooks feels about them, that they have no right to be discontented. But the analysis of that discontent, that "starvation," may well tell as much about the deprived female destiny as do accounts of suffering from the sterner and more obvious forms of oppression. To transform the private ambition to the public record is always difficult for women; if one can speak on behalf of an oppressed or despised group, one is more easily encouraged by that fact to take up the pen of self-revelation. To say this is not to try to annoint the woman of "privilege" with the stigma of suffering. Rather it is to suggest that the very fact of "privilege" has prevented the women who supposedly "enjoy" it from acknowledging or recording their own profound dissatisfaction.

37. Maxine Kumin, *To Make a Prairie* (Ann Arbor: University of Michigan Press, 1979), p. 305.

4

Lesbian Identity and
Autobiographical Difference[s]

Biddy Martin

No theoretical reading of "lesbian autobiography" can fail to take up the question of the category itself. Under the circumstances, it seems almost obligatory to begin with a set of questions designed to introduce some margin of difference into that apparently airtight package. To write *about* lesbian autobiography or even lesbian autobiographies as if such a totalizable, intelligible object or its multiplication simply existed would be to beg a number of questions, for example, what a lesbian life is, what autobiography is, and what the relation between them could possibly be. There is no singular answer to such questions, however ingenious the attempt to mask partial, provisional, interested responses with claims to generality, universality, or authority. Any attempt to give a definitive or singular answer to these three questions must be rendered suspect.

Much recent lesbian writing is autobiographical, often taking the form of autobiographical essay and coming-out stories, and I will return to that writing. There are full-blown, bound autobiographies by authors who define themselves quite explicitly as lesbians. If we lend credence to the lesbian reader's sensitivity to the ways in which lesbianism is encoded in only apparently "straight" autobiographical accounts, then there are many more lesbian autobiographies. And if we abandon the obsession with the author's identity, the text's mimetic function and the reader's necessary identification, if we then consider the reader's pleasure, the ways in which she feels addressed, her desire engaged, then the question of what is lesbian about a life or an account of a life shifts much more dramatically. In 1978 Bertha Harris suggested that lesbian writing engaged a desire and an excess that defied the fixity of identity, the boundaries drawn round individual subjects, around all forms of categorization and normalization. Her lobbying efforts for an avant-garde or modernist writing included the infamous and curious claim that *Jaws,* in its celebration of unassimilable monstrosity, was a far more lesbian novel than the far more "conventional" fiction written in the 1970s by self-declared lesbians.[1] In 1987 there are surely (lesbian) readers who would find, say, a Roland Barthes to be a far more "lesbian" autobiographer than some explicitly lesbian writers. I would not ordinarily go so far, but here, under the weight of that certain identification "lesbian autobiography," such extreme claims acquire a certain allure. They also constitute a certain danger, given the institutional privileges enjoyed by those who can afford to disavow "identity" and its "limits" over against those for whom such disavowals reproduce their invisibility.

Of course, "lesbian autobiography," in its bound singularity, could appear to be a match made in a rather conventional heaven, plagued as both terms are historically by "facile assumptions of referentiality."[2] Their combination brings out the most conventional interpretation in each, for the *lesbian* in front of *autobiography* reinforces conventional assumptions of the transparency of autobiographical writing. And the *autobiography* that follows *lesbian* suggests that sexual identity not only modifies but essentially defines a life, providing it with predictable content and an identity possessing continuity and universality. Set apart in a volume on women's life stories, "lesbian autobiography" suggests that there is something coherently different about lesbians' lives vis-à-vis other lives and that there is something coherently the same about all lesbians. We could attempt to introduce difference into the category by speaking of lesbians' autobiographies and emphasizing the differences between the experiences of various lesbians. Many of the collections of coming-out stories and autobiographical narratives are organized on this very principle. However, differences, for example, of race, class, or sexuality, are finally rendered noncontradictory by virtue of their (re)presentation as differences between individuals, reducible to questions of identity within the unifying context of feminism. What remains unexamined are the systemic institutional relationships between those differences, relationships that exceed the boundaries of the lesbian community, the women's movement, or particular individuals, and in which apparently bounded communities and individuals are deeply implicated.

1. Bertha Harris, "What We Mean to Say: Notes toward Defining the Nature of Lesbian Literature," *Heresies: A Feminist Publication on Art and Politics—Lesbian Art and Artists* (Fall 1977): 5–8. Harris's distinction between a literature of the grotesque and a literature of "winkieburgers" is certainly unsatisfying. For those, however, who felt somewhat isolated in 1977–78 in our critical response to increasingly homogeneous narratives of lesbian experience, Bertha Harris's pleas for monstrosity had particular polemical value.

2. Paul de Man, "Autobiography as Defacement," *MLN* 94 (Dec. 1979): 920.

The isolation of lesbian autobiography here may have strategic political value, given the continued, or perhaps renewed, invisibility of lesbians even in feminist work, but it also marks lesbianism in a way that gives "women's autobiography" a curiously unmarked and unifying quality, reproducing the marginality of lesbianism and its containment in particular types of people. Lesbianism loses its potential as a position from which to read against the grain of narratives of normal life course, and becomes simply the affirmation of something separated out and defined as "lesbian." Of course, the problem of essentialism inevitably plagues not only scholarly volumes committed to representing differences among women; it has plagued and continues to plague lesbian and gay politics and writing as well. In fact, it is the risk taken by any identity politics. Claims to difference conceived in terms of different identities have operated and continue to operate as interventions in facile assumptions of "sisterhood," assumptions that have tended to mask the operation of white, middle-class, heterosexual "womanhood" as the hidden but hegemonic referent. Challenges to the erasure of difference in the name of another identity, however, limit the potential for subversion and critique by recontaining the discursive/institutional operations of "differences" in discrete categories of individuals, thereby rendering difference a primarily psychological "problem." A number of marginalized communities now face important questions about the possibility of reconceptualizing identity without abandoning it and its strategic deployment altogether. I suggest that such reconceptualizations of identity and of community have emerged in recent autobiographical writing and on the very grounds of identity and community.

The work of Michel Foucault has been essential in gay studies to a critique of identity politics, of the ways in which sexuality comes to constitute the ground of identity, and autobiographical gestures the exclusive ground of politics.[3] Several claims have made their way into gay historiography and into discussions of the politics of "coming out": first, that homosexual identity, the "homosexual" as a particular type of personality, was an invention of the late nineteenth century, and further, that the creation of the homosexual as type was, in the words of Jeffrey Minson, part of "the efforts in the human sciences to regulate and control by way of the construction of definite categories of personality."[4] At the same time that "deviance" and "perversion" were located and confined in marginal types and communities, sexual pathologies of all

---

3. I am interested here in the impact of Michel Foucault's *The History of Sexuality,* vol. 1 (New York: Pantheon Books, 1978).

4. Jeffrey Minson, "The Assertion of Homosexuality," *m/f* 5 (1981): 22. Also see Minson, *Genealogies of Morals: Nietzsche, Foucault, Donzelot and the Eccentricity of Ethics* (New York: St. Martin's Press, 1985).

kinds were discovered to be potentials in "the normal family," justifying the intervention of pedagogical, medical, psychiatric, and social welfare experts. At stake in late nineteenth-century Europe was the health of the "family" and its role in securing the health of the "race." Foucault locates the deployment of sexuality at the center of a racist eugenics.[5]

In contrast, then, to conventional assumptions that the Victorian age was characterized by the repression of sexuality, Foucault argues that sexualities and discourse on sexuality proliferated in the late nineteenth century; moreover, he asserts that the deployment of sexuality as an apparatus of normalization and control involved the inducement to speak the truth of one's sexuality, to locate the truth of one's self in a buried sexual essence, and to confuse autobiographical gestures with liberation. The "repressive hypothesis" itself served to mask the actual workings of power. Laying claim, then, to one's sexuality and the rights associated with it, insisting on the freedom to speak freely of one's sexuality, risks subjection to regulation and control. Foucault's critique of the association of sexuality and truth and their location in the depths of the only apparently autonomous individual externalizes questions presumed to be internal and psychological by throwing them onto social and discursive axes. Hayden White characterizes Foucault's challenge to the illusions of the bourgeois subject: "Foucault resists the impulse to seek an origin or transcendental subject which would confer any specific 'meaning' on human life. Foucault's discourse is willfully superficial. And this is consistent with the larger purpose of a thinker who wishes to dissolve the distinction between surfaces and depths, to show that wherever this distinction arises, it is evidence of the play of organized power."[6] Foucault challenges any belief in the autonomy of the psychological, thereby contesting what Arthur Brittan and Mary Maynard have called the derivation of both racism and sexism "from the operation of the irrational, from the hidden depths of the human psyche."[7] Foucault's critique pushes "identity politics" off the exclusive grounds of identity to questions of alternative social and communicative forms, away from claims to "rights" and "choice" to questions about "the social relationships in which choice becomes meaningful."[8] It may

5. I have argued this point in more detail in "Feminism, Criticism and Foucault," *New German Critique* 27 (Fall 1982): 3–30.

6. Hayden White, "Michel Foucault," in *Structuralism and Since,* ed. John Sturrock (Oxford: Oxford University Press, 1979), p. 82.

7. Arthur Brittan and Mary Maynard, *Sexism, Racism, and Oppression* (Oxford: Basil Blackwell, 1984), p. 29. Brittan and Maynard use the work of Foucault to critique orthodox Marxism, Frankfurt School Critical Theory, and radical feminisms for treating racism and sexism as derivative of more primary contradictions.

8. Jeffrey Weeks, *Sexuality and Its Discontents: Meanings, Myths and Modern Sexualities* (Lon-

also, however, as a number of feminist critics have noted, work to suppress questions of subjective agency, indeed, to render self-determination unthinkable.

Teresa de Lauretis remains one of the most persistent critics of Foucault and discourse theory for neutralizing gender by conceiving it as pure discursive effect and for suppressing questions of subjective agency and self-representation. In her introduction to *Technologies of Gender,* de Lauretis also uses Foucault's work to criticize American cultural feminists for reproducing conceptions of gender as "sexual difference," i.e., woman's difference from man.[9] She identifies the heterosexual social contract and its constant assumption in feminist as well as nonfeminist writing as a primary site for the reproduction of "just two neatly divided genders." Such assumptions obscure the ways in which gender is constructed across a range of discursive and institutional lines, and always at the intersections of class, race, and ethnicity. Drawing on Foucault's technologies of sexuality, de Lauretis's conception of the "technologies of gender" serves not only to separate gender from any apparent continuity with biology but also to suggest that there is no one monolithic ideology of gender.

De Lauretis's double-edged critique of American feminist identity politics and of Foucault points to the importance of reconceptualizing "experience" and "identity" without abandoning attention to "the semiotic interaction of 'outer world' and 'inner world,' the continuous engagement of a self or subject in social reality."[10] To her earlier formulation of the tensions between that ideological distillate "Woman" and historical, empirical "women," de Lauretis adds a third term, "the sub-

don: Routledge and Kegan Paul, 1985), p. 218. I agree with Weeks's reading of the strategic political implications for gay politics in Foucault's work, in particular his emphasis on reconceptualizing rights and choices in terms of the social conditions that make such notions meaningful.

9. Teresa de Lauretis, *Technologies of Gender: Feminism, Film and Fiction* (Bloomington: Indiana University Press, 1987), p. 1. De Lauretis works with and against Louis Althusser as well as Foucault. Her critique of Althusser draws on the interesting and important work of Wendy Hollway, "Gender Difference and the Production of Subjectivity," in Julian Henriques, Wendy Hollway, Cathy Urwin, Couze Venn, and Valerie Walkerdine, *Changing the Subject: Psychology, Social Regulation and Subjectivity* (London: Methuen, 1984), 225–63. For an excellent discussion by the German feminist Argument Collective of the uses of and problems with Foucault for feminists, see *Female Sexualization,* ed. Frigga Haug et al., trans. Erica Carter (London: Verso, 1987). Haug et al. make a critique of the suppression of subjective agency in Foucault's work which is very similar to that made by de Lauretis. The *Argument* Collective is interested in mobilizing historical memory in order to expose both processes of "individualization" and possibilities of resistance. See also *Feminism and Foucault,* ed. Irene Diamond and Lee Quinby (Boston: Northeastern University Press, forthcoming).

10. De Lauretis, *Alice Doesn't: Feminism, Semiotics, Cinema* (Bloomington: Indiana University Press, 1984), p. 182.

ject of feminism," the space of an "elsewhere," in order to point to the irreducibility of "women" to any one ideology of gender:

> By the phrase "the subject of feminism" I mean a conception or an under-
> standing of the (female) subject as not only distinct from Woman with the
> capital letter . . . but also distinct from women, the real historical beings
> and social subjects who are defined by the technology of gender and actu-
> ally engendered in social relations. The subject of feminism I have in mind
> is one *not* so defined, one whose definition or conception is in progress.[11]

According to de Lauretis, this subject must be sought not in particular persons or groups—i.e., not in identities—but in "micropolitical prac-tices," practices of self-representation which illuminate the contradic-tory, multiple construction of subjectivity at the intersections, but also in the interstices of ideologies of gender, race, and sexuality.

De Lauretis draws on the autobiographical writing of women of color to suggest that identity can be reconceptualized on its very grounds. She is one of several feminist critics who read recent autobiographical writ-ing by women of color in the United States as "representational prac-tices" that illuminate the "contradictory, multiple construction of sub-jectivity." This autobiographical writing actually complicates de Lauretis's own earlier formulation of the inevitable tensions between the negativity of theory and the positivity of politics by robbing theory of its exclusive claim to negativity and suggesting a new imbrication of theory and personal history.

I am interested here in recent autobiographical writings that work against self-evidently homogeneous conceptions of identity, writings in which lesbianism comes to figure as something other than a "totalizing self-identification" and to be located on other than exclusively psycho-logical grounds.[12] These recent writings necessarily take up, even as they work against, already conventional lesbian-feminist narratives of lesbian experience. Encounters between and among feminists over rac-ism and anti-Semitism have played a crucial role in pushing identity politics, generally, and lesbian identity, in particular, beyond the appar-ent impasses of the late 1970s and early 1980s. The autobiographical contributions to *This Bridge Called My Back,* edited by Cherríe Moraga and Gloria Anzaldúa (1981), serve as a concrete example of how the politics of identity has been challenged on its very grounds. For the writings of Moraga, Anzaldúa, and others participate in attempts to attend to the irreducibly complex intersections of race, gender, and

11. De Lauretis, *Technologies of Gender,* pp. 9–10.

12. I am indebted to Jeffrey Minson's "Assertions of Homosexuality" for this formulation and for his use of that formulation to criticize particular forms of the politics of coming out.

sexuality, attempts that both directly and indirectly work against assumptions that there are no differences within the "lesbian self" and that lesbian authors, autobiographical subjects, readers, and critics can be conflated and marginalized as self-identical and separable from questions of race, class, sexuality, and ethnicity. I will conclude with a discussion of how the encounter with racism and its complexities has informed the autobiographical writing of two southern white lesbian writers, Minnie Bruce Pratt and Mab Segrest. In the exchange between the work of women of color and that of white lesbian writers, only apparently discrete and unified identities are rendered complex by attention to the imbrications of different personal and community histories.

Before I take up these exchanges in more detail, let me recall the forms of lesbian identity against which recent autobiographical texts implicitly, when not explicitly, react and on which they necessarily rely. In her review of the most widely read collections of coming-out stories and autobiographical essays of the 1970s and early 1980s, Bonnie Zimmerman argues that the centrality of autobiography in lesbian writing is fundamentally connected with the emergence of a lesbian-feminist politics of experience and identity.[13] Self-worth, identity, and a sense of community have fundamentally depended on the production of a shared narrative or life history and on the assimilation of individuals' life histories into the history of the group. This autobiographical writing has specific purposes in the (not always synchronous) histories of the community and of the individuals who write or read them; it aims to give lesbian identity a coherence and legitimacy that can make both individual and social action possible. The coming-out stories and autobiographical essays collected in such volumes *The Coming Out Stories, The Lesbian Path, The New Lesbians* are responses to the at least implicit question of what it means to be a lesbian, how lesbianism figures in a life, what it means to come out. In a stricter sense, they are accounts of the process of becoming conscious of oneself as a lesbian, about accepting and affirming that identity against enormous odds, including, of course, the authors' own resistance to the label. Hence, lesbianism becomes the central moment around which women's lives are reconstructed. These narratives appear in journals and anthologies committed quite explicitly to making the realities of lesbians' lives visible in accessible terms, committed, in short, to presence. They are addressed to a reading community assumed to be (or to have the potential to be) lesbian. They asume a mimetic relationship between experience and writing and a relationship

13. Bonnie Zimmerman, "The Politics of Transliteration: Lesbian Personal Narratives," in *The Lesbian Issue: Essays from Signs,* ed. Estelle B. Freedman, Barbara C. Gelpi, Susan L. Johnson, and Kathleen M. Weston (Chicago: University of Chicago Press, 1985), pp. 251–70.

of identification between the reader and the autobiographical subject. Moreover, they are explicitly committed to the political importance of just such reading strategies for the creation of identity, community, and political solidarity.

In an important sense, these written stories are imitations of oral narratives, the coming-out stories at the heart of community building, at the most everyday level. Indeed, many of the stories read as if they had been transcribed from taped accounts. But the oral exchange of stories is, of course, impossible to reproduce, despite the obviously dialogic quality of the individuals' written narratives, which identify the lesbian community as their origin and end. Like all spoken language, the language of many written coming-out stories is necessarily reductionist, all the more so in published accounts, for the pleasures and subtleties of oral exchange and storytelling traditions are eradicated. Here the communicative, performative, and provisional aspects of coming-out stories are subordinated to the claims of recorded speech; in print, the coming-out story appears to hold more claims on the "truth" of the life as a whole.

Telling, writing, and reading autobiographical stories are linked to the perceived importance of countering representations that have rendered homosexuality invisible, perverse, aberrant, or marginal. In her collection of autobiographical essays titled *My Mama's Dead Squirrel: Lesbian Essays on Southern Culture,* Mab Segrest attempts to link antiracist literary traditions with lesbian writing by suggesting that autobiography constitutes a critical "decolonization of self" in the lesbian community. Further, she defines lesbian storytelling as part of larger struggles for self-determination among oppressed and silenced groups.

> Now this literature I stumbled into was very different, you had better believe it, from what I had been reading while struggling to acquire a Ph.D. in English. . . . Most of the "great works" of this century traced the dissolution of Western white male culture, by male writers who could only identify with its demise. . . . With lesbian literature I remembered how it's supposed to be. No lesbian in the universe, I do believe, will tell you there's nothing left to say. We have our whole live to say, lives that have been censored, repressed, suppressed and depressed from millennia from official versions of literature, history and culture. . . . The lesbian's knowledge that we all have stories to tell and that each of our cultures produces its own artists lessens the suicidal modern alienation between writer and audience. Lesbian literature, like all the best women's writing is fueled by the knowledge that what we have to say is essential to our own survival and to the survival of the larger culture which has tried so hard to destroy us. The

lesbian's definition of herself is part of the larger movement by all oppressed people to define ourselves.[14]

Rendering lesbianism natural, self-evident, original, can have the effect of emptying traditional representations of their content, of contesting the only apparent self-evidence of "normal" (read heterosexual) life course. Lesbian autobiographical narratives are about remembering differently, outside the contours and narrative constraints of conventional models. Events or feelings that are rendered insignificant, mere "phases"—or permanent aberrations when a life is organized in terms of the trajectory toward adult heterosexuality, marriage, and motherhood—become differently meaningful in lesbian stories. They become signs that must be reread on the basis of different interpretive strategies. Whether the emphasis is on a tomboyish past, on childhood friendships, or on crushes on girl friends, teachers, or camp counselors—all now the stock-in-trade of lesbian humor—these narratives point to unsanctioned discontinuities between biological sex, gender identity, and sexuality.

But lesbian autobiographical writing has an affirmative as well as a critical relationship to questions of identity and self-definition. And lesbian identity comes to mean quite particular things in the seventies under the impact of feminist struggles for conceptual and political unity. It is now quite common to reconstruct the history of those struggles among American feminists as a shift from a "radical" to a "cultural" feminism concerned only with psychology and identity and guilty of reproducing the very gender divisions radical feminism set out to question.[15] A particular construction of lesbianism as a political stance for all women is seen to be at the heart of that shift, to have enabled and

14. Mab Segrest, *My Mama's Dead Squirrel: Lesbian Essays on Southern Culture* (Ithaca, N.Y.: Firebrand, 1985), pp. 101–2.

15. For two of the most influential reconstructions, see Alice Echols, "The Taming of the Id: Feminist Sexual Politics, 1968–83," in *Pleasure and Danger: Exploring Female Sexuality* (Boston: Routledge and Kegan Paul, 1984), pp. 50–72; and Echols, "The New Feminism of Yin and Yang," in *Powers of Desire: The Politics of Sexuality,* ed. Ann Snitow, Christine Stansell, and Sharon Thompson (New York: Monthly Review Press, 1983), pp. 439–59; see also Hester Eisenstein, *Contemporary Feminist Thought* (Boston: G. K. Hall, 1983). Ellen Willis, "Feminism, Moralism and Pornography," in *Powers of Desire,* pp. 460–67, has also popularized a narrative that moves from "radical" to "cultural" feminism. To the extent that these reconstructions rely on only apparently self-evident taxonomies, even as a position from which to assess the use of certain taxonomies, they tend to reproduce the problems they expose. Despite the importance of Echols's critique of what she calls "cultural feminism," the danger exists that all manner of cultural practices will be ossified as mere symptoms of a feminism gone wrong. It is also not clear what the status of "culture" is in many of these critical reconstructions. Since at least some such reconstructions have emerged in the context of a self-identified "socialist feminism," there is some danger that conventional distinctions between "real politics" and "cultural preoccupations" are reproduced in another guise.

supported it. "Elevating" lesbianism to the status of a "sign" of political solidarity with women worked to challenge the homophobic reduction of lesbianism to sex. Alice Echols has argued that the "desexualization" of questions of lesbianism may have been the condition of possibility for any unity between lesbians and feminists at all, given the virulent homophobia in the women's movement and the use of homophobia to attack the movement from without.[16] It also had more positive effects, providing a name and a visibility for interpersonal and political solidarity among women and for the pleasures that women, whatever their sexuality, take in each other's company. As a political fantasy, it allowed for the convergence of legitimate (because not explicitly sexual) desire and political liberation. And it provoked and enabled analyses of the intersection of gender division and a heterosexist social contract. In the place of the "sexual minority," however, another figure emerged, one that could encompass both lesbians and heterosexual women, the "woman-identified woman" with a legacy in the history of (romantic) female friendship, a figure that proved disabling and reductionist in its own way. By the late 1970s, when pornography and sexual violence had become the focus of what are now called "cultural feminist analyses," heterosexuality itself, not just particular institutionalized forms and normalizations of heterosexuality, had been identified as the source of women's dependence and oppression. In the context of this emerging critique of heterosexuality, lesbianism came to figure more and more significantly as what Katie King has called "feminism's magical sign of liberation."[17] For the key to opposing male supremacy and the forms of false consciousness imposed on women through the myths of heterosexual desire and pleasure was withdrawal from men, now named lesbianism.

One of the effects of the monolithic and universal division between men and women suggested by this work was the disappearance of institutional analyses, a focus on psychology, and the suggestion that politics could be derived directly from experience or identity. In King's words, "Identifying with lesbianism falsely implies that one knows all about heterosexism and homophobia magically through identity or association. . . . The power of lesbianism as a privileged signifier makes analysis of heterosexism and homophobia difficult since it obscures the need for counter-intuitive challenges to ideology."[18] At the heart of the

16. Echols, "The Taming of the Id," pp. 55–56.
17. Katie King, "The Situation of Lesbianism as Feminism's Magical Sign: Contests for Meaning and the U.S. Women's Movement, 1968–1972," *Communication* 9 (1986): 65–91. King's work provides an explicit and implicit critique of historical reconstructions of feminism that rely on taxonomic identification and linear historical narratives.
18. King, p. 85.

division is a conception not only of an inside and outside of oppression but of an inside and outside of ideology. Drawing on the work of the Furies Collective in the mid-1970s, Zimmerman suggests that the unity constructed between lesbianism and feminism and the links established between "the personal" and "the political" resulted in "a radically rationalistic rewriting of personal history" to conform to political stance[19]—hence, the often formulaic and noncontradictory quality of some autobiographical writing, hence, too, the forms of moralism and voluntarism that inhere in such demands for the identity of sexuality, subjectivity, and political stance.

As many critics have now argued, Adrienne Rich's "Compulsory Heterosexuality and Lesbian Existence" (1980) constitutes the ultimate formulation of a particular conception of the relationship between sexuality and politics, explicitly marking off lesbianism as an issue of gender identification and contrasting the interests of gay men and lesbians.[20] Indeed, Rich's essay can be read as the culmination of a textual and political tendency that begins with the Furies Tracts of the early 1970s, namely, the construction of lesbianism as "feminism's magical sign of liberation." Rich uses Freud himself to argue for the primacy and naturalness of women's erotic bond with another woman. The daughter is violently separated from the mother by the imperative of heterosexuality, a social imperative and a form of violence which serves to consolidate male power and to blind women to their own supposedly "essential" love or desire. The ultimate formulation of a politics of nostalgia, of a return to that state of innocence free of conflict conceived as women's primary emotional bonds with one another, enacts its own violence, as all dreams of perfect union do. A number of lesbian critics have remarked that Rich's lesbian continuum effectively erases sexuality and robs lesbianism of any specificity. As Hilary Allen argues, "In conventional terms, whatever is sexual about Political Lesbianism appears to be systematically attenuated: genitality will yield to an unspecified eroticism, eroticism to sensuality, sensuality to 'primary emotional intensity,' and emotional intensity to practical and political support."[21]

19. Zimmerman, p. 255.

20. Adrienne Rich, "Compulsory Heterosexuality and Lesbian Existence," *Signs* 5 (1980): 631–60.

21. Hilary Allen, "Political Lesbianism and Feminism—Space for a Sexual Politics?"*m/f* 7 (1982): 15–34. Allen's essay provides a particularly lucid exploration of the contradictions on which a political lesbian stance has relied, contradictions in the category "woman" and in conceptions of sexuality. For one of the most successful critiques of that once hegemonic figure, the "woman-identified-woman," and its effects on conceptions of lesbian sexuality, see Esther Newton's discussion of Radclyffe Hall, "The Mythic Mannish Lesbian: Radclyffe Hall and the New Woman," in *The Lesbian Issue,* pp. 7–25.

Many of the coming-out stories and autobiographical narratives collected in the 1970s quite clearly display the effects of feminist rhetoric on definitions of lesbianism. The narratives are written against the notion that lesbianism can be explained in terms of "penis envy" or the desire to be or imitate a man. And indeed, sexual desire is often attenuated and appears as "love" in these narratives. Lesbianism, understood to be first and foremost about love for other women and for oneself as a woman, becomes a profoundly life-saving, self-loving, political resistance to patriarchal definitions and limitations in these narratives. Virtually every contributor to *The Lesbian Path* and *The Coming Out Stories* acknowledges her debt to feminism for giving lesbianism the meaning it has come to have. A feminist analysis of the suppression of love and solidarity among women in a sexist society and the ensuing celebration of women's relationships with one another provide the lever with which many of the authors pry lesbianism loose from its homophobic reduction to sex, suggesting that the reduction of their desires and their relationships to sex stood in the way of their ability or willingness to accept a lesbian identity. Feminism and the collective rereadings and redefinitions it facilitated are credited with having created the possibility of taking on and redefining the label.

The debt is particularly clear in the editors' presentations of these collections. *The Coming Out Stories* are organized, according to the editors, on the basis of each author's access to a language for her feelings and desires.[22] The book begins with the stories of those contributors who came out when there were no words for the feelings they had, or only words that rendered them perverse, sick, or male; they end with the stories of those who could name their experience woman identification. The cover blurb of *The New Lesbians* makes the impact of feminist politics even more apparent; it suggests that "a majority of lesbians are woman-identified: they do not want to act like or look like men or to practice role-playing."[23] *The Lesbian Path* is introduced as "the book I never had: true stories of strong, women-identified women."[24] The opposition between negative stereotypes and new "truths" about the majority of lesbians masks the role of rhetoric in constructing this majority. The "old" lesbians, those who came out prior to feminism are rendered invisible, made anachronistic, or converted.

Clearly, access to lesbian and feminist communities, to the collective interpretive strategies and rhetoric developed there have made positive

22. *The Coming Out Stories,* ed. Julia Penelope Stanley and Susan J. Wolfe (Watertown, Mass.: Persephone Press, 1980).

23. *The New Lesbians,* ed. Laurel Galana and Gina Cavina (Berkeley: Moon Books, 1977).

24. *The Lesbian Path,* ed. Margaret Cruikshank (San Francisco: Grey Fox Press, 1985).

self-definition and political activism possible. As Joan Nestle suggests in her contribution to *The Lesbian Path*, self-definition shifts and changes as lesbian communities shift and grow. Nestle describes her own transformation under the impact of feminism from the bar butch/fem culture of the 1950s and 1960s to a lesbian-feminist culture of woman identification.[25] Joan Nestle has since become one of the most articulate critics of the constraints imposed on what it means to be a lesbian by the woman-identified woman, the rhetorical figure that effaced the subtleties of legacies other than romantic female friendship.[26] In the context of the "sexuality debates," renewed interest in butch/fem relationships, in role playing, and in sadomasochism has restored attention to the discontinuities of sex, gender, sexual desire, sexual object choice by introducing the elements of fantasy and play. This work not only has fractured the unity achieved in the woman-identified woman between lesbianism and feminism but has exposed the absence of any consensus about the definition of lesbian identity and its relation to politics.[27]

Many of the coming-out stories are tautological insofar as they describe a process of coming to know something that has always been true, a truth to which the author has returned. They also describe a linear progression from a past shrouded in confusion or lies to a present or future that represents a liberation from the past. Coming out is conceived, then, as both a return to one's true self and desire and a movement beyond distortion and constraint, grounding identity and political unity in moral right and truth. The titles alone, according to Zimmerman—*The Lesbian Path, Lesbian Crossroads, Coming Out Stories*—point to the conception of lesbianism and of life story as a journey, as a "metaethical" journey à la Mary Daly from patriarchal distortion to a woman-identified consciousness, a choice, finally, to be who one is in a new world of women.[28] The "happy end" to internal struggles,

25. Joan Nestle, "An Old Story," in *The Lesbian Path*, pp. 37–39.

26. For more detailed autobiographical accounts and analyses of the lesbian culture of the 1950s, see Nestle's collected essays, *A Restricted Country* (Ithaca, N.Y.: Firebrand Press, 1987).

27. Gayle Rubin has gone as far as to suggest that sexuality constitutes a separate axis, which intersects with but is irreducible to gender, so that feminism becomes inadequate to an analysis or politics of sexuality. Though Rubin's work on lesbian sadomasochism has been legitimately criticized for reproducing identity politics in the name of a different sexual community and for tending toward a sexual essentialism, it has served to contest the only apparent hegemony of particular constructions of lesbianism by introducing a complicating axis. See in particular Rubin's "Thinking Sex: Notes for a Radical Theory of the Politics of Sexuality," in *Pleasure and Danger*, pp. 267–319. For a critical assessment of the "prosex" and "antisex" divisions in the sexuality debates, see the review of the texts and major conferences of the so-called sexuality debates by B. Ruby Rich, "Feminism and Sexuality in the 1980s," *Feminist Studies* 12 (Fall 1986): 525–63.

28. Mary Daly, *Gyn/ecology: The Metaethics of Radical Feminism* (Boston: Beacon Press, 1978).

doubts, and contradictions in many coming-out stories depends, in part, on forgetting that "the community" and the feminist literature on which it relies construct rather than simply reflect the truth of experience and identity. It depends, moreover, on suppressing the fact that the past has been rendered not more diverse but homogeneous in a new way. Despite the dialogic exchange between individual and community, these narratives tend to erase the individual's and the group's active participation in their formation as social beings by relying on apparently transcendent "essences" lying in wait for discovery and language. The increasingly exclusive focus on shifts in consciousness and on identification with women leads Zimmerman to conclude that "although lesbian feminism evolved during the 1970's as a politics of transliteration, this power of the word has been used primarily to name, and thereby control, individual and group identity."[29]

In her review of lesbian autobiographical writing, Zimmerman points out that the critiques of lesbian-feminist unities by women of color, Jewish women, and sex radicals have themselves proceeded by way of autobiographical texts committed to the affirmation of multiple identities. In some sense, according to Zimmerman, anthologies like Evelyn Torton Beck's *Nice Jewish Girls* and Moraga's and Anzaldúa's *This Bridge Called My Back* reproduce a cultural politics that places its faith in identity and in writing.[30] Zimmerman warns against the fragmentation that results from the search for more authentic unities based on multiplication of identities. Like other critics of "cultural feminism" and identity politics, she concludes with an appeal for institutional analyses in place of the focus on identity. Challenges to increasingly identical constructions of the unity of "women" *have* at times simply expanded the con-

---

29. Zimmerman, p. 270.

30. Zimmerman characterizes *Nice Jewish Girls: A Lesbian Anthology*, ed. Evelyn Torton Beck (Watertown, Mass.: Persephone Press, 1982) and *This Bridge Called My Back: Writings by Radical Women of Color*, ed. Cherríe Moraga and Gloria Anzaldúa (Watertown, Mass.: Persephone Press, 1981), both now published by Firebrand Books, as "more political": than *The Coming Out Stories* or *The Lesbian Path*, both of which include work primarily by white, middle-class women. According to Zimmerman, however, "it is the intensity and power of self-affirmation that dominates these volumes" (p. 265). I am less interested in contesting Zimmerman's assessment of the differences, an assessment with which I basically agree, than in specifying the differences between conceptions of identity in the two sets of texts in terms other than "political" versus "self-affirmative." Zimmerman also points to a number of what she calls imaginative personal narratives or autobiographical texts by women of color, which are producing "a new, more inclusive, and more accurate politics" (p. 264). She notes, in particular, Audre Lorde, *Zami: A New Spelling of My Name* (Trumansburg, N.Y.: Crossing Press, 1983); Michelle Cliff, *Claiming an Identity They Taught Me to Despise* (Watertown, Mass.: Persephone Press, 1980); Anita Cornwall, *Black Lesbian in White America* (Tallahassee, Fla.: Naiad Press, 1983); Cherríe Moraga, *Loving in the War Years* (Boston: South End Press, 1983); and Gloria Anzaldúa, *Borderlands/La Frontera: The New Mestiza* (San Francisco: Spinsters/aunt lute, 1987).

ception of personal and group identities arithmetically without changing entrenched notions of identity and without furthering what Barbara Smith has called "our ability to analyze complicated intersections of privilege and oppression."[31] The autobiographical writings of women of color, however—indeed, the conception of that category itself—also have the potential to challenge conventional assumptions of identity and its relationship to politics and writing.[32]

I would like to look more closely at *This Bridge Called My Back: Writings by Radical Women of Color,* a collection of autobiographical essays, poems, and letters that move questions of identity off exclusively psychological ground. *This Bridge Called My Back* is a collection of writings by and for radical women of color which also addresses white feminists both directly and indirectly. *This Bridge* is a provocation to white feminists to educate themselves about racism, about the material lives and realities of communities other than their own, about the relationship between the histories of their communities or growing-up places and those of people of color in the United States and elsewhere. It also insists that we cease locating "race" in those individuals or groups in whom it is supposedly embodied, that we abandon the notion that to be "white" is to be unmarked by race. And further, it is a provocation to white feminists and lesbians to render their own histories, subjectivities, and writing complex by attending to their various implications in overlapping social/discursive divisions and their histories.

By demonstrating the complex discursive and institutional intersections of race, class, gender, and sexuality and their inscription on the bodies and psyches of women, these autobiographical essays, poems, and letters relate psychic and political struggles in ways that make "identity" irreducible to consciousness. Not all the contributors to *This Bridge* are lesbians; even for those who identify themselves as lesbians, sexual identity is not a singular focus. *This Bridge* is conceived as a discussion, between and among "women of color," of the contradictions, conflicts, and possibilities in that constructed but "potent fusion of outsider identities."[33] It is a text committed to exposing the complexities of "race" in the United States, complexities too often reduced to a black/white divide. The contributions of women from a range of racial, ethnic, even

31. Barbara Smith, "Between a Rock and a Hard Place," in *Yours in Struggle: Three Feminist Perspectives on Anti-Semitism and Racism* (New York: Long Haul Press, 1984), p. 81.

32. For an excellent discussion of the possibilities of "postmodern autobiography," see Caren Kaplan, "The Poetics of Displacement in *Buenos Aires,*" *Discourse: Journal of Theoretical Studies in Media and Culture* 8 (Fall-Winter 1986–87): 84–102.

33. I am indebted for this formulation to Donna Haraway's discussion of "women of color" as a category and a form of coalition in "A Manifesto for Cyborgs: Science, Technology, and Socialist Feminism in the 1980s," *Socialist Review* 80 (April 1985): 93.

national communities complicate "race" by focusing on the relationship between the histories and the current situations of different communities and individuals. The category "women of color," as it is elaborated in *This Bridge,* stands in a critical relation to assumptions of unity based on identity, assumptions of a "unity of the oppressed." For the forms of solidarity forged here are based on shared but not identical histories, shared but not identical structural positions, shared but not identical interests. Moreover, the forms of solidarity suggested here are grounded not in claims to victimization but, as Chela Sandoval has argued, in the convergence of shared perspectives, shared competences, and shared pleasures. For Sandoval, the very category "women of color" eschews reference to an essential, pregiven, natural, or self-evident "home" or whole; it is a category that operates as a form of "oppositional consciousness" as well as a source of new political unities, new pleasures and communities.[34] In her critique of Susan Krieger's work on lesbian communities, Sandoval formulates the challenge: "United States Third World feminists are pointing out the differences that exist among all women not in order to fracture any hope of unity among women but to propose a new order—one that provides a new possibility for unity without the erasure of differences. This new order would draw attention to the construction and ideological consequences of every order, of every community, of every identity."[35] The category "women of color" amounts to an acknowledgment of what Erica Carter, in her introduction to the work of a German feminist collective on ideology, has called "the disappearance of *any* one coherent subject whose history (individual or collective) might be mobilized as a force for political action," this without abandoning personal histories or politics altogether.[36]

The very title of *This Bridge* suggests its connections with a metaphorical tradition in lesbian-feminist writing of journeys, paths, and transformations.[37] Donna Rushin's "The Bridge Poem," however, and Moraga's preface suggest from the outset that *This Bridge* is critical of that tradition. Audre Lorde's "Open Letter to Mary Daly" makes it quite clear that too many lesbian-feminist "metaethical" journeys to an assumed new world of women have passed over the bodies, the differences, of women of color. And the text as a whole lodges a double-

34. Chela Sandoval, "Dis-illusionment and the Poetry of the Future: The Making of Oppositional Consciousness" (Ph.D. qualifying essay, University of California–Santa Cruz, 1984), quoted in Haraway, p. 73.

35. Sandoval, "Comment on Susan Krieger's 'Lesbian Identity and Community: Recent Social Science Literature,'" in *The Lesbian Issue,* p. 241–44.

36. Erica Carter, Introduction to *Female Sexualization,* p. 15.

37. Zimmerman calls attention to the prevalence of such metaphors and their implications in her review essay, p. 258.

edged critique of feminist and antiracist politics, both of which can erase the interests, indeed, the very existence of women of color; again and again, the critiques echo the analysis embedded in the title of Barbara Smith and Gloria Hull's introduction to black women's studies, *All the Women Are White/All the Blacks Are Men/But Some of Us Are Brave*.[38]

Moraga asks in her preface, "How can we—this time—not use our bodies to be thrown over a river of tormented history to bridge the gap?" For the contributors to this volume, the journey, and hence the narrative, is neither coherently linear nor tautological. There is no linear progression toward some other world or new "home" with women and no restored origin in innocence and wholeness. In fact, for women of color, the very conception of a linear passage from the old to the new, the expectation that women shed a patriarchal past for a new home with women constitutes a form of cultural imperialism. For the feminist dream of a new world of women simply reproduces the demand that women of color (and women more generally) abandon their histories, the histories of their communities, their complex locations and selves, in the name of a unity that barely masks its white, middle-class cultural reference/referent. In the words of Judit Moschkovich,

> When Anglo-American women speak of developing a new feminist or women's culture, they are still working and thinking within an Anglo-American cultural framework. This new culture would still be just as racist and ethnocentric as patriarchal American culture. I have often confronted the attitude that anything different is male. Therefore if I hold on to my Latin culture I am holding on to hateful patriarchal constructs. Meanwhile, the Anglo woman who deals with the world in her Anglo way, with her Anglo culture, is being "perfectly feminist."[39]

Moraga complicates the question of lesbian journeys and paths by beginning her preface with a description of her trip from the white suburbs of Watertown, Massachusetts, to black Roxbury.

> Take Boston alone, I think to myself, and the feminism my so-called sisters have constructed does nothing to help me make the trip from one end of town to another. Leaving Watertown, I board a bus and ride it quietly in my light flesh to Harvard Square, protected by the gold highlights my hair dares to take on, like an insult, in this miserable heat. **I transfer and go underground.** I am a lesbian. I want a movement that helps me make

38. *All the Women Are White / All the Blacks are Men / But Some of Us Are Brave: Black Women's Studies,* ed. Gloria T. Hull, Patricia Bell Scott, and Barbara Smith (Old Westbury, N.Y.: Feminist Press, 1982).

39. Judit Moschkovich, "—But I Know You, American Woman," in *This Bridge Called My Back,* p. 83.

some sense of the trip from Watertown to Roxbury, from white to Black. I love women the entire way, beyond a doubt.

The passage, for Moraga, must be "*through,* not over, not by, not around, but through."[40]

For the contributors who identify themselves as lesbians, lesbianism clearly does not figure as the exclusive ground of either identity or politics; however, it is neither divisible from nor subordinate to other identities. Moraga, for example, rejects the concept of separate, even if multiple, identities by refusing to isolate the "self" and then divide it into neat and hierarchical categories. Even as attention to racism interrupts any conception of lesbianism as the exclusive ground of identity and politics, lesbianism interrupts other potentially totalizing self-identifications. For it often works to expose the exclusions required by the dreams of heterosexual complementarity and wholes which organize so many fantasies of "home" and unity. Lesbianism represents the threat of rejection "by one's own kind."[41] Conceived here too as women's love for other women and for ourselves as women, lesbianism is politicized less as an identity than as a desire that transgresses the boundaries imposed by structures of race, class, ethnicity, nationality; it figures not as a desire that can efface or ignore the effects of those boundaries but as a provocation to take responsibility for them out of the desire for different kinds of connections. Lesbianism, for Moraga, for example, is about connection but not about a total or automatic identification; it marks a desire for more complex realities, for relationships filled with struggle and risk as well as pleasure and comfort.

> I would grow despairing if I believed . . . we were unilaterally defined by color and class. Lesbianism is then a hoax, a fraud. I have no business with it. Lesbanism is supposed to be about connection. What drew me to politics was my love of women, the agony I felt in observing the straight-jackets of poverty and repression I saw people in my own family in. But the deepest political tragedy I have experienced is how with such grace, such blind faith, this commitment to women in the feminist movement grew to be exclusive and reactionary. *I call my white sisters on this.*[42]

For a number of contributors, lesbian and not, the love of women, the pleasure in women's company, is said to sustain political analysis and struggle across divisions. This sense of a desire for connection, however partial and provisional, gives the pieces a particular force.

40. Cherríe Moraga, Preface to *This Bridge Called My Back,* pp. xiii–xix.
41. See Barbara Smith's introduction to *Home Girls: A Black Feminist Anthology* (New York: Kitchen Table Press, 1984).
42. Moraga, Preface, p. xiv.

There is no attempt to specify the relationships among gender, sexuality, race, and ethnicity in the abstract; Moraga and other contributors instead address the question of relationships and priorities by examining how they intersect at specific historical sites. A significant number of poems and autobiographical narratives begin with the memories of the crowds, the noises, the smells, the languages of the streets, concrete sites that evoke memories of home even as they suggest a kind of homelessness. The invocation of the sights, smells, sounds and meanings of "the street" works to locate the author concretely in geographic, demographic, architectural spaces, spaces with permeable boundaries and heterogeneous collectivities and communities. In "The Other Heritage," Rosario Morales uses the streets of Spanish Harlem to challenge the effects of racism and cultural imperialism on historical memory:

> I forgot   I forgot the other heritage   the other strain refrain   the silver thread thru my sound   the ebony sheen to my life   to the look of things to the sound of how I grew up which was in Harlem right down in Spanish Harlem El Barrio and bounded I always say to foreigners from Minnesota   Ohio and Illinois bounded on the North by Italians and on the South by Black Harlem. . . . What I didn't forget was the look of Ithaca Rochester Minneapolis and Salt Lake. . . .   so how come I come to feel   safe!   when I hit Harlem   when I hit a city with enough color   when a city gets moved in on   when Main Street Vermont looks mottled   agouti   black and brown and white. . . . [43]

Such attention to the ideological quality of memory itself interrupts conventional assumptions of a logical continuity between the past and present self, exposing the means by which such continuities are manufactured.

Virtually every contributor addresses the complex politics of language in postcolonial contexts, underlining the absence of "natural" linguistic unities. Donna Haraway has characterized Moraga's work in/on language: "Moraga's language is not 'whole': it is self-consciously spliced, a chimera of English and Spanish, both conqueror's languages. But it is this chimeric monster without claim to an original language before violation, that crafts the erotic, competent, potent identities of women of color."[44] Haraway's characterization of Moraga's work holds for many of the other contributors to *This Bridge* as well. The question of language is thrown onto historical axes that exceed and construct individual personal and community histories. The attention to "histories" carries an implicit, when not explicit, critique of the "dream of a common

43. Rosario Morales, "The Other Heritage," in *This Bridge Called My Back,* p. 107.
44. Haraway, p. 94.

language," calling attention to the impossibility of neutral or unmediated speech.[45] These texts work concertedly against the ways in which "experience" has been coded within feminist texts so as to render the complex realities of everyday life invisible.

The critique of a reduction of politics to psychology is also manifest in the call for a "theory in the flesh," in the use of a language of the body's physical pains and pleasures and of the materiality of psychic and social life. Moraga suggests that "the materialism in this book lives in the flesh of these women's lives, the exhaustion we feel in our bones at the end of the day, the fire we feel in our hearts when we are insulted, the knife we feel in our backs when we are betrayed, the nausea we feel in our bellies when we are afraid, even the hunger we feel between our hips when we long to be touched."[46] The contributions to *This Bridge* concretely describe the inscription of social and institutional constraints but also the lived pleasures and sensations of community in/on their bodies, drawing attention to the imbrication of "inner and outer world" without reducing one to the other. "Here," writes Moraga,

> we introduce you to the "color problem" as it was first introduced to us: "not white enuf, not dark enuf," always up against a color chart that first got erected far outside our families and our neighborhoods, but which invaded them both with systematic determination. . . . We were born into colored homes. We grew up with the inherent contradictions in the color spectrum right inside those homes: the lighter sister, the mixed-blood cousin, being the darkest one in the family. . . . We learned to live with those contradictions. This is the root of our radicalism.[47]

For Moraga, who describes herself as a light-skinned Chicana lesbian, the contradictions that she lives in and on her body provoke important questions about the workings of privilege and power, the difficulties of unities and of identities, the complexities, therefore, of her relations with other women of color. "Sisterhood" with other women of color, according to Moraga, is achieved, not assumed; it is based on affinities and shared but not identical histories. The attention to the difficulties of community are counterbalanced by the emphasis on its importance and its pleasures. These authors seek connections and forms of community that are chosen, negotiated, achieved, not simply given. But they do not

45. In her call for a postmodern socialist feminism, Donna Haraway works quite explicitly against political myths like Adrienne Rich's *The Dream of a Common Language* (1978), the title of one of Rich's collections of poetry, and a section title in Haraway's "Cyborg Manifesto."

46. Moraga, Preface, p. xviii.

47. Moraga, Introduction, to "Children Passing in the Street: The Roots of Our Radicalism," in *This Bridge Called My Back*, p. 5.

deny the importance or the pleasure of shared memories, shared histories, of identifications, partial and provisional though they may be. They avoid an overly rationalistic critique of identity and unity as dangerous fictions, curable through rational thought and theoretical negativity.

Several of the lesbian contributors speak openly of the importance of making connections with lesbians who share their ethnic, linguistic, or racial backgrounds, connections that allow them to combine their politics with the pleasures and safety of "home." The sense of safety and security in being with one's own kind is not explained with recourse to essential identities or natural connections but described quite concretely in terms of histories that are erased by all forms of "unity through incorporation or appropriation."[48] In the company of lesbians with similar histories, it becomes possible to live rather than cut off the languages, the forms of social interaction and humor, the smells, the tastes, the sights of those growing up places in oneself. What becomes crucial is knowing how to distinguish between the indulgence of home and the forging of political coalition, knowing how to indulge the provisional, though no less essential, pleasures of "home" without retreating into what Bernice Johnson Reagon has called "little barred rooms" in which differences are held at bay.[49]

In these narratives, "family" figures in complex and critical ways. The authors refer to neighborhoods, kin networks, communities that include aunts, grandmothers, mothers, fathers, sisters, brothers, neighbors, and friends. Families still operate as constraints and obstacles to particular forms of self-expression and freedom but also provide support, warmth, security, solidarity, sensuality. Moreover, working through memories and relationships with kin constitutes a resistance to internalized negations or denigrations of the authors' pasts, of families and communities that "fail" to mirror a white, middle-class Christian ideal:

> I don't really understand first-hand what it feels like being shitted on for being brown. I understand much more about the joys of it—being Chicana and having family are synonymous for me. What I know about loving, singing, crying, telling stories, speaking with my heart and hands, even having a sense of my own soul comes from the love of my mother, aunts, cousins. . . . But at the age of twenty-seven, it is frightening to acknowl-

48. Haraway, p. 67. She gives a critique of both radical and socialist feminism for reproducing conceptions of unity that amount to incorporation, appropriation, and erasure of differences.

49. Bernice Johnson Reagon, "Coalition Politics: Turning the Century," in *Home Girls,* pp. 356–68.

edge that I have internalized a racism and classism, where the object of oppression is not only someone outside of my skin, but the someone inside
my skin. In fact, to a large degree, the real battle with such oppression, for
all of us, begins under the skin. I have had to confront the fact that much of
what I value about being Chicana, about my family, has been subverted by
anglo-culture and my own cooperation with it.[50]

However great the actual physical or emotional separation between
mothers and daughters, a great many of the narratives, poems, and
letters are addressed directly to the authors' mothers, or to that relationship. This particular "thinking back through the mothers" involves neither disavowal nor total identification. Merle Woo, Moraga, and Aurora Levins Morales point to the negative legacies in forms of denial and
self-contempt, but they also draw on the skills, the strengths, the confidence that constitute the positive legacy, the legacy of survival. The
struggles to "unravel the knot" demonstrate the complex imbrication of
interpersonal, intrapsychic, and social relations in histories of colonialism, racism, and sexism. Aurora Levins Morales, daughter of Rosario
Morales, another contributor to *This Bridge,* describes the work:

I'm a latin woman in the United States, closely involved with Latin American movements in the rest of the continent. I *should* write about the connection. But when I tried, all I could think was: No, write about the
separation. For me the point of terror, the point of denial is the New York
Puerto Rican. My mother was born in New York in 1930, raised in Spanish
Harlem and the Bronx. I represent the generation of return. . . . For my
mother, the Barrio is safety, warmth. For me, it's the fear of racist violence
that clipped her tongue of all its open vowels, into crisp, imitation British.[51]

Finally, such attention to detail rather than to coherent life history succeeds in illuminating discontinuities between past and present and, as a
consequence, opens up possibilities for a different future. In her account
of the importance of personal historical memory to theoretical work on
ideology, German feminist Frigga Haug characterizes the "object" of
memory in terms that could describe the work in *This Bridge*: "Day-to-
day struggles over the hearts and minds of human subjects are not
located only within social structures or within the individual but in the
process whereby they perceive and appropriate the outer world . . . in a

50. Moraga, "La Güera," in *This Bridge Called My Back,* p. 30.
51. Aurora Levins Morales, ". . . And Even Fidel Can't Change That!" in *This Bridge Called
My Back,* pp. 53–56.

field of conflict between dominant cultural values and oppositional attempts to wrest cultural meaning and pleasure from life."[52]

The work of Minnie Bruce Pratt and Mab Segrest, both of whom identify themselves as southern, white, lesbian writers, demonstrates the impact of feminist encounters over racism and identity. In an autobiographical essay, "Identity: Skin Blood Heart," Pratt sets out to locate her own personal history in concrete histories of racism and anti-Semitism.[53] Pratt begins by identifying herself as a white, southern, middle-class, Christian-raised lesbian and then proceeds to explore the exclusions and repressions that support the seeming homogeneity, stability, and self-evidence of those identities. As Chandra Mohanty and I have argued elsewhere, Pratt situates herself quite concretely in relation to geographical, demographic and architectural sites, working to expose the illusory coherence and inclusiveness of the positions from which she is taught to see and to speak.[54] Like so many of the narratives in *This Bridge,* Pratt's begins on a street, on H Street, NW, in Washington, D.C., her current "home," a place that doesn't exist on most white folks' map of the city, except as "'the H Street Corridor,' as in something to be passed through quickly, going from your place, on the way to elsewhere" (p. 11). Pratt chooses to live in and to write about a space that daily brings her face-to-face with the relationship between her own personal history and the very different but overlapping histories of the people and the communities among whom she now lives.

Lesbianism figures in Pratt's narrative as a basis for her political vision. It is also that which her "identity" and privilege as a white, middle-class, southern woman disallows; its denial is the price of her privilege and her acceptance, of her welcome in a number of "homes." Pratt succeeds in showing that the exclusions required of conventional "homes" include parts of her self as well as others. Lesbianism then figures as desire, pleasure, and possibility, as a desire that transgresses conventional boundaries, not only the boundaries between self and others but the boundaries around "identity" itself. That desire, however, is easily recontained when it simply reproduces a nostalgia for safe places, for sameness, for Reagon's little barred rooms. Far from guaranteeing political correctness, innocence, and truth, lesbianism, when it is conceived

---

52. Haug, *Female Sexualization,* p. 41.

53. Minnie Bruce Pratt, "Identity: Skin Blook Heart," in Elly Bulkin, Minnie Bruce Pratt, and Barbara Smith, *Yours in Struggle: Three Feminist Perspectives on Anti-Semitism and Racism* (Brooklyn, N.Y.: Long Haul Press, 1984, now published by Firebrand Books), pp. 11–63, hereafter cited in the text.

54. See Biddy Martin and Chandra Talpade Mohanty, "Feminist Politics: What's Home Got to Do With It," in *Feminist Studies/Critical Studies,* ed. Teresa de Lauretis (Bloomington: Indiana University Press, 1986).

as automatic and essential commonality, can indeed stand in the way of analysis and of coalition. As for Moraga, lesbianism for Pratt is about connection but no longer about automatic connections or about substitute "homes." Pratt takes up the dangers of such substitutions: "Raised to believe that I could be where I wanted and have what I wanted, as a grown woman I thought I could simply claim what I wanted, even the making of a new place to live with other women. I had no understanding of the limits that I lived within, nor of how much my memory and my experience of a safe place was based on places secured by omission, exclusions or violence, and on my submitting to the limits of that place" (pp. 25–26). The connections Pratt struggles to make are conceived as expansions of a "constricted eye," a "living on the edge of the skin," on the borders, and are contrasted to the fearful isolation of homogenous "homes." Clearly, for Pratt a feminism that reproduces the constraints of the white, middle-class home constitutes a severe impoverishment of reality, a blindness to its complexities. Pratt's expansions proceed by way of her own efforts to educate herself about the histories of her family and of the peoples whose histories have been systemically obliterated, obscured by a systematic, an institutionalized and passionate forgetfulness, by racism and anti-Semitism.

Pratt attends quite concretely to her own family's implication in those histories and in their suppression. Pratt's return to her childhood home is rendered particularly complex and subtle by virtue of her attention to racism. Here, there is no attempt to efface either positive or negative connections with her past for the sake of coherence or political purity; rather, she attempts to work through her contradictory implication in structures of privilege and oppression, pain and pleasure by repeatedly relocating herself in relation to concrete structures and institutional forms. She, too, reconstructs and sorts through positive and negative legacies, the materiality, the very physicality of her connections with "home"; she opens the enclosed space of the family, the illusory promises of home to analysis and critique. Through specific demographic and architectural sites and figures, Pratt locates herself in a web of relationships of difference and similarity with her family, her father, their vision, and their deeds. For in Pratt's words, "I was shaped by my relation to those buildings and to the people in the buildings, by ideas of who should be in the Board of Education, of who should be in the bank handling money, of who should have the guns and the keys to the jail, of who should be *in* the jail; and I was shaped by what I didn't see, or didn't notice on those streets" (p. 17). The only apparent self-evidence and neutrality of her father's "white male" identity are exposed as bounded in terror and defense: "A month after I dreamed this he died; I honor the grief of his life by striving to change much of what he believed in: and my own grief by acknowledging that I saw him caught in the grip of racial, sexual, cultural fears that I still am trying to understand in myself" (p. 53). "Unraveling the knot" between herself and her father, working through the ways in which she is her father's daughter become central to Pratt's enterprise.

Antiracist politics inform Mab Segrest's autobiographical writing as well. Segrest also identifies herself as a white, southern, lesbian writer whose personal history is deeply implicated in the history of racism and bigotry in the South. In her attempt to draw connections between southern lesbian writing and antiracist writing, Segrest inevitably comes counter to a lesbian feminism that assumes the unity of women or of lesbians to be primary and essential, overriding other divisions and loyalties. In her critique of certain forms of lesbian autobiography, Segrest writes: "The assertion of the decolonized self . . . can trap the fugitive into a need to be too pure, too free—which leads back into a new repression, into another death-dealing denial of our complex selves. And if the decolonized self slips into the born-again self, we are really in trouble."[55] Racism, beginning with the forms it takes in her family and the community in which she grew up, becomes the lever by which she uncovers the stakes in particular forms of community and unity in the South and, indeed, in the women's movement. Like Pratt, Segrest recalls the pleasures of her family's brand of southern humor, social manners, styles of communication, and storytelling. Both succeed in working through the complex links between the pleasures of those social forms and the pain of the racism, misogyny, and homophobia inextricably embedded in them.

> Southerners raise their indirection to an art and call it *manners*. Manners are one thing that still, to this day, separate Southerners from Yankees. It is my experience that Yankees have a hard time believing that Southerners can have so many manners, and Southerners cannot believe that Yankees do not. . . . Manners, lies and truth were all intertwined in the world I grew up in. Manners were, in fact, elaborate rituals for getting at or avoiding the truth. . . . "Courtesy," my mother explained, "is the mortar of civilization." And anger, she implied, destroyed both. I think as a white Southern mother she knew her "civilization" needed a lot of mortar.[56]

Segrest's essays, ordered chronologically, move from the more exclusively autobiographical to several final pieces that document her antiracist work in Klanwatch in North Carolina. In fact, Segrest recon-

55. Segrest, p. 127.
56. Ibid., pp. 63–64.

structs the history of lesbian writing in such a way as to emphasize the ongoing links between antiracist and southern lesbian writing. This attempt to establish a tradition of southern antiracist lesbian writing leads Segrest to the work of Angeline Weld Grimké, Carson McCullers, Lillian Smith, and more recently, Barbara Deming, Pat Parker, Judy Grahn, and Minnie Bruce Pratt. Segrest locates the roots of contemporary southern lesbian writing in the early antiracist work of the Combahee River Collective in Boston;[57] in so doing, she challenges reconstructions that make lesbianism the origin and end of a coherent tradition, reconstructions that too often represent a lesbian-feminist tradition (from the perspective of white lesbian feminists) in such a way as to suggest that the problem of racism was "discovered" at a particular point in a fairly linear history. For Segrest, an antiracist lesbian tradition stands in a critical relationship to "southern gentlemen" and the "disciplinary power" of the agrarians, or New Critics, Allen Tate, John Crowe Ransom, Donald Davidson, Robert Penn Warren, Stark Young, and John Peale Bishop, the guardians of traditions she studied as a graduate student in English literature. Segrest suggests that the "arrogance in this New Critical approach is the assumption that white, class-privileged, European men have produced a *complete* tradition; in Tate's words, 'the whole of experience . . . the true knowledge which is poetry,' as opposed to society's 'unremitting imposition of partial formulas.'"[58] Though Segrest's polemical consolidation of antiracist and lesbian writing in opposition to white male culture tends to reproduce an overly simple division between oppressors and oppressed, it also represents the important effort to work back through the complex coimplication of histories in the South without completely reducing the relation between different histories to analogy.[59]

Segrest's work participates in attempts to remove questions of identity from the exclusive ground of the psychological or interpersonal and to open up questions about the relations between psychic and social life, between intrapsychic, interpersonal, and political struggles. Identity is thrown onto historically constructed discursive and social axes that crisscross only apparently homogeneous communities and bounded subjects. Experience itself, now exposed as deeply ideological, no longer guarantees knowledge and political correctness. In fact, experience and the identities on which it is presumed to rely stand in the way of

57. "The Combahee River Collective Statement," in *Capitalist Patriarchy and the Case for a Socialist Feminism,* ed. Zillah Eisenstein (New York: Monthly Review Press, 1979), pp. 362–72.

58. Segrest, pp. 111–12.

59. The consolidation also constitutes the basis for Segrest's humor and are therefore more complex than I render them here.

analysis and solidarity. The circuits of exchange between the work of Moraga, Anzaldúa, Pratt, and Segrest, whether direct or indirect, have moved autobiographical writing in this context onto a different plane. In these exchanges there is no longer a simple side by side, but a provocation to examine the coimplication of "my" history in "yours," to analyze the relations between.

As a consequence of these developments, lesbianism ceases to be an identity with predictable contents, to constitute a total political and self-identification, and yet it figures no less centrally for that shift. It remains a position from which speak, to organize, to act politically, but it ceases to be the exclusive and continuous ground of identity or politics. Indeed, it works to unsettle rather than to consolidate the boundaries around identity, not to dissolve them altogether but to open them to the fluidities and heterogeneities that make their renegotiation possible. At the same time that such autobiographical writing enacts a critique of both sexuality and race as "essential" and totalizing identifications, it also acknowledges the political and psychological importance, indeed, the pleasures, too, of at least partial or provisional identifications, homes, and communities. In so doing, it remains faithful to the irreducibly complex and paradoxical status of identity in feminist politics and autobiographical writing.

PART II

COLONIZED SUBJECTS
AND SUBVERSIVE
DISCOURSES

5

"Not Just a Personal Story": Women's *Testimonios* and the Plural Self

Doris Sommer

At first, I assumed rather naïvely that the testimonials I had been reading by Latin American women were "autobiographical." As such, their most salient feature, for me, was an implied and often explicit "plural subject," rather than the singular subject we associate with traditional autobiography. Domitila Barrios, for example, begins her testimony like this: "I don't want anyone at any moment to interpret the story I'm about to tell as something that is only personal. . . . What happened to me could have happened to hundreds of people in my country."[1] Similarly, Rigoberta Menchú opens by disclaiming her particularity. "I'd like to stress that it's not only *my* life, it's also the testimony of my people."[2] And Claribel Alegría's testimonial montage of the already-martyred heroine in *No me agarran viva* (They won't catch me alive) starts with this prologue: "Eugenia, exemplary model of self-sacrifice and revolutionary heroism, is a typical and not an exceptional case of so many Salvadoran women who have dedicated their efforts, and lives, to the struggle for liberating their people."[3]

I thank Eve Kosofsky Sedgwick, Andrew Parker, George Yúdice, and Leah Hewitt for their very valuable comments and generous encouragement.

1. Domitila Barrios, *Let Me Speak! Testimony of Domitila, a Woman of the Bolivian Mines*, written with Moema Viezzer, trans. Victoria Ortiz (New York: Monthly Review Press, 1978), p. 15, hereafter cited in the text. Originally published as *"Si me permiten hablar . . ."; Testimonio de Domitila, una mujer de las minas de Bolivia* (Mexico: Siglo XXI Editores, 1976).

2. Rigoberta Menchú, *I Rigoberta Menchú: An Indian Woman in Guatemala*, ed. and introduced by Elisabeth Burgos-Debray, trans. Ann Wright (London: Verso Editions, 1984), p. 1, hereafter cited in the text. Originally published as *Me llamo Rigoberta Menchú y así me nació la conciencia* (Barcelona: Ed. Argos Vergara, 1983).

3. Claribel Alegría and D. J. Flakoll, *No me agarran viva: La mujer salvadoreña en lucha* (Mexico: Serie Popular Era, 1983), p. 9, my translation. The book has been published in English under the title *They'll Never Take Me Alive* (London: Women's Press, 1986).

I began to worry that my assumption about the autobiographical nature of testimonials might represent a contradiction in terms, since autobiography is precisely that genre which insists on singularity. When women write it they tend to distinguish themselves from others and to assume what they consider to be more differentiated, male personae, as Nancy Miller has shown for France.[4] Or as Elaine Marks puts it, women's autobiographies proclaim, "I am my own heroine."[5] Of course, some autobiographers assume that they represent others, and that the reader is ideally among them.[6] And even where there may be no such assumption, the "I" of the writer inevitably spills over to stand in for the reader, who, paradoxically, achieves a kind of specialness by identifying with the heroic autobiographer.

But the testimonial "I" does not invite us to identify with it. We are too different, and there is no pretense here of universal or essential human experience. Rigoberta, for example, ends her book by reminding us of the necessary limits she has respected in her apparent intimacy and confidence: "I'm still keeping secret what I think no one should know. Not even anthropologists or intellectuals, no matter how many books they have, can find out all our secrets" (p. 247). The protestations of collectivity, then, do not necessarily argue that the testimonial "I" can slip uncritically from identifying herself in the singular to assuming that she is typical enough to stand in for the "we." Instead, her singularity achieves its identity as an extension of the collective. The singular represents the plural not because it replaces or subsumes the group but because the speaker is a distinguishable part of the whole. In rhetorical terms, whose political consequences should be evident in what follows, there is a fundamental difference here between the *metaphor* of autobiography and heroic narrative in general, which assumes an identity by substituting one (superior) signifier for another (I for we, leader for follower, Christ for the faithful), and *metonymy*, a lateral identification through relationship, which acknowledges the possible differences among "us" as components of the whole.

To banish my doubts, I reasoned that the rhetorical construction of an often explicitly collective subject behind the first-person narrator of

---

4. Nancy K. Miller, "Writing Fictions: Women's Autobiography in France," this volume.

5. Elaine Marks, "'I Am My Own Heroine': Some Thoughts about Women and Autobiography in France," in *Teaching about Women in the Foreign Languages: French, Spanish, German, Russian,* ed. Sidonie Cassirer, prepared for the Commission on the Status of Women of the MLA (Old Westbury, N.Y.: Feminist Press, 1975), pp. 1–10.

6. Violette Leduc begins her autobiographical *La Bâtarde* (Paris: Gallimard, 1964) by claiming: "Mon cas n'est pas unique." And Michel Leiris has devoted practically a lifetime to writing an autobiography as a representative man of a particular context. See *La Règle du jeu,* 4 vols. (Paris: Gallimard, 1948–76).

testimonials did not really seem so striking a departure as to constitute a separate genre. Whatever the differences, testimonials were life histories narrated in a first-person voice that stressed development and continuity, were they not? In fact, the full title of Rigoberta's book could be literally translated as "My name is Rigoberta Menchú and this is how my consciousness was raised"—a regular Bildungsroman! So I simply tried to frame testimonials within what I considered the more general category of autobiography. But by now my confidence was shaken. At what political and aesthetic price could I favor one genre over the other? I should point out that the specific books that most challenged me (and from which I chose to theorize generic categories) fit somewhere at the seam of testimonials themselves, related, as it were, metonymically but not as typical or substitutable exemplars of the genre.[7] When women in Latin America enter politics as an extension of the domestic realm and narrate their life stories to journalists or anthropologists (who have sought out these sometimes illiterate informants as representatives of particular historical struggles), we can hardly place the results in the familiar category of autobiography or even the heroic testimonial norm of male informants. Rather, these intensely lived testimonial narratives are strikingly impersonal. They are written neither for individual growth nor for glory but are offered through the scribe to a broad public as one part of a general strategy to win political ground.[8] One part of the strategy is simply to record the history of popular struggles, as Domitila argues: "And there should be testimony. That's been our mistake, not to write down everything that happens. Very little has been set down in writing. Like the testimonies that we had in the union, or on the miners' radio stations, like for example recordings; they were taken or destroyed by the army. And all of that would have been so useful to us, even just to think about what we were doing and criticize it, you know?" (p. 40). Or again: "Some of us have to suffer, play the role of martyr, others have to write our history" (p. 44). Another part of the strategy is to pry open the process of subject formation, to rehearse it with the reader in a way that invites her to hook into the lateral network of relationships that assumes a community of particular shared objectives rather than interchangeability among its members.

7. See George Yúdice on testimonials as a form of aratology, or narrative of heroic, exemplary lives. Most Latin American testimonials fit this category.

8. John Beverley offers similar observations about the impersonal nature of testimonial narrative. He wisely concludes that one of the common denominators of the varied testimonial genre in Latin America is that it always challenges the political status quo, even when the challenge is not explicitly intended. See his "Anatomía del testimonio," chap. 7 in *Del Lazarillo al sandinismo: Estudios sobre la función ideológica de la literatura española e hispanoamericana* (Minneapolis: Institute for the Study of Ideologies and Literature, 1987), pp. 157–205.

It may be objected that this strategic difference is one of intentionality and that to make a generic distinction between autobiography and women's testimonials on this basis would be naïve, since the very act of rewriting history through the first person will inevitably color the narrative with the same blush of intimacy and particularity that makes the autobiographer glow as she distinguishes herself from the rest. This is to some degree a valid objection, as I hope to show. But I will argue here that the intentional difference in the writing goes far beyond a possible fallacy on the reader's part. In fact, we will see that several formal characteristics follow from the testimonial's insertion within a more general discourse of metonymy designed to challenge the hegemonic language of metaphoric substitution.

After closely examining women's testimonials, we may indeed find it legitimate to classify them as a variation of autobiography or perhaps to see them as contiguous categories. On the other hand, the differences may be too significant, too politically loaded, to risk the economy of fewer generic categories and a neat subordinating organization. My own casual impulse to recuperate testimonials into autobiography, for example, dramatizes at least one danger for First World readers. By understating the difference, we may miss the potential in what I am calling the testimonials' collective self: the possibility to get beyond the gap between public and private spheres and beyond the often helpless solitude that has plagued Western women even more than men since the rise of capitalism. To read testimonials as if they were merely a variation of autobiography would reinforce a blind-spot that the difference in genre could help to locate. The blindness I am referring to is the habit of conflating human culture and history with the lives of extraordinary individuals.

Since Georges Gusdorf published "Conditions and Limits of Autobiography" (1956) and especially since James Olney's translation (1980), students of the genre have had to consider its originally parochial and then imperializing nature: "It would seem that autobiography is not to be found outside of our cultural area; one would say that it expresses a concern peculiar to Western *man*, a concern that has been of good use in *his* systematic conquest of the universe and that *he* has communicated to *men* of other cultures."[9] Not surprisingly, the autobiography is a latecomer to Western literature, associated with the focus of humanism

---

9. Georges Gusdorf, "Conditions and Limits of Autobiography," in *Autobiography: Essays Theoretical and Critical,* ed. James Olney (Princeton: Princeton University Press, 1980), p. 29, my emphasis, simply to point out how even Gusdorf is complicitous in the exclusion to which he refers.

on "the singularity of each individual life." Says Gusdorf, "Throughout most of human history, the individual does not oppose himself to all others; he does not feel himself to exist outside of others, and still less against others, but very much with others in an interdependent existence that asserts its rhythms everywhere in the community." Even if the genre began with Saint Augustine, "at the moment when the Christian contribution was grafted onto classical traditions,"[10] autobiographies became really popular during the Renaissance and Reformation, when self-made men became the rage.

The phenomenon of a collective subject of the testimonial is, then, hardly the result of personal preference on the part of the writer who testifies. It is a translation of a hegemonic autobiographical pose into a colonized language that does not equate identity with individuality. It is thus a reminder that life continues at the margins of Western discourse, and continues to disturb and to challenge it. But this relative autonomy may be on the eve of capitulation, for as Gusdorf continues, the very fact that a first-person singular is marshaled to narrate a plural history is a symptom of Western penetration. "When Gandhi tells his own story, he is using Western means to defend the East."[11] At the same time, though, testimonials also point beyond the dialectic of resistance and capitulation. They are models of experimental syncretism which represent a "return of the repressed" in both traditional and Westernizing discourses. That this return occurs at the margins of the same imperializing language it challenges, that it helps to define that language by showing what has been excluded, is evident from the countertradition of Black autobiographies in the United States. It has provided an organizational principle for Black Studies courses, as James Olney observes, because it preserved the particular history that standard North American historiography ignored.[12] Gusdorf might have called Black autobiography "a revenge on history." Olney's observations may serve to indicate the slippery, Janus-faced nature of autobiography. Is it the model for imperializing the consciousness of colonized peoples, replacing their collective potential for resistance with a cult of individuality and even loneliness?[13] Or is it a medium of resistance and counterdiscourse, the legitimate space for producing that excess which throws doubt on the coherence and power of an exclusive historiography? The slippage be-

10. Gusdorf, p. 29.

11. Gusdorf, p. 29.

12. James Olney, "Autobiography and the Cultural Moment: A Thematic, Historical, and Bibliographical Introduction," in *Autobiography*, p. 16.

13. Roger Rosenblatt develops this argument in "Black Autobiography: Life as the Death Weapon," in *Autobiography*, p. 169.

tween attention to one's individuality and a focus on the social constraints of that individuality prompts Roger Rosenblatt to conclude that
"all autobiography is minority autobiography."[14] Perhaps we will conclude that all autobiography is really testimonial, the only difference
being that the autobiographer nurtures an illusion of singularity, an
illusion of standing *in* for others as opposed to standing *up* among them.

What follows is not a point-by-point comparison between autobiographies and testimonials by women, which would only return us to
my initial and facile subordination of the "marginal" genre to the one
considered paradigmatic for Western humanism. Contrasts will inevitably suggest themselves, but I would like to focus on the particular
generic logic of Latin American women's testimonials, on their characteristic features, and on their relationship to literary and political
history.

Why, to begin, does the testimonial seem to flourish today? If Gusdorf considers autobiography to be peculiar to the West and to a late
period of development at that, one would have to observe that the
testimonial is more narrowly localizable and so recent that it hardly has
any age at all. Perhaps we could date it from the 1960s, when intellectuals began to doubt whether they could adequately reconstruct their
national histories in a way that would help to plot directions for change.
The challenge, even mandate, to do so is self-evident for many Latin
American intellectuals, because the privilege of education often brings
with it a combination of guilt, social responsibility, and a kind of superiority that breeds messianism. The distinctions among intellectual, artist,
and activist tend to blur for many Latin Americans. Throughout the
nineteenth century and well into the twentieth, for example, the so-
called fathers of their countries, master statesmen and political architects, have also been the most notable novelists. Romantic or historical
novels in Latin America often turn out also to be analyses of national
frustrations and projected histories of improvement.[15]

Jean Franco describes the public nature of art clearly and simply in the
contrast she draws between Latin America and the traditions of Europe
and North America: "An intense social concern has been the characteristic of Latin-American art for the last hundred and fifty years. Literature—
and even painting and music—have played a social role, with the artist
acting as guide, teacher and conscience of his country. Latin America
has generally viewed art as an expression of the artist's whole self: a self

14. Ibid.
15. See my "National Romance and Populist Rhetoric in Spanish America," in *Europe and Its Others,* ed. Peter Hulme (Colchester: University of Essex, 1985), pp. 33–45.

which is living in a society and which therefore has a collective as well as an individual concern. Conversely, the idea of the moral neutrality or the purity of art has had relatively little impact."[16] Franco certainly does not deny the countertradition that made art a cult, beginning with *modernismo* at the turn of the century through to a Borgesian distancing from any immediate and changeable cares. But she reminds us that this pose is less frequent. And we might add that even where she sees social irresponsibility, for example, in the experimental "Boom" novels of the 1960s and 1970s,[17] a different reading would discern the novelists' social criticism in the form of impatience with standard social-narrative projects gone sour.[18] Given this general sense of responsibility, one can imagine the frustration of the Latin American intellectual-artist, who because of class, racial, and cultural barriers cannot even feel himself or herself to be an "organic intellectual," to use Antonio Gramsci's term. To be an intellectual is precisely not to come from the people or, as Domitila Barrios complains, not to return to them (p. 59). Therefore, socially responsible writers in Latin America have had to come to terms with their unrepresentativeness. One response, at the turn of the century and into the 1920s and 1930s was a literary movement called indigenism, a romanticization of pre-Hispanic cultures and a denunciation of the suffering caused in the name of Europeanization. Socialism and communism colored another wave of denunciation, focusing on class rather than racial exploitation. In either case, those who spoke for the masses were not of them and, in the worst case, could portray them as practically dehumanized, helpless except for the outrage they inspired in their white, city-dwelling advocates.[19]

The mandate to rewrite Latin American history from the "people's" perspective was renewed with a greater sense of cultural independence after the Cuban Revolution. This imperative followed the experimental "Boom" in narrative, which had succeeded in debunking some romantic and positivist assumptions about inevitable progress in history but offered little in their place. When the "Boom" went bust, however, little serious interest remained in reviving a discredited heroic "populist"

16. Jean Franco, *The Modern Culture of Latin America: Society and the Artist* (New York, 1967), p. 1.

17. Jean Franco, "The Crisis of the Liberal Imagination and the Utopia of Writing," *Ideologies and Literature* 1 (Dec. 1976–Jan. 1977): 5–24.

18. George Yúdice and Doris Sommer, "Latin American Literature from the 'Boom' On," *Postmodern Fiction: A Bio-bibliographic Guide,* ed. Larry McCaffery (Westport, Conn.: Greenwood Press, 1986), pp. 189–214.

19. See, for example, Jorge Icaza, *Huasipungo* (1934) and Franco, *Modern Culture of Latin America,* chaps. 3 and 4.

narrative and the historiography that went with it.[20] By the 1960s, after Cuba's "assault on the impossible"[21] turned into a triumphant revolution and after the imported economic theories of modernization and developmentalism gave way to the local critique of "dependency," some Latin American writers began to rethink their position in society and to experiment with an entirely different technique for overcoming the marginality that privilege imposed. Instead of designing programs for "civilization" to conquer "barbarism," straining to overcome what the positivists had called "racial backwardness" or appointing themselves apostles to the exploited, some intellectuals began to realize that the people whose causes they advocated were subjects, not the objects, of national history.

It must have dawned on these writers that for years a more or less well intentioned intellectual elite had been missing the point. The point is that historical change cannot be mandated from the top down, that, rather, the process is a complex of local and more general developments in which the intellectual can choose to intervene. Therefore, some journalists, anthropologists, and literati left their writing desks to become scribes. The women writers stood to gain the most; they could address their double marginalization by helping to portray other women as workers, militants, strategists. To repeat, this decision to interview women in struggle was made by intellectuals; it was not spontaneously generated by those interviewed. This means, among other things, that the testimonies do not exactly set up what Philippe Lejeune called an "autobiographical pact"[22] in intimacy with the reader, although they conform to his criterion of sincerity. Testifying is always a public event. Some of the accounts are, in fact, ghostwritten. One such is anthropologist Miguel Barnet's widely read *Autobiography of a Runaway Slave* (1968) about Estéban Montejo. Another is journalist Elena Poniatowska's *Hasta no verte Jesús mío* (1969), a novelized testimony of Jesusa Palancares, which tells of her part in the Mexican Revolution and of her working

20. Nevertheless, there are significant throwbacks to the populist narrative. Perhaps the most evident example is Manuel Cofiño López, *La última mujer y el próximo combate* (Havana: Casa de las Américas, 1971). The title itself, "The last woman and the next battle," predicts the narrative. Here, heroic "Marxism," which celebrates the young and innocent blonde heroine, is dedicated to work and associates the irresistibly sexy woman with all uncontrollable desires, including the irrational counterrevolution.

21. A characterization coined by Mario Benedetti, a Uruguayan poet, intellectual, and editor of *Revista Casa de las Américas*.

22. See Philippe Lejeune, *L'Autobiographie en France* (Paris: Armand Colin, 1971); and his *Le Pacte autobiographique* (Paris: Seuil, 1976). Lejeune is still associated with this position more for convenience's sake than to accurately represent his own thinking. Even Nancy Miller cites Lejeune's idea of pact in her essay only to point out later that he too has come to modify it substantially in "Le Pacte autobiographique," *Poétique* 14 (1973): 137–62, esp. 160–62.

life until 1968. Other, apparently more direct transcriptions are Moema Viezzer's compilation of interviews with Domitila Barrios, *Si me permiten hablar* (1977) (a rhetorically humble "If you allow me to speak" translated rather gracelessly as *Let Me Speak!* [1978]); the anthropologist Elizabeth Burgos-Debray's presentation of *I Rigoberta Menchú: An Indian Woman in Guatemala*; the poet Margaret Randall's interviews with Cuban and Nicaraguan women; and the poet Claribel Alegría's *They'll Never Take Me Alive* (1983), an experimental mirror image of testimonial subject construction in which a community of narrators reconstructs the life of a single revolutionary in El Salvador. Part of an international trend to promote oral history, the interviews in Latin America also responded to the early days of the Cuban Revolution. The relatively brief period of cultural laissez-faire and euphoria fostered a spirit of cooperation among Latin-American intellectuals and established new challenges for literature. Perhaps the main response came later, though, after the break with liberal Latin American intellectuals over the "hardening" of the Soviet line in Cuba.[23] It was then that Cuba's cultural clearinghouse, Casa de las Américas, legitimated the testimonial as a genre somewhere between novel and essay by instituting a prize category for testimonials among other (traditional) genres. Clearly, the ideological purpose was to represent the "people" as agents of their own history. Whether or not the genre would have flourished without this stimulus, the Cuban promotion is undeniable. Testimonials surely existed before the 1960s, but they were relatively isolated, even ignored. One example is *Benita*, Benita Galeana's account of her orphaned childhood during the Mexican Revolution and of her militancy within the Mexican Communist party. Originally published in 1940, it waited over thirty-five years to be reprinted, and by 1979 it appeared in a third edition. Similarly, Carolina Maria de Jesus had for years been writing her diary of life in a São Paulo *favela* (as well as poems and stories that never attracted the intelligentsia's attention) before a journalist "discovered" her testimony in 1958 and published it first in his paper and then as a book called *Child of the Dark*. Ironically, the very act of legitimating these narratives as a genre may have been the kiss of death. Instead of writing and reading them as resistances to institutionalization, testimonials now may seem standardized and lose the power of their unpredictability. It is perhaps as a consequence of this very institutionalization that the Cubans themselves have recently lost interest in testimonials. This abandonment, of course, argues for Cuba's political and aesthetic

---

23. I am indebted for this specific point and in general to George Yúdice's excellent "Central American Testimonial" (unpublished manuscript), p. 8.

open-mindedness. On the other hand, it is possible that the rejection owes more to an assumption that testimonials of suffering and struggle are no longer necessary in an era of "already existing socialism." It is significant, I think, that although feminism is still considered to be a social battlefront, I know of no testimonials of Cuban women confronting those challenges.

The job of supplementing official history extended to novelists as well. For some of them (Alejo Carpentier, Guillermo Cabrera Infante, José Donoso, Augusto Roa Bastos, Carlos Fuentes, among others) there was a sense that standard histories falsified the past, that they presented barriers or denied opportunities for change. Novelists responded by constructing alternative versions of the past. Their target texts ranged from the first chronicles of the Conquest to periods of recent memory. The model for this kind of rewriting or unwriting in Latin America is as old as the chronicles themselves. Those first Spanish texts in America are far from a coherent or self-identical canon. On the contrary, the chronicles describe a field of authorized discourse and a variety of counterdiscourses competing for authority. Bartolomé de Las Casas wrote his defense of the Indians against the calumnies published by Fernández de Oviedo, chronicler to the king; and Bernal Díaz wrote his account of the campaigns in Mexico because he and his fellow officers were given short shrift in the official reports of López de Gómara and Hernán Cortés. Conquerors and adventurers also wrote a particular type of uninvited brief, the *relación*, addressed to an emperor who could choose to favor the author, or at least to pardon him for some offense reported by another. Alejo Carpentier revisited this dialectic of information and counterinformation in his novel about Columbus' (ad)ventures, *El arpa y la sombra* (1979). From the admiral's diaries, Carpentier managed to read out a series of inconsistencies, statements in bad faith born of Renaissance opportunism and a medieval fear of divine retribution. The inconsistencies are felt even more keenly when the events are part of living memory, as in the case of *One Hundred Years of Solitude* by Gabriel García Márquez.[24]

24. Gabriel García Márquez, *One Hundred Years of Solitude* (New York: Harper and Row, 1970), originally published as *Cien años de soledad* (Buenos Aires: Sudamericana, 1967). This is probably the best known example for English-language readers of a contemporary novel that tries to set the record of recent history straight. The novel challenges innocuous official history with a tragic version of the Banana Strike in Colombia in 1927, the year of García Márquez's birth. He reports a massacre that was prepared by the "hermeneutic delirium" of official discourse. Since the government found the workers' demands absurd, it concluded that the conditions they reported did not exist and, for that matter, that there were no workers, only day laborers. Once they were erased in the discourse, rubbing the workers out in the flesh was easy. In some ways, the book seems motivated by a necessarily frustrated desire to fix that event in language. The irony of fixing anything in language is not lost on the author. He is a

At this point I would like to make a tentative observation about a general consequence that followed from the gesture of returning to the chronicles and to other historical documents right after the "Boom." The return implied a simultaneous but unarticulated acknowledgment that no one version of history can be ultimately authoritative. From the beginning, Latin America was a series of confrontations between blueprints for progress and mutually inexplicable indigenous pre-texts, between constructing a "rational order" and enjoying the return of the repressed, the excluded (indigenous cultures, languages, the "barbarous" land, non-Europeans, and women). Of course these oppositional terms do little justice to the mediating powers of José Martí, along with José Carlos Mariátegui and others, who understood the particular cultural, ethnic, and geographic conditions of "Our America."[25] In their majority, nevertheless, Latin America's political architects came to work with ready-made plans for which variations were more annoying than inspiring. And so there was always a particular legitimacy associated with the vanquished (never entirely silenced) indigenous or otherwise oppositional voices. European models were obviously imported and therefore arbitrary. Latin America did not merely inherit them; it often chose in a free marketplace of ideas, at least since the independence movement, when British ideas of free-trade liberalism found support in Spain's colonies while Britain funded the revolutionary wars. Monopoly trade and the inquisitorial orthodoxy of the Spanish empire were no more natural to Latin America than were France's enlightenment and England's liberalism. Rationality almost inevitably collided with demands for "authenticity," a word that keeps losing its moorings in a context of competing traditions and competing truths. Therefore, contemporary intellectuals did more than rewrite what had apparently been fixed as the very foundation of Hispanic Americanness; they also evoked this conflictual field of historical writing. Knowing that some corners of the contemporary field of historical experience, maybe even the center, have either been excluded from historical discourse or represented through intellectual and therefore perhaps marginal positions, the testimonial "scribes" set out to perform a corollary recuperation of others' experience into published discourse.

The oral quality of the informants' narratives, though, is unmistak-

---

master at desacralizing his own myths, too. But at least his version of the strike is provocative enough to startle us out of complacency. Even if the strike did not end in a massacre of the magnitude that he reports, the narrative makes us worry about the possibility that it did; it puts us on guard against other more unbelievable (official) versions.

25. José Martí, "Nuestra América," originally published in the Mexican newspaper *El Partido Liberal,* 30 Jan. 1891, often reprinted and translated into English as "Our America."

able, even in the edited and polished versions that reach us. And as a device, the orality helps to account for the testimonials' construction of a collective self. For unlike the private and even lonely moment of autobiographical writing, testimonies are public events. Autobiography, to make a stylistic distinction, strains to produce a personal and distinctive *style* as part of the individuation process, but testimonial strives to preserve or to renew an interpersonal *rhetoric*.[26] That rhetoric does not need to postulate an interchangeable "I" of the ideal reader, as autobiography does. Instead, it addresses a flesh-and-blood person, the interviewer, who asks questions and avidly records answers. The narrative voice, therefore, sometimes shifts into a second person. The interlocutor and, by extension, each reader is addressed by the narrator's immediate appeal to "you." This appeal is not only consistent with existing cultural assumptions about community as the fundamental social unit; it has political implications that go beyond, perhaps to corrupt, the cultural coherence the narrators seek to defend. When the narrator talks about her*self* to *you*, she implies both the existing relationship to other representative selves in the community and potential relationships that extend her community through the text. She calls us in, interpellates us as readers who identify with the narrator's project and, by extension, with the political community to which she belongs. The appeal does not produce only the admiration for the ego-ideal we might feel for an autobiographer who impresses us precisely with her difference from other women; nor does it encourage the consequent yearning to be (like) her and so to deny her and our distinctiveness. Rather, the testimonial produces complicity. Even if—perhaps because—the reader cannot identify with the writer enough to imagine taking her place, the map of possible identifications through the text spreads out laterally. Once the subject of the testimonial is understood as the community made up of a variety of roles, the reader is called in to fill one of them. One lesson of these narratives may be that our habit of identifying with a single subject of the narration (implicitly substituting her) simply repeats a Western logocentric limitation, a vicious circle in which only one center can exist. If we find it difficult to entertain the idea of several simultaneous points of activity, several simultaneous and valid roles, the testimonials help to remind us that politics is not necessarily a top-down heroic venture.[27]

26. Fredric Jameson makes this provocative distinction in his "Criticism in History," in *Weapons of Criticism: Marxism in America and the Literary Tradition,* ed. Norman Rudich (Palo Alto, Calif.: Ramparts Press, 1976), pp. 31–50.

27. For a recent and rather compelling theoretical discussion of the democratic promise in decentered politics, see Ernesto Laclau and Chantal Mouffe, *Hegemony & Socialist Strategy: Towards a Radical Democratic Politics* (London: Verso, 1985).

We can see how this self-construction differs from autobiography. An autobiographer such as Jean-Paul Sartre may be representative for his class and generation; but this observation is often not the autobiographer's. It is made easier by the distance of time or of person, as when theorist Paul John Eakin reads Sartre.[28] In any case, the autobiographer does not call in readers to recognize themselves in a metonymic relationship of shared experience and consciousness. Instead, she or he tends to play out the metaphoric drama of representation by substitution. By now we are used to conceiving of autobiography as the "self-invention" of a particular, though paradoxically repeatable, self. At least as early as Gusdorf's essay, autobiography has been read as a self-reconstitution from memory, one that translates disparate experiences into a story of development and a more or less pleasing coherence.[29] Paul de Man took this observation a step further to question the referential value of autobiography. "We assume that life *produces* the autobiography as an act produces its consequences, but can we not suggest, with equal justice, that the autobiographical project may itself produce and determine the life and that whatever the writer *does* is in fact governed by the technical demands of self-portraiture and thus determined, in all its aspects, by the resources of his medium?"[30] Here de Man turns the tables on the idea that language is used as a theater of self-expression and self-discovery; it is no medium but the subject itself. He shifts the focus from the portrait produced to the productive trope of self-reference.

Testimonials, on the other hand, never put the referentiality of language into question. Therefore, they resist both de Man's coyness and, for example, Joan Didion's journalistic-touristic reports of alienated horror. In *Salvador*, Didion almost revels in a kind of sublime unrepresentability of Salvadoran reality. Her language no longer refers, perhaps because she maintains the distance between it and a world that eludes her, as she walks "straight ahead, not wanting to see anything at all,"[31] when, say, a youth gets herded into an army van. Where they see victims of the army and of "cultural impotence," the female narrator of Manlio Argueta's *One Day of Life* and the women recorded by Claribel Alegría know the satisfaction of fighting back. As part of that fight, the

28. Paul John Eakin, *Fictions in Autobiography: Studies in the Art of Self-invention* (Princeton: Princeton University Press, 1985), p. 128: "In a second interview, in 1957, Sartre maintains this historical interpretation (drafting in 1939 was pivotal) suggesting the extent to which his own story represents the experience of an entire generation of bourgeois intellectuals."

29. Gusdorf, p. 35.

30. Paul de Man, "Autobiography as Defacement," quoted in Eakin, p. 185. The quotation continues: " . . . does the referent determine the figure, or is it the other way round: is the illusion of reference not a correlation of the structure of the figure?" See also de Man's "Sartre's Confession: *The Words* by Jean-Paul Sartre," *New York Review of Books*, 5 Nov. 1964.

31. Joan Didion, *Salvador* (New York: Washington Square Press, 1983), p. 36.

"testimonies" of those who are herded or those who resist are speech acts of the most passionate and militant variety. If particular words miss their marks or if an entire Western language, such as Spanish, violates the reality of indigenous peoples whose cultures survived the Conquest, testimonials understand these failures or impositions as errors or falsehoods. Whether or not they are the inevitable ironies and excesses that post–Saussurians find in any arbitrary system called language, they constitute a challenge to knowing rather than an insuperable barrier.[32]

In testimonials, too much hangs on the reality to which words refer for meaning to be indefinitely delayed. Inadequacy of words to their referents reflects on an imperfect and necessarily evolving language rather than on some notion of necessarily unstable or unreachable referents. "For me," writes Argueta, "everything was part of nature. . . . I used to believe in those things. If one is poor, well, that's life. . . . Until we began to discover the meaning of the word exploited."[33] To doubt referentiality in testimonials would be an irresponsible luxury, given the urgency of the call to action. If the narrator has been raped countless times by Somoza's National Guardsmen (Amada Piñeda interviewed by Randall) or if she has followed the slow stages of her mother's torture at the hands of the Guatemalan army (Rigoberta) or had the baby in her womb literally kicked out of her during torture in a Bolivian prison (Domitila), just to give a few examples, she might well wonder at the academic pause we take in considering how delayed or artificial her reality is.

This is not to say that testimonials lack irony or that they doggedly defend a particular code of description or a single program of action. On the contrary, one of the most fascinating features of these texts is their unpredictable pattern, the sense that the discourse of analysis and struggle is being created in an open-ended and syncretic process of trial, error, and surprise. When Domitila challenges some soldiers to bring her children and herself to where they detained her husband, she says, "Then with dirty words they answered me and asked if they had fathered my children. So I asked them, with even dirtier words, if they thought they were men enough to do that" (p. 137). As working-class or peasant women involved in political, often armed, struggle, the subjects of these narratives move about in a largely unmapped space. Or it is a space on which competing maps are superimposed, where no single

32. I am generally indebted to George Yúdice's "Central American Testimonial," in which he gives a fuller discussion of the differences between contemporary Latin-American writing and "postmodernism."

33. Manlio Argueta, *Un día de vida* (San Salvador: UCA/Editores, 1980), p. 70; trans. by Bill Brow as *One Day of Life* (New York: Vintage Books, 1983).

code of behavior can be authoritative. "Well, señora," says her cell mate after the prison guards have given Domitila the choice between naming names and losing her children, "I think you have gotten yourself into a tight spot. Your people must have seen something good in you in order to appoint you to the position you have. You shouldn't think only as a mother, you've got to think as a leader" (p. 125).

Conscious of working in a translated, borrowed language, they do not have to be reminded of the arbitrary nature of the sign. They live the irony of those linguistic dis-encounters. From their marginal position vis-à-vis existing discourses, they may typically adopt features of several not because they are unaware of the contradictions among being a mother, a worker, a Catholic, a Communist, an indigenist, and a nationalist but precisely because they understand that none of the codes implied by these categories is sufficient to their revolutionary situation. Rigoberta Menchú's community, for example, will adapt the story of Moses by shifting the focus of heroism and leadership from one to many: "We compared the Moses of those times with us, the 'Moses' of today" (p. 157). As for feminism, by the way, it generally figures only insofar as it promotes class interests (see Domitila, p. 41). The trick is not to identify the correct discourse and to defend it with dogmatic heroism but to combine, recombine, and continue to adjust the constellation of discourses in ways that will respond to a changeable reality. This flexibility or eclecticism is doubtless why, despite Havana's initial promotion, women's testimonials outside Cuba tend to be written just beyond the constraints of party lines, or any lines. "I want to emphasize that," Domitila says, "because it seems there are people who say that they made me, their party made me. I don't owe my consciousness and my preparation to anything but the cries, the suffering, and the experiences of the people. I want to say that we have a lot to learn from the parties, but we shouldn't expect everything from them. Our development must come from our own clarity and awareness" (p. 163).

About her community's use of Catholicism (considered heretical by the priests and nuns who could not win the Indians' trust), Rigoberta writes: "In this way we adjusted to the Catholic religion and our duties as Christians, and made it part of our culture. As I said, it's just another way of expressing ourselves. It's not the only, immutable way" (p. 81). Her multiple unorthodoxies constitute what poststructuralists might call an exercise in decentering language, sending the apparently stable structures of Western thought into an endless flux in which signifiers are simply destabilized, not abandoned. But there are several contradictions built into this freedom from predictability. First, the power of the testimonial discourse derives from its collective use, which can temper or delay innovation. Similarly, the lack or paucity of foremothers gives the narrators a mandate to construct themselves, and us along with them, in ways that respond to particular historical conditions and not to existing models. But at the same time, foremothers are necessary in the interest of collectivity and continuity. Already Rigoberta's and Claribel Alegría's texts echo something of Domitila's. If these are examples of political continuity and canon formation, however, there seems little danger of losing originality and discursive daring. These seem to be the lessons that revolutionary foremothers teach best as long as they remain relatively autonomous from the fathers.

Unfortunately, some academic readers of testimonials have fixed on only part of their language lesson, the part that insists on the reality of reference. Therefore, they tend easily to agree that the signified determines the signifier. To worry about the instability of the signifier and the need to reinvent language as part of political struggle would seem treacherous to them; it would tend, so the argument goes, to reinforce the system of oppression by doubting the efficacy of that or any other system. The response is consequently to affirm the power of the existing order, in order to affirm the efficaciousness of struggle against it. What is lost here, evidently, is, first, the irony that can help to wither the apparent stability of the ruling structure and, second, the testimonials' playful—in the most serious sense of that term—distance from any preestablished coherence. That distance creates the space for heteroglossia, the (battle)field where revolutionary discourse is not given but made. In terms of contemporary, neo-Gramscian, political theory, what is lost is a strategy for establishing a socialist hegemony as opposed to the insistence on a Leninist party-centered politics.[34]

Although Eakin does not write about testimonials, he too finds de Man's position on the "performative" nature of autobiographical writing to be extreme; for Eakin, language is not the subject but the condition for subjects to constitute themselves. And by extension, autobiography turns out to be almost a necessary stage in developing the human character to its full potential. A Lacanian reading of development would reinforce this contention, since for Jacques Lacan the self derives from the dialectic of the subject and the fictions he or she projects onto the mirror or onto any other structure that returns a coherent image. Eakin calls autobiography the third and culminating stage in the process of personal maturation and individuation. After the acquisition of language follows the consciousness of one's individuality; autobiography is a self-conscious consciousness of the self.[35] Eakin's scheme suggests a significant difference from the way consciousness is understood in the

34. See Laclau and Mouffe.
35. Eakin, p. 8.

testimonials. There it is a political consciousness that can be raised, as in the Spanish title of Rigoberta's book, which, as we saw, announces the story of "how my consciousness was raised." In her self-construction, Rigoberta does not find one pleasing face as she gazes in the mirror; instead the mirror returns an image of a community that gives her an identity and in which we are potential members.

In other words, it would be a mistake uncritically to attribute intimacy and individuation to the first-person-singular pronoun in testimonials, not a categorical mistake but a relative one that may blind us to the tension in the testimonial "I." Breaking, or at least cracking, as she does, the cultural forms that privilege community over individual, the first-person narrator finds herself in a contradiction. To save the culture she must violate it. It appears that the tension insists on being resolved in favor of stability and community, even while the shift to first person challenges that coherence. The narrator often strains between affirming her singularity and denying it in favor of the first-person plural. "I" is the part that represents "we"; at least this is the conscious assumption made in the face of the Westernizing temptation to slide from the metonymy of the communal to the metaphor of a single subject that replaces the contiguous and more collective sign. I do not wish to deny or even to minimize the relevance of heroic historical models or ideal characters for the process of self-construction in the testimonials but simply to observe that these models are ideal because they represent communal values. And more significant, they are necessarily destabilized, tampered with. Moses, for example, gets pluralized, and Christ turns into a political militant. That is why the testimonial does not have to apologize for, or justify, a personal and irreducible difference between text and interpretation, between model and disciple. Significantly, the narrator's provisional ideal is often her father, the guardian and guide to the communal code. For instance, Domitila Barrios's mother died when the girl was only ten, leaving her responsible for four younger sisters and the companion to her adored father who had been a leader in the 1952 Bolivian Revolution. Jesusa Palancares also lost her mother early in childhood and loved her father jealously, consciously imitating him in order to become a better companion. And although Benita Galeana was also her father's favorite after her mother died, his own early death left her truly orphaned and at the mercy of exploitative sisters. In her case, the model was Manuel, the handsome Communist "husband" she found in the capital. She lost him later, but that loss did not alter her militancy; rather, it reinforced the critical distance she brought to party politics. Only Margaret Randall's subjects for *Sandino's Daughters* refer consistently to their mothers. Or is that merely the reader's impression from the photographed interviews, which juxtapose revolutionary daughters with their proud but worried mothers? The idea for conducting the interviews in this way does not seem to follow from political alliances; in fact many of the mothers knew very little about their children's activity until their struggle succeeded. The impression may come from Margaret Randall's desire to see ideal alliances between women across generations. In any case, the English title of her book, which was published in Spanish as *Todas estamos despiertas* ("All us [women] are awake"), certainly returns the father to his exemplary role.

One could conclude that these women, like the French autobiographers about whom Elaine Marks writes, value themselves only to the extent that they are valued by superior men. "The search for the superior man as lover is common to all women autobiographers who are not . . . profoundly lesbian." Whether the source of self-esteem is male or female, the "woman autobiographer loves herself being loved," because, unlike the male autobiographer, who tends to be narcissistic, the woman sees herself "as if she were being seen or looked at; her judgment is not sufficient. Someone else must look at her and approve."[36] Mary G. Mason makes a similar observation for England, where, she says, the first and model women autobiographers constructed themselves "in relation to" a superior earthly or divine husband.[37] Certainly the same could be said for Spanish America. Victoria Ocampo, for example, fills much of her five-volume autobiography with the admiration and desire great men have felt for her.[38] She also bears out Marks's comment about the long-windedness of female autobiographies, as if each detail were a defiance of annihilation. Another telling example is María Luisa Bombal's autobiographical novella "The Final Mist," in which the narrator's fragile sense of worth during a loveless marriage comes from a one-night affair with an unknown man. Her "lover" brings her to life by acknowledging her beauty, just as the prince's kiss brings back the sleeping princess. "I burn with the need for him to see me naked, for my lovely body at last to receive the homage it deserves."[39] But the fairy tale has a tragic twist here not only because the beginning of the affair was also the end but because the lover turns out to have been blind.

36. Marks, pp. 3, 4.
37. Mary G. Mason, "The Other Voice: Autobiographies of Women Writers," this volume.
38. Victoria Ocampo, *Autobiografía*, 4th ed. (Buenos Aires: Sur, 1982).
39. María Luisa Bombal, "The Final Mist," in her *New Islands and Other Stories,* trans. Richard Cunningham and Lucía Cunningham (New York: Farrar, Straus, Giroux, 1982), p. 16, originally published as *La última niebla* (Santiago de Chile: Ed. Orbe, 1976). See also p. 19: "The years go by. I look at myself in the mirror and see those undeniable little wrinkles under my eyes that before only appeared when I laughed. My breasts are losing their roundness, their fullness—once they were as firm as hard green fruit. My flesh sticks to my bones, and I am no longer slender, but angular—like one of Picasso's nudes. But I don't care! What matter though my body withers, if it has known love!"

Nevertheless, the comparison between women's autobiographical writing and women's testimonials strains and finally cracks even on this point of the requisite male admirer. In the testimonial, the "superior" man may initially be the narrator's object of desire and source of approbation, but she gets beyond her dependence upon any particular man. More than a love object, he represents goals and ideas with which the narrator falls in love. It is in the nature of the genre to proceed from demanding the personal love one man can give to desiring love and approbation from the public. And unlike autobiographers, the writer of testimonials has more tools than language with which to act upon the world. Marks describes the impotent rage that sours women's autobiographies because their "visceral emptiness is filled (only) with language. Language is all women possess."[40] Not if you have joined the guerrillas, or the Communist party, or the militant "Housewives' Committee" in Bolivia.

These women who take up men's tools also use language in a way that doesn't fall into a "visceral emptiness" but rather adjusts and challenges the very codes they adopted from their admirable men. The safety net is to use language collectively, perhaps institutionally. Domitila, for instance, understands this need because the impressive list of heroic but isolated foremothers she quotes from Bolivian history never produced a language of political legitimacy for women (p. 70). So Domitila's generation formed what was to become a prototypical nationwide organization parallel to the miners' union, the Housewives' Committee of Siglo Veinte (the name of the mining town means "twentieth century"), and their early campaign was directed against the very men whom she and her compañeras had organized to support.

> When we organized a demonstration to demand more job openings in 1973, some five thousand women participated. And when they went back to their homes, lots of workers beat their wives and said they were housewives and had nothing to do with politics and that their obligation was to be at home. Until, finally, we said we were going to criticize them on the radio, which we did. We said: "Those compañeros who beat their wives must be government agents. That's the only thing that can explain the fact that they're opposed to their compañeras' demanding what in all justice is ours. And how can they be annoyed by a protest which in the end benefits everyone?" . . . Happily, these new ideas concerning women have jelled very well, and we've won our place in the struggle. (Pp. 77–79)[41]

40. Marks, p. 7.

41. Domitila prefaces this incident of the committee's media terrorism with the context: "But you should have heard the guffaws from the men at that time. They'd say: 'The women have organized a committee! Let them! It won't last even 48 hours.' . . . In the first demonstra-

For cultural and political reasons Rigoberta Menchú's "subversion" of traditional codes is far more problematic than Domitila's. As a Guatemalan Indian, Rigoberta strives to safeguard her tradition. It is the mark of cultural independence from the Westernizing elite. Her objective is to stabilize the community by reaffirming its pre-Hispanic culture. To do this, though, she must engage in political activity outside the community and its codes and so bear a burden of inevitable contradiction, nostalgia, and hints of guilt. The brutal repression in Guatemala and the urgency of Rigoberta's work makes her decide to renounce even motherhood, the most sacred responsibility for a Quiché woman—all this in the name of preserving tradition. In practice, Rigoberta continues to violate codes, both her own and those she borrows, because those codes become the raw material of a political language that demands results, not prescribed formulae.

Paradoxically, in this heteroglossic tug-of-war, pulling back from the "modernizing" Western codes to the indigenous ones may be going forward. The daughters' subversion sometimes brings back the forgotten egalitarian assumptions of the community's "law" and promises to replace the phallocentric European "law of the father" with that of Indian parents. I am thinking specifically about Rigoberta Menchú's use of the Popol Vuh, the cosmogony and "paideia" of the Guatemalan Indians. It is not exactly an epic, according to translator Munro S. Edmonson. "Although it belongs to a heroic (or near-heroic) type of literature, it is not the story of a hero: it is (and says it is) the story of a people, and the text is bracketed by the opening and closing lines declaring and affirming that intent."[42] Rigoberta's frequent references to this sacred pre-Hispanic tradition is probably typical. To read early Spanish translations of the "Book of Counsel" one would think that patriarchy was at least as fundamental to the ancient Guatemalans as it is in the West. In fact Edmunson seems to miss his own point about the non-hierarchichal and communal nature of this tradition when he reports

---

tion in Siglo XX after they came back from La Paz, the compañeras went up on the balcony of the union hall to speak. The men weren't used to hearing a woman speak on the same platform as them. So they shouted: 'Go back home! Back to the kitchen! Back to the washing! Back to your housework!' And they jeered and booed them." (p. 74) "I think that there are still about 40 percent of the men who are against their compañeras' organizing. For example, some of them are afraid they'll get fired from the company, or that there'll be reprisals like those my husband had to suffer because of my involvement. Others are afraid people will say bad things about their wives. Because, in spite of our behavior, in spite of the fact that the men in the leadership respect us, there are still people who speak badly of us, especially people who don't understand those who are *machistas,* you know, people who say that women should stay at home and only live for the family and not get mixed up in politics." (pp. 77–78).

42. Translator's Introduction to *The Book of Counsel: The Popol Vuh of the Quiché Maya of Guatemala,* trans. Munro S. Edmonson (New Orleans: Tulane University Press, 1971), p. xiv.

that, "traditional Quiché life revolves around a patriarchal, patrilineal, and patrilocal family."[43] His translation, nonetheless gives a clue to the opportunities the book offered Rigoberta, for along with the "somber" or sacred feeling of responsibility, it describes an egalitanianism in gender that Western monotheism finds heretical. That equality was lost in older translations in which the term "father" achieved the broad meaning of parent through a synechdochal evaporation of the whole. This recuperation of the female into the male may have been prepared by the Spanish language, in which the plural of father means parents, *padres.* Or it may be a more general habit in the West since the monotheistic editors of the Old Testament tipped the balance of the first version of human creation, "male and female he created them," to the myth of Adam's original loneliness, which made him help to engender Eve. Whatever his interpretation, Edmunson's translation of the Quiché cosmogony provides the term "engenderers," male and female, to replace the "fathers" of earlier translators. "It was told, / By the Former / And Shaper, / The Mother / and Father / Of Life / And Mankind / . . . Children of the Mother of Light / Sons of the Father of Light" (p. 8). With insistent repetition, the females precede the males: "They produced daughters; / They produced sons" (p. 24).

The gender equality extends to communal organization, as Rigoberta tells us in her recently acquired Spanish, a hierarchical language that only barely accommodates the system she describes.

> In our community there is an elected representative, someone who is highly respected. He's not a king but someone whom the community looks up to like a father. In our village, my father and mother were the representatives. Well, then the whole community becomes the children of the woman who's elected. So, a mother, on her first day of pregnancy goes with her husband to tell these elected leaders that she's going to have a child, because the child will not only belong to them but to the whole community, and must follow as far as he can our ancestors' traditions. The leaders then pledge the support of the community and say: "We will help you, we will be the child's second parents." They are known as *abuelos,* "grandparents" or "forefathers." (P. 7)

43. Ibid., pp. xv–xvi. The principles of hierarchy and authority are greatly emphasized and are reflected in daily life in respect form in speech (p. xv). Young Quichés sometimes choose to speak Spanish to avoid the deference exacted by the Quiché pronouns towards older brothers. The discharge of one's duty to one's elders is the fundamental axiom of social existence, and the psychological tone of Quiché culture is somber and guilty. Outside the family one's obligation to the community is a sober discharge of the civic and religious duties. Modern Indians are linked to it (Popol Vuh) by their religion, which is perpetuated on the one hand in family life and community organization, and on the other in an oral and written literature (pp. xv–xvi).

Evidently Rigoberta loses power from having to use a language borrowed from the oppressive "ladinos," or Spanish speakers. The loss is common to all colonized peoples, as María Lugones reminds us when she defines the racial and class exclusivity of existing feminist theory: "We and you do not talk the same language. When we talk to you we use your language. . . . We try to use it to communicate our world of experience. But since your language and your theories are inadequate in expressing our experiences, we only succeed in communicating our experience of exclusion."[44] Without minimizing the importance of this complaint, I think there is another equally valid, if less apparent, consequence of borrowing the politically dominant language; it is the transformative process of borrowing. Rigoberta's Spanish is qualitatively different from that of the "ladinos" who taught it to her. And her testimony makes the peculiar nonstandard Spanish into a public medium of change.

The flavor of translation consistently refreshes her use of language, because, just to give one stunning feature, the figural assumptions embedded in Spanish seem to be lost on her. Therefore, her own Quiché associations are allowed to disturb what would otherwise be a rather closed and less promising code. In Spanish, as in many Western languages, the word *earth* is regularly metaphorized as woman; that is, woman is substituted by the land, which is the prize of struggle between men as well as their material for (re)production. On the other hand, man is metonymized as her husband; his agency and power are extended through the figure. From this preconception follows a scheme of associations including the passive and irrational female contrasted to the active, reasoning male. This opposition has generated a populist rhetoric in Spanish America that functions left, right, and center of the political spectrum. The bitterest enemies will agree that the people's goal is to preserve or repossess the beloved land from a usurper.[45] Rigoberta would surely sympathize, but first she would know who the people are and how they relate to the land; her gender lines are quite different: "The earth gives food and the woman gives life. Because of this closeness the woman must keep this respect for the earth as a secret of her own. The relationship between the mother and the earth is like the relationship between husband and wife. There is a constant dialogue between the earth and the woman. This feeling is born in women because of the responsibilities they have, which men do not have" (p. 220).

44. María Lugones and Elizabeth Spelman, "Have We Got a Theory for You! Feminist Theory, Cultural Imperialism and the Demand for 'The Woman's Voice,'" *Women's Studies International Forum* 6 (1983): 573–81.

45. See my *One Master for Another: Populism as Patriarchal Rhetoric in Dominican Novels* (Lanham, Md.: University Press of America, 1983).

Her consciousness of those responsibilities steels her against the machismo of her male comrades.[46] It may, therefore, not surprise the reader to find that despite Rigoberta's cultural context for male-female equality, she too preferred to model herself after her father, even though her mother outlived him. Both had been community leaders, and both died in the struggle to save its land from appropriation by the landowners with the help of the government. But Rigoberta's mother was drawn fully into the resistance only after the suffering affected her family directly, after her husband was blown up during the protest occupation of the Spanish embassy and after she saw her son tortured to a slow death by Guatemalan soldiers. Her father was active much earlier; it was his insistence on the connection between local demands and national politics that sent him on endless journeys to the capital and to other communities and helped to establish the Committee of United Peasants for which he prepared Rigoberta as a leader. "When he had meetings with people, he'd choose me first, so I'd stop keeping my opinions to myself. I didn't like intruding. . . . So my father taught me how to speak. 'You must speak here,' he'd say" (p. 194). It appears, then, that in these testimonials, women acquire a degree of freedom or militance by privileging male models over female, even though they can get beyond an apprenticeship. This privileging suggests an analogy with the French autobiographers in Nancy Miller's essay and reminds us that whatever the cultural and political distances between them, professional European writers and Latin-American working women share a condition of relative subordination and domestication. Machismo is one form of oppression related to others that the testimonials denounce and alter.

One way of marking the difference between women's testimonials and autobiographies, a difference that should nag any reader who attempts to account for one genre in terms of the other, is precisely the testimonials' insistence on showing relationships. These can be among forms of oppression and among those who suffer or profit from it. We have seen that (1) testimonials are related to a general text of struggle. They are written from interpersonal class and ethnic positions. (2) But the narrator's relationship to her social group(s) is as a particular individual. Therefore, she represents her group as a participant, rather than as an ideal and repeatable type. This positioning allows a further relation-

46. Rigoberta reasons that her leadership of men as well as women follows naturally from women's special type of agency. "That is how I've been able to analyse my specific task in the organisation. I realize that many compañeros, who are revolutionaries and good compañeros, never lose the feeling that their views are better than those of any women in charge of them. Of course we mustn't dismiss the great value of those compañeros, but we can't let them do just whatever they like. I have a responsibility, I am in charge, and they must accept me for what I am" (p. 220).

ship with readers, who can be called into the text without their assuming an identity with the writer or with her group. Identity is unnecessary and impossible in the acknowledgment of differences that testimonials impose on their readers. The reader can be linked at a respectful distance, metonymically, as an extension of a collective history. (3) To make the reader's interpellation possible, the narrator and her public must assume that language always relates to the world, even when it does so imperfectly. (4) One symptom of language's imperfection is the limit or boundary of any one code. In women's *testimonios*, apparently incompatible codes, such as Catholicism and communism, militance and motherhood, are syncretized to produce a flexible field of signification and political intervention. (5) Finally, male models are adapted to a different but related female experience. This insistence on relationships can, in fact, be understood as the testimonial's goal: to raise the reader's consciousness by linking her to the writer's testimony.

Autobiographers may share this last characteristic to the extent that they describe their condition as shared with other women or with a particular ethnic group or class. In that case the autobiography presents the personal as also political and either denounces or implies a denunciation of a group's marginality. If all women's first-person writing does this, then perhaps it is all testimonial in a subtle way. But more often, or at best, women's autobiographies are accounts of one isolated being speaking for other isolated readers, not for a community. They tend, on the contrary to value marginality as a mark of personal distinctiveness rather than as a measure of political inequality. Autobiographers can enjoy the privilege and the privacy of being misunderstood, whereas those who testify cannot afford or even survive it.

6

In Other Words: Native
American Women's Autobiography

HELEN CARR

As an Englishwoman writing about Native American women's autobiography, I am at a double remove from my subject; yet I hope that
remove may have its advantages. There is a sense in which it is easier—
perhaps deceptively so—for the colonizing nations to grasp one another's dubious imperial histories rather than their own. When George
Catlin brought his Indian Gallery—his exotic collection of portraits,
artifacts, and dances—to London in the 1840s, enthusiastic British re-
viewers were quick to castigate the U.S. government for its Indian
policy, apparently without reflecting on parallels that might be drawn
with British India or the treatment of the Irish. Similarly, toward the
end of the century, British public opinion was shocked by the behavior
of the Belgians in the Congo; it was in the United States that there was
an outcry against British conduct in South Africa. American anthropology in the interwar period, on which I concentrate here, was in many
ways rather more enlightened than British. Although I criticize some
Euro-American anthropologists, it is not in any spirit of English virtue
but from an urgent sense of the shared need to understand and come to
terms with the discourses that still entrap relationships between First
and Third World peoples.

To anyone not familiar with Native American autobiographies, this
may seem an oblique beginning to this essay. But the role of anthropologists is crucial for any interpretation of the texts discussed here.
Their production was complex, and the interwoven strands that form
them are not easily unraveled. Several different kinds of work shelter
under the term "Native American autobiography." I would distinguish
three main forms, though other observers have suggested different divisions: first, some early self-written accounts by Christianized Indians;

second, a group of life histories and personal recollections recorded by anthropologists, largely during the interwar period; and third, more recent autobiographies written and published in the Euro-American autobiographical tradition.[1] I shall look at the second group in this essay. The methodological problems raised by the more recent works are not so different from those of any other form of Western women's autobiography. The first group, while important in the genre of Native American autobiography, contains very few written by women.

Autobiography as the European or Euro-American tradition knows it is not an indigenous Native American form. One might argue that there is something close to the autobiographical impulse in the shamanic songs that record visionary journeys or in the brief death songs, but they are hardly comparable to the autobiographies recorded by anthropologists in the 1920s and 1930s. These accounts were solicited, translated, and edited by white anthropologists and their assistants. They were valued within the profession because they gave the imprimatur of authenticity to a "total" cultural picture that was based on the anthropologist's observations. Published with introductions and notes of varying length, these "autobiographies" could endorse and validate the anthropologists' interpretation of Native American life.

Reading these texts now, it is essential to be aware that they have been structured, consciously or unconsciously, to serve particular "white" purposes, and to give credence to particular "white" views. This is not to suggest that these documents are marred by crass racism. On the whole, that is very far from the case. During this period of American anthropology, the pervasive intellectual drive came from the liberal and enlightened Boasian school, which collected customs, rituals, artifacts, myths, songs, as well as some life histories, to create a full and sympathetic picture of a culture.[2] Franz Boas and his followers argued against the previous century's assumption that "primitive" societies presented

1. See Arnold Krupat, "The Indian Autobiography: Origin, Types and Function," in *Smoothing the Ground: Essays on Native American Literature,* ed. Brian Swann (Berkeley: University of California Press, 1983), and Arnold Krupat, *For Those Who Come After* (Berkeley: University of California Press, 1985). See also Gretchen Bataille and Kathleen Sands, *American Indian Women: Telling Their Lives* (Lincoln: University of Nebraska Press, 1984). I am indebted to Arnold Krupat both for his published work on Native American autobiography and for conversations and written communications. I am also indebted to David Murray for published and unpublished work, and for conversations and advice. Bataille and Sands's book contains much valuable information, though I feel their reading of these texts lacks consideration of the complex circumstances of their production.

2. Intensive fieldwork in the language was held to be the key to success. The study of linguistics surged forward, transformed by Edward Sapir's (a student of Boas) realization that Indian languages, like their cultures, had their own complex structure and were not to be seen as inferior forms of Latin. This approach made possible the recording of autobiographies from informants who had had little contact with whites (and therefore English).

earlier stages of evolution, which the white man had left far behind. Ethnographic data from the nineteenth century were used to construct a universal evolutionary ladder, leading from primitive to civilized. Boasians rejected this model of human development and the rigid hierarchy of cultures that went with it, maintaining that non-Western cultures had their own intrinsic value and validity. Every culture formed a complex whole, and it was the function of their research to collect the data necessary for understanding that totality.

In consequence, where earlier ethnographers such as Henry Schoolcraft or John Wesley Powell wanted to understand the "savage" mind, Boasian anthropologists were more often interested in understanding the Winnebago or the Papago or the Fox.[3] As cultural relativists, they were deeply opposed to racism.[4] Yet even though they eschewed the crude assumption of white superiority in nineteenth-century texts, problems remain in their work. The usual accusation leveled against the Boasian school—that they haphazardly heaped up facts for their own sake—does not really explain these problems.[5] For one thing, an anthropological "fact" is no self-evident commodity. The Boasians' "facts" included a wealth of detail about aesthetic, emotional, and conceptual life and a close study of language and oral traditions. Economic pressures and power structures seemed less important, and the contemporary historical reality of relations between Native Americans and white society went largely unrecorded.

3. The number of books published with the word *primitive* in their title might seem to go against my point—for example, *Primitive Art* (1927) and *The Mind of Primitive Man* (1916), by Franz Boas, and *Primitive Man as Philosopher* (1927), and *Primitive Religion* (1937), by Paul Radin. But these books stressed the heterogeneity of the different cultures labeled primitive and insisted that there was no essential difference between "advanced" and "primitive" minds.

4. For example, Ruth Benedict's famous work *Patterns of Culture*, published in 1935, begins with an argument against the notion of racial purity. Boas's own writings were burnt in Munich by the Nazis. Boas was himself a German Jew, his face bore scars said to have been acquired in a duel with anti-Semites, and his work commonly carried implicit pleas for appreciation of Indian humanity. He ends one of his very earliest ethnographical publications by expressing the hope that his work "will show that the mind of the 'savage' is sensible to the beauties of poetry and music, and that it is only the superficial observer to whom he appears stupid and unfeeling." Franz Boas, "Poetry and Music of Some North American Indian Tribes," *Science* 9.230 (1987): 383–85.

5. Here I differ from Krupat (*For Those Who Come After*, p. 77). The reaction against Boas's atheoretical work in our period of high theorizing has been extensive, but in many ways the limitations of his viewpoint in coming to terms with the historical process of dispossession were shared equally by the contemporary British structural anthropologists. See Paul Bonte, "From Ethnology to Anthropology: On Critical Approaches in the Human Sciences, Part I," *Critique of Anthropology* 2 (Autumn 1974): 36–67. Boas's own uncertainty about actual autobiography springs from his awareness of the problem of using the idiosyncratic individual memory for the kind of general truths he sought, and his caution did not inhibit the impetus given to such life histories by his "desire to grasp the meaning of a culture as a whole . . . [to] understand the individual as living in his culture; and the culture as lived by individuals." Ruth Benedict, *Patterns of Culture* (London: Routledge and Kegan Paul, 1935), p. x.

In their apolitical, subjectivist appraisal of what was relevant, Boasians had the strengths and weaknesses of much early twentieth-century liberal humanism. They reacted, like many other intellectuals, against the reductiveness of nineteenth-century positivism, no longer believing that human societies could be explained by scientific laws deduced from a few observations. Their imaginations were seized by the rich variety and heterogeneity of social groups, making them wary of premature, oversimplified conclusions. Boas in particular was reluctant to advance theoretical explanations of social structures, stressing rather the need to gather as much information as possible in order to understand a culture's complexities.

Yet even if the overall attitude of these anthropologists was sympathetic to Native American culture, they were part of the power structure that oppressed it; they had inherited beliefs and discourses that supported and legitimated that power. Even if in some respects they were alert to the prejudices of their predecessors, that inheritance needs to be borne in mind when approaching these autobiographies.

First, their analysis could still slip insidiously into traditional constructions of the Indian, whether as inadequate savage or noble primitive. In *Autobiography of a Fox Woman,* for example, Truman Michelson, embarrassed by gynecological details, refuses to translate them on the grounds that this language is too "naïve" for white readers, reinvoking the notion of the native as child—quite ironically in a period when leading white artists would have found such frankness sophisticated. More often, it is the primitivist strain that emerges, as in my second text, Ruth Underhill's *Autobiography of a Papago Woman.* Additionally, in trying to grasp the distinctiveness of other societies, some of Boas's followers projected a homogeneity of character that did not exist, most famously, perhaps, in Ruth Bunzel and Ruth Benedict's idealization of the tranquility of Zuni life.

Second, like earlier ethnographers, most anthropologists in this period continued to search for Native American culture in what they saw as its "real" form, that is, its form before contact with Europeans, which might be very different from its actual contemporary practice and position. Indeed, the Boasians' very anxiety to document these "different" cultures in their totality gave a new urgency to this pursuit of the past, this "salvage anthropology," which they then often continued to write in what has been called the ethnographer's present. They were forever pursuing an essence, a discrete and integral whole that had perhaps never existed. In this atomistic view, the liens of the existing power relation remained invisible while the actual conditions in which Native Americans lived in the United States were, on the whole, ignored in favor of a reconstruction of what might have been their past.[6] The visual equivalent between 1910 and 1930 was the romantic photography of Edward Curtis, who would persuade the Indians to change their usual Westernized clothes for the still carefully preserved traditional costumes and then would pose them not in front of reservation shacks but against a natural background of rocks, trees, or water.

Last, and specifically relevant to the women's autobiographies, was the assumption that men were representative of their cultural group in a way women could not be; women featured at best as a subgroup. For this reason far fewer life histories of women exist, and those that do concentrate on "women's concerns"—childbirth, marriage, first menstruation. Gretchen Bataille and Kathleen Sands's recent account of Native American women's autobiographies suggests that these women were less interested in contemporary history than were the men—a dubious supposition. Again, these are not texts from which such straightforward deductions can be made. There is little to indicate that anthropologists would interview female informants about public events.

Collecting an autobiography in that period entailed finding a "typical" figure who could represent not just a present tribal group but the "true" nature of that group before its disruption. Toward World War II, as interest grew in psychology (the "culture and personality" movement in anthropology), the problems that hover round this use of first-person narrative became harder to ignore. The very form of autobiography subverts the aim of exemplifying a representative other. The subject of the life story becomes a comparable self, asking to be understood in terms of Western individualism. Paul Radin, for example, moves from his insistence on the typicality of Crashing Thunder's autobiography, which "should be taken as an inside view of Winnebago culture, rather than a careful analysis of a human life,"[7] to his later individualism: "It is not, for instance, a Crow Indian who has made such and such a statement, uttered such and such a prayer, but a particular Crow Indian. It is this particularity that is the essence of all history."[8] Radin's retreat to history is a symptom of the problems anthropology faced in writing about dispossessed people, apparently from their viewpoint yet without acknowledging the process and results of their dispossession. In nineteenth-century Indian autobiographies the narrative structure moves to-

6. Boasians took account of historical developments within Native American culture, but rarely of what later anthropologists euphemistically call its acculturation.

7. Radin quoted by Clyde Kluckhohn, "The Personal Document in Anthropological Science," in *The Use of Personal Documents in History, Science, and Sociology,* ed. L. Gottschalk (New York: Social Science Research Council, 1947), p. 87.

8. Radin quoted by Marvin Harris, *Rise of Anthropological Theory* (London: Routledge and Kegan Paul, 1968), p. 300.

ward closure, Arnold Krupat has shown, with the acceptance of the inevitable disappearance of the Indian.[9] At this later period no coda can so easily resolve the contradictions of the texts.

In the terms Edward Said uses in *Orientalism* (his study of the ideology by which the West has asserted a right to dominate the East), this ethnographic discourse is the "manifest" version of the process by which Native Americans have been placed, defined, controlled by the dominant American culture. (The "latent" is the unconscious assumptions current in society and social discourse at large.) How then does one read—or deconstruct—such texts? I am certainly not arguing that the "real" Native American women are to be discovered behind the layers of anthropological distortions. Such an ambitious and dubious claim pursues as volatile an essence as the Boasian "culture as a whole" and hardly advances on Clyde Kluckhohn's illusory wish to separate out in these autobiographies what is "individual" from what is "cultural." Human subjects are formed within culture and are not separable from it.

Instead, I suggest that these life stories present in sharp focus the central problem we have in reading any women's autobiographies: interpreting a text in which a marginalized subject speaks a dominant discourse. Toril Moi, in her recent book, *Sexual/Textual Politics,* distinguishes two main currents of feminist literary theory that are useful in this context. Some feminist critics—particularly pioneer feminist literary critics in the United States during the 1970s—have stressed the imperative right of women to have a "voice," their need to express their different experience, and the importance of uncovering suppressed and forgotten female texts. On the other hand, the feminist literary theory that emerged under the influence of French poststructuralism and Lacanian psychoanalysis sees such privileging of the expressive as naïve and treacherous realism. Language is a symbolic system within which woman is always inscribed as other and inferior: texts give no direct access to an "author" or to "true" women's experience. To ignore the formation of women's texts within a phallocentric discourse is, they insist, to collude with that discourse. For them, it is only in the gaps and ruptures that what is excluded or unnamed in the phallocentric symbolic order may emerge. Like most feminist critics today, I am conscious of the heritage of both these approaches. Reading these texts, with their doubly marginalized subjects, one must, like the latter critics, employ Ricoeur's "hermeneutics of suspicion."[10] But also, like the former, one must recognize the political importance of these women's challenge to

9. Krupat, *For Those Who Come After,* p.48.
10. Paul Ricoeur, quoted by Toril Moi, "Sexual/Textual Politics," in *The Politics of Theory,* ed. Francis Barker et al. (Essex: University of Essex, 1983), p. 1.

Western and patriarchal assumptions. Jacqueline Rose has argued that the revolutionary catalyst of Freud's work was his "talking cure." His case histories have become valuable to feminists because Freud allowed his patients to become subjects. The analogy between the case history and the Indian autobiography is an important one. They grow out of the same form, the scientific and medical case study of the nineteenth century. Although Freud's cases are presented as dialogues and narratives, and the autobiographies in apparently discrete voices (the informant's text, the anthropologist's appendixes), the ordering of material shares many similarities.[11] The overall structure is that of the analyst's or anthropologist's explanation; it is in the byways and interstices that other possibilities and desires emerge.

The remainder of this essay explores possible ways of reading two autobiographies from the period in order to illustrate the complex issues they raise. One was collected by a male anthropologist, the other by a woman. One is presented baldly; the other organized into a literary form. One has an extensive ethnographic and linguistic apparatus; the other had none in its original publication. The first, "The Autobiography of a Fox Indian Woman," was published in 1925 by Truman Michelson, an ethnologist who produced many papers on the Fox (or the Mesquakie, as they prefer to be called), a central Algonkin group from southwest of the Great Lakes. At that time, Michelson points out, this first-person life history of an Indian woman was almost unique. Her story had been recorded in 1918 by Michelson's assistant, Harry Lincoln, who was half Fox and half Winnebago. Originally written in the Fox syllabary, it was later rewritten phonetically by Lincoln's wife, a Fox Indian. After translation by another assistant and Michelson, the autobiography finally appeared between the stiff green, gold-embossed boards of the Fortieth Annual Report of the Bureau of American Ethnology, one of the several contributions by Michelson in that volume.[12] Lodging it between the myth of the origin of the White Buffalo Dance and an account of Fox mortuary customs and beliefs, Michelson appended a brief introduction and many notes to the work.

The translation makes few concessions to literary style. We are told in the introduction that it "has been made as literal as possible without vio-

11. This similarity seems to have struck Arnold Krupat, at least subliminally. See Krupat, "The Indian Autobiography," p. 279, where the notes refer to *"Autobiography of a Fox Woman,"* a parapraxis perhaps formed by analogy to Freud's Rat Man.

12. Truman Michelson, "Autobiography of a Fox Indian Woman," in *Bureau of American Ethnology Fortieth Annual Report, 1918–19,* hereafter cited in the text. The translation process is not entirely clear. Michelson says, "The English translation is based on a paraphrase written by Horace Poweshiek, supplemented and corrected by a grammatical analysis of the text by myself" (p. 295).

lence to idiomatic English usage" (p. 295). Yet the story shows considerable life and vigor, in striking contrast to the desiccated pedantry of Michelson's notes. Its liveliness comes partly from Michelson's decision to incorporate the woman's extensive use of reported conversations and thoughts recounted as inner dialogue. The outline of the tale is briefly this: The storyteller ("unnamed by agreement") describes her life as a child—her toys, games, and gradual training in women's skills such as washing, cooking, making bags, mats, and moccasins. She describes her first, terrifying menstruation and the instruction she was given then by a "grandmother" from the village. When she reached marriageable age, she became deeply attached to a young man of whom her family did not approve. Under pressure she marries someone else. After she gave birth to a child, her husband was told about her earlier attachment. He became jealous and began to beat her. The baby died, perhaps, she thought guiltily, because of the anger between herself and her husband. She went through a very unhappy period when she would have liked a divorce, but her mother refused to consider the idea. Only after her mother's death did she finally divorce her husband, with her uncle's approval. She eventually married the original lover, now himself a widower. They were idyllically happy, apart from the loss of their only child. When this husband died, she was devastated. She had to "walk far off to cry" so that no one would say of her "Heavens! she must be very sorry, even as if she were related to him." After four years of mourning she married once more, unenthusiastically, as the first time. She had several healthy children, and after this third husband's death, she thought, "Well, I shall never marry again . . . for these children of mine will help me (get a living)" (p. 337).

What were Michelson's motives for using this story? What was the woman's motivation for telling it? Its placement in the volume (alongside myths and mortuary customs) and Michelson's comments (noting the typicality of details) suggest that he saw it impersonally, as useful ethnographic data. Unlike the Boasians, most of whom were affiliated with universities, Michelson was a Bureau of American Ethnology anthropologist. Although he was influenced enough by the Boasian climate to collect this life history, he shows no concern for the woman's subjective experiences. The introduction says that "no attempt was made to influence the informant in any way; so that the contents are the things which seemed of importance to herself." It is most unlikely that this statement is true, although it may have been what Harry Lincoln told Michelson. The precision and detail with which the woman describes her training as a girl, her introduction to puberty, the rites associated with childbirth and funerals would be superfluous and irrelevant for a Fox woman speaking to a half Fox married to another Fox woman, unless she had been specifically asked for such an account. What Michelson had here was unusual anthropological material, which he could proceed to publish.

The question of why the woman told her story seems more complex. The ending would suggest that it probably was not for money, since she has children to support her. There may have been many factors, but two chief desires emerge from her text: one is to clear her name from accusations of immorality; the second is to exorcise, or at least order, ambivalent feelings of gratitude and anger toward her mother.

The question of immorality is first raised when she is eighteen. Her mother tells her she must not "talk to" any young men (an activity which appears to be equivalent to and as ambiguous as what whites would call going out, or dating) apart from the man she is to marry. She disobeys, "talking to" the young man who later becomes her second husband. She seems to imply that they did not become lovers, though she never explicitly denies this. What she insists on very firmly, however, is that she was wholly faithful to her first husband once she had married. She places a long and perhaps overly emphatic speech in her second husband's mouth which supports her claim of innocence and confirms her first husband's unreasonableness.

Michelson never comments directly on this aspect of the tale, but his notes form a disapproving counterpoint. For example, when her first husband begins to beat her, her mother visits her to let her know that she had brought this upon herself by her previous defiance of parental advice. Her mother warns her that the trouble between her and her husband may make their baby sicken and die, as it indeed does. Michelson's response to this painful moment is to gloss the mother's words with a note that says, "It is a fact that Fox women who have good reputations do exactly as the mother advised her daughter" (p. 343). What does Michelson mean by the phrase "it is a fact"? Surely it implies definite sympathy for the mother's punitive viewpoint and questions the autobiographer's assertion of innocence. This comment echoes the emphasis of an earlier note on a strawberry-picking expedition at which she first met her young man: "A girl is not supposed to go off by herself unless she has some good reason. If a girl gads about and does no housework she soon acquires an unenviable reputation." (p. 342).

Michelson also reacts in a curious way to her divorce. The woman anxiously stresses how justified this was, even though her mother had disapproved. Her maternal uncle, the relative with the greatest claim to the obedience of a Fox woman, is the one who finally advises her to divorce her violent husband, as Michelson himself explains, apparently without accepting the uncle's lengthy justification of the divorce:

> No one will reproach you if you think of being divorced. I myself will not scold you. It is a rule that a married couple should alike treat each other well. As for me, I treat the one with whom I live . . . well and she treats me well. . . . And if I were suddenly to treat her badly while she was still treating me well and while she was still living morally, were I to become jealous over something without reason, her relatives would not like it. For I surely would be doing wrong. If she cast me off none of her relatives would scold her. Every one, all over, would be glad of what happened to me. (P. 325)

Michelson's comment is again oblique:

> It is to be regretted that at the present time divorces are extremely prevalent among the Foxes; there is hardly a girl or boy 21 years old who has not been married at least twice. It may be noted that Forsyth's statement that a man could force his wife, willy-nilly, to a certain extent still holds good. If a woman leaves her husband and right away starts to go with another man with a view to marriage, the former husband will beat her. Formerly adultery on the part of the woman was punished by cutting off her ears, nose, or even killing her. A husband might kill her lover if the latter was caught red-handed. (P. 343)

Michelson's deliberate inclusion of an irrelevant selection of facts about divorce among the Fox betrays his own preoccupations and contradicts his implied scientific detachment. The increase in divorce excites his moral opprobrium. Details of how women's adultery used to be punished are given without mentioning that this text asserts emphatically that this particular wife has not been guilty of infidelity. For Michelson, her original disregard for appearances has branded her as improper, sexually smirched, and therefore indefensible. The likeness of her uncle's argument to contemporary liberal white views may be part of what has provoked, under the cover of objectivity, Michaelson's aggressively violent response.

Here, as elsewhere, Michelson's regulating commentary contains and smoothes over these disturbing aspects of the text. For example, Michelson indicates that dances encourage immorality even though the second husband points out that since they are public events, they afford little opportunity for improper behavior. His editing has veiled the tensions and passions of the story so effectively that the woman's personal traumas have since been ignored, even though her autobiography has been analyzed by two feminist anthropologists and adapted as a feminist novel for girls.[13] Neither the anthropologists nor the novelist recognizes her anxieties about her actions or her need to prove them acceptable. Bataille and Sands accept Michelson's presentation almost without question, describing her tale as bland, her character as passive.[14] They even rebuke the woman for taking no interest in the contemporary split between progressives and conservatives in the Fox community.

Like Michelson they find the story most useful for its detailed account of a girl's upbringing, and like him they pay scant attention to the tensions between the woman and the powerful mother. The girl resents her mother's strictness, yet as far as the teaching of skills is concerned, accepts it as inevitable. Her mother explains that her own upbringing was the same and that the girl, like her, will be grateful in the future: "So very likely when you think of me, you think, 'She treats me meanly.' It is because I am fond of you and wish you to know how to make things. If I were not fond of you, I would not order you around (to do things). . . . I would think, 'I don't care what she does.' If you are intelligent when you are grown and recollect how I treated you, you will think, 'I declare! My mother treated me well'" (p. 301). Her mother's prediction seems accurate. The woman recalls that when she was twenty-five and her husband was growing increasingly brutal, she thought: "Surely my mother treated me well in teaching me how to make things. What would have happened to me if I had not known work suitable for women? I should have been even poorer, if my mother had not instructed me" (p. 321). Yet this tenuously achieved, baroquely recorded gratitude is interwoven with bitter clashes with her mother over her sexuality. Twice she defers to her mother's wishes and advice, and twice the mother is proved wrong—over the first marriage and over the refusal to countenance divorce. Her real happiness, she insists, comes only when she finally rejects her mother's advice, divorces her first husband, and marries the man she prefers. Although she is emphatic in her justification of that act, her anxiety and guilt over her defiance emerge as the generative force behind the story.

We Are Mesquakie, We Are One (which acknowledges advice from Bataille), a novel written for teenage girls, draws on the Fox woman's account for information about her upbringing rather than the story of her life. The novel is set at the time of the removal of the Fox to Kansas

13. Bataille and Sands, American Indian Women; Hadley Irwin, We Are Mesquakie, We Are One (London: Sheba Feminist Publishers, 1984).

14. They point out that the Fox prefer the term Mesquakie and criticize Michelson's translation of a word in the passage about the first menstruation. The word he translates as "evil" should, they say, be "bad" or "unclean." Some of their statements about this text are contradictory; cf. p. 38 and p. 164.

and their heroic return to Iowa. Painted with a sentimentalizing feminist-separatist gloss, it presents an unproblematic solidarity among Fox women, who happily accept the distinctiveness of women's role. Even though the book has the historical setting of Mesquakie dispossession, it evades the unpalatable nature of Indian-white relations by blaming everything on a distant government or absent agents. All the whites who actually appear in the story are portrayed as benevolent.[15]

It can be argued that this is fiction, and so the authors can do what they like with the original and with history. Yet that seems to be a mistaken way to attempt to reclaim this text. If Michelson was unprepared to hear what the woman wished to say about her life, it is tragic that feminists have continued to silence her. This autobiography does not, as Bataille and Sands suggest, ignore the tensions and changes in Mesquakie society; it is permeated by them. The woman's sense of moral confusion and her baffled anxiety to do right are the products of the increasing pressure on the structure of Mesquakie culture. Margaret Mead has shown the strains to which women were particularly subject as white society eradicated traditional ways of life. The changing sexual mores here are the visible signal of the political and economic changes that are only hinted at.[16]

Michelson collected two other women's life stories, in which he once again lingers over such issues as whether Arapho women's dubious reputation is justified, leading one to suspect he is drawn to these women's narratives by a puritan prurience.[17] But this condemnatory unease is not unique to Michelson. The correlation of Indian otherness with dangerous (often female) sexuality has been part of the discourse of dispossession since the seventeenth century, just as the present idealization of Native American women's lives by some white feminists is an extension of the primitivist tradition that in its own way equally denies the human complexity of Native Americans.[18]

15. I have reviewed this novel at greater length in *Dragons Teeth*, no. 22 (London: National Committee on Racism in Children's Books, 1985).

16. Margaret Mead, *The Changing Culture of an Indian Tribe*, Columbia University Contributions to Anthropology Series 15 (1932), passim, but especially the chapter "Maladjustment as an Index of Conflict," pp. 186–222. This was a pioneer study in accultural disruption. Mead shows the painful confusion surrounding women's sexual mores in a changing society, though she points out that women are in some ways better able to keep in touch with traditional customs than men, for theirs are domestic and familiar rather than concerned with public ritual life.

17. I am not, of course, suggesting that depicting sexual mores is itself "prurient." After all, many anthropologists at that period were realizing the importance of sexual habits. It is his mixture of avid fascination and unexamined disapproval that makes Michelson's interest appear prurient.

18. I have looked at some aspects of the correlation between female sexuality and Indians in "Woman/Indian: 'The American' and His Others," in *Europe and Its Others*, ed. Francis Barker et al. (Essex: University of Essex, 1985).

I have already suggested that Truman Michelson is committed to "autobiography" only as an alternative net for anthropological facts, and that for him, anthropological facts do not include Indian subjectivity or a woman's emotional experiences. As a first-person life story, "Autobiography of a Fox Indian Woman" is apparently not influenced beyond its title by the Western literary genre. For other anthropologists, the very naming of these accounts as "autobiographies" claims and produces likeness to the Western mode. My second text is a particularly striking example of this transmutation. The older life-and-times, first-person history has always been primarily associated with men, whose lives are more obviously touched by public events. Women informants were not encouraged to frame their lives in that way. Their lives are more easily restructured as romantic autobiography, the secular but still veridical descendant of the confession. With its emphasis on childhood, natural surroundings, peaks of experience, and introspection, it is already a "feminized" form, and its conventions sometimes figure in the production and reading of these texts.[19]

Ruth Underhill draws extensively on this model for "Autobiography of a Papago Woman," which begins with a brief, vivid description of Maria Chona's childhood home and preserves this awareness of place throughout. Chona's consciousness is the center of the story. We are given her reaction to events, not merely told how or why they happen. The story moves from heightened moment to heightened moment, giving most space to the excitements, delights, and pains of her earlier life and ending with the melancholy regretfulness of age.

Underhill collected this life history when she was sent by Boas, as what we would now call a "mature" graduate student, on her first field trip in 1931. She spent several months in Arizona with the Papago, returning intermittently over the next four years. Maria Chona, who acted as her "informant, hostess, guide," was almost ninety, somewhat confused, but an impressive character, still proud of her father's position as government-appointed chief of her village. She knew little English and Underhill was just becoming acquainted with Papago, but they both spoke some Spanish and were aided by local interpreters. Like the Fox woman's story, the 1936 autobiography was published as a professional anthropological paper, in the *Memoirs of the American Anthropological Association*.

Underhill claims no literal fidelity to Chona's random and repetitive memories, admitting frankly that the arrangement and emphases are her own. She is telling an Indian tale "to satisfy whites, rather than Indi-

---

19. Note, for example, that Bataille and Sands feel compelled to explain or justify the lack of introspection or description in these texts (e.g., p. 17).

ans."[20] She weaves in the natural descriptions characteristic of our own urban culture, not found in Papago or other Native American literary forms, where the surrounding region may provide a symbolic landscape but is not overtly described.[21] The picturesque atmosphere owes much to the many colorful small details she has elicited—tattooing with cactus thorns and greasewood juice, Gauguinesque girls with their red-painted bare breasts—and to her evocative translations of place names such as "Where the Water Whirls"; friends called "Leaf Buds," "Rustling Leaves," "Windy Rainbow," or "Dawn Mist"; dates such as the "month of the Pleasant Cold" or the "year the world went wrong." Underhill candidly acknowledges her reworking, her excisions, her imperfect knowledge of the language, and the result has been variously appraised. L. L. Langness called this memoir one of the "finest professional documents" of its time. Clyde Kluckhohn more cautiously noted that her "treatment has surely enhanced the literary effectiveness of the story (from a European point of view) but equally surely the scientific value has been diminished."[22]

Certainly, Underhill tells Chona's story skillfully, unobtrusively introducing information about war ceremonies, rainmaking rituals, medicine men, and other aspects of traditional Papago life into the narrative. Chona recounts her childhood with a hero-father, a meekly conscientious mother, the sisters and brothers of her extended family. She describes her nerve-wracking arranged marriage to a shaman, whom she later came to love deeply. To survive, they would go each dry season to work in Mexico. Though she had six children, only one daughter survived. When her husband brought home a second wife, Chona left, taking her daughter and a butcher knife in case her husband followed. Her second arranged marriage was to a singer, a much older, richer man. Although somewhat consoled by the birth of several healthy children, Chona missed her first husband and had little affection for the older man. The winters were spent working profitably for whites in Tucson. Back home one summer, when their group was decimated by "falling-sickness," a disease introduced by the whites, she discovered

20. Ruth Underhill, "Autobiography of a Papago Woman," *Memoirs of the American Anthropological Association* 46 (1936): 4.

21. Bataille and Sands say of this account: "Like all works of American Indian literature, Maria Chona's autobiography is permeated with a sense of place, the inextricable weaving of language and landscape; the concept of the land is not merely the setting for the story, but that the story is formed and shaped by the land, and the land is given significance and vitality in language." *American Indian Women*, p. 49. This is an unhelpful confusion of two separate cultural traditions.

22. L. L. Langness, *The Life History in Anthropological Science* (New York: Holt, Rinehart and Winston, 1965), p. 9; Kluckhohn, "The Personal Document in Anthropological Science," p. 90.

her own gifts as a song maker and shaman, particularly her skill in curing babies. In this she took great pride, and from it she gained prestige. After her second husband's death, she lived with her daughter. The account ends poignantly with Chona saying, "It is not good to be old. Not beautiful. When you come again, I will not be here."[23]

Underhill's approach to her material, in some ways so painstaking, in others so cavalier, springs from motivations very different from Michelson's. Although the story was published in a professional forum, its appearance there, bare of the expected accompanying notes, is a clear statement of Underhill's individualistic approach to anthropology. Not for her the 142 footnotes that went into Kluckhohn and Leland Wyman's paper in the same volume. If Boasian anthropology could be construed as either a social science or one of the humanities, for her it was very much the latter. Her unconventional presentation was bold for a graduate student young in the subject if not in years, but it also indicated how closely she was in sympathy with the Boasian desire to understand the Native American experiential world. Ruth Benedict wrote an introduction to the autobiography in 1933 (although it was not published until the republication of the autobiography in 1979) in which she praises the work in terms that strikingly recall Virginia Woolf's essay on the fact-laden realism of "Modern Fiction" through which "life escapes."[24] In the past, Benedict says, anthropology detailed kinship, agriculture ritual patterns—the "formal outlines" of a culture—but "too often in the business-like account everything is told except the essential matter; all that is left out is what manner of men and women these are, and how long they live and die and pursue their chosen goals."[25]

When Underhill went into anthropology after various experiences in welfare work ("to know more about PEOPLE," as she later wrote), she "fell permanently in love" with the Papago.[26] Besides her anthropological works, she went on to produce a number of popular books, and later television programs, whose aim was to draw the white public into an imaginative appreciation of Native American culture and people. What was vital for Underhill was not just the accumulation of "objective" scholarly ethnography but that her text should convey Maria Chona's human dignity and worth. She wanted to extend knowledge, but in order to evoke sympathetic insight. Not surprisingly, she was glad to republish the autobiography in 1979 in a more accessible format, adding

23. Underhill, "Autobiography of a Papago Woman," p. 64.
24. Virginia Woolf, "Modern Fiction," *The Common Reader: First Series* (London: Hogarth Press, 1984), p. 149.
25. Ruth Benedict, Introduction to Ruth Underhill, *Papago Woman* (Prospect Heights, Ill.: Waveland Press, 1979), p. vii.
26. Underhill, *Papago Woman*, pp. ix–x.

extra explanatory chapters and an introduction that served as her own brief autobiography.

This fusion of professional and humanistic zeal finds expression at the early stage of her career in the language of primitivism, the discourse that has traditionally distanced and romanticized the disadvantaged, associating them with natural surroundings of fitting beauty, from which they emerge in their innocence and incapacity. Underhill dwells on the Papago's poetic past, avoiding if she can the current modernization of their culture. In *Singing for Power,* an account of Papago rituals based on the same research, she writes:

> In describing the ceremonies, I do so in the present tense. There has been a change, almost within a generation. People who went naked under the Arizona sun have put on the white man's clothing and built adobe houses. . . . I have preferred to use the method of the old men who gave me the poetry and to draw the picture as though all of it were still to be found in the present. . . . The beauty of the ceremony came from the loneliness of the naked figures against the stark desert. Blue jeans, calico dresses, and the waiting automobiles of the Whites make them look pathetic. Yet they are majestic. Therefore I have felt that their words, holding both sound and meaning and containing much of that majesty, should be preserved.[27]

Chona, at ninety, has memories and words that go back long before jeans and automobiles to that unsullied "majesty." Underhill was attracted by the Papago as one of the least acculturated groups of Native Americans. Their culture, like that of the Pueblos, had been only slightly modified by the Spaniards, who had little concern for their impoverished northern territories. After the transfer of the territory in 1853, the United States government was slow to regulate the lives of these peaceful groups. In the 1920s and 1930s these southwestern cultures became the focus of a revival of artistic primitivism. Mary Austin, Mabel Dodge Luhan, and D. H. Lawrence were among those who wrote admiringly of an instinctual link between these people and their land, which contrasted so tellingly to twentieth-century rootlessness.[28]

Underhill's text echoes this artistic primitivism. It is a critique of

27. Ruth Underhill, *Singing for Power: The Song Magic of the Papago Indians of Southern Arizona* (1938; rpt. Berkeley: University of California Press, 1976), pp. 8, 19.

28. In *Modern Indians,* David Murray discusses this attitude, with "its contrast between past cultural coherence and present degradation. . . . Proper, pure Indians are noble. Anything less does not deserve to exist. Eventually many of the Indians subjected to this idealization tired of their role. One publicly offered to exchange his home for Mabel Luhan's, with its modern construction, when she tried to block the modernization of the Taos Pueblo by the introduction of sanitation" (British Association for American Studies, Pamphlet 8).

modern life, stressing the Papago's sensitivity to natural rhythms, and their perception of the literally awe-ful responsibilities of those who take life in war. (Her only previous publications seem to have been two Red Cross reports in 1918 and 1919, fruit of her own wartime experiences.) Underhill has chosen to emphasize the rituals and harmonies of Chona's life. Relations with government officials, references to the support the Papago gave to the United States against the Apache, the eventual establishment of the reservation—all which must have been part of her experience—never appear. The dual allegiance of the Papago to Catholic and native religious rituals is touched on only evasively. Shortages, most bereavements, illnesses (apart from their shamanic cures) are passed over. The only distresses the narrative encompasses are romantic ones: Chona's mourning for her first husband, not abated until the second husband severely lectures his rival's bones; the loss of a son, drawn to his death by the dangerous charms of a "wild woman"; the muted sadness as she herself faces death. Yet, although Underhill concentrates on the past, although the presence of the whites is so subdued that even the work done for them in Tucson is never specified, the Papago's Euro-American oppression cannot be entirely effaced. It emerges obliquely in scattered references to the disruptive power of white urban culture, illnesses, and alcohol.

Underhill was not usual among Boasian anthropologists in seeking the pure essence of the precolonial. Ruth Benedict's introduction to Papago Woman actually recommends the autobiography, by saying "Chona spent her girlhood . . . under conditions differing very little from those of pre-Spanish days."[29] Significantly, when Ruth Underhill later wrote her account of her time with Chona, therefore being forced to describe the Westernized Papago life she encountered, she relied even more heavily on a romantic sense of place than in the autobiography itself, beginning her account, "'I was born there,' breathed Chona reverentially, 'on the Land.'" The details of her own visits to the modern ceremonies are submerged into an exotic landscape: "Ahead rose the feathery green of a paloverde tree, with a stump of thorny sahuaro cuddled under beneath it. . . . Before us was a gentle hillside without undergrowth. . . . I saw Lulita eyeing the tops of the cacti where white flowers once had been. Now there were red fruits, pear-shaped, perching against the tops. . . . It was wonderful to sleep that night under the open sky. . . . Its color was deep indigo, not black; and the stars were almost within reach of one's hand."[30] Again here the conflict between the Papago and whites over the land (central to the account, because

29. Benedict, in Underhill, *Papago Woman*, p. vii.
30. Underhill, *Papago Woman*, p.19.

getting access to the reservation was one of Underhill's main problems) becomes more an indication of white spiritual insensitivity than of political exploitation.

Another, in some ways contradictory dynamic behind this account is Underhill's fascination with Chona as an individual and a woman; her sense, as she put it later, that they were "two of a kind."[31] Underhill was keenly aware that anthropologists had shown little professional interest in women. In an introduction to Nancy Lurie's *Mountain Wolf Woman* (1961) she wrote:

> In early monographs that tried to map and relate the patterns of American Indian life, women often appear merely as links in the kinship system. The ceremonial spotlight caught them briefly at the high points of puberty, childbirth and widowhood, and the economic spotlight when their marriages were arranged and paid for. Otherwise they formed, in most cases, an undifferentiated mass of female workers, excluded from council, and often, from ceremonies.
>
> True, women could be shamans in California and, to a lesser degree, in some other areas. True, the women of the Plains and of the Pueblos had some ceremonies of their own. Still, even in matrilineal and matrilocal society, the main figures in war, government and ceremony were men. So were the ethnologists who studied them.[32]

Even women anthropologists worked with male informants, she notes. Unlike Michelson, Underhill is intrigued with Chona as a Papago woman not because she is in search of typical, traditional female customs, which have a limited place in the text. On the contrary, she is attracted to Chona because, like Underhill herself, she is an unusual, ambitious, and forceful woman who does not entirely conform to her society's expectations, yet retains respect and prestige.

In the brief autobiographical note that precedes the 1979 edition, Underhill describes how, as a young woman leaving Vassar before World War I, she rejected the two professions offered to her ("the choice was marriage or teaching: both seemed tame"), turning to more adventurous activities. Two decades later, enjoyably yet nervously conscious of her maverick position as an older woman with a personality "inclined to be independent and executive" (as she says of Chona) setting out in this still new and bizarre profession, she found an alter ego in this proud and decisive woman, who, among a people who gave women com-

31. Bataille and Sands, *American Indian Women*, p. 64.

32. Ruth Underhill, Introduction to *Mountain Wolf Woman, Sister of Crashing Thunder: The Autobiography of a Winnebago Indian*, ed. Nancy O. Lurie (Ann Arbor: University of Michigan Press, 1961), p. vii.

paratively limited power, "ruled her whole connection with a competent hand."

Chona's ambition is shown chiefly in her desire to be a maker of songs. Underhill passionately admired the Papago's high regard for poetry and song, contrasting them again with soulless modern society: "What of a society which puts no premium whatever on aggressiveness and where the practical man is valued only if he is also a poet?" Underhill interweaves Chona's story with songs, in Papago fashion, and Chona's "urge to accomplish" as a song maker is an important recurring motif. For Underhill, whose own writing is so self-consciously literary, the song making is an extra strand to her identification with Chona. That Chona was only partially successful, lacking sufficient opportunity and possibly even talent, is perhaps another.

This empathy with Chona has an important, though oblique influence on the text. Underhill was perturbed by the clash between her admiration for Papago culture and her unease at the position of their women. In her 1936 preface, one of her main concerns was to see how Papago women coped with their people's "fear of woman's impurity with all its consequent social adjustment." Although in the introductions she lays increasing emphasis on Chona's toughness and independence, she is aware that Chona cannot be constructed on the model of the Western feminists, who demand equal opportunities and power. Chona is not a Rebecca West who will not put up with H. G. Wells. Underhill realizes that Chona's advanced age has made possible a forcefulness unacceptable in a younger Papago woman. Chona's moment of decision when she leaves her first husband is dramatically told, and her self-possession is always underlined. But in general she accepts male directives about whom to marry, how to avoid contaminating men, when she should have her shaman's crystals cut out, and she believes that as a woman she must work all the harder. In her anxious honesty Underhill abandons her literary paring down of repetitions, leaving as a leitmotif Chona's reiterated declarations of her acceptance of a woman's lot.

This problem nags away not only within the main text but also in Underhill's accompanying writing. In her original introduction, following Ruth Benedict's arguments in *Patterns of Culture,* she says merely that, although Chona was not "the ideal Papago type" of woman, "in the end she did all that her culture would allow her towards satisfying her desires and was not unhappy."[33] By 1961 she has found a white Ameri-

---

33. Underhill, "Autobiography of a Papago Woman," p. 3. Benedict believed that the configurations of a culture naturalize and encourage certain forms of behavior. Individuals conform to them with greater or lesser ease depending on the degree to which their personality coincides with the social norm.

can analogy which makes sense of this lack of outrage at confinement within conventional womanly roles: "In most cases, the Indian woman's life appeared very similar to our pioneer great-grandmothers. Her work, like theirs, was done apart from men."[34] In the 1979 edition, she worries about the issue both in the introduction and the afterword. She finally reconstructs a conversation with Chona in which she, the Westerner, is convinced by the Papago insistence that women need no share of male social or ceremonial power because women have babies: "'We make the men.' That delightful attitude I should have been glad to take home with me," she says carefully, protected by the qualifying conditional. Pointing out that Papago women are now beginning to take on positions of authority, she suggests that their move toward equality will be accomplished through the Papago "peaceful" way. In this brief passage, without abandonment of Western rational commitment to equality, the emotional dynamics reassert Papago moral superiority.[35]

In terms strikingly like those of traditional Christianity, Underhill expresses concern about the Papago belief in "women's impurity," a position modified in this later work. She accepts that her rationalist feminism is inadequate for an understanding of a Papago woman's life. Bataille and Sands's more essentialist and separatist feminism idealizes the role of Native American women, particularly in their positive acceptance of women's maternal power. They misread Chona's life in these terms, ignoring the events recorded in her story: "Of all the autobiographies of American Indian women, Maria Chona's *Papago Woman* best demonstrates the power and strength of traditional Indian women within their own society. . . . The contemporary reader must wonder at the independence and mobility of Maria Chona's life, especially in the light of the stereotypes of Indian women as domestic drudges."[36] Their desire to avoid that stereotype is understandable and admirable, but by employing this Native American woman as a critique of Western faults, they refuse to see her in her psychological, social, and colonial complexity.

Why did Chona tell her story to Underhill? It is perhaps not suprising that an old woman, proud of her family and people, would enjoy recounting her early days—though there are reports of her irritation at Underhill's repetitive questioning. Her reasons are difficult to extract. Underhill has taken great care in creating a "Chona" we will respect and admire, and so the text is much more homogeneously and opaquely Underhill's. Ironically, her writing is a much more successful colonizer of the Native American mind than Michelson's less sensitive reportage.

34. Underhill, Introduction to *Mountain Wolf Woman*, p. viii.
35. Underhill, *Papago Woman*, p. 92.
36. Bataille and Sands, p. 51.

Chona may or may not have been the observant child and resourceful, stoical woman Underhill has drawn from "the disjointed statements of an ancient Papago woman, too old to organize and tell a connected story." What we know is that large parts of Chona's life are yet again silenced. The text is full of fascinating, intriguing details of Papago life, which in factual terms are undoubtedly largely reliable. What Underhill was most interested in—Chona's "innerness"—fragments and dissipates. The possibility of such a coherent, graspable identity is nullified by the multistranded, pluralistic world in which Maria Chona exists.

The literary, primitivist, and early feminist discourses that in one way or another frame this tale all claim to present Chona's subjectivity, yet they lead us to what they cannot encompass—the central oppressive power in Chona's life, which is that of the Euro-Americans, not of Papago men. Chona's refusal to admit her domination by men mirrors and justifies Underhill's constant emphasis on Papago artistic otherworldliness, which demands no part in the power relations of modern society. Underhill can create symbolic liberation for Chona from male domination only by having her defeat the white woman. Underhill's disturbance at the law in her imaged Papago world is the register of her unease at her colonial relationship to it.

The text throughout undermines the notion of the separate wholeness of Papago life. In the introduction, Underhill commended Chona's bravery in leaving her first husband in a way considered "unnatural" for a Papago shaman's wife. Underhill, far more intellectually sophisticated than Michelson, is very much a cultural relativist in her desire to challenge Western notions of the natural. Writing after Margaret Mead's influential work, she frequently alerts her readers to the difference of cultural norms. (Much emphasis, for example, is given in the text to Shining Evening, Chona's man-woman brother-in-law). Papago shamans, she points out, traditionally have four wives, although other Papago men have only one. To make her point here she already seems to be straining the concept "natural" for what was a minority Papago situation. In our culture Roman Catholic priests are celibate, but no one suggests it is "unnatural" when one renounces his vows and marries. More important, the Papago, though less Westernized than many Native American groups, were, this story itself shows, in much closer contact with white mores than Underhill cares to acknowledge. Before this time, Chona has had her baby baptized by a priest ("we were modern"), and has given her father (who was a U.S. government appointee and named José Maria) a Christian-influenced burial. For Maria Chona, colonial disruption had already called in question the notion of the "natural." Chona is clearly not seen as deviant by her pluralistic community, as Underhill herself asserts when she points out that Chona is not the kind of "aberrant" informant on whom earlier anthropologists naively relied. Yet Underhill's use of "aberrant" denotes her belief in a unified culture, which her text scarcely bears out.[37]

One last point I want to raise is Underhill's surprisingly dismissive attitude toward Chona's powers as a poet and shaman. She writes: "Chona was no poet by nature. . . . She learned a manipulation of sick babies that was much respected. Very possibly she had observed its performance by her first husband . . . but did not . . . recognize this."[38] In ironic contrast to her express contempt for the businesslike, what Underhill actually seems to acknowledge most in Chona is her "competence." Yet the life itself stresses the centrality of Chona's visions (in one of which the Virgin Mary figures) for resolving crises and regaining self-respect. Part of what lies behind Underhill's attitude is her own insecurity as a woman. In spite of her intellectual assertions, she finds it hard to maintain a woman's inherent worth without the male structure of values within which she and Chona live. In 1936 she justifies her recounting of a woman's life by reference to Chona's powerful husband and father. She significantly speaks of the "honored man," not woman, as a singer and, of course, is technically justified in that the majority of singers were men. Yet one of the most impressive Native American shamans whose work has been recorded was a Papago woman—Owl Woman—whose songs were taken down by Frances Densmore.[39]

All this is not said to belittle Underhill's project. In many ways she succeeded in her wish to win appreciation for this culture from Euro-Americans. As in all these "autobiographies," the decision to present the Native Americans as the subjects of their own lives allows their perspective, or even the possibility of their perspective, to challenge Western preconceptions, including the anthropologist's own. Autobiography inevitably makes an ahistorical primitivism impossible. The subject can only live in history, and the multistranded production of these texts denies the myth of separate existence. Colonial power pervades these life histories, even though it is superficially absent. Its presence both works within and calls attention to the split between their own human-

---

37. Underhill, "Autobiography of a Papago Woman", p. 4.
38. Ibid.
39. Frances Densmore, *Papago Music* (Washington: Bureau of American Ethnology), Bulletin 90 (1929), pp. 114–30. In *Papago Indian Religion,* Columbia University Contributions to Anthropology Series, 33 (1938; rpt., New York: AMS, 1946), p. 267, Underhill comments that women rarely become shamans till they are past childbearing age. Their healing, she says, as with white women doctors, is often confined to the care of children. Again Owl Woman did not follow this pattern, but would this general information have added to her identification with Papago women's limited opportunities?

itarian, libertarian ideals, and the oppressive power relations within which they work. The Boasians could only maintain the former by ignoring the latter. Consequently, colonial power was made invisible. Caught in the mesh of colonial discourses, Euro-Americans still have no easy understanding of non-Western peoples; what is needed is a closer view of how a shared, unequal history has formed the First World construction of the Third World, most complexly, the women of that world. When Maria Chona found a cure difficult she sang this song:

> 'Haya, sickness!
> I can't find you!'
>
> I tried
> I could not see.
> I sat back.[40]

Westerners have assumed that they can see and judge the inhabitants of the Third World more clearly than they do themselves, just as women have been traditionally evaluated by the male gaze. But in both cases the gaze has been myopic, selective, reifying. These autobiographies, with all their limitations, remind us of the need for sensitive agnosticism and for the acknowledgment of other subjectivities, other points of view.

40. Underhill, "Autobiography of a Papago Woman," p. 61.

7

Between Two Worlds: The Formation of a Turn-of-the-Century Egyptian Feminist

Leila Ahmed

Autobiography is an anciently known form in Islamic-Arabic letters. Famous early autobiographical works include one by the religious scholar and philosopher Al-Ghazzali (d. 1111) *Munqidh min al Dalal*, and another by Usamah ibn Munqidh (d. 1188) *Kitab Al-I'tibar.*[1] Indeed, there are even distinguishable varieties of Islamic autobiography, including autobiographies of rulers, religious-mystic autobiographies, and the autobiographical accounts of scholars.[2] Georges Gusdorf's statement that autobiography is not to be found outside the Western cultural area and that it expresses a "concern peculiar to Western man" (a concern he finds expressed also in Western man's "systematic conquest of the universe") is, therefore, at least with respect to Islamic and Arabic civilization, quite simply incorrect,[3] as is his further statement that autobiography evolved in non-Western cultures only following the colonial impact. It is true, however, that Arabic letters underwent a major literary and intellectual transformation after Arab societies were opened to the West and that this period witnessed the emergence of the novel and of a kind of autobiographical writing that differed from the "classical"

---

1. Al-Ghazzali, *The Confessions of Al-Ghazzali*, trans. W. M. Watt (London: John Murray, 1909); and Usamah ibn Munqidh, *An Arab-Syrian Gentleman and Warrior in the Period of the Crusades: Memoirs of Usamah ibn Munqidh*, trans. Philip K. Hitti (New York: Columbia University Press, 1929).

2. On Arabic autobiography, see Franz Rosenthal, "Die arabische Autobiographie," *Studia Arabica* (Rome: Pontificium Institutum Biblicum, 1937), pp. 1–40. On Islamic scholars' autobiographies, see Georg Misch, *Geschichte der Autobiographie.* vol. 3: *Das Mittelalter,* pt. 2: *Hochmittelalter im Anfang,* 2d half (Frankfurt am Main: Verlag G. Schulte-Bulmke, 1962), pp. 962–1006.

3. Georges Gusdorf, "Conditions and Limits of Autobiography," trans. James Olney, in *Autobiography: Essays Theoretical and Critical,* ed. James Olney (Princeton: Princeton University Press, 1980), p. 29.

or "traditional" type. The emergence of the Arabic novel and of "modern" autobiography were intertwined events.[4] A number of early novels were markedly autobiographical, and one autobiography, Taha Husain's *Al-Ayyam,* the first volume of which was published in 1924, is regarded as central to the development of the Arabic novel. Distinctive for its limpid prose and its narrative power, it is regarded as a major, and sometimes even *the* major, literary work of the modern age.[5]

The question of how modern Arabic autobiography differs from the classical is part of the broader question of how modern Arabic literature more generally differs from the classical, and whether the emergence of modern literature marked a complete break with the traditional past and reflects a transformation in consciousness or whether, as some argue, for all its novelty, it essentially continues the classical modes and thus expresses a fundamental, if subterranean, continuity with the past. Questions that autobiographical texts in particular promise to illuminate, and with respect to which they have yet to be explored, include questions relating to the nature of self as construct, such as the differences between the concept of self in classical and modern literature, or between either and the Western.

No autobiographies by women exist in classical Arabic literature. In this century, however, many women's autobiographies have been published. *The Memoirs of Huda Sha'rawi*, published posthumously in 1981, is among the first autobiographical works in Arabic by a self-defined feminist and, indeed, among the first autobiographical undertakings by an Arabic-speaking woman. Sha'rawi dictated the work to her male secretary, principally because her mastery of written Arabic was not adequate to the task. Huda Sha'rawi (1879–1947) who founded the Egyptian Feminist Union in 1923 and headed it until her death, was prominent among the articulate and active Egyptian feminists of the first half of the twentieth century. Indeed, she was the public figure most associated with the demand for women's rights. She fought for reform in the laws governing marriage, divorce, child custody, and other aspects of family life, and she advocated education for women. In 1923 she became the first upper-class woman formally and publicly to renounce the veil. Peasant women had all along been unveiled, but for urban women, and in particular upper- and middle-class women, the veil had been the rule. The question of whether veiling was necessary

4. On the Arabic novel see Roger Allen, *The Arabic Novel: An Historical and Critical Introduction* (Syracuse, N.Y.: Syracuse University Press, 1982); and Hamdi Sakkut, *The Egyptian Novel and Its Main Trends, 1913–1952* (Cairo: American University in Cairo Press, 1971).

5. See Fadwa Malti-Douglas, *Blindness and Autobiography: Al-Ayyam of Taha Husain* (Princeton: Princeton University Press, 1988).

began to be raised in the latter part of the century, along with other issues pertaining to the status of women, and in the nineties these questions were debated in the periodical literature. In 1899 with the publication of Qasim Amin's *Tahrir Al-Mara's* ("The liberation of woman") a work which has been described as provoking a controversy of unprecedented proportions in Arabic letters, the debate reached new levels of intensity, and the veil, which Amin took a strong stand against, took on central emblematic significance in the battle between "modernity" and "tradition."[6]

Two years before her death, the state awarded Huda Sha'rawi the Nishan al-Kamal, the highest possible state decoration. That award was a measure not only of the prominence Sha'rawi had attained as leading advocate of women's rights but also of the enormous transformation Egyptian society had undergone in the first half of this century. A society in which women of Sha'rawi's (upper) class were veiled and invisible and could have no presence in the world of public and political activities had become one in which they were visible and active in the public domain, in which their activities were reported in the papers (accompanied by photographs of their unveiled faces), and in which the state and the secular-minded politicians, literati and intellectuals of the day recognized women's contributions. Society had changed, and the state at midcentury proclaimed itself committed to the kinds of changes that were in process. Indeed, by awarding its highest distinction to a woman whose achievements were on behalf of women, the state was proclaiming its commitment to the advancement of women.

But that was in 1945. It would be difficult to imagine in today's changed ideological atmosphere a Middle Eastern Muslim state decorating anyone, man or woman, for advocacy of women's rights. Even in her own day Sha'rawi's activities and the reforms she called for on behalf of women were not universally regarded with favor. Sheikhs (the "clergy" of Islam or, more accurately, since Islam has no clergy, the guardians of the socioreligious norms of the society) opposed Sha'rawi, sometimes attending her public lectures to denounce her views.[7] Today, as a religious vision of the future gains ground in Egypt, as elsewhere in the Middle East, Sha'rawi's "feminism" is liable to be dismissed as a product of the Westernized—and thus inauthentic, un-Islamic—vision of their society adopted by the old upper classes. The slur is com-

6. See Mukhtar Al-Tuhami, *Thalath Ma'arik Fikkriyya* (Cairo: Dar Al-Ma'mun lilTiba'a, 1976), p. 8.
7. Ruth F. Woodsmall, *Moslem Women Enter a New World* (New York: Roundable Press, 1936), p. 121.

pounded by the further accusation that Sha'rawi's father was among those who had facilitated the British occupation of Egypt in 1882.

Sha'rawi's first public political action was as leader of a delegation of upper-class Egyptian women demonstrating in the streets in 1919 against the British presence in Egypt. Although Egyptian women had participated in street protests long before Western penetration, it is unlikely that Sha'rawi was inspired by, or even knew of, such examples. She probably took her cue from the British suffragettes, whose activities were reported in the press in the decades of Sha'rawi's adolescence and young maturity. In many other ways also Sha'rawi was undoubtedly influenced by developments in Western societies. However, the notion that her ideas for women's advancement came entirely from the West and that Arab societies were innately and in all respects more restrictive for women than Western societies bears reexamination. For example, in the nineteenth century, particularly in the reign of Mohamad Ali (1805–1848) and again under Ismael (1863–1879), the state had actively interested itself in education for girls and women and in the 1830s had instituted a college (the School of Maternity) to train women as midwives and doctors. The British occupation in fact retarded women's education in a number of ways. In the first decade of occupation the number of girls attending state schools dropped.[8] When, by the turn of the century, the state (under the British) began to revive its interest in education and to bring schools under government control, the curriculum, which had been the same for both sexes in the traditional local *kuttab* (schools), was changed for girls to include the subjects the British thought appropriate—needlework, child care, cookery, laundry work.[9] Also under the British, the School of Maternity, which had given women medical training of the same duration as the men's training at the School of Medicine, was down-graded and its graduates, who had previously practiced as doctors, were restricted to midwifery. Even though women had been active in medical service for most of the nineteenth century, Lord Cromer, the British consul general in Egypt, considered the local view that women preferred to be treated by women unreasonable. "I am aware," he said, "that in exceptional cases women like to be attended by female doctors, but I conceive that throughout the civilized world, attendance by medical men is still the rule."[10] Thus, it appears

8. Amir Boktor, *School and Society in the Valley of the Nile* (Cairo: Elias Modern Press, 1936), p. 134.

9. Judith E. Tucker, *Women in Nineteenth-Century Egypt* (Cambridge: Cambridge University Press, 1985), p. 126.

10. United Kingdom Foreign Office paper: FO 633/8, Cromer Papers, Lord Cromer to Mr. Davidson, Cairo, 23 Jan. 1900, fol. 252, cited in Tucker, p. 122.

that in the matter of women's rights the rhetoric and some styles of demand and protest (in other words, the couching of the matter in political terminology) were borrowed from the West, but some indigenous attitudes were potentially and actually less confining for women than contemporary Western ideas. Such indigenous attitudes may have engendered in women a strong sense of self-worth and the desire, though not perhaps the political tools, to resist the injustices of society (including those of their British overlords). Sha'rawi lived at that turning point in Egyptian society when Western economic and cultural penetration and internal change would shortly and irrevocably transform the society and women's role in it. Because she was a member of the first generation of Egyptian women exposed to a fair degree to Western ideas and, at the same time, a member of the last, or almost the last, generation of women to have experienced in childhood and early adulthood the secluded life of upper-class women, her life is especially appropriate ground for an examination of how Western political ideas, and in particular those of feminism, intersected or combined with the social and psychological structures that were the given realities of Egyptian upper-class life.

Pursuing this examination entails the exploration of Sha'rawi's self-representation on a complex of issues: what, as she came to consciousness, being female meant to her or, more exactly, how she negotiated her sense of self in relation to the structures of gender imposed by the culture and the people who mediated the culture; how she experienced (or represented herself experiencing) the imposition of those structures; what those structures actually were as they impinged on or altered or constricted her life; in what way she perceived these as sources for her later commitment to change; and whether she conceived of her feminism as influenced by Western ideas. Because essentially these are questions about her *formation* as a feminist, it is Sha'rawi's childhood and adolescence which are most relevant to this inquiry, and which will be focused on here.

Sha'rawi herself foregrounds in her account those childhood experiences she considered formative to her development as a feminist. In the later chapters, which are more impersonal in tone and content, she is particularly concerned with chronicling her activities as a feminist. Written in her later life and possibly even begun after her decoration by the state, the memoir is decidedly an account of self, for the record, by a public personage of recognized achievement, prepared with the object of detailing the genesis and course of those activities that had brought her distinction. Her self-representation is not the confessional narrative an American woman might offer either to her analyst or in autobiographical writings. The memoir contains nothing, we may be sure, that the "respectable" members of Egyptian society would have considered improper or unseemly. Propriety was characteristic of Sha'rawi's life and also of her demands as a feminist, which were always such as the "respectable" liberal men and women of her society could, and did, assent to. That is, her feminism did not challenge the fundamental structures of her society and its gender arrangements to any large degree; instead it was a practical feminism, aimed at fundamentally modifying discrimination against women in education and law, a feminism that probably ultimately achieved more than a radical vision could have done.

Sha'rawi's account of the discrimination and rejection she experienced, as well as the support she received, is interesting not only for what is explicitly recounted but also for what is incidentally revealed of her family background. The inner geography of familial relations in the period before Egyptian society began radically to change—even of what constituted the family—is as yet a largely unknown landscape. Much has been written about the Middle Eastern family in its externals—we know, for example, about polygamy, male precedence, and other aspects—but there are no accounts, not even imaginative or fictional ones, by women of how in practice these social structures affected individual interiority.

The psychoanalyst Alan Roland maintains that it is psychoanalytic imperialism to approach non-Western cultures as though the paradigms of the West are universal and ought to apply. Instead, he insists, different paradigms of psychoanalytic processes and development must be developed for the analysis of subjects whose formation and evolution as selves occurs within the matrix of other cultures.[11] It is in this sense that the inner territory of self, with respect to the subject in the premodern Middle East, is as yet fundamentally unknown.

In a similar vein, Vytautas Kavolis stresses that autobiographical texts must be read with the clear awareness that social relations and their meanings are culturally specific.[12] For these, as for the basic territory of inner geography, Sha'rawi's text offers the possiblity of a preliminary charting on the basis of the experiences of one consciousness. Possibly when other texts, contemporary or near-contemporary with it, have also been studied, we will begin to discern a recognizable common

11. Alan Roland, "The Self in India and America: Toward a Psychoanalysis of Social and Cultural Contexts," in *Designs of Selfhood*, ed. Vytautas Kavolis (London: Associated University Presses, 1984), pp. 171–72.

12. Vytautas Kavolis, "Histories of Selfhood, Maps of Sociability," in *Designs of Selfhood*, p. 21.

landscape. Meanwhile, we cannot extrapolate from Western meanings and experience. For example, a Western psychoanalytically biased reading of Sha'rawi's text might conclude that she was "in love" with her brother. To take her account as evidence of such a relationship would be to read the text as transparent rather than as the author's presentation of self in terms of the norms and assumptions of her own society. Moreover, in that the autobiography is the self-presentation of a public personage, and not a confessional outpouring, the fact that Sha'rawi foregrounds her love for her brother and even emphasizes that it was the deepest and most intense love of her life, suggests that this was a form of love her society sanctioned, and even that the brother-sister relation was one the culture particularly valorized. Indeed, it was among the few cross-sexual relations permitted to flourish openly, in a society in which cross-generational relationships were strongly hierarchical and in which marriage was not generally contracted on an affective basis and often was, for both men and women, an intensely lonely and noncommunicative relationship.[13] Oral histories of women near to Sha'rawi's generation confirm the central emotional importance of brothers. Beyond knowing that they were important, we know little of the nature and content of such relations. On this as on other matters pertaining to the inner and the personal, research initially can only be, as in the following pages, primarily exploratory and descriptive.

Sha'rawi grew up in a large household, consisting of her parents, her siblings and half siblings, her father's wife, nurses, guardians, slaves and maids. Sporadically the household also embraced more transient relatives, occupants, and visitors. We are far here, it need hardly be pointed out, from the nuclear family. Perhaps it barely needs stating also that so large a household—and the consequently relationally rich environment in which Sha'rawi was nurtured—to the extent that it was typical, would have been typical only of the wealthy upper classes.

Sha'rawi singles out a number of individuals within this household as having hurt her because they gave different, preferential treatment to the boys in the family. Others she describes in ways that affirm, at least implicitly, that they were not guilty of discriminating against her. Chief among those who wounded her by discriminatory treatment was her mother, while her father and brother Sha'rawi represents as free of such bias. The father died when Sha'rawi was five. Noting that she has few recollections of him, Sha'rawi offers only one: "I would go to my father's room every morning to kiss his hand, and I would be accompanied on this trip by a brother I had by another mother, called Ismael. We would find father sitting cross-legged on his prayer rug, telling his

---

13. See, for example, Qassim Amin, *Tahrir al-Mar'a* (Cairo: Dar al-Ma'arref, 1901), the section "Al-'A'ila: al-Zawajj," pp. 139–48.

rosary beads, and we would kiss his hand and he would kiss us; then he would rise and open his book cabinet and extract from it a piece of chocolate for each of us, and we would take it and leave cheerily."[14] Noticeably, the scene shows the father treating boy and girl alike and not—as her mother and guardian do (as will be seen)—favoring the boy. Two details in Sha'rawi's self-presentation suggest that her father was important to her internal organization of self and particularly, perhaps, to her ability (in a male-dominated and patriarchal society) to annex authority to herself. She devotes the long second chapter of her memoirs to an account of her father's involvement in the political events that led to the British occupation of Egypt—an account that exonerates him from charges of complicity with the British. It is not, however, so much the chapter's content that suggests her father's importance in developing her sense of self but rather that she felt a chapter about him belonged at the forefront of her account of herself. The second detail suggestive of his importance is a scene in which a father figure attempts to pressure her into accepting a situation she finds unjust and unacceptable by invoking the memory of her father and declaring that this is what her father would have wished. She suddenly finds herself able to resist the man and assume control of the situation by countering his version of her father with the father of her memory—a "just and compassionate father" who would never have tolerated injustice for his daughter (p. 87). Since her father died when she was very young, it is likely that this just and kindly father was, at least in part, a father figure of her own creation. Memory or creation, he was a figure that *she* could invoke and wield with great practical effectiveness.

I have already referred to the enormous love that bound Sha'rawi to her brother Omar, her only sibling by the same mother as well as father. She writes in her memoir that on his death, which occurred when she was in her late thirties, "all my hopes died," and but for a sense of duty toward her children, "I would not have survived him by an instant" (p. 157). They developed in childhood a bond of loyalty and love against the world of adults. For Sha'rawi the bond was sealed when, swearing him to secrecy, she revealed to Omar that their father was dead and not simply away, as the adults claimed. Despite the tears and illness to which this information reduced him, and despite the entreaties of their mother and the entire household that he reveal the cause of his distress, Omar, who was two years her junior, never betrayed her.

One other relative who never slighted her, Sha'rawi says, is her fa-

14. *Mudhakirat Huda Sha'rawi,* ed. Abdel Hamid Fahmy Mursy (Cairo: Al-Hilal, 1981), p. 11, hereafter cited in the text. All translations are my own. For a discussion of the differences between this text and Margot Badran's English translation, *Harem Years: The Memoirs of an Egyptian Feminist, 1879–1924* (London: Virago Press, 1986), see the *Women's Review of Books,* Nov. 1987.

ther's widow, whom she called Mama al-Kabira (Big/Senior Mama). Sha'rawi's own mother in her daughter's account was also a wife/widow of her father's, but external evidence indicates that she was in fact his concubine—that is, a slave, whom he did not liberate and marry.[15] Mama al-Kabira, an invalid who had lost a son, is the only adult in the household the young Sha'rawi trusts completely, "because of her kindness and openness" (p. 40). She would often obtain her mother's permission to spend nights with Mama al-Kabira, full of delight over sharing the older woman's bed because, like herself, Mama al-Kabira loved to sleep with the windows open. Waking early to the sound of birds and to "nature, in whose beauty I lost myself," she writes, she loved sharing the thoughts of this kindly woman "because of the great affinity of our tastes in all things" (p. 40).

While father and brother are represented as never discriminating against her, Mama al-Kabira alone consoles Sha'rawi for the discrimination she experienced as a female child: "I remember I asked her one day," she writes, "to explain to me why my brother was preferred over me. She replied with her sweet smile, 'Do you not feel/understand now the difference between you and he?' I said, 'Yes, but I am the elder and first; my share should be larger than his, and my place above his.' She said, 'But you're a girl and he's a boy . . . and not only that but also you're not the only girl and he's the only boy, whose responsibility it will be to perpetuate the family name'" (p. 42). This response briefly assuages the child's anguish over the matter, and she finds herself comprehending now that her brother will keep alive her "beloved father's name," loving the brother all the more for it. Mama al-Kabira, understanding "how [Sha'rawi] suffered from these feelings," adds in further explanation, "Your brother's constitution is frail and they therefore fear for his health and are kind to him, whereas you are strong and healthy" (p. 42).

"I loved this woman greatly," Sha'rawi writes, "and she returned my love" (p. 33). Throughout her life she kept on her finger a ring Mama al-Kabira had given her. Shortly before Sha'rawi's marriage at the age of about twelve to her guardian, a man in his forties—a marriage arranged by Sha'rawi's mother and her guardian—Mama al-Kabira died. Just before her death, Sha'rawi had run in to her to show her and share with her her pleasure in some jewelry her mother had given her, and Mama al-Kabira, although her illness had taken an acute turn for the worse, rejoiced with her. The jewelry her mother had given her on the pretext that it was a gift to celebrate Sha'rawi's convalescence from an illness

---

15. This is mentioned in Badran, *Harem Years*, p. 139.

was, in reality, part of the formalization of the arrangements for Sha'rawi's marriage, arrangements the mother concealed from her daughter. Had Mama al-Kabira lived, Sha'rawi notes, "I would have learned the truth from her, alas, after her death there was no one to reveal the truth to me or to explain to me what I did not understand" (p. 71).

Mama al-Kabira's explanation that it was her brother's frailty in contrast to her own robustness which in part accounted for the love lavished on him had left Sha'rawi longing to become ill "so that I could equal my brother in my mother's love." Soon after, an infectious illness begins to spread through Cairo, and Sha'rawi does in fact fall ill—much to her gratification. Briefly her mother becomes greatly concerned, and the family doctor is sent for. Then her brother comes down with the same illness, and the entire household is plunged into agitation, doctors flocking to attend him, then departing without so much as noticing her, though she lay in a bed alongside his. This experience, she says, affected her deeply, causing her illness to worsen. She came to see the incident as a turning point. After the illness she withdrew all the more into herself, bitterly resentful of those around her. Thenceforth, "I would spend most of my free time after lessons in our garden, which was like a small forest, and I loved animals, and I would imagine that they understood me and lamented my plight" (p. 42).

The chief, most painful source of the discrimination Sha'rawi experienced was her own mother. If Sha'rawi's mother was indeed concubine rather than wife to her father, her overriding concern about the health of her son is intelligible. Unlike wives, concubines had no rights of inheritance. Their children could inherit, provided the father acknowledged them, and the mother would then be entitled to maintenance as the children's caretaker. Without a son, such a woman would be in a precarious economic position when the children reached adulthood. At best she would continue to be, as must have been the arrangement on the death of Sha'rawi's father and when the children were minors, under the legal guardianship of a male relative of the father's. On her son's majority, however, she would pass to his guardianship.

Sha'rawi's mother, who was born in Turkey, never explained to her how she had come to find herself in Egypt and in her present situation. Instead, a maternal uncle related a convoluted tale that sometimes strains credulity. Her mother's family had found themselves refugees as a result of Turkish wars, and therefore they sent their daughter, for her own protection, to a relative in Egypt. When, because of the machinations of his wife, the relative failed to acknowledge the girl, she was left in the keeping of another family with whom the child's traveling companion was friendly. They raised her and eventually gave her in marriage—or sold her if she was a concubine—to Sha'rawi's father. The sale of daughters and also sons was occasionally practiced by the poorer communities among the Circassians, who, because of their reputed good looks and abilities, were among the most desirable slaves. It is at least possible that the mother had been sold by her parents rather than merely sent to Egypt for her own protection. If so, Sha'rawi's mother's situation would have been unusual, for by the latter part of the nineteenth century, slavery had become rather rare (it was banned in 1890).

Sha'rawi quite explicitly refers to her mother as married to her father, but she also tacitly acknowledges an intrinsic painfulness to her mother's plight, a painfulness which she represents her mother as masking with silence, just as she represents herself as retreating into silence when wounded. "The truth is I never dared ask my mother of her origins or of how she came to be in Egypt," Sha'rawi begins; "she was, God have mercy on her, spare in her words about herself, little given to complaining or speaking openly of her pain, controlling her feelings and concealing in the depths of herself all that pained her" (p. 37). Pain (the word is as obtrusively repetitious in the Arabic as in the English translation) and the silence with which she surrounds it are presented as the essence of her mother's situation. One day, however, she recounts how her mother, while helping Sha'rawi's father dress, glanced out of the window, glimpsed an approaching guest who reminded her of a brother, and found herself in tears. The father then learned for the first time of her relatives in Turkey and at once arranged for them to be brought to Egypt. The ensuing reunion brought tremendous joy to the mother and altered her life. Thus for the mother, in Sha'rawi's account, speaking of her pain brought about a measure of resolution.

A number of elements link Sha'rawi's presentation of key moments in her mother's life and in her own. A central pain, a pain too lonely and intense for speech, is at the heart of those moments for both mother and daughter. For both, the pain ensues from the fact of their being female in their society. The one was physically rejected (sent away), and the other was, or felt herself to be, emotionally rejected. Both were consigned to sexual/marital relations (in both cases to men considerably older than themselves) that took no account whatsoever of themselves as persons. Yet, though centered on suffering, those moments are also shot through with a sense of loveliness, guessed at though beyond reach, which helps to assuage and, in her mother's case at least, even to resolve the suffering. Repeatedly, in Sha'rawi's evocations of particularly charged moments in her own early life, as in this account of her mother, gardens or windows looking onto gardens reappear, often forming the background against which a foregrounded pain is achingly juxtaposed (and always it is the pain of being female). Gardens seem to bespeak the wealth of loveliness and possibility inhering in life, which human arrangements stupidly and wantonly waste, abridge, or destroy.

Two passages in which gardens or windows figure in this way have already been referred to. Sha'rawi dwells on the delight of spending the night with Mama al-Kabira in her open-windowed room and her joyous pleasure in waking there to the sounds of birds and to "nature," and she describes her withdrawal into herself and retreat into the garden when her illness, far from gaining for her an equal place in her mother's love, results instead in the bitter reinforcement of the fundamental inequality between herself and her brother. A garden, into which she looks from a window, again figures in her recapitulation of another moment charged with possibilities, yearning, pain, and irretrievable waste and loss: the morning following the consummation of her marriage.

Her husband is a man she both disliked and feared from earliest childhood. When he had visited the family, as the legal guardian, he invariably ignored her and addressed only her brother, on whom he lavished attention. When she learned of the plans for her marriage, she resisted the arrangement by such feeble means as were at her disposal—tears and refusal—without success. As the elaborate arrangements for the wedding are reaching their peak, however, and she is shown over the newly and sumptuously furnished wing of the family home being prepared for her occupation, she begins to be seduced both by the gorgeousness of the affair and by her own importance. The seduction is completed by the lavish three-day wedding itself, for which canopies have been erected in the garden and throughout which she feels herself dazzled and intoxicated with the excitement of being richly dressed and bejeweled among throngs of bejeweled, gift-bearing female guests, intoxicated above all at finding herself the center of attention. The festivities culminate with the withdrawal of the women when the groom is led in, after which the bridal pair shares the customary cup of red sherbet.

Sha'rawi writes of the morning after the wedding: "The following morning I looked out of the window to cheer myself with the sight of the large tents with their fine carpets . . . that had enchanted me the previous evening." But the tents are gone, and so are the trees, which had been cut down to make way for the tents:

All those trees I had loved and found companionship in and climbed and returned to in childhood, and which had been planted by my father and

which he had loved as I had and which he had cared for. . . . Destroyed for
the sake of one night that I had imagined would endure in its splendor and
majesty, but how quickly it had passed, like a beautiful dream.

   I cried for my trees, I cried for childhood, and I saw in this barren garden
a picture of the life I would live, bereft of all that was companionable and
pleasing to me. (Pp. 76–77)

In her mother's case, pain dissolves into speech at the instigation of
the figure in the garden, and the result is an easing and some measure of
resolution, but there is no such resolution in the passages relating to
herself. To Mama al-Kabira she speaks around but not of her pain.
Taking refuge and finding solace in the garden from the wounding
neglect of her mother, it is with animals and trees, with those who are
mute, that she feels kin. And the scene in which she views the devastated
garden, reflecting her devastated self, is characterized by silence. Thus,
her pain does not dissolve into speech and the release of speech—in the
text. Sha'rawi's future life, however, dedicated to speaking out for
women and changing the human arrangements stupidly crippling them,
and to the composition of her memoirs, constituted precisely a refusal of
mute pain, and a speaking out and breaking of the silence around the
female condition.

   It is striking in the memoirs that for all the centrality Sha'rawi gives
her sense of emotional rejection, nowhere does she indicate that she was
ever told that by virtue of her gender, she was intrinsically inferior. On
the contrary, among the reasons she is given for the discriminatory
treatment she experiences is that she is *superior*, more robust than the
weak male, the brother. The only other reason she is given similarily
does not suggest innate inferiority but only a difference in the roles and
responsiblities society assigns.

   A second point of interest is Sha'rawi's relationship with her father, a
figure interesting both for its presence in her mind and for its actual
absence. It is apparent that she invokes her father as a means of affirming
the rightness of her own point of view and of gaining her own ends
against opposition. *He* had loved the trees as she did, trees destroyed in
the service of her ugly and unjust marriage; *he* would have supported
her in her decision not to return to her husband. In reality, of course, he
was dead. And even before his death, experientially in her world he was
a remote figure of nebulous significance, encountered for a few moments a day, praying and dispensing chocolate. Even before his death,
that is, he was all but absent. Accounts of the Middle Eastern family
suggest that in these societies, in which segregation was the norm, male
presence in the home was relatively limited, particularly among the

wealthy who could afford the luxury of space that makes segregation possible. Significantly, the only male individual with whom Sha'rawi forms a deep and intimate relationship in childhood is her brother, and presumably, since she was both older and more robust, it was a relationship in which she would often have been dominant.

Thus, the presiding presences and the authority figures in Sha'rawi's experiential world are women. Two women, a biological mother and a second mother (literally Big Mother), oversaw a household of both male and female slaves and servants. Nominally after the father's death a male cousin was guardian, but he appeared only sporadically and experientially would have been no more than an occasional intruder. Until his marriage to her, even if his decisions were important, Sha'rawi did not perceive them to be so. Even her marriage to him she describes as an arrangement brought about by her mother as well as by the guardian. (Practical reasons could well have inspired the marriage: since women inherit in Islam, Sha'rawi's marriage outside the family would mean the loss of her considerable inheritance to the family.)

The societal arrangements that made two women the presiding, dominant presences in Sha'rawi's (and her brother's) childhood were polygamy, legally regulated concubinage, and the practice of segregation. Thus the customs that we have learnt, in the wake of Western cultural hegemony, to see as oppressive and confining to women (and indeed women are not treated equally in Islamic personal law, and segregation does confine them) paradoxically may also be sources of psychological strength for women. Cooperation between wives or between wives and concubines and cross-mothering of each other's offspring must obviously have varied from household to household, but clearly, it did occur. The sense of women as the presiding presences would obviously also have increased with an increase in the number of wives and concubines, provided, that is, that they, or some of them, lived collaboratively. Moreover, even when there were no cospouses (and by and large polygamy and the keeping of concubines was limited to the upper classes), the practice of segregation and the importance of the larger, as opposed to nuclear, family would make women the presiding presences in many households. This phenomenon, as part of the order of childhood, could contribute to a strong sense of self-worth and personal empowerment for girls and women; such an order could nurture a conviction of the innate and "natural," even though not societal, ascendancy of women. In this case the society's formal and explicit gender system, valuing boys over girls, could have been experienced by girls as bizarre, unreasonable laws, manifestly flying in the face of the "real" and "natural" order of things. That is, it could have been experienced as an affront not only to their sense of self-worth but to reality—to *their* experiential reality—and thus as intrinsically preposterous.

The large and varied household and its domination by two women, to both of whom Sha'rawi related intimately, though differently, are important in the further sense that society's codes and imperatives regarding gender came to her mediated through a range of individuals, each pursuing different interests and thus mediating the culture's imperatives differently. Considering the contrasting treatment Sha'rawi received from her own mother and from Big Mother, it is evident that the one had everything to gain materially by falling in with the cultural ascription of greater value to the boy, and the other nothing to lose or gain by ignoring that ascription.

Finally, it is striking that though Sha'rawi conjures a father figure to give herself strength to stand up to the unjust demands of others, the adult with whom she had shared love and contentment was an older woman who mothered her. And it was a physical reminder of this woman, the ring Mama al-Kabira had given her, that she never removed from her finger throughout her life.

Such then were the formative elements in Sha'rawi's familial background. She was also, of course, influenced by her education and by sources she presents, either explicitly or implicitly, as those from which she developed her feminist ideas.

Sha'rawi received instruction alongside of and on equal terms with her brother and the other children of their large household. Their mornings were spent learning Arabic, Turkish, and French. Sha'rawi, who liked music was given a piano when her brother got a pony, and she also took piano lessons.[16] She was taught to read/recite the Koran, which she completed at the age of nine. This accomplishment was lavishly feted: her mother held a party—the first festivities in the house since the death of Sha'rawi's father—and Mama al-Kabira celebrated the occasion with the gift of the ring Sha'rawi was always to wear.

As the celebration indicates, a certain amount of education was approved for girls of her class.[17] It is in progressing beyond this basic knowledge, particularly to acquire mastery of written Arabic, that Sha'rawi found herself actively obstructed. The individual who blocked her acquisition of Arabic was Said Agha, the person (probably a eunuch) who had charge of her brother and herself. "I loved the Arabic lan-

16. Sha'rawi had wanted a pony also, arguing, when told that girls did not ride, that the daughter of their neighbor, a military officer, both rode and drove her own carriage (p. 47).

17. By the late nineteenth century it was common for upper-class families to hire foreign (often French) women tutors to instruct their daughters in the sciences and arts and French language. Yacoub Artin Pasha, *L'Instruction publique en Égypte* (Paris: Ernest Leroux, 1890), p. 130.

guage," Sha'rawi has her secretary write. When her teacher explains to her that the reason she cannot read the Koran without mistakes, as he does, is that she has not studied grammar, she begs him to teach her. He is happy to be asked, she reports, agreeing "with pleasure," and arrives the following day with a grammar book under his arm. "Said Agha asked him with an arrogant air: 'What's that book?' He said a grammar book. Agha laughed and said: 'Take your book. No need for grammar—she's not one day going to be a lawyer.'" This rebuff to her desire to learn "affected me deeply," says Sha'rawi; "despair began to seep into my heart and lassitude and disinterest took hold of me so that I neglected my studies. I came to hate my femaleness because it deprived me of the pleasures of learning and of the physically active life which I loved, as it would later come between me and the freedom I longed for" (p. 43).

Knowledge of the written tongue, of the language that would enable one to compose and discourse—as distinct from simply speak—was, it would seem, linked for Sha'rawi with the idea of mastery, authority, and an empowered self; and it was linked in particular with the empowering of women to deal as equals with men. In Sha'rawi's account of Khadija, a poet who often came to visit with them during Sha'rawi's childhood and whose visits reinforced her "inclination" to poetry, the link is quite explicit. A room would be given over to the poet during her visit, to which the child would go every morning:

> I would find her under the mosquito net, writing in her papers. If I asked, "What are you writing?" She'd say, "poetry." I would ask her to read it to me and she would read what she had composed. I loved poetry so much then that I asked her to teach me to compose poetry. She said it required knowledge of a number of [linguistic] sciences, of grammar . . . of which I was completely ignorant. I admired this woman greatly because she attended men's gatherings and discoursed with them on literary and social matters, while the ignorant women I saw were full of fear, and their brow would break out in sweat if they happened to speak to a man, even from behind a curtain. I got from this the idea that women could equal men if not surpass them . . . and my admiration for her was all the greater and I longed to be like her, despite her ugliness. (P. 46)

In the short term, Sha'rawi's marriage interrupted such formal education as she had been receiving. For a time her access to education was confined to what she might glean from her brother's account of school and from his school books. The boy visited her faithfully every day on his return from school, and he sometimes left her his books "to amuse" herself with (p. 78). She probably read some fiction, for she tells of often carrying a book with her during this period specifically for the purpose of concealing her unhappiness: that is, if someone should see her in tears she could claim it was because of the sad events she was reading about. If this speculation is correct, then the fiction she was reading would have been Western, whether she read it in Arabic translation or in French. Books that might leave one in tears—novels and romances presumably—only began to be written in Arabic a few years later in the century. By the last decade of the nineteenth and first decade of the twentieth centuries, however, many such works were available in translation.

The marriage was not a happy one. After an initial period of kindness following their marriage, Sha'rawi's husband began forbidding her to visit her female friends and relatives, interrogating her about their conversations when they called on her, and sending her instructions, whenever she played the piano, to desist.

Marriage, however, and more particularly their separation fifteen months later, opened educational opportunities, both formal and informal, not available to an unmarried girl. Even before their separation, for example, Sha'rawi was invited to join a committee of socially prominent Egyptian women formed to organize aid to Turkey during its wars in the 1890s. This proved a highly educational experience and helped draw her out of her misery. It was her first "public, humanitarian" endeavor, and it made her aware for the first time of the individual's duty toward society and of the effectiveness of collaboration. It left her also with a new sense of her own value (p. 80).

Some short while after their marriage, Sha'rawi's husband, in breach of their marriage contract, secretly resumed seeing the woman (presumably a concubine) who had already borne him several children. Sha'rawi received the news from her mother by joyfully clapping her hands (to the astonishment of her mother, from whom she had concealed her unhappiness) and rushed to congratulate her similarly astounded husband on his concubine's pregnancy. Then she at once left their domicile for her mother's wing of the house, thus initiating the separation she was to maintain, despite the attempts of her husband and others to effect reconciliation, for seven years—years that were to be crucially formative in her education. She wrote, "I remained separated for seven years, and I shaped/created myself well in knowledge during the period" (p. 83). She resumed her French and piano lessons and, with an autonomy she had not enjoyed as an unmarried girl, arranged for a suitably elderly sheikh from the ancient university at Cairo to teach her Arabic. The household, however, soon put a stop to the Arabic lessons.

At this stage of her life, friendships also provided exposure to books and ideas. Four friendships were particularly important. One was with 'Adila Nabarawi, the daughter of a diplomat, who had been raised in

Paris and with whom Sha'rawi especially enjoyed going to the opera. Another close friend was a French woman of Sha'rawi's own age, the daughter of a neighbor. She visited Sha'rawi almost daily, and they would spend their time "reading French stories, and literature and poetry, or playing piano" (p. 85). A third friend was 'Atiyya, a woman in her thirties related to Sha'rawi's mother, who, in flight from a miserable marriage, took up residence with them for five years, during which period she and Sha'rawi became "like sisters," though 'Atiyaa was not much interested in the studies Sha'rawi invited her to join.

The fourth friend is presented as the most influential on the direction of Sha'rawi's life and the stances she was later to take as feminist leader. Sha'rawi met Mrs. Rushdi Pasha, a Frenchwoman, at a party, and they were drawn to each other. Soon after, in the course of a day's pleasure outing by boat down the Nile taken by Egyptian women and some European women, their friendship began to develop. Mrs. Rushdi had married an upper-class Egyptian and had converted to Islam, a conversion not merely of form, Sha'rawi reports her as saying. She was the author of a book on Egyptian women, which, she informed Sha'rawi, she had written with the objective of correcting the mistaken ideas of Europeans about the lives of Egyptian women (presumably their extreme oppression). She wanted to make them aware that matters were not so different from those experienced by European women. At the time Mrs. Rushdi was becoming friends with Sha'rawi, she was writing another work on Egyptian women, she informs Sha'rawi, this time to expose the distressing realities Egyptian women were in fact often subjected to because the society failed to respect the laws of Islam and instead followed customs that had departed from the Islamic code. Sha'rawi (whose most famous public act was that of casting off her veil in 1923) records that she often discussed the status of Egyptian women with Mrs. Rushdi, who, she recalls, considered the veil an unfortunate custom because, among other reasons, it stood in the way of women's education and physical activity. Sha'rawi notes also that Mrs. Rushdi was admired by such friends of Mr. Rushdi's as Qassim Amin (author, as noted earlier, of "The liberation of woman") and Mohamad 'Abdu, a leading Egyptian intellectual and public figure who also called for reform in the position of women. Mrs. Rushdi often spoke with these men, Sha'rawi informs us, and would later relay the content of their discussions to Sha'rawi, who, of course, at this stage of her life was segregated and could not meet and converse with her male contemporaries. Mrs. Rushdi, despite her "progressive" views, evidently also supported some of society's notions of proper conduct, for she had an important role in bringing about Sha'rawi's reconciliation with her husband (p. 103). She seems generally to have cast herself in the role of Sha'rawi's mentor as well as friend. She urged Sha'rawi to attend her weekly salons for women, helped her with her French, advised her on which books to read, and discussed with her those she read. Sha'rawi was immensely grateful for these attentions.

In about 1901, at the age of twenty-one or twenty-two, Sha'rawi returned to her husband. According to her account, her brother, who had become engaged, had vowed not to celebrate his marriage until she returned to her husband. Not wanting to stand in the way of her brother's happiness, she agreed to a reconciliation, but not before she stipulated certain conditions, to which her husband agreed. What those conditions were she does not say, but it is clear that she took up her marriage now as a mature young woman with her own views and a habit of independence. Dates are infrequently given for this period of her life and are difficult to establish, but after the birth of her two children and an initial preoccupation with them, particularly her daughter who as an infant was seriously ill, Sha'rawi reestablished her connections with friends. She keenly felt the loss of Mrs. Rushdi, who had died in 1908, but she set about the business—arranging meetings, attending and organizing lectures—of advancing the cause of women.

What Sha'rawi recounts of her friendships suggests an unmistakable pattern. Those with whom she shared books and ideas and intellectual pleasures were European (French) or, like 'Adila Nabarawi, who was raised in Paris, profoundly shaped by European ideas. The only friend she describes who does not belong in this category is also the friend who, she tells us, had no interest in books and book learning. Sha'rawi is thus herself identifying the West and Western influence, or more exactly people and books from the West, as the sources of her intellectual life. In addition, it is noteworthy with respect to Mrs. Rushdi that Sha'rawi not only writes of how grateful she was for her attention but also notes that Mrs. Rushdi talked to her of her ideas about and opposition to the veil and that she discussed with Sha'rawi the two books on Egyptian women she had written. Clearly, Sha'rawi's intention in detailing such points is that of acknowledging a debt to Mrs. Rushdi in the area in which Sha'rawi would distinguish herself.

That Sha'rawi herself traced the sources of her intellectual life and her feminism to ideas that came to her from Westerners, however, is not to say that she was entirely correct. Like many colonized people, she identified the colonizer as the source of enlightenment; she accepted and internalized the notion that advancement came from and with the West, and she believed herself personally indebted to Westerners and their ideas. In fact, the situation and the sources of her feminism are much more nuanced and complex than that. For example, Mrs. Rushdi's views on Egyptian women and on the veil, to which Sha'rawi reports herself indebted, were in no way novel or original views in Egypt in the 1890s. Since the 1830s, when Tahtawi had written advocating women's education, and when the first college to train women doctors was opened, the subjects of women's education, women's position, and finally the issue of veiling progressively became issues that Egyptian society grappled with, both on the level of social experimentation and in printed discussions published in books and newspapers. In the 1870s the state opened the first state-sponsored girls' schools and already whether schoolgirls should be veiled or unveiled was an issue. In the 1890s the issues of women's education and of the need for reform in conceptions of women's responsibilities were being discussed not only by men and some women writers in men's newspapers but also in women's journals—the first of which was launched in 1892. Even schoolgirls by this point were taking up these issues as a set topic for their presentations. Reporting on the examination results at the American College for Girls in 1890, for example, a journal noted that two of the graduating students spoke, one on "what women of the East have gained in the last fifty years," and the other on "the role of women in society."[18] Two of the men that Sha'rawi mentions Mrs. Rushdi had discussions with, Mohamad 'Abdu and Qassim Amin, were both figures who joined in this debate initiated by Egyptian intellectuals earlier in the century and who took strong stands on the need for social reform, 'Abdu in variety of fields, including in matters affecting women, and Amin specifically on the position of women. Mrs. Rushdi's views on the veil and her opinion that the low status of women in Muslim countries was due to un-Islamic customs that a regenerated Islam should cast off in fact reiterated the positions that, by the 1890s, were those of liberal Egyptian intellectuals. These points thus suggest that Mrs. Rushdi's role, through books addressed to Europeans and her conversations with Sha'rawi, was essentially that of a mediator and conduit of the ideas of Egyptian intellectuals, rather than originator herself of such ideas. Thus, while Sha'rawi was in her debt for conveying the ideas, she was in reality indebted for the ideas themselves to the climate of the day among the intellectual and social leaders of Egyptian society. All this is not to deny but only to set in perspective Sha'rawi's subjective perception of a debt to Westerners and Western ideas.

How the reading of novels and the sharing of conversations with

18. *Al-Lata'if,* 15 June 1890, cited in Bryon D. Cannon, "Nineteenth Century Arabic Writings on Women and Society: The Interim Role of the Masonic Press in Cairo (*Al-Lata'if,* 1850–1882," *International Journal of Middle East Studies* 17 (Nov. 1985): 476.

Western or Western-influenced friends shaped her ideas is finally imponderable but by no means necessarily of negligible importance. Also imponderable in the final analysis are some of the elements of the familial setting—particularly polygamy—which seem unexpectedly to have formed a source of strength for women and endowed them with an innate sense of self-worth and authority. It is remarkable that Sha'rawi undertook what was arguably her most daring and authoritative act at the age of about thirteen, when her exposure to Western ideas was minimal. It was then that she took the defiant and powerful step of leaving her marriage and insisting on her right to a separation. She not only took that position but stood immovably by it until the resumption of her marriage was no longer a threat to her sense of herself and her interests and concerns in life. The act speaks volumes about her early sense of her right to autonomy, her right to follow her moral code, even in the face of opposition from mother, husband, and every male or female authority they mustered to their aid.

8

Race, Gender, and Cultural Context
in Zora Neale Hurston's
Dust Tracks on a Road

Of late, scholars interested in minority group or women's autobiography have begun to challenge many of the epistemological assumptions of white Western male critics who are concerned only with the autobiographies of white Western male subjects. These scholars have denied the universality of the criteria put forth by several of the most prestigious "deans" of the genre as requirements for the successful production of autobiography, particularly the view that individualism is the most important factor in the Western autobiographical endeavor.[1] Scholars opposed to this view have demonstrated that for those outside the dominant group, identification with community is pervasive for the unalienated self in life and writing. For instance, Susan Stanford Friedman (relying heavily on the work of Nancy Chodorow on the psychology of gender socialization and that of Sheila Rowbotham's, on the role of cultural representation and material conditions in the formation of "women's consciousness") points out that the importance of group identification repeatedly surfaces in womens' and minority group autobiographies. It is vital, Friedman notes, in theory as well as in practice, for it enables these individuals to move beyond alienation within the dominant culture to construct meaningful lives in writing and otherwise. Community identity permits the rejection of historically diminishing images of self imposed by the dominant culture; it allows marginalized individuals to embrace alternative selves constructed from positive (and more authentic) images of their own creation. Such im-

---

1. See *Autobiography: Essays Theoretical and Critical,* ed. James Olney (Princeton: Princeton University Press, 1980). In this collection, the essay by Georges Gusdorf, is one of the most respected by those who accept the idea of individualism as a central force in Western autobiography. The collection contains essays that subscribe to and disagree with this theory.

175

ages, Friedman insists, come from the merging of the individual with a collective group identity and not from within the individualist, isolated self.[2]

Critics of Afro-American autobiography have also subscribed to the collective nature of the genre for blacks.[3] In one of the earliest studies on the subject, Stephen Butterfield noted the conscious political nature of black autobiography from its beginnings to the present. The black self, he says, is conceived as part of a group, with inseparable "ties and responsibilities" to the rest of the group in the creation of the individual self in narrative.[4] Among others, William L. Andrews, in his comprehensive study of the first century of Afro-American autobiography, reinforces Butterfield's political argument by asserting that the antebellum slave narrative provided the "rhetorical mode that would conduct the battle against racism and slavery on grounds other than those already occupied by pro- and antislavery polemics." In the context of the social situation of black people within American culture, the early Afro-American autobiography revised the "myths and ideals of America's culture-defining scriptures . . . [and demanded] new insight of white readers to recognize the ways in which [black] autobiography had [also] become a mode of Afro-American scripture."[5] Stated differently, in all aspects of its creation, early black autobiography altered the terms for the production of Western autobiography as they had been defined by the dominant culture. The central aim remained the promotion of an authentic self-in-writing, and that self originated from a source other than the alienated self within the dominant culture. Critics opposing the individualistic model agree that identity originates not in the self but in relationship to the other within the culture of the self's unique community.

The theoretical framework on which the autobiographies of black women in America are constructed is located at the intersection of the creative processes that form white female and black male selves. As Elizabeth Fox-Genovese argues, it is not enough to say simply that black women suffer the double oppression of race and gender and to regard the autobiographies as the mathematically predictable result of

2. Susan Stanford Friedman, "Women's Autobiographical Selves: Theory and Practice," in *The Private Self: Theory and Practice in Women's Autobiographical Writings,* ed. Shari Benstock (Chapel Hill: University of North Carolina Press, forthcoming).

3. I deliberately used the lowercase *b* for black and *w* for white. Most Afro-American, as well as other, scholars agree that the terms *black* and *white* are purely descriptive.

4. Stephen Butterfield, *Black Autobiography in America* (Amherst: University of Massachusetts Press, 1974), p. 3.

5. William L. Andrews, *To Tell a Free Story: The First One Hundred Years of Afro-American Autobiography* (Urbana: Illinois University Press, 1986), pp. 5, 14.

this dual oppression. For the identity of these women is grounded "in the historical experience of being black and female in a specific society at a specific moment and over succeeding generations," and this recognition demands a "theory and method that respects . . . the distinctiveness" of the group.[6] In constructing their personal narratives, black women negotiate the dangerous shoals of white male and female race and class oppression and white and black male sexism. Connected to black men by the history of class and race, to white women by sex and configurations of gender roles, and to both by the politics of writing from the outside, they have, from the beginning, created unique selves-in-writing to document their individual and collective experiences.

Differences between the autobiographies of women and men have been evident within the Afro-American tradition from its beginning. In spite of the common racial experience and some shared qualities, women's slave narratives diverged in content and emphasis from those of the men. For instance, women who escaped from slavery stressed family ties, identified with older female relatives, and wrote of a supportive community of white and black women within the dominant patriarchy to a far greater extent than did men.[7] Slave women who escaped often credited the efforts of others, black men as well as black and white women, for their good fortune. Male escapees were more inclined to take full credit for individual initiative and bravery. To some extent, differences in the processes of male and female identity formation among black slaves influenced these differing perspectives on self. First, although racism threatened the identity of all black slaves, both male and female, sexism ensured the black female her sexual identity. In a world dominated by white men, not only did the absence of black male authority figures have a negative effect on the self-concept of male slave children, but this condition was doubtless exacerbated by the continual degradation of adult male slaves, especially in their roles as husbands and fathers. Equally important, in the face of their oppression, young female slaves could expect the support of mothers, grandmothers, and other female relatives and friends and could depend on them for maternal nurturing well beyond childhood. And as each female slave matured she assumed similar responsibility for girls and younger women. In addition, white women within the slavocracy occasionally formed se-

6. Elizabeth Fox-Genovese, "To Write Myself: The Autobiographies of Afro-American Women," in *Feminist Issues in Literary Scholarship*, ed. Shari Benstock (Bloomington: Indiana University Press, 1987), p. 161.

7. In *To Tell a Free Story*, Andrews discusses differences in male and female narratives. Also see Frances Foster, "'In Respect to Females . . .': Difference in the Portrayals of Women by Male and Female Narrators," *Black American Literature Forum* 15 (Summer 1981): 66–70.

cret bonds with black women against the oppressive white male world.[8] In the world of slave children the models for strong black female identity formation were considerably more accessible than they were for black males.

After the Civil War, the rhetoric of black men's and women's narratives moved closer together, united by group efforts against discrimination and racism and the struggle to secure human rights for all black people. Ida Wells Barnett's *Crusade For Justice* (1970), published almost seventy years after her death, and Mary Church Terrell's *A Black Women in a White World*, published in 1940 when she was more than eighty years old, present good examples of the representative black female self engaged in the collective struggle for black human dignity in much the same way as W. E. B. Du Bois or Walter White. For forty years Barnett, a journalist, was one of the most valuable workers in the antilynching campaign of the late nineteenth and early twentieth centuries. She ignored threats against her own life, often visiting the sites of recent lynchings to collect firsthand information that could be used to seek legal redress. Her autobiography, like the slave narratives, documents the group terror perpetrated against the entire black community. Terrell, an educator and one of the first black women to graduate from Oberlin College, was a tireless worker for black civil rights and black women's rights. Although her class and Caucasian features insulated her from a great many of the indignities that poor black people suffered, she chose to identify with the problems of the group and shaped her narrative around issues of race, gender, and class oppression. "Negro Uplift" was the rallying cry among blacks between the 1870s and the 1920s, a slogan that had great impact on the autobiographies of black men and women of that period.

Many black women continued in the tradition of autobiography centered upon their overt political activities on behalf of the black community into the late twentiety century, as Daisy Bates's *The Long Shadow of Little Rock* (1970), Angela Davis's *Autobiography* (1975), and Anne Moody's *Coming of Age in Mississippi* (1970) indicate. But others, while remaining solidly within the racial community, have grounded their identities in more narrowly focused community issues. They show concerns for the welfare of black youth and for health and education in the black community. Gender issues have also become more prominent, and black women focus on black female development and on black

8. In *To Tell a Free Story*, pp. 249–63, Andrews shows how some white women secretly helped black women in their fight against white slave owners, especially when the issues were connected to sexism. Also see Minrose C. Gwinn, *Black and White Women of the Old South* (Knoxville: University of Tennessee Press, 1985), for an extended discussion of women's cross-racial relations in the South in American literature.

women's lives as well. It is not surprising that twentiety-century auto-biographies by black female schoolteachers are exceeded in number only by those of twentieth-century black female entertainers.

The audience for the black narrative has changed since the nineteenth century, when part of the aim of Afro-American autobiography was to persuade white men and women that people of color were just as human as white people and deserving of humane treatment. Today's black writer addresses a sophisticated multiracial audience through a text that lends itself to multiple levels of reading. At the same time, the issues have become more diverse, sometimes less overtly political and more personal. Nevertheless, group identity remains at the center of the self emerging from contemporary black male and female personal narra-tives. For black women, this group identification also denotes a self that trancends socially imposed limits of race, class, and gender. Black female autobiographers perceive their triumphs and failures against a background of the historical experiences of the women who went before them; they respect their voice-enabling traditions, but they are not af-raid to revise the terms of discourse in the interests of personal freedom and autonomy.

Among the most problematical of autobiographies by black women is Zora Neale Hurston's *Dust Tracks on a Road,* first published in 1942. By that date Hurston was a seasoned writer; she had already published three novels and two collections of folklore, generating a good deal of critical controversy. *Dust Tracks* sold well, and the book received favorable reviews in several influential newspapers and magazines. The *Saturday Review* even awarded Hurston a prize of one thousand dollars for the book's "contributions to race relations." Most critics, however, have expressed keen disappointment in this book.[9] Even those who most admire Hurston's work for its delineation of the values of black folk culture and its representation of women who transcend the stereotypes so often presented in black and white American literature, have had trouble with *Dust Tracks.* Much has been written about the "lies" in the autobiography, its evasions and lack of honest self-disclosure, including Hurston's misrepresentation of the date of her birth, which confuses the historical context in which the events of her life occurred—her devia-tions from the strict patterns that defined early black autobiography, and her nonconfrontational racial politics. To the Hurston scholar none of these charges is wholly unexpected. Hurston rejected racial group

9. See Robert Hemenway, *Zora Neale Hurston: A Literary Biography* (Urbana: University of Illinois Press, 1977), p. 288. In this comprehensive biography of Hurston, as well as in his introduction to the recent edition of the autobiography, Hemenway strongly criticizes *Dust Tracks.* Fox-Genovese, "I Write Myself," also discusses some of the failings of this book.

oppression as a characteristic identity trait. She preferred to celebrate black strength and transcendence. In the autobiography and elsewhere, her statements provoked the wrath of black civil rights activists and other black writers, who complained that her quest for individualism was detrimental to the group fight for racial justice.

In the tradition of black women's autobiographies, *Dust Tracks* is a transitional text, in which Hurston makes a radical break with rhetorical patterns in the slave narrative and opens the way for even bolder experiments with form and content.[10] *Dust Tracks* is the first autobiography of a black woman who is a creative writer, but it does not reveal intimate details of the writer's life. Nor is it a polemic on racial injustice. Yet, even though she blatantly rejects the idea of her autobiography as a race-representative document, Hurston never separates herself from the black community. Instead, in her bid for independence she changes the traditional system of signs and shatters the boundaries of previous forms of black self-representation. For example, in place of the former slave's overweening claims to "authentic" self-representation, as Fox-Genovese observes, Hurston, without much subtlety, offers her text as the "statue" of the "self" she wishes the world to see.[11] Hurston's "life" and her autobiography are not one and the same; nor did she intend them to be. It is unproductive to continue to focus on the discrepancies between text and life, however problematical. Instead, we need to find new areas to explore. We need to come to terms with the very conflicts out of which the text was made, or what Barbara Johnson refers to as Hurston's strategies rather than her truths.[12]

It is useful to keep in mind that Hurston was not the first black writer to create an image that did not offer a wholly accurate reading of the self. In "The Literature of the Slave," Henry Louis Gates, Jr., examines new biographies of Frederick Douglass which reveal the discrepancies among Douglass's three narratives. Douglass was less interested in documenting facts than in employing rhetorical strategies that enabled him to replace the erroneous identity the dominant culture had bestowed on him with an "equally fictitious," "stolid black self." His inaccuracies do

---

10. Here I think especially of Gwendolyn Brook's *Report from Part One*, an autobiography that visually resembles a collage, and reads like a long prose poem.

11. Zora Neale Hurston, *Dust Tracks on a Road*, ed. Robert Hemenway (Urbana: Illinois University Press, 1984), p. 34, hereafter cited in the text. See Fox-Genovese, p. 173, for her comment on the anxieties in Hurston's question "What if there is no me like my statue?" Many critics of Hurston, including Nathan Huggins and Barbara Johnson, have observed that Hurston's manipulation of language leaves us wondering who fooled whom?

12. Barbara Johnson, "Thresholds of Difference: Structures of Address in Zora Neale Hurston, *"Race," Writing, and Difference,* ed. Henry Louis Gates, Jr. (Chicago: University of Chicago Presss, 1986), p. 324.

not diminish his historical standing, nor was Douglass an anomaly among black autobiographers. Gates concludes that a significant aspect of the black autobiographical tradition is "the positing of fictive black selves in language, in a mode of discourse traditionally defined by large claims for the self. The self, in this sense, does not exist as an entity but as a coded system of signs, arbitrary in reference."[13] In attempting to cope with the powerlessness and vulnerability of the racial self, blacks have employed language strategies, particularly artifice and concealment, in their relations with white America. Even though audience strongly influences the nature of both the hidden and the fictive black self, and Douglass's audience was extremely different from Hurston's, one has little difficulty recognizing that *Dust Tracks* conforms to the paradigm Gates identifies. Hurston's claim of impartiality toward race, for instance, is only one of the "large" claims that emerge from her book. Also important with regard to issues of identity and self-representation is Hurston's depiction of the cultural context of portions of her early life.

As the narrator of her text, Hurston's position is analagous to her childhood "seat on the top of the gate-post" in the all-black township of Etonville, "the first Negro community in America . . . to be incorporated [in the 1870s], the first attempt at organized self-government" on the part of black people (p. 4). From here, she watched the world go by and often, defying her parents, walked a short distance with white travelers passing through town (p. 45). Barbara Johnson has noted that this "lucrative" activity (travelers often gave her silver coins to "speak pieces" and sing for them), presages the position Hurston would often occupy in later life, somewhere between the white world and the black.[14]

As a child, in addition to the financial rewards of the gatepost seat, Hurston loved the attention it brought her and the "show" she could enjoy as both audience and actor. There is little question that the adult woman continued, in similar roles, to enjoy the "show," and unfortunately, *Dust Tracks* has often been perceived as another instance of "speaking pieces" to the white world for no more than "silver change."

13. Henry Louis Gates, Jr., *Figures in Black: Words, Signs, and the "Racial" Self* (New York: Oxford University Press, 1987), pp. 119, 123.

14. Johnson, p. 318. In "How It Feels to Be Colored Me," *World Tomorrow* 11 (May 1928): 215–16, Hurston admitted that passersby generously gave her silver coins for her "gate-post" performances. Hurston's time as a student at Barnard College, during which she refers to herself as "Barnard's sacred black cow" (*Dust Tracks,* p. 169), and her association with Mrs. Osgood Mason, the woman who supported her through much of the time she did anthropological research in the South, are two instances when she must have felt herself literally stationed between the black and the white worlds.

Hurston's reluctance to write her autobiography and the outcome of the pressure put on her to do so are well known. At the time she needed money, a situation familiar to her throughout her adult life. Lippincott, her publisher, insisted on the autobiography in place of the novel she was trying to write, but as she confided to a friend later, it was not an easy project for her to undertake.[15] Considering the conflicts she had previously experienced with black intellectuals, Hurston no doubt could have predicted the negative reaction they would have toward *Dust Tracks*. In Eatonville her family had often punished her for her gatepost activities; in New York, among the Harlem literati, her punishment was denunciation.

Elizabeth Fox-Genovese claims that "the tension at the heart of black women's autobiography derives in large part from the chasm between the autobiographer's intuitive sense of herself and her attitude toward her probable reader."[16] The statement seems fully justified in *Dust Tracks*. Pressured to undertake the project, Hurston found it impossible to reveal her "self" in the genre. She produced a fictive self that, ironically, seemed to deepen the chasm between the autobiographer and her black audience while bridging the gap between her and her white readers. Despite appearances, however, it is entirely possible, given her aptitude with coded signals and her many language poses in this book, that Hurston was playing the trickster on all her readers.

It is significant to note, especially in the first part of *Dust Tracks*, that Hurston reinforced her identity within the black community not as autobiographer but as self-appointed cultural interpreter for the community from which she came. As the only southerner associated with the Harlem Renaissance, Hurston carried out this role as few others could. She knew that the qualities of black culture which the artists in that movement were striving to capture resided in folklore. Unlike most of them, she also knew that the folk represented not an aesthetic or a spiritual force to be merely intellectualized in art but rather a people struggling for life in all its positive and negative aspects. There can be no question that the narrator of *Dust Tracks* derives her identity from rural black people and takes her stance as their cultural interpreter. In this respect, Hurston's claims on Eatonville verify the contention of Mary G. Mason, Susan Friedman, and others that women form their identities by linking the individual self with "another consciousness." Friedman and Mason also argue that unlike white male autobiographers, women and minorities discover identity through acknowledgment and recogni-

15. Hemenway, *Zora Neale Hurston*, p. 278.
16. Fox-Genovese, p. 169.

tion of another presence.[17] Regina Blackburn and Bernice Johnson Reagon have made similar claims for black women's identity formation.[18]

Hurston's narrative opens with the announcement that before she can inform her readers about her "self," she must make them aware of the "time and place" from which she comes and to which she rightly belongs, since those things were the "materials that went to make [her]" (p. 3). Although the promise of self-revelation against the background of the group is never satisfactorily fulfilled, the collective self of Eatonville with which she identifies comprises the racial and female selves that are evident inside and outside of *Dust Tracks*. In respect to race, the community Hurston claims might strike us as romantically idealized, but the specialness of its history is in the deprivileging of and liberation from the supremacy of American slave history over other aspects of the black American experience. Eatonville, in Hurston's mythology, may initially have come into being as the result of the thirst for more adventure by three white soldiers of fortune at the close of the Civil War, but the men had fought on the side of right and later established their own domain on principles modeled from the ideals of democracy as these had never been envisioned by the framers of the American Constitution. Black people arrived, first in white Maitland, then in black Eatonville, adjacent to Maitland, in the late 1870s and the 1880s not in slave ships or on chain gangs but of their own free will. They stayed because the work was easier than what they had left behind in the bordering states, the pay was good, and there was an opportunity for them to live without the constant fears and indignities of unrelenting racial hostility. In Eatonville they flourished and kept their culture and closeness to nature, not losing them to the onslaught of industry and mechanization as their children would do in the next century in the North. Jean Toomer immortalized the remnants of these "back-country" people in his modern classic, *Cane*, the first full-length book to emerge from the Harlem Renaissance.[19]

In assuming the role of the historian-storyteller as the point of departure for her personal story, Hurston remains faithful to the tradition of collective responsibility that is the hallmark of black and women's auto-

---

17. Mary G. Mason, "The Other Voice: Autobiographies of Women Writers," this volume; Friedman, "Women's Autobiographical Selves."

18. See Regina Blackburn, "In Search of the Black Female Self: African-American Women's Autobiographies and Ethnicity," in *Women's Autobiography: Essays in Criticism,* ed. Estelle C. Jelinek (Bloomington: Indiana University Press, 1980), pp. 133–48; Bernice Johnson Reagon, "My Black Mothers and Sisters; or, On Beginning a Cultural Autobiography," *Feminist Studies* 8 (Spring 1982): 81–95, cited by Friedman.

19. Jean Toomer, *Cane* (New York: Boni and Liveright, 1923).

biography. But she revises the terms of that collectivity as it had previously appeared in black autobiography. As narrator, she resembles more the African *griot*, whose memory preserves the sense of a past culture, than the political activist in the struggle to improve contemporary black life. In this she foreshadows later characters in black women's literature, such as Paule Marshall's Merle, the protagonist in her novel *The Chosen Place, the Timeless People*, who insists on teaching the children the history of their ancestors' resistance to slavery.[20] Hurston initially finds her "self" as part of a black community with a history of autonomy that it is generally believed black people in America never possessed. The idea and existence of Eatonville constituted the kind of radical thought and act in American history which mirrored her own attitudes toward white-over-black authority.

The narrative continues with the story of Hurston's immediate family. If race is her first reference point for identity, it did not take her a long time to discover that gender was as powerful a force to deal with within the racial community, inside and outside of her family. Hurston's mother, Lucy Ann Potts Hurston, although a diminutive woman, was a great deal stronger in character and will and abler in mind than her robust husband, John. She was the source of and guide for his civic, religious, and social successes, and she encouraged her children, including her daughter, to "jump at de sun." She did not want to "squinch [their] spirit[s]." Forced at times to defend the child against her husband's anger, Lucy Potts Hurston claimed this daughter's disposition as her own. Hurston enjoyed a warm and satisfying relationship with her mother. "Mama never tried to break me," she wrote of the times when her high spirits carried her away. Often she would confide to her mother the stories she had made up, although other family members saw the tales as "lies"—the work of the devil. Lucy Potts Hurston would "listen sometimes, and sometimes she wouldn't. But she never seemed displeased" (p.72). On her deathbed, it was to nine-year-old Zora that her mother confided her final wishes. The little girl could not carry them out, but she grieved the loss of her mother for a long time.

Lucy Potts Hurston was not the only woman in Eatonville from whom Hurston learned to resist restrictive gender roles. One chapter in *Dust Tracks*, "My Folks" (it might well have borne the title "My Women Folks"), celebrates the strength of the women in Hurston's early life,

20. Paule Marshall, *The Chosen Place, The Timeless People* (New York: Vintage Press, 1969). The novel is set in a West Indian island that was a British colony. Merle Kinbona, the protagonist, like Hurston, is out of step with many of her cohort group because of her concern for the internal life of the "little fella." She loses her job as a schoolteacher because she insists on teaching black revolutionary history to the island children rather than the English history that had been mandated for them.

women who successfully asserted themselves in a world in which men attempted to dominate them. But Lucy Potts Hurston was the most important influence. The death of the mother was also the death of the child, for with her mother's passing out of life Hurston passed from the innocence and freedom of childhood into the world of responsibility to the self. "That moment [of death] was the end of a phase in my life," she wrote. "I was old before my time with grief of loss. . . . No matter what the others did, my mother had put her trust in me. . . . Mama died at sundown and changed a world" (p. 89). If Hurston took her racial identity from the autonomous black community of Eatonville, she derived her gender identity from the communion of closeness that she felt with her mother. In her self-representation she was her mother's child—an example of the continuity Friedman finds in mother-daughter relationships.[21]

As Hurston tells her story, her childhood behavior in Eatonville reflects her choice of an identity that would later transcend socially imposed boundaries of race and gender. In "The Inside Search," the longest and most reflective chapter in the narrative, self-representation unveils a portrait foreshadowing the woman who refused to subscribe to collective black oppression, who insisted upon the inherent richness and emotional security of the nonmaterialistic, preurban black culture. While still very young, Hurston confided to her best friend, Carrie Roberts, a desire to walk to the edge of the horizon to see what the "end of the world was like" (p. 36). She asked her friend to accompany her because she thought she was too young to face the hazards of such a journey alone. At first Carrie agreed, but then she reneged on her promise. Zora was angry but undeterred. If Carrie would not go with her on this great adventure, she would wait for a time when she could ride a horse and so make the trip by herself. "For weeks," she said, "I saw myself sitting astride of a fine horse. My shoes had sky-blue bottoms to them, and I was riding off to look at the belly-band of the world" (p. 38).

Nor did the matter end there. Later that same year, when asked by her father what she wanted for Christmas, Hurston requested "a fine black riding horse with white leather saddle and bridle" (p. 38). The request so stunned her father that she escaped a whipping only by making a hasty retreat from the room. Hurston retaliated by resorting to her imagination. "Since Papa would not buy me a saddle horse I made me one up. No one around me knew how often I rode my prancing horse, nor the things I saw in far places" (p. 39). This was the kind of imagination and strong will that characterized the Hurston we know from the rest of her

21. Friedman, "Women's Autobiographical Selves."

writings and the more factual biography. They carried her into strange and sometimes dangerous times and places, especially during much of her anthropological research in Florida and the West Indies; and among her peers of the Harlem Renaissance and beyond they made her the "uppity" black woman who insisted on going her separate way.

The reaction of Hurston's father to her request for a saddle horse was consonant with what he imagined her place in the world to be, as defined by race and gender. John Hurston had come from Alabama, escaping, only after marriage, the backbreaking work and dehumanization of the southern black sharecropper. Having done so, he did not intend to transgress against the status quo. Eatonville afforded him a place to avoid the racial conflicts he had seen in his youth, but he did not intend to raise his children with illusions that they would ever be safe from the kind of vulnerability he must have felt. He shared the attitudes of perhaps the majority of southern black parents of that time, who, out of concern for the safety of their children, tried to modify the goals and behavior of those of the younger generation who seemed to be stepping outside the realm of white-accepted black behavior.[22] John Hurston was particularly distressed by his daughter's audacity, and he often predicted that she would come to no good end. It was not the fantasy of riding to the edge of the horizon that upset him but the idea that a black girl child would dare to formulate such a dream and then imagine herself carrying it out on no less than a black horse with white leather saddle and bridle, as though she were white and male.

Although the story may well be one of the large claims that Hurston makes for herself in *Dust Tracks*, the truth or fiction of the child's request is not the issue. The anecdote is as important to the image that Hurston projected of herself as her romanticized depiction of Eatonville, and it is her strategy of self-representation that is the interesting element. In the depiction of Afro-American autonomy in Eatonville and in the young girl's wish for a horse can be seen a deliberately constructed explanation of Hurston's later refusals to conform to the expectations of either the black or the white world. By foregrounding her rejection of certain limitations on her individuality, her childhood rebellion and transcendence, the woman manages to remain within the community identity while asserting the self from it. Other people in the community were like Carrie, for whom Zora's scheme was "too bold." They were not as brave or imaginative or willing to take the risks Hurston found exciting, and she did not understand why not.

22. See Richard Wright, *Black Boy* (New York: Harper and Row, 1945), for an account of how young black boys in the South were treated by their parents as a way of teaching them how to stay alive.

Like many other writers, Hurston's fell in love with books when she was very young; her preference was for tales of fantastic adventure, carried out by heroic men—Thor and Odin, Hercules, Moses, and King David among them. At the same time, her youthful admiration for strong black women did not extend to an identification with most girls of her age group, for she was not drawn to "lady-like" activities. She preferred to play with boys and was as tough as they were. Dolls, except the ones she made for herself, looked "too different" from her, and "caught the devil around" her, getting into fights, leaking sawdust, jumping off the barn, and trying to drown themselves in the lake. Driven inward by an active imagination, she describes her unseen life as rich and exciting: "My soul was with the gods and my body in the village. People just would not act like Gods. . . . Raking back yards and carrying out chamber pots, were not the tasks of Thor. I wanted to be away from drabness and to stretch my limbs in some mighty struggle" (p. 56). Eatonville's racial autonomy and the hardy, aggressive black women there gave her a secure identity, but her own spirit needed wider spheres in which to find fulfillment. As a child, she says, she was happiest when she was alone in the woods, where she made friends with all of nature. She had a special feeling for one large tree, which she named the "loving pine." The symbolism can hardly be lost on us.

In Eatonville, the favorite communal pastime was storytelling. At the end of the day's work, this was the town's entertainment. Long before she could fully understand the importance of her curiosity, Hurston was drawn to the stories she heard on the porch of Joe Clark's store, "the heart and spring of the town." Here in "lying sessions," the men "strain[ed] against each other in telling folktales" (p. 63). As a child, Hurston greatly enjoyed the yarns they spun, but "lying" was a man's prerogative. The store was a male province that admitted women only to congregate around the porch on Saturday nights or to order household provisions, so testifying to the prosperity and generosity of their men. But if women were forbidden to participate in the male ritual, there was no forbidding the mind of the child Zora, who not only made up stories of her own but used "the glints and gleams of what [she] heard [on the porch] and stored away" for her own tales. She even recalls some of her most delightful early creations. Years later, after college, she returned to Eatonville and its environs and collected many of those tales in her celebrated *Mules and Men*.

Dust Tracks on a Road is a deliberately staged work, and Hurston knew exactly what she wanted her readers to know. In its considered design, she presents her life as a search for autonomy, which she claimed no less in "autobiography" than in her better-received works. If the text lacks self-disclosure and bombards us with factual inaccuracies, its absence of bombast and arrogance, for one of Hurston's standing, is also quite remarkable. Unlike many other writers of the Harlem Renaissance, as Hazel Carby notes, Hurston had no literary class confrontation in the milieu in which she wrote. She was free to establish her reputation as a representative of the "people" through a reconstruction of the "folk," who figured so prominently in the early stages of her identity formation.[23]

If *Dust Tracks on a Road* is Hurston's statue, it celebrates a black woman who wanted us to know that very early in her life she decided to ride to the horizon on the finest black riding horse with the shiniest bridle and saddle she could secure. The fact that she was black and a woman did little to dampen her enthusiasm or willingness to go. Equally important, if one of her desires for her book was to present a more balanced view of the effects of racism on black life, it was not because Hurston was unaware of the seriousness of racial politics. She simply refused to accept the oppression of blacks as a definition of her life. And she did not want to contribute to the race literature of her day. By 1942 Hurston had "touched the four corners of [her] horizon." *Dust Tracks on a Road* gave her a chance to pull it in, and like Janie Killicks Starks Woods in *Their Eyes Were Watching God*, to drape it over her shoulder for a moment. In the act of creating her life-in-writing Hurston brought to consciousness a special understanding of her own experiences at a particular moment in her own time. Factually accurate or not, *Dust Tracks* presents a view of black female identity that justifies its existence. We need not only be concerned about Hurston's answer to: "What if there is no me in my statue?"

23. Hazel Carby, "The Quicksands of Representation: Race, Sex and Class in the Black Text" (Unpublished paper, American Studies Association, San Diego, Nov. 1985).

9

Structures of Liberation: Female Experience and Autobiographical Form in Quebec

Mary Jean Green

Among critics who have devoted their attention to autobiographies written by women, there is ready agreement that these works challenge critical assumptions about autobiography as a genre, assumptions that have developed primarily through the study of male autobiographers. In the growing corpus of critical work on women's autobiographical writings, certain traits have repeatedly been noted as characteristic of these gender-marked narratives.

One such feature is a focus on relationships with others rather than, as in men's autobiographies, on the development and successful accomplishments of the self. In her examination of the earliest women's autobiographies written in English, Mary G. Mason finds that "the self-discovery of female identity seems to acknowledge the real presence and recognition of another consciousness, and the disclosure of female self is linked to the identification of some 'other.'"[1] Estelle Jelinek, too, in the introduction to her collection of essays on women's autobiography, notes an "emphasis by women on the personal, especially on other people."[2] The stress on relationships with others which feminist literary critics have found in women's autobiographies would seem to bear out the findings of much recent work on female development. In particular, Nancy Chodorow's influential study *The Reproduction of Mothering* stresses that, because of the nature of the mother-daughter relationship, women's sense of self is continuous with others and that, unlike men, women experience themselves relationally.[3]

1. Mary G. Mason, "The Other Voice: Autobiographies of Women Writers," this volume.
2. *Women's Autobiography: Essays in Criticism,* ed. Estelle C. Jelinek (Bloomington: Indiana University Press, 1980), p. 10.
3. Nancy Chodorow, *The Reproduction of Mothering: Psychoanalysis and the Sociology of Gender* (Berkeley: University of California Press, 1978).

In women's literary works, the other may function in a variety of ways. An important central figure may serve as an alter ego, as is the case in Simone de Beauvoir's autobiography, which is shaped by her relationships with her childhood friend Zaza and, subsequently, with Jean-Paul Sartre. Alternatively, relationships with several others may give rise to a series of episodes, as, most notably, in Lillian Hellman's *Pentimento,* where each section is centered around a particular person.[4]

The others who preoccupy female autobiographers generally belong to the world of their personal and private experience rather than to the wider domain of political history, which has long been the favorite subject of male autobiography. Apparently, even in autobiographies written by women who have actively participated in public life the private sphere receives relative emphasis. This phenomenon is perhaps not without its relevance to the fact that women's autobiographies have often been treated as marginal texts, as women's life experiences themselves have been treated as historically marginal.[5] As Jelinek points out, "The consensus among critics is that a good autobiography not only focuses on its author but also reveals his connectedness to the rest of society; it is representative of his times, a mirror of his era."[6]

Another recurrent characteristic of female autobiography is an apparent formlessness. Jelinek notes that the narratives of women's lives are "often not chronological and progressive but disconnected, fragmentary," and she speculates that such discontinuous forms may tend to mirror the "fragmented, interrupted and formless nature of their [women's] lives."[7] This "formlessness" of women's autobiography becomes most evident when the life studies of women are contrasted with the highly structured autobiographies of men. Annette Kolodny, in her discussion of critical response to Kate Millett's *Flying,* is led to question the "heritage of male autobiography," which seems to prescribe a certain type of structured literary form. Arguing that "the fine distinctions between public and private, or trivial and important, which had served as guides for the male autobiographer have never really been available to

4. See Marcus K. Billson and Sidonie A. Smith, "Lillian Hellman and the Strategy of the 'Other'" in *Women's Autobiography,* pp. 163–79.

5. Gerda Lerner, for example, notes that the criteria of historical significance have long been defined by men and in relation to male-dominated activities, a situation that the study of "women's history" is beginning to change. Lerner quotes her predecessor Mary Beard on this point: "History consists of threads . . . selected from men's activities in war, business and politics, woven together according to a pattern of male prowess and power as conceived in the mind of man. If the woman's culture came into this pattern in any way, it is only as a blurring of a major concept" (*The Majority Finds Its Past* [1979; rpt., New York: Oxford University Press, 1981], p. xxii). See also Lerner's introduction to *The Female Experience* (Indianapolis: Bobbs-Merrill, 1977).

6. Jelinek, p. 7.

7. Jelinek, pp. 17, 19.

women," Kolodny asserts that "any demand that women write the same kind of formal, distilled narrative we usually get from men implies a belief that women share the same kind of reality as men; clearly, this is not the case."[8] Because women's autobiographies often fail to conform to the criteria of "orderliness, wholeness or a harmonious shaping,"[9] which have been used to characterize autobiography in general, a number of feminist critics have argued that the study of women's autobiographical writing calls for an extension of the definition of the genre to include such less-structured literary forms as memoirs and even diaries or journals.[10]

Nancy Miller, in her investigation of autobiography in the work of Colette, has pointed out that the traditional limitations of the genre pose other problems for the reader who seeks the "inscription of a *female* self."[11] Referring to the work of Philippe Lejeune, whose *Autobiographie en France* has established the autobiographical "canon" in French literature, Miller finds that much important writing about women's life experiences is excluded by Lejeune's insistence on the concept of an "autobiographical pact"—a pact that assures the reader of autobiography that the author, narrator, and main character are one and the same person. In Miller's view, women's formal autobiographies are often inadequate as a record of the authors' specifically female experience because of their tendency to exclude such experience—"to cast out the parts that don't add up"—in their attempt to present their lives in a way that can be universally understood: "One has the impression reading Stern, Sand, and Beauvoir that the determination to have their lives make sense and thus be susceptible to *universal* reception blinds them, as it were, to their own darkness; the '*submerged* core,' 'the sexual mystery that would make drama.'" In order to "provide a more sensitive apparatus deciphering a female self," Miller goes on to advocate a "dialectical practice of reading," a "double reading," of autobiography with fiction. This type of reading is well illustrated by Germaine Brée's study of the work of George Sand, where the triangular configuration of the child torn between mother and grandmother is seen to function as the "matrix of fabulation" for both Sand's autobiography and her fiction.[12]

Miller's restatement of the problematic of women's autobiography is

---

8. Annette Kolodny, "The Lady's Not for Spurning: Kate Millett and the Critics," in *Women's Autobiography*, pp. 240–41.

9. Jelinek, p. 19.

10. See especially Jelinek, p. 19; and Nancy K. Miller, "Writing Fictions: Women's Autobiography in France," this volume.

11. Miller, this volume.

12. Germaine Brée, "George Sand: The Fictions of Autobiography," *Nineteenth-Century French Studies* 4 (Summer 1976): 438–49.

an important point of departure for the study of women's use of autobiographical form in Quebec, because it opens the field of inquiry to
major works that fail to meet the conditions of Lejeune's autobiographical pact and whose status as autobiography is unclear on the basis of
external evidence. An important work of the literary explosion that
surrounded Quebec's *Révolution tranquille* is Marie-Claire Blais's trilogy *Manuscrits de Pauline Archange* (the second and third volumes were
published under the title *Vivre! Vivre!* and *Les Apparences*).[13] Blais's
trilogy does conform to what Lejeune calls the "internal" characteristics
of autobiography: "The retrospective narrative in prose that someone
writes about his own existence when he emphasizes his individual life,
in particular the history of his personality."[14] However, it fails to meet
the "external" criteria, since the author's name on the volume is not
Pauline Archange but Marie-Claire Blais. Although critics have per-
sistently suspected that the experiences of Pauline Archange closely re-
semble those of the author herself as a young girl and aspiring writer in
Quebec City,[15] such an identification cannot be made with certainty. It
has, indeed, been denied by the author[16]—who is, however, known for
guarding the privacy of her personal life. However this may be, Blais's
trilogy is clearly an important example of the use of autobiographical
form by a major woman writer to describe the experience of growing
up in Quebec. To attempt to draw the line between "fictional fiction"
and the "fictions of autobiography" may prove to be an impossible and,
as Miller and Brée have shown, largely meaningless endeavor in the case
of women's writing.

Moreover, *Manuscrits de Pauline Archange* reveals important similarities to a second major work of the 1960s in which the autobiographical element is clear: Claire Martin's *Dans un gant de fer* (the second
volume is also known as *La Joue droite*).[17] The work of an established
writer of fiction and winner of the 1965 Prix France-Québec (which it

13. Marie-Claire Blais, *Manuscrits de Pauline Archange* (Montreal: Editions du Jour, 1968);
Vivre! Vivre! (Montreal: Editions du Jour, 1969); *Les Apparences* (Montreal: Editions du Jour,
1970). The English translation of the first two volumes is titled, *The Manuscripts of Pauline
Archange*, trans. Derek Coltman (New York: Farrar, Straus and Giroux, 1969, 1970). The third
was translated as *Durer's Angel*, trans. David Lobdell (Vancouver: Talonbooks, 1976). Further
references to these works will appear in my text.

14. Philippe Lejeune, *L'Autobiographie en France* (Paris: Armand Colin, 1971), p. 14. See also
Lejeune, *Le Pacte autobiographique* (Paris: Seuil, 1975).

15. See, for example, Thérèse Fabi, *Le Monde perturbé des jeunes dans l'oeuvre de Marie-Claire
Blais* (Montreal: Editions Agency d'Arc, 1973), p. 4; and Roger Duhamel in *Livres et auteurs
canadiens 1968,* p. 41.

16. I had the opportunity to discuss this question briefly with the author on 4 Oct. 1981.

17. Claire Martin, *Dans un gant de fer,* I: *La Joue gauche* (Montreal: Pierre Tisseyre, 1965); II:
La Joue droite (Montreal: Le Cercle du Livre de France, 1966). The English translation is titled,
In an Iron Glove trans. Philip Stratford and *The Right Cheek,* trans. Philip Stratford (Montreal:
Harvest House, 1975). Further references to the translation will appear in my text.

shared with Marie-Claire Blais's masterpiece, *Une Saison dans la vie d'Emmanuel*), *Dans un gant de fer* has the merit of conforming exactly to the terms of the "autobiographical pact." Both of these major texts, then, will be the focus of an investigation of women's use of autobiographical form in this important period of Quebecois literary history.

Like many other female autobiographies, Claire Martin's *Dans un gant de fer* is centered around the writer's relationships with others from the first words of the text. The dominant other in her life—who appears on the first page simply as LUI (capital letters in the text)—is Martin's father, portrayed as almost a caricature of patriarchal authority. Much of the text is taken up with describing new variations of the abuse to which he subjects his many children, particularly the frequent near-fatal beatings he administers arbitrarily, not to punish but apparently to provide an outlet for some unarticulated rage against the entire world. Equally cruel is his determination to cut the children off from contact with the outside world: when they are not imprisoned in closely supervised convent schools, they are confined to a rural house chosen especially for its physical isolation. The father justifies his programmatic cruelty as an attempt to protect the children from threats to their physical and spiritual well-being, threats that seem particularly connected with sexuality. As an adolescent, the young Claire is forced to conceal her body in outmoded clothes several sizes too large, and as a small child, she is even accused by her father of carrying on incestuous relations with her brother and of molesting her infant sister. Through her early memories of her maternal grandparents' home, however, it is apparent to the child that what her father is really repressing is love, in all its forms, and the possibility of happiness in life.

The father's repressive efforts are seconded by an unholy succession of teaching nuns, whose ignorance is surpassed only by their lack of compassion. The convent reveals the same rigid authoritarianism, the same suppression of physical reality, the same interrogations, the same punitive gestures, the same arbitrary pattern of punishment, and the same implicit contempt for women as the home; the child's angry rejection of the nuns follows naturally upon her rejection of her father. She says of one teaching sister, "I felt the same suspicions about her as I did about my father: whatever she said couldn't be anything else but wrong" (p. 133). By pointing out the parallels between the actions of the father and the attitudes of the nuns, Martin makes it clear that her condemnation of her father extends beyond the individual paternal figure to encompass an entire patriarchal system of values supported by the authority of the church and administered in the institutions of family and school.

The child must even refuse to identify with her beloved mother, whose pious submission to this system has resulted in a life of suffering for herself and her children: "I think I resented the fact that she had married that man, that she had given him to me as a father, that she was too weak to bring him down to size" (p. 98). As the girl begins to look toward her own marriage, she is emphatic in rejecting the model represented by her mother: "Ah, no! I wasn't going to be treated the way Mother had been, not me!" (p. 266).

The structure of *Dans un gant de fer* appears to be based on a loose chronology, and many of its episodes are repetitive. However, the relationships with others which form the center of the text also provide it with another structure: a movement on the part of the protagonist at first of rejection and then of progress toward rebellion and ultimate liberation. Initially articulated in the outburst "I wish he were dead," a wish the child is powerless to carry out, this attitude of rejection slowly extends beyond the father to all the other authority figures in her life: "But I wished so many people would die, and only the ones I loved did" (p. 236). In the course of the autobiography, however, this negative attitude evolves into a covert resistance that will eventually lead to the liberation promised at the end.

At the origin of this movement is the one positive vision of the other presented in the text, the description of the loving atmosphere of the grandparents' house, where the children live during their parents' brief separation. It is the positive relationship with the grandparents which later gives rise to the older children's organized efforts to escape the father's authority and, for Claire herself, to her first attempts to write (the reader is not really surprised to learn that in signing her work the author has divested herself of her father's name and assumed her mother's). The final act of liberation, of course, is taking place before the reader's eyes, as the act of writing, initiated to maintain clandestine contact with the grandmother, is continued in defiance of a patriarchal authority that, at home and in the convent school, has sought to deny women access to the tools of language and culture: "We had no right to knowledge, either general or specialized. But yearly maternities, sleepless nights and dreary days, nursing children, washing, cooking, finished off with eclampsia or puerperal fever—no objection to that. Feminine vocation" (p. 273). In this attitude, ironically, the upholders of the status quo can be seen to have displayed great "foresight": Martin's autobiography is a vivid demonstration of the way in which these cultural tools may be used by the victim of a repressive system to analyze its functioning and, in so doing, free herself from its iron grip.

A similar pattern of rejection, resistance, and liberation is present in Blais's *Manuscrits de Pauline Archange*. Here, however, the oppressive forces the protagonist rejects are not summed up in a larger-than-life father figure but exist in diffuse form throughout the world in which she moves, even threatening to corrupt the child herself.

Like Martin, Blais begins by evoking the presence of others: "Like the chorus of my distant miseries, . . . the old nuns, who once cradled my life in their cruel kindness, still keep their eyes on me" (p. 3). This long meandering opening sentence, of which I have quoted only a small part, mirrors the form of the work itself and establishes the nature of Pauline Archange's relationship with the others who dominate her narrative. It is, in fact, the desire to reconstruct images of others in her life, particularly her mother and her persecuted cousin Jacob, which inspires in the child, if only in the inner recesses of her mind, her first desire to write: "And my mother, who had always had so little existence in her own eyes, never having lived except for others, my mother emerged from the shadows like an unfinished portrait, and the void where her frightened features should have been seemed to be saying, 'Finish this brief sketch of me'" (p. 80).

If the world of Claire Martin is one of victims and torturers, the universe of Pauline Archange is populated by victims and judges, both of which roles the child immediately rejects. The judgmental nuns of the opening sentence, who are shown denying the child both material and spiritual nourishment, are treated as harshly by Blais as by Martin, and Pauline Archange loses no time in joining with her independent-minded friend Louisette Denis, "a sister in combat," to revolt against them. Her ready identification with Louisette Denis suggests the possibility of a positive alliance with others, but in the world of Pauline Archange such relationships cannot survive. Louisette returns subdued from her two-year stay at a sanatorium, just as Pauline's rebellious cousin Jacob loses his mind in the asylum where he is confined by his family. Pauline's more distant attitude toward the newly recovered Louisette, like her earlier rejection of her beloved and humiliated friend Séraphine, suggests her innate refusal to identify with those condemned to be victims.

Her dual rejection of both victims and judges explains the child's ambivalence toward her parents. The family unit is first presented as a group of inquisitors, a "tribunal fermé," whose main function is to pass judgment on Pauline's heartlessness. In the first scene with her mother, Pauline refuses to come home for dinner, fleeing "an authority that I condemned as monstrous" (p. 14). Yet, as she soon admits, her deeper reason for rejecting her mother is a recognition of her status as a victim; she pities "this young woman, already failing in health and worn out by work" (p. 19). While she admits feeling pity, she quite consciously refuses to make the affectionate gesture that would affirm the identity of mother and daughter. She is "afraid, above all, of snapping our fragile bond of reticence and silence by making the consolatory gesture that she was expecting of me, and thus proving that we did not belong to the same martyred tribe" (p. 19).

Her father, too, plays the role of a harsh judge, cutting short her schooling, forcing her into a world of mind-destroying jobs and, at the end of the trilogy, constantly threatening to take away the typewriter that holds the concrete possibility of her liberation. Yet she can see that her father, too, is a victim, especially of the harsh rural environment of Quebec in which he has been raised and which is shown in the trilogy through Pauline's catastrophic vacation with her paternal relatives. As he reproaches her early attempts at writing, recalling his own youth spent as a factory worker, Pauline's response is clear. "No one is ever going to work the clothes off my back, no one is going to humiliate me like that" (p. 135). The father of Pauline Archange is not the clearly deranged child-abuser of *Dans un gant de fer* (although his brother does come close to this model); yet, like Claire Martin's father, he becomes the spokesman for a traditional patriarchal order that preaches submission to authority and humiliation of body and spirit.

Unlike Claire Martin, Pauline Archange has the opportunity of making contacts beyond the world of family and convent school, and in this wider world she can examine more positive models for her own projected existence in the lives of two women who have achieved some independence from traditional female roles. The writer Romaine Petit-Page at first excites Pauline's admiration because of her life devoted to poetic creation. Very quickly, however, Pauline comes to realize that the woman poet has built around herself a "royaume artificiel" (*Vivre! Vivre!* p. 113), creating illusions belied by the reality presented by the narrator of the trilogy. Pauline often finds herself contrasting her own perceptions with those of the poetess. When Romaine and her admirers exclaim over "la belle neige qui neigeait," the narrator observes drily, "'The lovely snow it's snowing now.' It had been snowing for three days, and the sidewalks were lined on either side by mountain ranges of less than pristine whiteness, but they did not seem to notice that" (p. 149). As her poetic vision of snow bears little relation to the dingy reality of the city, Romaine Petit-Page cannot see that the "garden of wearisome virginity" (p. 149), the vision of childhood purity that dominates her poetry, flies in the face of the real childhood existence of Pauline Archange. A caricature of a certain type of sentimental and moralizing writer, Romaine Petit-Page is, in the end, thoroughly rejected by her would-be follower.

The figure of Germaine Léonard, the woman doctor who takes a charitable interest in the young girls at the convent, occupies a place of disproportionate importance in the trilogy, playing a role in each of the volumes and threatening, at one point, to run away with the third. As a woman who has rejected the traditional female roles and the religion that has upheld them, Germaine Léonard exerts a powerful fascination on the young Pauline. Yet if her character is analyzed at such length, it is because she does not live up to the promise she holds forth. For all her apparent liberation, she has not succeeded in piercing through the "appearances"—the title of the third volume—of the world around her; she still subscribes to the rigid conventions of socially acceptable behavior on which she has been raised. She is repeatedly shown displaying an irritating "moral superiority," judging Pauline severely for having the attitudes and aspect of a child of her social class. When she sees Pauline on the street selling newspapers, the child is aware of her contempt: "I knew immediately that in her eyes I was 'one of that gang of guttersnipes' and that she had condemned me" (p. 138). And when at the end of the trilogy, the unemployed and practically destitute Pauline goes to ask Germaine Léonard for a loan needed to save her typewriter, the older woman judges her only on her shabby clothing: "You're as poorly dressed as ever. And that's surely a sign of apathy!" (p. 101).

Although the protagonist ages in each succeeding volume of the trilogy, scenes of any single volume are only loosely bound by chronology, and Blais's critics have often been disconcerted by an apparent lack of order or direction. One complained of "a structure which does not always favorise immediate comprehension," and another declared that *Vivre! Vivre!* possessed "neither logic nor chronological order."[18] Unconsciously echoing the critical judgment of many women's autobiographical narratives, Roger Duhamel lamented, "Throughout all these pages, nothing really happens"—nothing, that is, but "incidents of her daily existence, as banal as those of most children."[19] Yet, like *Dans un gant de fer, Manuscrits de Pauline Archange* is structured by the evolution of the child's—and, in this case, also the narrator's—relationships with the others of her text.

The characteristic response of the young Pauline Archange in the first volume is one of impotent rejection. When she is temporarily blinded by the whipping administered by her country uncle, she revels in the possibility of cutting herself off from the world: "I had hoped to become blind, to follow the opaque trajectory of a wholly inward vision" (p. 53). It is this capacity to isolate himself from the world which attracts

18. Pierre Chatillon, "Marie-Claire Blais telle qu'en elle-même," *Livres et auteurs canadiens 1968*, pp. 243–45; Yvan Lepage in *Livres et auteurs québécois 1969*, pp. 24–26.

19. In *Livres et auteurs canadiens 1968*, p. 41.

her to her retarded infant brother Emile: "Emile's fragility, his exiled existence, made me understand that there perhaps existed a mysterious race of men, not subject to our ordinary laws, but living according to the dictates of their hearts" (p. 103).

Toward the end of this volume, however, she begins to realize that "resurrection" will come not through an impossible retreat into the self but through an active re-creation of the elements of her own life: "And if I was destined to survive it one day, then it would perhaps be simply in order to go down into that depth of mud and dried leaves to take a last look at all the living and the degenerate dead from whom, more than my birth, more than my life, I had to extract my resurrection" (p. 93). Whereas Martin's narrator maintains an ironic distance from her material from the very beginning, as has been noted by Philip Stratford and others, the narrator of *Manuscrits de Pauline Archange* often seems uncomfortably close to the events she describes.[20]

By the third volume of the trilogy, however, the narrative itself reveals the beginning of this process of resurrection. As the protagonist begins to embark on her career as a writer, the narrator, too, seems to have gained the ability to look back on the people in her life with sympathetic understanding. *Les Apparences* begins with an attempt to recapture a positive moment of childhood, a vision, like Martin's, of the maternal grandmother. The narrator enters into a long and sympathetic examination of the life of Germaine Léonard and presents the work's first moving portrait of a teaching nun, who, like Pauline herself, is waging a persistent battle against the mediocrity of her cultural environment. Finally, she conjures up for herself a positive vision of a kindred spirit, which she first sees pictured in Durer's *Melancolia* and then encounters in the person of her acquaintance André Chevreux, whose appearance points to the possibility of a new type of relationship with others and the world.

Both of these autobiographical narratives can be seen to have a common structure: the female protagonist displays a clear pattern of rejection of the others whose presence dominates both her life and her narrative, a rejection that, in each case, is a necessary prelude to the attainment of individual autonomy. Although both texts have been perceived as relatively unstructured, the focus on relationships with others is in both works the basis of a clearly discernible structure.

The two narratives also, of course, conform to a third characteristic of female autobiography, that of concentration on personal rather than political history: events occurring outside of home and school have no

20. Philip Stratford, *Marie-Claire Blais* (Toronto: Forum House, 1971).

impact at all on the life of either female protagonist. It is somewhat ironic, then, that the structure of personal development in the auto-biographies should reveal similarities to the structure of Quebec's politi-cal development in the period following the *Révolution tranquille,* the era in which both works were written and published. With the *Révolution tranquille,* the people of Quebec began questioning, if not rejecting outright, a rigid authoritarianism in religious, political, educational, and familial institutions and initiated a search for a new autonomous identity on an individual and collective level. While neither these political devel-opments nor any others play a role in either text, their narrative struc-ture and the structure of the collective political movement are clearly homologous.

Many explanations of this homology suggest themselves, and surely, historical and literary as well as biographical factors are involved. The least that can be said is that in Quebec such female autobiographical narratives have transcended the peripheral status usually accorded them and have demonstrated their intimate connection with the central politi-cal and intellectual movements of their time. The recognition of these parallels suggests one possible answer to the now famous questions posed by the feminist writer Nicole Brossard at the opening of the inter-national colloquium on women and writing held in Montreal in 1975: "How is it that women have played such an important part in our literature: Gabrielle Roy, Anne Hébert, Germaine Guèvremont, Marie-Claire Blais. How come, in particular, that their works were able to reach a wide section of the Quebec public? With what collective schizo-phrenia did their own phantasms connect? On what oppression did they throw light?"[21]

21. Christiane Makward, whose translation is used here, quotes Brossard's statement in her important introductory article, "Quebec Women Writers," *Women and Literature* 7 (Winter 1979): 3. Brossard's remarks were reprinted in *Liberté* 18 (July-Oct. 1976): 13.

PART III

DOUBLE MESSAGES: MATERNAL LEGACIES/ MYTHOGRAPHIES

10

Revisions of Labor in
Margaret Oliphant's Autobiography

GAIL TWERSKY REIMER

An unusual document in the literature of self-explanation, Margaret
Oliphant's autobiography is a particularly rich text for the feminist critic
concerned with the relationship of feminism to mothering and the relationship of both to women's autobiography. Oliphant's efforts to imagine and represent herself as a mother not only defy the conventions of
Victorian autobiography but challenge prevailing assumptions of how
women ought to define themselves while also highlighting the problematic position of a woman who wishes to speak as a mother. The challenge, of course, is muted, dispersed, and disguised, embedded in a text
designed to satisfy the Victorian reader's expectations of women, even
while disappointing his or her expectations of autobiography. But that
strategy should not mislead us into believing that in the autobiography
Oliphant simply retreats into woman's conventional role. To emphasize
the womanhood rather than the writerhood of the woman-writer is to
risk reinscribing maternity as woman's crowning achievement, but
Oliphant is too convinced of a pervasive dismissal of maternal experience to be aware of this risk. Her goal is to gain a hearing for *procreativity*
in a genre dedicated to the exploration of *creativity*.

The male Victorian autobiographer typically explored his own creative mind and imagination with the consciousness that he was a "hero"
of the age, whose vocation could be best understood through analysis of
past experience. Seeking to trace a continuity from early childhood to the
defining idiom of his adult life, i.e., his work, he concerned himself less
with the actual events in his life than with re-covering or dis-covering a
unitary self by probing the life of the mind.[1] This characteristic focus of

1. Oliphant's absence from most works on Victorian autobiography is not altogether
surprising inasmuch as the authors of these works derive their definitions from male models of
the genre. See for example Jerome Hamilton Buckley, *The Turning Key: Autobiography and the*

Victorian autobiography disturbed Oliphant. Herself a biographer and critic of autobiography, Oliphant punctuated her own autobiography with references to other biographies and autobiographies, comments that testify to her awareness of, and discomfort with, the conventions and expectations of the genre. At the outset, invoking Trollope's auto-biography, Oliphant insists that though her autobiography, like his, is rooted in the "fashion of self-explanation which belongs to the time," she will follow this fashion "in another way."[2] Only much later, recalling yet another contemporary autobiography, does Oliphant hint at the nature of the difference: "I have been reading the life of Mr. Symonds, and it makes me almost laugh (though little laughing is in my heart) to think of the strange difference between this prosaic little narra-tive, all about the facts of a life so simple as mine, and his elaborate self-discussions. I suppose that to many people the other will be the more interesting way, just as the movements of the mind are more interesting than those of the body, or rather of the external life" (p. 80).

Embedded in this passage of all-too-obvious self-denigration, is a serious challenge to the conventional discourse of autobiography and the assumptions that underlie that discourse. Even as she participates in the self-deprecation Elaine Showalter identifies as characteristic of Vic-torian women novelists,[3] Oliphant refuses to align herself with the "many" who find the prosaic ("the usual experiences of women") lack-ing in interest and resists the privileging of a particular category of experience. But in her effort to disengage herself from the dominant (masculine) mode of autobiography, Oliphant falls victim to the dualist perception of existence at the root of Western patriarchal thought. By opposing the movements of the body to the movements of the mind, Oliphant betrays her acceptance of body and mind as antithetical modes of orientation to experience, and by substituting "external life" for "body" she reveals her own internalization of the familiar analogies that are generated by, and continue to sustain, this dualism—mind is to body as spirit is to matter, as internal experience is to external fact. And yet, while the passage clearly operates within a dualist mode of thought, the slippage from "body" to "external life" simultaneously exposes Oliphant's discomfort with dualism. With mind opposed to external life, body can be reclaimed as something neither opposed to mind nor

Subjective Impulse since 1800 (Cambridge: Harvard University Press, 1984); and Avrom Fleish-man, *Figures of Autobiography: The Language of Self-Writing in Victorian and Modern England* (Berkeley: University of California Press, 1983).

2. *The Autobiography and Letters of Mrs. M. O. W. Oliphant,* ed. Mrs. Harry Coghill (New York: Dodd, Mead, 1899), p. 4, hereafter cited in the text.

3. Elaine Showalter, *A Literature of Their Own: British Women Novelists from Bronte to Lessing* (Princeton: Princeton University Press, 1977), p. 83.

analogous to external life. Body thus becomes a distinctive category of experience which mediates internality and externality and therefore might prove particularly fertile ground from which to discern the meaning of a life.

Reclaiming the body as a source of knowledge sounds like a peculiarly modern feminist project, and arguing for its presence in Oliphant's autobiography may seem ridiculous, given the absence in the text of any discourse of the body. But as I have already indicated, Oliphant's resistance to the way experience is shaped by masculine autobiographers is quite explicit and recurs at several points in her text. In addition to acknowledging a gap between her story and men's stories of their experience, Oliphant hints at a new ground upon which her own story might be built. She can do little more than hint, for the culture offered her no suitable discourse for describing the physical and emotional movements of the maternal body. And the hint itself is potentially so dangerous that the text (whether consciously or not matters little) suppresses it by substituting "external life" for "the movements of the body" and thus reinscribes the conventional dualisms it seeks to disrupt.

A parallel substitution is at work throughout the autobiography, seemingly moving it in the direction of memoir and thus accounting for the work's inferior evaluation as autobiography.[4] To fault a work, however, for not living up to a standard that the work sets out to challenge is to put the cart before the horse. I want instead to read Oliphant's focus on external life as a substitution, an attempt to cancel/conceal the more profound challenge to Victorian culture implicit in her refusal of the dominant discourse of Victorian autobiography.

Each articulation of her own perception of self and world is followed by a gesture of suppression. The feeling that initially motivates the writing—"self-compassion," sympathy with her own experience and what it meant to her—quickly gives way to "self-explanation," the effort to translate her experience into the culture's terms. This pattern is already evident in the opening pages of the autobiography, which begins with an explicit refusal of the discourse of work and productivity.

> When people comment upon the number of books I have written, and I say that I am so far from being proud of that fact that I should like at least half of them forgotten, they stare—and yet it is quite true; and even here I could no more go solemnly into them, and tell why I had done this or that, than I could fly. They are my work, which I like in the doing, which is my *natural* way of occupying myself, though they are never as good as I meant them to be. And when I have said that, I have said all that is in me to say. (P. 5, my emphasis)

4. On the distinction between memoir and autobiography, see Karl Weintraub, "Autobiography and Historical Consciousness," *Critical Inquiry* 1 (June 1975): 821–48.

By refusing the discourse of work, Oliphant strikes at the heart of what Victorian culture held most sacred. But with her subsequent invocation of Browning's Andrea del Sarto, she suppresses her challenge and presents her life in a form acceptable to her audience, a form that, rather than confront prevailing assumptions of what is worth recording, apologizes for not being able to record it. To focus on the obstacles to vocational success, as Browning's Andrea does, is nevertheless to see vocational success as the defining idiom. Oliphant draws upon Andrea's apology for failing to produce first-rate works comparable to those of Michelangelo or Raphael to explain her own failure to produce works comparable to those of George Eliot; yet even as she does so, she recognizes this form of self-presentation as "altogether self-defense" (p. 7). And while the autobiography can and has been read as an apology for her failure as an artist, we should not lose sight of the fact that the story she tells in the autobiography is not that of Browning's Andrea.

The failure that looms largest in Oliphant's autobiography is not her failure as an artist but her possible failure as a mother, and the pathos of the autobiography lies in her struggle to make sense of the maternal efforts of a lifetime in light of their impoverished results. It is relatively easy for the artist to admit that her works are never as good as she intended them to be and to wish that she had not written half of them. But what of the mother disappointed in her children? Oliphant began her autobiography at a time when neither of her grown sons was able to settle into a career. Her elder son, Cyril, had recently returned home from Ceylon sick, leaving behind the first and only self-supporting job he ever held, and her younger son, Cecco, was having difficulty securing a position. Can she admit that they did not turn out as well as she had hoped? Can she express the wish that half of them had not been born? And what of the childless mother, the artist-mother who has not only outlived her own reputation but, as becomes the case midway through Oliphant's autobiography, has outlived all five of the children she bore as well? Must she feel herself a "failure all round"?

Oliphant's emphasis on the maternal, her primary identification of herself as a mother, has been noticed before. Too often, however, this emphasis is read as a defense arising from Oliphant's "difficulty imagining and representing herself autobiographically in the role of literary artist," rather than as a courageous choice, a desire to represent herself autobiographically in the role of mother.[5] To insist on the courage involved in this choice is to recognize that in spite of the oft-cited

<hr/>

5. Linda H. Peterson, "Audience and the Autobiographer's Art: An Approach to the Autobiography of Mrs. M. O. W. Oliphant," in *Approaches to Victorian Autobiography*, ed. George P. Landow (Athens: Ohio University Press, 1979), p. 167.

Victorian idealization of motherhood, *reproduction*—childbearing and childrearing—commanded little respect in a society dedicated to *production*. Maternal experience, or what Oliphant refers to as the "usual experiences of woman" (p. 8), impressed nobody, for being a mother was, after all, only natural. But Oliphant resists the conflation of the usual with the natural and insists upon "a sort of whimsical injury" in the denigration of the experience of motherhood. Oliphant's "droll little complaint" follows directly upon her self-pitying recognition that, unlike George Eliot, whose biography she claims as the stimulus to her own autobiographical writing, she herself will not be thought worthy of a biography. "I am in very little danger of having my life written, and that is all the better in this point of view—for what could be said of me?" (p. 7). What indeed, if the usual experiences of women are taken to be biological rather than biographical, if motherhood is taken to be women's natural rather than chosen vocation? Yet from the start Oliphant affirms the maternal self-image at the expense of the authorial one, repeatedly insisting that she is by nature a writer—"I have written because it gave me pleasure, because it came natural to me, because it was like talking and breathing" (p. 4)—and by circumstance and choice a mother.

The tendency to read Oliphant's emphasis on motherhood as defensive rather than assertive betrays the critic's own participation in these "Victorian" assumptions, for what is ruled out at the start is the possibility that Oliphant may value her role as mother more than her role as literary artist. More important, the critic who rejects the possibility that the representation of motherhood constitutes Oliphant's autobiographical project is inevitably blinded to the difficulties Oliphant encounters in imagining and representing herself as a mother. Yet only by exploring these difficulties can we begin to see the magnitude of the problem faced by the female autobiographer.

Resisting the shape of male autobiography is only the beginning. The female autobiographer must also resist cultural pressure to remain silent. The pressure is all the more intense if she wishes to speak as a mother, for as recent feminist and psychoanalytic theorists have shown, the central project of our (patriarchal) culture necessitates the mother's absence and silence.[6] It is not simply that the woman writer experiences her writing as literally in conflict with her mothering, though the consequences of this conflict ought not to be minimized. Comparing her own life to George Eliot's, Oliphant views herself as "handicapped," noting, "It is a little hard sometimes not to feel with Browning's Andrea, that

6. For a summary of the Lacanian account of language acquisition and its implications for mothers who write, see Margaret Homans, *Bearing the Word: Language and Female Experience in Nineteenth-Century Women's Writing* (Chicago: University of Chicago Press, 1986), chap. 1.

the men who have no wives, who have given themselves up to their art, have had an almost unfair advantage over us who have been given perhaps more than one Lucrezia to take care of" (pp. 5–6). Beyond this literal conflict, however, is the symbolic one outlined in Lacan's psychoanalytic account of language, in which writing (representation) and motherhood are not merely incompatible but antithetical, and maternal discourse a theoretical impossibility. Mothers can, of course, write; Oliphant can, that is, record her struggles as a writer. But they cannot write *as* mothers. While the culture tolerated and (as Elaine Showalter argues in *A Literature of Their Own*) even admired writers who were also mothers, it denied these women the possibility of recording their struggles as mothers. The myth of maternal love rendered such a record taboo, and the Lacanian myth of what enables and constitutes the symbolic order helps explain why even the mother who might resist the taboo would have difficulty finding a language in which to record the feelings and experiences most specifically hers.

Unable, then, to explore maternal experience in the voice of the mother, Oliphant uses the conventional autobiographical exploration of childhood experience to uncover maternal experience in the voice of the daughter. Yet, while the recollections clearly reveal the child's sensibility, the narrative strains toward an adult (mother's) understanding of the mother. Oliphant's first recollection of her mother is not the idealized portrait one might expect. Oliphant does present her mother as devoted, nurturant, and all-giving, but to her son, not to her daughter: "I can see myself, a small creature seated on a stool by the fire toasting a cake of dough which was brought for me by the baker with the prematurely early rolls which were for Frank. . . . And my mother, who never seemed to sit down in the strange, little warm bright picture, but to hover about the table pouring out tea, supplying everything he wanted to her boy (how proud of him, how fond of him!—her eyes liquid and bright with love as she hovered about)" (p. 9). This description, perhaps more revealing than Oliphant intends, points to her own sense of secondariness or inferiority. Clearly, the mother who was "all in all" to her daughter (p. 11), did not consider her daughter the all in all. Oliphant recalls delight in the cake of dough, but that cake is available only because her brother is home and rolls are brought for him. The mother she introduces into this scene is wholly engaged with her son rather than with her daughter. Any doubt about the envy implicit in the parenthetical statement is dispelled later in the autobiography when Oliphant recalls other sister-brother scenes in which her sense of loss and deprivation is exacerbated by her brother's presence. One particularly memorable scene occurs shortly after her husband's death during a "not very successful" visit with her brother's family. "I think it was rather more than I could bear," Oliphant recalls, "to see his children rushing to the door to meet him when he came home, and my fatherless little ones ready to rush too, though it was so short a time since their father had been taken from them" (p. 66). It seems that Oliphant is distressed by her children's insensitivity, the ease with which they replace one father with another, but the comment with which she concludes this recollection reveals a different source of her pain. "It is a perilous business, when one is very sorry for oneself," she writes, "and the sight of happy people is apt, when one's wounds are fresh, to make the consciousness keener" (p. 67). The self-pity aroused by her children's willingness to rush into her brother's arms suggests that she is once again feeling displaced by her brother. And significantly, the "happy people" she sees when her "wounds are fresh," are always the same one person—her brother.[7]

It is her brother, far more than the women novelists invoked at the start of the autobiography, who inclines Oliphant to cry over her "poor little unappreciated self—'Many love me (i.e., in a sort of way), but by none am I enough beloved'" (p. 8). It would be fairly easy to explain Oliphant's need for "love" along psychoanalytic lines as a need for the mothering she never got. We could even read her choice to focus on motherhood as an attempt to gain the approval she never had from her mother.[8] But in pursuing such interpretations we would necessarily be engaging a set of assumptions about motherhood which the autobiography is itself protesting. Begun at a time when her sons were facing their own failures and quite possibly blaming her for them, the autobiography tentatively but consistently resists the temptation to hold mothers accountable for the failures or problems of their children.

What is perhaps most striking about Oliphant's remembrances of her mother is her seemingly modern feminist effort to "move beyond the myths and misconceptions embodied in the fantasy of the perfect mother."[9] Not only does Oliphant resist blaming her mother, but she implicitly questions the legitimacy of the child's interpretation of the mother's behavior. "She was of the old type of Scotch mothers, not

7. Similar envy and resentment of her brother is expressed after her daughter's death. See *Autobiography*, p. 94.

8. For an exploration of the consequences for women's lives of unsatisfied wishes for nurturance from the mother, see Jane Flax, "The Conflict between Nurturance and Autonomy in Mother-Daughter Relationships and within Feminism," *Feminist Studies* 4 (June 1978): 171–91.

9. Nancy Chodorow and Susan Contratto, "The Fantasy of the Perfect Mother," in *Rethinking the Family: Some Feminist Questions*, ed. Barrie Thorne and Marilyn Yalom (London: Longmans, 1982), pp. 54–75.

demonstrative, not caressing, but I know now that I was a kind of idol to her from my birth" (p. 11), writes Oliphant, and, "I was not petted nor called by sweet names. But I know now that my mere name meant everything to her. I was her Maggie" (p. 12).

The repeated phrase "I know now" calls attention to the belatedness of this perspective as well as to its difference from an earlier view; I know now, Oliphant says, what I did not know then. We could of course read this as the retrospective idealization of a problematic and painful mother–daughter relationship. But Oliphant initially began writing the autobiography for her sons in an effort to secure their "strong affection," to gain for herself, in her sphere as mother, the kind of affection that George Eliot had secured in another sphere. Moreover, she began writing in a time of crisis in her sons' lives. We might, therefore, consider the possibility that she purposely rejects and erases the child's interpretation of her mother's behavior in order to show her children how they might reinterpret their own mother's behavior, in order, that is, to give a hearing to the maternal perspective.

Oliphant, as she tells us, offered her children the "narrative of [her] life" in the hope that they "might cast an interpretation of love" upon "some things" (p. 81). Her understanding of how the child might (ought to) interpret the mother's behavior can be gleaned from her own interpretation of moments in her mother's life. As she recalls her child-hood from the perspective of the adult-mother, she shapes her memo-ries of her mother by empathy and identification, providing her sons (and us) with a model of how one might (must) sacrifice one's own infantile feelings in order to understand who the mother was and how she felt. Oliphant acknowledges what a difficult task this is for the adult as well as the child. "How little one realizes the character or individu-ality of those who are most near and dear," she writes. "It is with difficulty even now that I can analyze and make a character of her" (p. 12). But as she grapples with the effort to understand her mother she recognizes that the point is not to "make a character of her" but rather to recognize the complexity of her mother's life, to see her in her particu-larity: "She herself is there, not any type or variety of humankind" (p. 12).

Refusing to assimilate her mother into a type, Oliphant begins the autobiography resisting Victorian ideology about motherhood. Wheth-er Oliphant's effort to identify with, rather than rage against, her moth-er led to her decision to claim attention for maternal experience or was determined by it, this identification was unusual for the feminine novel-ist. As Elaine Showalter has noted of nineteenth century women novelists, "A factor that recurs with remarkable frequency in the backgrounds of these women is the identification with, and dependence upon, the father; and either loss of, or alienation from, the mother.[10] For Oliphant the reverse is true: "My father is a very dim figure in all that phantasmagoria. I had to be very quiet in the evenings when he was at home, not to disturb him; and he took no particular notice of me or any of us. My mother was all in all" (p. 11).

In addition to defining her allegiances, Oliphant draws attention, in this passage, to the conditions that foster the child's sense of the mother as "all in all." By recalling the father's absence before she claims the mother's omnipotence, she suggests that the mother's omnipotence (or, more precisely, the child's sense of the mother's omnipotence) is a consequence of the father's absence or withdrawal. Oliphant again alludes to the recognition that the father's presence might have altered family dynamics when she recalls the tensions of her early married life: "It looked all happy enough but was not, for my husband and my mother did not get on. My father sat passive, taking no notice, with his paper, not perceiving much, I believe" (p. 31). Had Oliphant stopped after the first sentence, or had she continued by elaborating upon the conflict between mother-in-law and son-in-law, the passage would have taken on a substantially different meaning. But by connecting the conflict to her father's passivity, Oliphant shifts responsibility from the mother's resistance or jealousy to the father's nonparticipation. This paternal noninvolvement leads in another context to what she refers to as her "indignation with the popular fallacy about mothers-in-law" (p. 59).

Oliphant's sensitivity to maternal isolation undoubtedly arose from her own sense of isolation. As she turns from recollections of her mother to her own maternal experience, she calls attention to how the pressures she faced were exacerbated by her husband's decision to move the family to a foreign environment, where she could not find other supports and was forced into a position of being "all in all" to her children. In the midst of remembering moving to Italy for a change of air to improve her husband's health, Oliphant breaks the sequence and refers to a later moment around the time of his death: "Afterwards in Rome, Robert Macpherson told me . . . that the doctors had told Frank his doom; that his case was hopeless, but that he had not the courage to tell me the truth. I was angry and wounded beyond measure, and would not believe that my Frank had deceived me, or told another what he did not tell me. Neither do I think he would have gone away, to expose me with

10. Showalter, p. 61.

my children to so awful a trial in a foreign place had this been the case. And yet the blessed deliverance of that moment was not real either. The truth most likely lay between the two" (p. 47).

If Oliphant genuinely believed that "the truth lay between the two," then she would have given that belief more narrative credibility, i.e., allowed the narrative of the move to Italy and Frank's eventual death to stand between the hope for a cure and the eventual revelation that no cure was possible. Instead, she prefaces the narrative of the move with Macpherson's claim that it was all for nought. The effort to spare her sons the full recognition of their father's irresponsiblity also shapes her description of Frank's death. But here again the measured tone only barely conceals Oliphant's rage at her husband: "Frank died quite conscious, kissing me when his lips were already cold, and quite, quite free from anxiety, though he left me with two helpless children and one unborn and very little money and no friends" (p. 63).

Sensitivity to maternal isolation does not of itself result in a more complex understanding of the mother and mothering. As Nancy Chodorow and Susan Contratto argue in their analysis of recent feminist literature on mothering, blaming conditions other than the mother's incompetence or malevolence for maternal behavior can still leave one mired in unrealistic expectations of the mother and thus can sustain rather than undermine the cultural ideology of maternal responsibility. Paying heed to the conditions that make mothering less than perfect still leaves women trapped in the belief that "perfect" mothering is both possible and desirable. Continued belief in this possibility, they claim, leads to a maternal identification "full of rage and fear, and a sense that the conditions of patriarchy totally oppress mothers and isolate them with their child."[11]

The rage and fear Chodorow and Contratto speak of is certainly present in the autobiography. But ultimately this rage does not prevent Oliphant from recognizing and insisting upon the limits of maternal responsibility. Constantly on the edge of claiming total responsibility for her sons' failures, she consistently pulls back: "My dearest, bright, delightful boy missed somehow his footing, how can I tell how? I often think I had to do with it, as well as what people call inherited tendencies, and, alas! the perversity of youth, which he never outgrew" (p. 147). The paragraph continues with a description of her son's responsibility for how he turned out, though Oliphant keeps reverting to her own "foolish ways," to what she had "to do with it." An expression of her ambivalence about maternal responsibility, the paragraph is prefaced by

11. Chodorow and Contratto, p. 67.

a question that reveals a crucial factor in maternal resistance to claiming development as interactive. "I do injustice," writes Oliphant, "to those whom I love above all things by speaking thus, and yet what can I say?" (p. 147). How, she seems to be asking, can the mother speak honestly without hurting the child she loves, without, in the end, hurting herself.

For Oliphant, the death of her children nullified the threat that exposing one's vulgar, unrefined, or unorthodox maternal feelings will adversely affect one's children. As noted earlier, Oliphant began writing her autobiography of the mother at a moment when she might reasonably have felt that her active mothering should have come to an end. Instead, her two sons, aged twenty-nine and twenty-six, were financially and emotionally dependent on her. The hope that Cyril might make a life of his own in the foreign service was short-lived. He returned home from Ceylon in less than six months, and about six months later Oliphant began her autobiography. Both her sons were dead before she was halfway through.

Whether or not the work was, as she tells us, originally meant for her sons, motherhood initially served Oliphant as a culturally legitimate rationale for writing her autobiography. She was writing her life for her children, just as she had lived it caring for others, rather than "being taken care of" like George Eliot (p. 5). Their deaths not only invalidated this rationale but also challenged her identity as a mother. Not surprisingly, the change in circumstances revived earlier doubts about representing herself in the "commonplace" role of mother: "When I wrote it for my Cecco to read it was all very different, but now that I am doing it consciously for the public, with the aim (no evil aim) of leaving more money, I feel all this to be so vulgar, so common, so unnecessary, as if I were making pennyworths of myself" (p. 75).

Paradoxically, these doubts arising from the death of her last child are quieted by the recognition that her children are dead. "Well," the passage continues, "what does it matter? Will my boys ever see it?" (p. 75). Childlessness simultaneously undermines the validity of maternal discourse and makes it possible. The childless mother can speak more freely, for she need no longer worry that her children might suffer as a result. But the mother without children may wonder whether she is indeed still a mother, whether the loss of her children does not also entail the loss of an identity, the very identity Oliphant chose to explore in her autobiography.

Oliphant resists this sense of loss by textually reproducing herself as mother. Cecco's death comes as she is completing the record of her husband's illness and death. Midparagraph, Oliphant interrupts her story and abruptly shifts from past to present, to the moment of writing:

"While I write, October 5, 1894, he, the last, is lying in his coffin in the room next to me. . . . All gone, all gone, and no light to come of this sorrow any more" (p. 64). This interruption, however, is followed by an equally abrupt shift in the next sentence back to the story she was telling: "When my Cecco was two months old we came home . . ." (p. 64). Returning to the past enables Oliphant to retain her maternal identity and to continue to explore maternal experience. Thus, it should not surprise us that the emphasis on motherhood is as prominent in the second half of the autobiography as it is in the first half, nor should it surprise us that the autobiography comes to a close as the narrative itself brings Oliphant to the moment of her last child's death.

As many theorists of autobiography have noted, the life story the autobiographer tells (the bios) is inherently incomplete. One option for the autobiographer is simply to bring the story up to his or her own present moment of writing, to write about the past up to the moment where past and present intersect. The ending, in this case, is likely to be abrupt and inconclusive, something like "and now here I am. I cannot write [retrospectively] any more" (p. 150). I am purposely drawing upon the final lines of Oliphant's autobiography because they come so remarkably close to this kind of abrupt closure, that it is easy to understand why the editor of the manuscript, Oliphant's niece Mrs. Coghill, experienced the ending as a simple "breaking off" and wished to "complete" the record of Oliphant's life by supplementing her manuscript with letters. As she wrote in her preface to the autobiography, "After 1892 there is nothing, and it seemed impossible to allow the later years of her life—full of work, full of varying scenes of interest—to remain altogether unrecorded" (p. ix). Mrs. Coghill misses the closure in Oliphant's final lines because she has missed (and altered) the beginning of the narrative.

The serial composition of the autobiography would have troubled Mrs. Coghill less, if the entries in Oliphant's book had followed a sequential pattern, if they had begun at the beginning of Oliphant's life and continued through to her late years. But because the manuscript she found did not begin with the beginning she expected, Mrs. Coghill assumed it had no beginning. "When those to whom she had intrusted it came to examine the manuscript," writes Mrs. Coghill, "a great disappointment befell them. It had no beginning; scraps had been written at long intervals and by no means consecutively" (p. ix). She notes two of the scraps: the first, written in 1860, "mentions, rather than records, the struggle of her early widowhood," and the second, written in 1864, "is the outpouring of her grief for the loss of her one daughter, her little Maggie." The next entry, the one Mrs. Coghill designated as Oliphant's

Dates of composition[a]	Content	Relevant life events at time of composition
	Section 1	
Feb. 1885–1888	Childhood through birth of 1st daughter, death of mother, birth and death of 2d daughter	July 1884, Cyril returns from Ceylon, sick, dependent on his mother, unable to hold his 1st and only job
	Section 2	
Jan. 1891–Christmas 1894	Birth of 1st child, death of 2d daughter, birth of 4th child[b] (1st son), death of husband, birth of 2d son (Cecco)	Nov. 1890, Cyril dies Oct. 1894, Cecco dies
	Section 3	
30 Dec. 1894–22 Jan. 1895	Life of widow with her two sons and daughter through death of daughter	
	Section 4	
1894–?[c]	Death of daughter through death of both sons	

[a]Dates of composition are those recorded in Oliphant's text.
[b]A third child died shortly after birth.
[c]The date of this section lacks the specificity of other dates (no month is recorded) and seems unlikely since Section 3 takes Oliphant into 1895.

autobiography is the "more connected and less sad record" Oliphant began in 1885. But even this record troubles Mrs. Coghill, for "the thread is snapped two or three times before it finally breaks off after the death of her sons" (p. ix).

The moments at which "the thread is snapped" in this more connected narrative, betray an underlying structure in this seemingly fragmentary autobiography, an internal logic that can be charted. Clearly, the autobiography is organized around Oliphant's life of mothering—the life she was writing and the life she was living while writing. By juxtaposing the dates of composition of each section with the life events that frame the composition (i.e., moments in the present) and the life events recorded in each section (i.e., recollections of the past), we can more easily recognize how central is maternal experience to the whole and how the divisions of the narrative further the exploration of maternal experience.

The chart calls attention to both the centrality and interrelatedness of birth and death in maternal experience, nowhere more apparent than in the tension between the content of Section 2 and the timing of its composition. Section 1 was completed in 1888. Oliphant returned to the autobiography in January 1891, two months after Cyril died, and ended this section of the autobiography two months after her last surviving child died. She resumed writing several days later but began a new section, suggesting a possible unconscious intentionality to the silent symmetry of children's deaths framing the second narrative section, which begins with the birth of her first child and ends with of the birth of her last child. The repeated record of that first birth, already set forth in Section 1, seems to underscore the complex relationship between maternity and mortality which women confront as they give birth to their first child.

A more significant symmetrical frame has been effaced by the well-intentioned but unfortunate efforts of Mrs. Coghill, for Oliphant had written some pages in 1864, and these Coghill inserted later in the text "so as to preserve the sequence of the narrative" (p. 3). The allusion in the first line of the pages begun in 1885 to "what is on the opposite page" suggests that Oliphant intended to preface the work with the pages she had written in 1864 following the death of her eldest daughter Maggie. These pages, I believe, constitute the appropriate beginning to the autobiography that Mrs. Coghill believed "had no beginning." Though they did not satisfy her concern with sequence, the pages she transferred to their rightful chronological place at the end of Section 3 could provocatively begin the autobiographical narrative that culminates in the death of Oliphant's last son and ends with the lines "And now here I am all alone. I cannot write anymore" (p. 150). The intense loneliness of the mother who has lost her child, "her ewe lamb," her "woman–child," recorded in the pages written in 1864 finds its apotheosis in the lines "Here is the end of all. I am alone. I am a woman" (p. 94). Mrs. Coghill's editorial changes retroactively confirm Oliphant's sense of loneliness, her feeling that she must "bear the loss, the pang unshared" (p. 94). For by reinserting the death of Oliphant's daughter in its "natural sequence," Mrs. Coghill "naturalizes" it and thus undermines what Oliphant apparently wished to emphasize by beginning her autobiography with the pages written in 1864—the horrible unnaturalness of losing one's own child. Significantly, as she begins the "more connected" narrative of 1885 she reminds us that there was no trouble in George Eliot's life "but the natural one of her father's death" (p. 7). And later in her text, when she recalls her own mother's death, which was shortly followed by the death of her second baby, she again emphasizes the difference between death in its natural sequence, painful though it be, and the death of a child: "My dearest mother, who had been everything to me all my life . . . did not give me when she died, a pang so deep as the loss of the little helpless baby, eight months old" (p. 33).

And because she fails to recognize the beginning of the autobiography, Mrs. Coghill also cannot recognize its end. "After 1892," she writes, "there is nothing." Yet, as I have already noted, the point Mrs. Coghill refused to see as an end is the point at which Oliphant records the death of her last child. The fact that Oliphant ended her autobiography with Cecco's death, although her life continued to be "full of work," is but another sign of her refusal to be defined by the discourse of work. And if the autobiography is read as the autobiography of a mother, then the moment of childlessness is painfully but peculiarly appropriate to ending the autobiography.

The significant repetition that enforces closure is the phrase "I am all alone," which signals that the loss of her children, or, more precisely, the loss of her vision of herself as a mother, has more profound consequences for Oliphant than the loss of her ability to write. Juxtaposing the last lines of her autobiography with the lines they recall and repeat (the lines, as I have tried to show, with which the autobiography should have begun) reveals a striking and, I believe, telling omission. The statement "I am alone" in the 1864 section is followed by "I am a woman." The simple, balanced lines suggest an equivalence; solitariness, loneliness, is the condition of woman. One wonders, then, why, at the end of the autobiography, when she is more alone than ever, Oliphant "omits" the line "I am a woman." The significant difference between these two moments is that in the former, though she had lost her child, she still had other children; she was still a mother. The "omission" at the end suggests Oliphant's fear that having lost all her children, not only is she no longer a mother, but she may also no longer be a woman. Having so totally fused her identity as a woman with her identity as a mother, the childless Oliphant finds herself unable (or unwilling) to assert her female identity.

This painful confusion, however, is not a simple capitulation to the cultural mythology that a woman alone is "redundant" or that a woman's raison d'être is motherhood. Quite possibly it is the inevitable result of creating a self out of the materials of maternal experience. If maternal experience is defined exclusively as the experience of women who bear and raise children, affirming the maternal self may not only divide the mother/woman from other women, as it does in a passage near the conclusion, which I shall examine shortly, but might ultimately divide the mother/woman from herself.

Both the most creative and the most destructive aspects of affirming the maternal self come to the fore as the autobiography draws to its end. Returning to a complaint with which she began her autobiography, Oliphant expresses her resentment of the "contemptuous compliments" she often received for her "industry" (p. 131). At the same time she seeks recognition, as she did at the start, for her "infinite labor." The distinction between industry and labor is puzzling unless we see Oliphant's insistent claim that she has led "a laborious life," as a possible play on the word *labor,* in service of her desire to assert the value of maternal experience. Symbolically, woman's labor, the process by which one brings a child into the world, is the central maternal task. Thus it is not surprising that Oliphant continues to call attention to the "infinitude of pains and labor" that characterize her life, even as she rejects the attention so often paid to her "industry." The specificity of "labor" as maternal work is reinforced by its conjunction early in the text with another aspect of pregnancy and childbirth. Contrasting the unlimited freedom of the Laurence Oliphants to do as they chose to her own freedom limited by the ties that bound her to others, Oliphant admits that she was no simple self-sacrificing mother. But while she often got what she wished, it was only "at the cost of infinite labor, and of carrying a whole little world with me whenever I moved" (p. 6). The juxtaposition of "labor" and "carrying" exposes an unconscious preoccupation with what it feels like to live in a woman's body.

Appropriately enough for a text focused on motherhood, reproductive labor becomes a central source of metaphor. Several times Oliphant refers to the "elasticity" that might account for a pattern of anxiety, despair, and deliverance which reasserted itself with remarkable frequency in her life. The final description of this pattern is worth quoting at length, for it suggestively highlights the connection between this pattern and the experience of childbirth:

> Lately in my many sad musings it has been brought very clearly before my mind how often all the horrible tension, the dread, the anxiety which there are no words strong enough to describe—which devoured me, but which I had to conceal often behind a smiling face—would yield in a moment, in the twinkling of an eye, at the sound of a voice, at the first look, into an ineffable ease and the overwhelming happiness of relief from pain, which is, I think, our highest human sensation, higher and more exquisite than any positive enjoyment in this world. It used to sweep over me like a wave. . . . I cannot explain, but if this should ever come to the eye of any woman in the passion and agony of motherhood, she will more or less understand. I was thinking lately, or rather, as sometimes happens, there was suddenly presented to my mind, like a suggestion from some one else, the recollection of these ineffable happinesses, and it seemed to me that it meant that which would be when one pushed through the last door and was met—oh, by what, by whom?—by instant relief. The wave of sudden ease and warmth and peace and joy. (P. 147)

The language of tension, dread, anxiety, of the overwhelming happiness of relief from pain, of waves and pushing, and yielding in a moment at the sound of a voice, at the very first look, will indeed be understood by "any woman in the passion and agony of motherhood," for it is the language of labor and parturition. The final vision, too easily dismissed as sentimentality, is both a strikingly original and remarkably daring vision of the entry into heaven as the final stage of labor and delivery, as well as a demythologizing of delivery itself. For the laboring woman, the "by what, by whom" at labor's end is at least momentarily, if not for much longer, overpowered by ending of the ordeal, "by instant relief."

The metaphor that animates this passage and the autobiography as a whole is a uniquely female one; throughout, Oliphant sees herself as a laboring woman and not, as has been suggested in the past, as a Victorian Andrea del Sarto. This rooting of the shape of her life experience in the physical and emotional experience of childbirth, in the fundamental movements of a woman's body, is what most crucially defines this text as a distinctively female autobiography.

The passage just quoted also provides another example of how Oliphant conceals the potentially powerful challenge to the conventional discourse of autobiography through a typical gesture of self-deprecation. Midway through her effort to explain the pattern of her life, she stops and almost gives up, claiming that she "cannot explain." But as she continues, we realize that what is at issue here is an unwillingness to explain rather than an inability to explain. In spite of its ineffability, the experience she is speaking of, Oliphant claims, will be "more or less" comprehensible to other mothers. To be sure a number of historical, cultural and psychological factors feed into Oliphant's reluctance to deal with the experience of childbirth more directly and explicitly. Feminine discretion and propriety certainly contribute to her resistance. But as the invocation of other women suggests, so does feminine solidarity. By resisting further explanation Oliphant makes the experience she is drawing upon inaccessible to those who have not had, and will never have, a similar experience and thus preserves for women something uniquely their own.

As the autobiography nears its end, Oliphant inadvertently reveals a possible source of the complex ambivalence she felt about writing her own autobiography. Fear of the appropriation of maternal experience betrays a recognition that in acquiring a speaking position in the dominant discourse, women may end up even greater losers. Significantly, this fear begins to surface when circumstances necessitate redirecting the autobiography initially written for Oliphant's sons to an unsympathetic public. "When I wrote it for my Cecco to read," Oliphant laments, "it was all very different, but now that I am doing it consciously for the public . . . I feel all this to be so vulgar, so common, so unnecessary, as if I were making pennyworths of myself" (p. 75). As she records the death of her last child, Oliphant can no longer escape the full impact of leaving behind a narrative that "will be touched and arranged by strange hands" (p. 81). And as the impulse toward self-preservation overwhelms the impulse toward self-representation, the autobiographer writes herself into silence. Oliphant finally responds to the dilemma of the feminist autobiographer by ceasing to write. The retreat into silence obviously threatens the project of gaining a hearing for maternal experience. But if, as ultimately happens in Oliphant's autobiography, maternal experience gets too narrowly or rigidly defined—i.e., as the experience of only those women who have given or will give birth to children and raise them—then gaining a hearing for maternal experience may also threaten the feminist project.

"A Nutmeg Nestled Inside Its Covering of Mace": Audre Lorde's *Zami*

CLAUDINE RAYNAUD

Audre Lorde's *Zami* is more than an "unfolding of [her] life and loves," it is a "biomythography."[1] Indeed, in Lorde's narrative the reflexiveness and the individualism of the autobiographical gesture give way to the construction of a mythic self: Zami, "the name given to women who work together as friends and lovers" (*Z*, p. 255). From the start, the question of the authenticity of autobiographical reconstruction becomes secondary. Lorde is not faithfully telling her life story: she is giving herself a new name; she is telling the story of Zami. The first name, *le nom propre*, the signature on the title page, will give way to the mythic name.[2] The black lesbian poet, then, can be said to be writing a biography of the mythic self. She herself called *Zami* "a biomythography, which is really fiction," declaring, "it has elements of biography

1. Audre Lorde, *Zami: A New Spelling of My Name* (Trumansburg, N.Y.: Crossing Press, 1983); and *Sister Outsider: Essays and Speeches by Audre Lorde* (Trumansburg, N.Y.: Crossing Press, 1984), p. 190, hereafter cited in the text, abbreviated *Z* and *SO*. Chinosole gives her view of Lorde in "Audre Lorde and Matrilineal Diaspora: Moving History beyond Nightmare into Structures for the Future . . . " (Unpublished paper, 1985), which explores more specifically how Lorde's autobiography integrates black history. I would like to thank Lemuel Johnson, Martha Vicinus, and Domna C. Stanton for their comments on the various drafts and Raymonde Carroll, Carol Tufts, and David Young for their help with the translation.

2. I am here referring to Philippe Lejeune's definition of autobiography in *Le Pacte autobiographique* (Paris: Seuil, 1975), p. 33: "For the reader, autobiography is defined, first and foremost, by a contract of identity sealed by the proper name." (Unless otherwise indicated all translations in this essay are my own.) An excellent critique of Lejeune's topological efforts by Michael Ryan, "Self-Evidence," *Diacritics* 10 (June 1980): 2–16, points to directions feminist critics should pursue. One point is that the contractual quality of the agreement ultimately excludes women. If autobiography is based on the notion of *nom propre*, what is a woman's "proper" name, what is the name that belongs to her? For further analysis of this critical issue, see Domna Stanton, "Autogynography: Is the Subject Different?" in *The Female Autograph*, ed. Domna Stanton (New York Literary Forum, vol. 12–13, 1984), pp. 5–23; and Germaine Brée, "Autogynography," *Southern Review* 22 (Spring 1986): 223–30.

and history of myth."[3] It is the mythmaking function of Lorde's narrative as she attempts to define her composite identity that I wish to
explore in this essay.

Although traditionally defined as nonfiction, autobiography is the
telling of a story, the re-creation in words of self, the invention of a
narrative of the past. In the face of this questioning of the truth-value of
autobiographical discourse, "authenticity" has to be redefined in the context of myth. Lorde's autobiographical narrative is the telling of a myth
that reenacts the beginning, goes back to the roots, the authentic, the
"native." Lorde wants to create a story that will be true for the lesbian
community, an empowering tale that women can live by and will perpetuate. In a sense, the political implications of myth are to be understood as the reality that myth actualized for traditional societies. The
mythic name is the true name.[4]

As they look for their origin, as they retrace the source of their creativity, female writers often go back to the ambiguous relationship with
their mothers.[5] Lorde is no exception; there is a complex interplay
between the maternal and the poetic as the female poet remembers her
coming to language and her *venue à l'écriture*.[6] At the same time, the
return to the mother becomes an evocation of her mother's mother as
Lorde describes the community of her female ancestors. Autobiographi-

3. Lorde, quoted in Claudia Tate, *Black Women Writers at Work* (New York: Continuum,
1984), p. 115.

4. See Mircea Eliade, *L'Univers fantastique des mythes* (Paris: Presses de la Connaissance,
1976), p. 18: "In societies where myth remains alive, people make a careful distinction between
myth, i.e., true stories, and tales and fables, which are called untrue stories." A thorough
analysis of the political implications of the utopian dimension of the mythic vision of black
female writers is called for. In Zora Neale Hurston's *Dust Tracks on a Road,* for instance, the
Greek myths reverberate tragically when juxtaposed with black history.

5. Béatrice Didier's analysis of the poet Kathleen Raine's autobiography leads her to the
conclusion that "the practice of poetry is closely linked to the mother. . . . Writing would be a
means of revealing the phantasms of the mother." *L'Ecriture-femme* (Paris: Presses Universitaires de France, 1980), p. 264. A case could be made that women write predominantly to
give their mothers a voice, to recover the hidden secrets behind their mothers' silences. Yet
such an idealization of the maternal does not always reflect the ambivalence of women's
feelings toward their mothers. For an analysis of that ambivalence in *Zami,* see Barbara
Christian, "No More Buried Lives: The Theme of Lesbianism in Audre Lorde's *Zami,* Gloria
Naylor's *The Women of Brewster Place,* Ntozake Shange's *Sassafras, Cypress and Indigo,* and Alice
Walker's *The Color Purple,*" in *Black Feminist Criticism* (New York: Pergamon Press, 1985), p.
199. Some women's autobiographies offer examples of matrophobia and describe the author's
strong identification with the father. See Lynn Z. Bloom, "Heritages: Dimensions of Mother-
Daughter Relationships in Women's Autobiographies," in *The Lost Tradition: Mothers and
Daughters in Literature,* ed. Cathy N. Davidson and E. M. Broner (New York: Ungar, 1980),
pp. 291–303.

6. Based on *Zami* and not dealing with Audre Lorde's poetic works, my thesis is opposed
to Jerome Brooks's essay "In the Name of the Father," in *Black Women Writers, 1950–1980: A
Critical Evaluation,* ed. Mari Evans (Garden City, N.Y.: Doubleday, 1984), pp. 269–76.

cal writing is the slow and compelling creation of a vision: a feminist—
or, more precisely, a lesbian— utopia. The foremothers of the magical
island of Carriacou join the women whom Lorde meets throughout her
life until Kitty, Lorde's last lover in *Zami* and an incarnation of the
African goddess MawuLisa, finally brings the circle to a close: Afrekete
reminds Lorde of her mother.

The evocation of a mythology that rests on matrilinealism is a conscious political act for Audre Lorde. As Jung describes matrilineal consciousness, "The individual's life is elevated into a type, indeed it becomes the archetype of woman's fate in general. This leads to
restoration or *apocatastasis* of the lives of her ancestors, who now,
through the bridge of the momentary individual, pass down into generations of the Future. . . . the individual is rescued from her isolation and
restored to wholeness."[7] Deliberately choosing African mythology as
the source of her vision, Lorde points to her own mythmaking. As
positive acts of self-definition, the affirmation of female African origins
and the resurrection of a mythic Caribbean past spell the freedom of the
black woman. Lorde believes in the power of myth to transform the
deepest structures of society.[8] In her lesbian utopia, a plurality of identities (black, female, lesbian), a line of women (her ancestors, her mothers, her lovers) coalesce into one name. The autobiographical "I" becomes a collective "we." Fragmentation is resolved into wholeness;
difference and sameness, no longer seen as opposites, exchange their
mutual power.

> I am the reflection of my mother's secret poetry as well as of her
> hidden angers.

Lorde is a poet, a "Black woman poet warrior" (*SO*, p. 41), and, like
most writer-autobiographers, she traces in her autobiography the gene-

---

7. C. G. Jung and C. Kerényi, *Essays on a Science of Mythology: The Myth of the Divine Child and the Mysteries of Eleusis* (Princeton: Princeton University Press, 1949), p. 162, quoted in Stephanie A. Demetrakopoulos, "The Methaphysics of Matrilinearism in Women's Autobiog-raphy: Studies of Mead's *Blackberry Winter,* Hellman's *Pentimento,* Angelou's *I Know Why the Caged Bird Sings* and Kingston's *The Woman Warrior,*" in *Women's Autobiographies,* ed. Estelle C. Jelinek (Bloomington: Indiana University Press, 1980), pp. 180–205. Demetrakopoulos presents a Jungian analysis of matrilineal consciousness in women's autobiographies. The universality of the Jungian archetypes overwhelmingly relies on their embodiment in Western tradition. Lorde's insistence on matrilinealism is explicitly inscribed in a different tradition (black, African).

8. Alicia Ostriker, in "Thieves of Language: Female Poets and Revisionist Mythmaking," *Signs* 8 (1982): 72, defines revisionist mythmaking as "ultimately making cutural change possible."

sis of her vocation. The aggressive bold print of one chapter heading in *Zami,* "How I Became a Poet," ironically recall traditional auto-biographical gestures of self-dramatization and self-aggrandizement. Yet she owes her creativity not to literary forefathers or to a remarkable incident but rather to her mother's special relationship to language. Anticlimactically responding to the boldness of the chapter heading, the poetic voice—the personal voice—speaks in italics. Lorde goes back to the relational, to the intimate. She sees it as her poetic mission to give life to what had remained secret and unsaid in her mother. Her mother's "picaresque constructions and surreal scenes" are the very material of her poems (*Z,* p. 32), but with a difference. Lorde mocks her mother's euphemisms for the unnameable parts of the body. Whereas in her family "the sensual content of life was masked and cryptic," Lorde will attempt in her autobiography to speak the erotic (*Z,* p. 32).[9] Yet, even when she conjures the power of the erotic—especially then—her link to language bears the imprint of her mother's relationship to words.

The words she cites as examples of the poetry of her mother's language recall home, the island of Grenada: "Impassible and impossible distances were measured by the distance from 'Hog to Kick'em Jenny'" (*Z,* p. 32). She teaches her reader two words, *cro-bo-so* and *zandelee,* which will reappear in her text at moments of emotional intensity. It is symptomatic of her relationship to her mother's language—and, beyond it, to her mother—that her lovemaking with Muriel is couched in her mother's words. With centuries of magical and healing knowledge in her hands, her mother does not massage her backbone but "raises her *zandelee.*" Later in her text, imparting the knowledge of the island women to her lover, Lorde will tell Muriel, "In the West Indies they call this, raising your *zandelee*" (p. 195). In another poignant recollection, she remembers being swung around by her father, who held both her mother and Lorde in his arms: "I remember being delighted and thrilled at his attention, as well as terrified by the familiar surroundings suddenly turning *cro-bo-so*" (*Z,* p. 57). This momentary re-creation of the familial triangle, with its mixture of pleasure and pain, its intimacy, calls for one of her mother's words. A few pages earlier, the reader had been introduced to Lorde's private language: "I never caught cold, but 'got co-hum, co-hum,' and then everything turned 'cro-bo-so,' topsy-turvy, or at least, a bit askew" (p. 32). The words of the mother used by the daughter erase exile, eliminate distance in space and time.[10] They lead the reader

9. In "Uses of the Erotic: The Erotic as Power," in *Sister Outsider,* pp. 53–60, Lorde opposes the sexual to the erotic. For her, the erotic is a way of knowing, a resource that women must recover.

10. Ostriker, p. 87, sees this fusion of past and present as an essential feature of women poets' revisionist mythmaking: she opposes it to male mythmaking, which "[represents] history as a decline, or [bemoans] disjunctions of past and present."

to the paradisiacal island, the vision of which is handed down across generations.

As a poet, Lorde will use the written word to translate the oral poetry of her mother's language, but writing is also associated with her mother, her first writing teacher: "I sat at the kitchen table with my mother, tracing letters and calling their names" (*Z*, p. 23). From the start, the visual and the aural are bound together; the mother asks her daughter to *call* the names of the letters (emphasis mine). Earlier on, in an attempt to retrace her filiation, Lorde had quoted the jingle the illiterate Carriacou women had devised to identify the tobacco shop: "3/4 of a cross / and a circle complete / 2 semi-circles and a perpendicular meet . . ." (p. 11). The poet wants to retain a certain quality of the letter which she links to her ancestors' illiteracy. For them, the letter is a line, a drawing, a design. Soon it also becomes a rhythm, a song, a melody. A trace of this attraction to the visual and concrete character of the letter can be detected in Lorde's use of the different possibilities offered by print: italics, bold characters of different typefaces, the spacing of the words on the line, the graphic reproduction of melodies. Qualifying the relationship between literacy and illiteracy, the black female poet strives to rescue the graphic beauty of writing.

The power of naming, the coincidence of the letter with identity, is stressed in a childhood episode in which Lorde suppresses the last letter of her name, disobeying her mother's injunctions: "I did not like the tail of the Y hanging down below the line in Audrey, and would always forget to put it on, which used to disturb my mother greatly. I used to love the evenness of AUDRELORDE at four years of age" (p. 24). The little girl literally sees her identity through the evenness of the spelling of her name, a sure sign of stability and wholeness. During another episode at school, she refuses to print only the first letter of her name; instead, she spells it across the page, filling two pages of her notebook. It is as if she feared that her self would be truncated, mutilated, if her name were not spelled in full. At that moment in the autobiographical text, collapsing the past of childhood and the present of reading, Lorde the autobiographer reenacts her childhood transgression as she reproduces her slanting name on the page (p. 25). Fusing past, present, and future, each reader will in turn repeat Lorde's action.

Her childhood gesture is also replayed by the bold spelling of Zami across the cover. Lorde in her role as writer is using the power of writing, already known to her as a child. All these episodes linking writing and identity contain the motif of self-assertion which Lorde develops as an adult woman. She insists that self-definition is the only way to fight oppression. Black women should not wait for other-imposed definitions but should name themselves: "For Black women as well as Black men, it is axiomatic that if we do not define ourselves for ourselves, we will be defined by others—for their use and to our detriment" (*SO*, p. 45). Lorde's conviction contrasts with a feminist approach that sees language as the place of women's subjection and hence ultimately advocates silence or a retreat into poetry.[11] Lorde does not see silence as a viable alternative: "I remind myself all the time now that if I were to have been born mute, or had maintained an oath of silence my whole life long for safety, I would still have suffered and I would still die" (*SO*, p. 43). A fiercely active denomination is the most crucial aspect of her militancy: "What is most important to me must be spoken, made verbal and shared, even at the risk of having it bruised and misunderstood" (*SO*, p. 40). Her parents refused to give racism a name (*Z*, p. 69), hoping they would eradicate it; Lorde, however, defines it.

To become a poet, Lorde has moved from the oral poetry of her mother to the written text, from the songs of the Carriacou women to the poems, from silence to language and, beyond language, to action. But in the chapter "How I Became a Poet" (*Zami*), she further locates her vocation in two intimate episodes that describe her physical, sensual relationship to her mother. What she owes to her mother has its source beyond language: "I think I got another message from her . . . that there was a whole powerful world of nonverbal communication and contact between people that was absolutely essential and that was what you had to learn to decipher and use" (*SO*, p. 83). Lorde's conception of the poetic reflects her attachment to the semiotic, to that "homosexual-maternal-facet," which Kristeva defines as "a whirl of words, a complete absence of meaning and seeing; it is a feeling, displacement, rhythm, sound, flashes and fantasied clinging to the maternal body as a screen against the plunge."[12] Lorde remained in a preverbal world until the age of four (*Z*, p. 31). In an interview with Adrienne Rich, she explains how gradual her coming to language was: "I kept myself through feeling—I lived through it. And at such a subterranean level that I didn't know how to talk. I was busy feeling out other ways of getting and giving information and whatever else I could because talking wasn't where it was at" (*SO*, p. 81). It is through her mother that she comes to understand feeling as a way of communicating, and this debt she acknowledges in her autobiography.

The depiction of a familiar scene, soon transformed into a symbolic

---

11. For a survey of the feminist debate on women's language, see Ostriker, pp. 71–72. Like Hélène Cixous, Lorde insists that writing is action, yet she does not advocate the radical disruptiveness of *écriture féminine* since she sees the "oppressor's language" as the product of sexism, homophobia, *and* racism.

12. Julia Kristeva, *Desire in Language: A Semiotic Approach to Literature and Art* (New York: Columbia University Press, 1980), p. 239.

birth, follows her reflection on her mother's language. The child Audre is sitting between her mother's spread legs; the mother is combing her daughter's hair: "I remember the warm mother smell caught between her legs, and the intimacy of our physical touching nestled inside of the anxiety/pain like a nutmeg nestled inside its covering of mace" (Z, p. 33). While acknowledging the tensions—the oneness with the mother is always already a separation—the image expresses her rapport with her mother, her sense of belonging to the island of Carriacou, and discloses the source of her lesbianism. The comparison with the nutmeg coalesces notions of closeness, of unity, and yet of difference, but a difference that spells complementarity rather than opposition. The protection of the mace recalls her mother's legs encircling her shoulders, her hair, her mother's pubic hair. The rich red color of the mace netting before the nutmeg is dried might even hint at the womb and the placenta, with its net of blood veinlets. The image evokes the envelope, the nest of the first abode, together with the richness of taste and the concentration of power. It is the secret sign of home, the island of Carriacou, of Grenada, one of the main producers of nutmeg.[13]

The same sort of intimacy is revealed in Lorde's recollections of the time spent in bed with her mother. The little girl would play with the water bottle, its softness and the liquid within suggesting uterine life. The playfulness and the eroticism emphasize the link between the lesbian and the maternal, the point on which Lorde purposely chooses to close her book: "There [in Carriacou] it is said that the desire to lie with other women is a drive from the mother's blood" (Z, p. 256).[14] The remembrance also echoes the sensuality of the prologue when Audre "[sits] and [plays] in the waters of [her] bath" (Z, p. 7). It is an attempt to eliminate difference, to reach identity/sameness by creating in words the sensations and the experience of the lost oneness. Yet, at the end of the episode, her mother finally gets up and leaves her alone. If poetry is an attempt to transcribe the mother's language, it is because the reality of

13. I see in this metaphor an answer to Luce Irigaray's suggestion that "common symbols must be created among women so that love between them can take place." Later on, Irigaray muses: "Both of them. Them both, within one and not closed. Constituting two in one un-looped, the sign of the infinite? Traveling in their mutual relationships the distance of the infinite, but an infinite always open, not finite." Ethique de la différence sexuelle (Paris: Minuit, 1983), p. 103, my translation. Irigaray's own symbolism, the mathematical sign of the infinite, contrasts with Lorde's. For the abstract sign of the female philosopher, the black female poet substitutes the concrete, the visual, natural image of the rich spice. Her metaphors insist on the sensual reference.

14. A thematics of blood runs through the book. Lorde stresses the importance of her first menstruation (Z, p. 74) and later records the pain of her abortion and her horrible bleeding (Z, pp. 109–15). In her feminist symbolism, blood becomes a sign of strength and knowledge shared by all women (Z, p. 78).

birth, history, the abruptness of the maternal dismissal, bring the writer back to the necessity of separation. Poetry and, in this case, autobiography can be described as an effort to erase the state of separateness between mother and child.[15]

In contrast to this desire to recover oneness with the mother, Lorde's actual relationship to her mother is fraught with tension. She even leaves home (*Z*, p. 10) and will feel free of her mother only when she acknowledges her mother's dependence on her father on the day of his death: "I saw my mother's pain, and her blindness, and her strength, and for the first time, I began to see her as separate from me, and I began to feel free of her" (*Z*, p. 143). The child Audre sometimes dreamt for herself a mother who corresponded to the image of the dominant ideology, "the blonde smiling mother in *Dick and Jane*" (*Z*, p. 55). Later, she reinterprets this feeling to trace a filiation: "As a child, I always knew my mother was different from the other women I knew, Black or white. . . . *Different how?* I never knew. But it is why to this day I believe that there have always been Black dykes around—in the sense of powerful and women-oriented women—who would rather have died than use that name for themselves. And that includes my momma" (*Z*, p. 15). Her whole mythmaking enterprise is an attempt to resolve the tensions, to find the intimacy of the newborn, to return to the female, to the same. Her text, however, spells the gap between her own awareness—she calls herself a "dyke"—and her mother's resistance, which she hopes to overcome by calling her "momma." Yearning for a reconciliation, Lorde unveils her most private desires. She makes explicit in its concrete implications the incestuous relationship of the mother and the daughter, a recurrent motif in lesbian mythmaking.[16] She remembers the day she first menstruated: "Years afterward when I was grown, whenever I thought about the way I smelled that day, I would have a fantasy of my mother, her hands wiped dry from the washing, and her apron untied and laid neatly away, looking down upon me lying on the couch, and then, slowly, thoroughly, our touching and caressing each other's most secret places" (*Z*, p. 78). The mythic vision finds its source in the physicality of her experience, in the privacy of her sexual fantasies.[17]

Another episode paralleling the ritual of hair combing takes place on the day of her first period. Pounding spices with a pestle to prepare a Caribbean dish, Lorde is holding her mother's mortar against her,

---

15. A similar position is argued by Lynn Z. Bloom in "Heritages."

16. See Tucker Farley, "Realities and Fictions: Lesbian Visions of Utopia," in *Women in Search of Utopia: Mavericks and Mythmakers,* ed. Ruby Rohrlich and Elaine Hoffman Baruch (New York: Schocken Books, 1984), p. 240.

17. Barbara Christian, in *Black Feminist Criticism,* sees the exploration of female sexuality as central to black American female writers' novels of the 1980s and insists that understanding society's oppression of different women is the task of the literary critic (p. 189).

"*Thud push rub rotate up*. The feeling of the pestle held between my curving fingers, and the mortar's outside rounding like a fruit into my palm as I steadied it against my body" (*Z*, p. 74). Making *souse* is a means for Lorde of recovering a world of scent, sensation, rhythm, and sound. The grinding of the spices on the day when she first menstruates becomes a ritual, "a piece of old and elaborate dance between [her] mother and [herself]" (*Z*, p. 76). It is this core of feeling which originates in the mother's womb, this preverbal erotic sensuality, which Lorde places at the basis of her poetry. She lingers in these moments of raw intimacy, her text an attempt at ritualizing the sensuous.

In her essay "Poetry Is Not a Luxury," Lorde writes: "The white fathers told us: I think, therefore I am. The Black mother within each of us—the poet—whispers in our dreams: I feel, therefore I can be free" (*SO*, p. 38). Such a position seems to be a restatement in feminist terms of the eternal feminine, of woman as the center of emotions, as the irrational, instinctual being that men have often said she was. In answer to Adrienne Rich, Lorde qualifies her statement: "Ultimately, I don't see feel/think as a dichotomy. I see them as a choice of ways and a combination" (*SO*, p. 101). Insofar as it can re-create a specific feeling, already experienced, female writers should see poetry as their language, long forgotten, long suppressed. Watching the little blind bird-boy Jeroméo, Lorde explains: "For the first time in my life, I had an insight into what poetry could be. I could use words to recreate that feeling, rather than to create a dream" (*Z*, p. 160). In *Zami*, Lorde is constructing a myth based on the poetic re-creation of intense past experiences. The feminist lesbian poet consciously recaptures past feelings translatable only by poetry, which is "a revelatory distillation of experience" (*SO*, 37).[18]

> Poetry is the way we help give name to the nameless so that it can be thought.

Lorde struggles with the traditional medium of autobiography, the narrative reconstruction of past experiences in a chronological sequence. She acknowledges her uneasiness with representation, the re-creation of a referential narrative through a set of conventions borrowed from the realistic novel, and she knows herself to be primarily a poet: "Communicating deep feeling in linear, solid blocks of print felt arcane, a method

18. For a poststructuralist view of the specificity and the authority of female experience, see Jonathan Culler, "Reading as a Woman," in *On Deconstruction: Theory and Criticism after Structuralism* (Ithaca: Cornell University Press, 1982); and Peggy Kamuf, "Writing like a Woman," in *Women and Language in Literature and Society*, ed. Sally McConnell-Ginet, Ruth Borker, and Nelly Furman (New York: Praeger, 1980), pp. 284–99. Lorde believes, however, that poetry can re-create a specific feeling already experienced.

beyond me" (*SO*, p. 87). This reluctance to use the conventions of realistic writing corresponds to new definitions of the autobiographical act. Elizabeth W. Bruss, for instance, comes to the conclusion that autobiography, though it appears to privilege chronological linearity, actually tends "towards discontinuous foci of attention."[19]

In *Zami* the constructed linearity of the autobiographical narrative is interrupted by poems, or it stops suddenly for poetic exploration and the re-creation of a remembered feeling, for the recapturing of a lost past sensation. Poetry surfaces at the crucial moments of Lorde's life story, as when her first love, Gennie, dies (*Z*, p. 103). Similarly, a poem marks her passage from the carelessness of childhood to the demands of life (*Z*, p. 97), and again, she quotes the poem of despair, when writing was her only way of feeling alive (*Z*, 118). It is through these self-quotations that Lorde identifies her commitment to poetry as well as her resistance to prose writing. Poetry shapes her life; it also dates her autobiographical text. It creates a plurality of textual selves. The surfacing of the poetic self through delineated, self-contained poems creates intense moments followed by gaps and breaks. In *Zami* the illusory fullness of linear realistic writing is the exception rather than the rule. Lorde's writing, however, never takes on the self-consciousness of, for example, Monique Wittig's in *Le Corps lesbien* or *Les Guérillères*. Wittig creates through language a lesbian subjectivity, sees language as the place and the material in which to construct the subject.[20] Lorde's myth-making does not entail such a radical reshaping of language.

Lorde often resorts to italics to break the rhythm of realistic writing, to modulate it, to blur the possible identification by the reader of the source of writing, of the voice. The autobiographical "I" of the prose narrative often disappears, replaced by the omniscient and yet paradoxically elusive voice in these italicized passages. Italics help to create polyphony and are uttered by other voices than that of the traditional autobiographical narrator.[21] Lorde gives us lists of women's names in

19. Elizabeth W. Bruss, *Autobiographical Acts: The Changing Situation of a Literary Genre* (Baltimore: Johns Hopkins University Press, 1976), p. 64.

20. For an analysis of Wittig's lesbian writing, see Namascar Shaktini, "Displacing the Phallic Subject: Wittig's Lesbian Writing," *Signs* 8 (Autumn 1982): 29–44. Bertha Harris's definition of lesbian writing—"If in a woman writer's work a sentence refuses to do what it is supposed to do, if there are strong images of women, and if there is a refusal to be linear, the result is innately lesbian literature"—is problematic, for it coincides with the experiments of a number of contemporary male writers, notably Roland Barthes and Michel Leiris. Harris is quoted by Barbara Smith in "Toward a Black Feminist Criticism," *Conditions: Two* 1 (Oct. 1977): 33.

21. In *Le journal intime* (Paris: Presses Universitaires de France, 1976), Béatrice Didier makes the comment: "Italics establish a contour. They correspond to underlining in a manuscript, i.e., to a line, a distinctly graphic element. . . . Italics will at times create a polyphony in a fundamentally monophonic text" (pp. 185–86). For Lorde, italics introduce a stronger voice, but they also work to reproduce the handwritten page of the diary.

italics (*Z*, pp. 14, 104, 158, 226, 255). Uttered by a collective voice instead of the writer's "I," they represent litanies that must be spoken out loud. Italics also introduce a rupture in the chronology when Lorde tells us that she met Muriel twenty years after the moment being recalled in the text (*Z*, p. 190). In another instance, the roles are reversed: the adult self comments on the adolescent "I" created through the narration in italics (*Z*, p. 141). Since Lorde does not use them consistently for the same purpose, italics can only be said to be the sign of the passage from one memory to the next, from one mode of remembering to another.

Habitually, however, italics signal a self-contained narrative, such as the episode of the Jewish man Sol (*Z*, p. 182) or the last of her childhood nightmares (*Z*, p. 198). The organization of these italicized narratives often revolves around a central sensual or poetic experience: the description of the pickle man (*Z*, p. 130), the picture of her lover Ginger (*Z*, p. 136) or the little blind boy Jeroméo (*Z*, p. 160). The intensity of these poetic passages culminates in the description of her lovemaking with Afrekete, which rises above the chronological sequence, expands the privacy of the feelings beyond the individual moment into a mythic encounter: "Afrekete Afrekete ride me to the crossroads where we shall sleep, coated in the woman's power. The sound of our bodies meeting is the prayer to all strangers and sisters, that the discarded evils, abandoned at all crossroads, will not follow us upon our journeys" (*Z*, p. 252). The urgency of the prayer makes it a powerful oracular plea for women's love.

Whereas italicized passages signal interruptions in the narrative, snatches of songs bridge the gaps between episodes. Lorde, in effect, dedicates her book to "the writers of songs whose melodies stitch up [her] years" (acknowledgments page). Songs offer a reconciliation between oral and written which linear narrative only faintly attempts. They are foils for intense moments in Lorde's life, echoing and replaying in their music and lyrics love encountered, love lost. Lorde tells us at the beginning of her autobiography that in her mother's native island songs are spontaneously made about people (*Z*, p. 11). It is the spontaneity and the naturalness of the songs, their humorous and ironic commentary on life that she wishes to preserve.[22]

Songs fuse different events in her life, crystallize the intensity of different moments. As counterpoint to her parting with Gennie, she offers Sarah Vaughan's "chocolate voice repeating over and over, I saw the harbor lights" (*Z*, p. 98). Fats Domino's "I found ma' thrill-l-l-l-lll / On Blueberreeeeee Hill—lllll" (*Z*, p. 136) comically punctuates

---

22. Martha Vicinus suggested this opposition to me.

her encounter with Ginger on a hill, and earlier on, Rosemary Clooney's voice, anticipating Ginger's offer, pleads: "*Come on a my house, my house a come on*" (*Z*, p. 130). When singing, Ginger mixes this song, the song Lorde associated with Gennie, and "*If I came home tonight, would you still be my. . .*" (*Z*, p. 138). The melodies replay life, comment upon it, telling always of going home, to the lover's home, or of leaving, of forever parting. Her sister's song, played over and over when her father dies, is a cruel reminder of the departure of death: "For I know you'll be gone / and I'll be here all alone" (*Z*, p. 144). Songs also accompany her life with her friends: Rosemary Clooney presides over her joy (*Z*, p. 191); Ruth Brown and Frank Sinatra are heard as women dance and talk (*Z*, p. 220). Doris Day's lyrics prophetically proclaim the uncertainty of the future: "Que Será, Que Será [*sic*]. / Whatever will be, will be" (*Z*, p. 228), and Lorde's love encounter with Afrekete is to the sounds of Frankie Lymon's "Goody, Goody," a Belafonte calypso, and a slow Sinatra (*Z*, p. 245).

Lorde literally owes her survival, after the end of her relationship with Muriel, to a spiritual she repeats in her head while she is graphically trying to bring to the reader's mind the power of the melody (*Z*, p. 238). It is a song of hope, of death and resurrection, a parallel to her own progress; after her emotional death when Muriel leaves her, she will finally emerge full of determination. The irony of Elvis Presley's "Heartbreak Hotel" will echo, at that time, her homelessness and love-lessness: "Now that my baby's left me I've found a new place to dwell. / It's down at the end of Lonely Street in Heartbreak Hotel" (*Z*, p. 240).

In contrast to these harmless melodies, Lorde quotes one song that, like the spiritual that gives her hope, spells the plight of the black woman. A tuneless song, it is the voice of the goddess speaking through one of the most victimized women in her story, Ella, Gennie's stepmother: "Momma kilt me / Poppa et me / Po' lil' brudder / suck ma bones. . ." (*Z*, p. 251). The song is from a story about a mother who kills her own child, an Afro-American version of a European tale, which was told by slaves. As Lawrence W. Levine relates the story, "The murderous mother, . . . after eating the possum her husband brings home for the entire family to share, becomes frightened and kills and bakes one of her children, serving it to the husband at dinner. While eating, the husband is informed of the murder, either by a bird who flies in and sings of the crime or by the child's spirit who sings: 'My mother killed me. / My father ate me. / My brother buried my bone / Under a marble stone?'"[23] Lorde rereads this story from her culture's folklore in a femi-

23. Lawrence W. Levine, *Black Culture and Black Consciousness: Afro-American Thought from Slavery to Freedom* (New York: Oxford University Press, 1977), p. 95.

nist context, seeing in it the story of a daughter, killed by her mother for the benefit of the male members of the family. The murder of the daughter, exemplified by the narrative of Gennie's suicide, contrasts with the myth Lorde ceaselessly constructs. The tale does not tell of women's innate wickedness; rather it epitomizes self-hatred, which is the result of a deeper crime identified by Hélène Cixous: "Men have committed the greatest crime against women. Insidiously, violently, they have led them to hate women, to be their own enemies, to mobilize their immense strength against themselves, to be the executants of their virile needs. They have made for women an antinarcissism!"[24] Denouncing the self-hatred mythically embodied in the murder of the daughter by the mother, Lorde strives to recapture the paradisiacal past of black women. She wants to reclaim what has been taken away from them: "What was native has been stolen from us, the love of Black women for each other" (*SO*, p. 175).

Overall, popular culture underscores personal emotional states, whereas African Caribbean myths describe Lorde's gradual achievement of identity. The popular songs, which deal with heterosexual love, are often used ironically. They bring comic relief and are a contemporary version of the songs created impromptu by the Caribbean women. One can easily appreciate the difference, however, and participate in Lorde's nostalgia. Together with the dated poems, they correspond on the textual level to an anchoring in time, which Lorde, as the autobiographer-narrator, needs. The Afro-American myths, on the other hand, transcend the limit of this chronology, since they define the mythic self.[25]

I coming out blackened and whole.

Zami's many starts formally echo the attempt to recapture cosmological time through the mythologizing of the female self. Typically, the beginning is delayed; the text refuses to give itself a start, an initial episode, a grounding event. The book is dedicated to three women, one of whom does not appear in the text at all; from the outset the reader's trust in the reliability of autobiography is undermined. The second

24. Hélène Cixous, "The Laugh of the Medusa," *New French Feminisms,* ed. Elaine Marks and Isabelle de Courtivron (New York: Schocken Books, 1981), p. 248. It would be interesting to examine this manifesto in the light of Lorde's "Poetry Is Not a Luxury." Both women insist on the urgency of writing for women; they both define or, in Cixous's case, at least suggest possible avenues. They both see women as dark. Yet, whereas Lorde can literally talk about "the Black mother inside each of us" (*SO*, p. 380), Cixous's reference to darkness is metaphoric.

25. See also Elizabeth Fox-Genovese, "To Write My Self: The Autobiographies of Afro-American Women," in *Feminist Issues in Literary Scholarship,* ed. Shari Benstock (Bloomington: Indiana University Press, 1987), p. 180, n. 27.

woman mentioned, Helen, could be Lorde's sister. The last one is the African goddess, who, incarnated in Kitty, is Lorde's last lover in *Zami*. The narrative itself starts with Grenada, the mother's land, the earth of the mother's home.

Along with the evocation of a community of women comes the notion of debt which defines the female self.[26] Lorde's writing is placed under the sign of "recognition": an acknowledgment of debt, an expression of gratitude, and, more deeply, a discovery of the self in others, a rebirth in the realization of the power of matrilineality. For the female poet, everything takes place as if writing, like living, signals a dependence. Commenting on *La Bâtarde*, Violette Leduc's autobiography, Martha Noel Evans defines the genre: "To write one's life, one's autobiography, is to recognize implicitly that existing is not enough to justify one's life; writing (graphy) compensates for this lack of being (bio) by allowing the writer to give herself a second self-generated (auto) birth. . . . Thus autobiography is nourished by a dream of self-genesis."[27] Lorde greatly departs from that individual dream of self-genesis. She is more interested in establishing, or rather unearthing and reasserting, a collective mythology through her writing than in grounding her identity on a purely reflexive (auto) gesture. She does not justify her life though her text; her writing does not fill in the gap of her being. It is instead an affirmation of being; it celebrates a myth, i.e., a truth, a power. When she writes "stories," Lorde prefers to sign with a pseudonym (*SO*, 87). *Zami* is somehow signed by both Lorde and Zami, by both the more personal "I" and the mythic self.

Lorde's biomythography is not an individual act of rebirth. Playing with the correspondence between writing (*graphein*) and life (*bios*), she tells us how, beyond the conception of her life, she also owes the conception of her book to women. She is "recreating in words the women who helped give [her] substance" (*Z*, p. 255). At another point, her lover's body becomes "a well-touched book" (*Z*, p. 248).[28] Echoing the

26. Didier, *Le Journal intime*, p. 41: "Women's diaries paradoxically succeed in referring constantly to other beings, whereas men's diaries are usually the epitome of egocentrism."

27. I am translating from Martha Noël Evans, "La Mythologie de l'écriture dans *La Bâtarde* de Violette Leduc," *Littérature* 46 (May 1982): 82. The essay has been adapted and translated in *The (M)other Tongue: Essays in Feminist Psychoanalytic Interpretation*, ed. Shirley Nelson Garner, Claire Kahane, and Madelon Sprengnether (Ithaca: Cornell University Press, 1985), pp. 306–17.

28. This writing of the body parallels Cixous's injunctions in "The Laugh of the Medusa," but it corresponds more precisely to Gloria Anzaldúa's "organic writing": "It's not on paper that you create but in your innards, in the gut and out of living tissue—*organic writing* I call it." "Speaking in Tongues: A Letter to Third World Women Writers," in *This Bridge Called My Back*, ed. Cherríe Moraga and Gloria Anzaldúa (Watertown, Mass.: Persephone Press, 1981), p. 172.

comprehensiveness and the urgency of the last list of women's names (Z, p. 255), the acknowledgments start with the making of the book and the women who helped her with her writing. They end with thanks addressed to her family, her mother, her children, and finally, to close the circle, to the women of Carriacou who "proofread [her] dreams." The metaphor is not innocent. Lorde reverses here the opposition between literacy and illiteracy. Her writing comes to life mediated, "proofread," by her female ancestors who in a way carry on performing, through her work, their offices as midwives.[29]

Lorde retells in her own words Alice Walker's powerful lesson about the source of black female creativity.[30] It is close to home, in the luxuriance and beauty of her mother's garden, that Walker finds the sure sign of the power of black women's imagination, that she realizes the lineage of creativity, in which she is only one manifestation. By signing her name as Zami, Lorde similarly acknowledges the source of her creative energy. Her life-giving ancestors help her create a book that is literally life-giving, since Lorde wrote it when she was fighting a battle against cancer. Surviving, like birth, signals a debt. She almost endlessly asks herself: "*To whom do I owe the symbols of my survival?*" (Z, p.3), and she will thus add other acknowledgments to the formal ones. Women have helped her survive, have contributed to her emergence from chaos, and she cannot resist the lesbian pun: "Images of women flaming like torches adorn and define the borders of my journey, stand like dykes between me and the chaos. It is the images of women, kind and cruel, that lead me home" (Z, p. 3). Telling her mother's story necessarily means retracing her genealogical tree. Beyond her own symbolic birth, she pictures her mother's: "My mother Linda was born between the waiting palms of [my great-aunt's] loving hands" (Z, p. 13). Returning to the past, Lorde discovers and recovers sameness, life as a continuum of women giving birth.

Her mother's land, Carriacou, becomes the occasion for the evocation of a lesbian paradise. Lorde never doubts the existence of this magical island, associated with childhood tastes and smells and handed down to her out of her mother's mouth: "*Carriacou*, a magic name like cinnamon, nutmeg, mace, the delicate little squares of guava jelly each lovingly

---

29. In "Towards a Black Feminist Criticism," Barbara Smith remarks on the way in which writers such as Hurston, Margaret Walker, Toni Morrison, and Alice Walker incorporate root working, herbal medicine, conjuring, and midwifery into the fabric of their stories. *All the Women Are White / All the Blacks Are Men / But Some of Us Are Brave: Black Women's Studies*, ed. Gloria T. Hull, Patricia Bell Scott, and Barbara Smith (Old Westbury, N.Y.: Feminist Press, 1982), p. 164.

30. See Alice Walker, *In Search of Our Mothers' Gardens* (New York: Harcourt Brace Jovanovich, 1983), pp. 229–43.

wrapped in tiny bits of crazy-quilt wax-paper cut precisely from bread wrappers, the long sticks of dried vanilla and the sweet-smelling tonka bean, chalky brown nuggets of pressed chocolate for cocoa-tea, all set on a bed of wild bay laurel leaves, arriving every Christmas time in a well-wrapped tea-tin" (Z, p. 14). The vividness of her mother's evocation transcends the "reality" of Carriacou "captured on paper" by colonizing map making, which Lorde will only discover at twenty-six. Picturing her mother's past as idyllic, Lorde resurrects a world of women, her ancestors as powerful and self-determined women. The lists of their first names recall the *feminaries* of Wittig's *Guérillères*.[31] At the call of their names, the island women gather strength, exalt their good qualities, and are gradually aggrandized into powerful mythic figures: *"Madivine. Friending. Zami. How Carriacou women love each other is legend in Grenada, and so is their strength and their beauty"* (Z, p. 14). Instead of choosing exile, Carriacou women send their men away, the better to love one another. They work together, cooperate, their individualities blending into the plural name of Zami.[32] Lesbianism is as natural to them as the blood that runs through their veins (Z, p. 255).

Lorde visualizes her lovers as part of a never-ending female chain of being: *"Their shapes join Linda and Gran'Ma Liz and Gran'Aunt Anni in my dreaming, where they dance with swords in their hands, stately forceful steps, to mark the time when they were all warriors"* (Z, p. 104). These women are warriors like her friend Eudora, who, having lost one of her breasts to cancer, will be described as an Amazon (Z, p. 167). Even when life in its banality and ordinariness resists the mythical thrust, Lorde manages to transform it, to incorporate it in her vision. She changes symbols of weakness into signs of strength.[33] Her joy as she, *"in libation, wet[s] the ground to [her] old heads"* (Z, p. 104) recalls the opening of *Les Guérillères*, in which women are urinating in a circle (Z, p. 9). The women in Mexico (Z, p. 158), those of the gay scene in the Village (Z, chap. 29), the sister-outsiders (Z, p. 226), are all listed throughout her work, and these women gather strength as they gather numbers: *"Ma-Liz, DeLois,*

---

31. In *Les Guérillères*, trans. David LeVay, Monique Wittig writes: "THAT WHICH IDENTIFIES THEM / LIKE THE EYE OF THE CYCLOPS, / THEIR SINGLE FORE-NAME" (New York: Viking Press, 1971), p. 13. The feminary "consists of pages with words printed in a varying number of capital letters. There may be only one or the pages may be full of them. Usually they are isolated at the center of the page, well spaced, black on a white background or else white on a black background" (p. 15).

32. "Zami" is *patois* for lesbians throughout the Caribbean, based on the French expression "les amies." Chinosole, p. 12.

33. Similarly, the Women's House of Detention becomes a symbol of power, "a defiant pocket of female resistance, ever-present as a reminder of possibility, as well as punishment" (Z, p. 206).

Louise Briscoe, Aunt Anni, Linda, and Geneviève; MawuLisa, thunder, sky, sun, the great mother of us all; and Afrekete, her youngest daughter, the mischievous linguist, trickster, best-beloved, whom we must all become" (Z, p. 255). This last litany links them all—the Carriacou ancestors; the loving aunts; Linda the brave mother; DeLois and Louise Brisco, black women, courageous and proud in the face of death and insult; Geneviève, the first love; the great androgynous goddess, MawuLisa, and Afrekete, the last lover, the black woman of the future.

Retracing her genealogy, Lorde will elaborate on African mythology as the source of her identity. Lovemaking with Afrekete takes place under the sign of Mawu, the African goddess of the moon: "I remember the full moon like white pupils in the center of your wide irises" (Z, p. 252).[34] In her poem-letter to Mary Daly, she asks the feminist critic why the goddess images she cites are white, Eastern European, Judaeo-Christian (SO, pp. 66–72). Similarly, the Jungian archetype of the relationship between the mother and the daughter is often described as the Demeter/Kore myth while the archetypal return of the goddess in Western art is explained in reference to Occidental mythology.[35] The point Lorde makes underscores the racism inherent in Daly's references, the de facto exclusion of women of color. Lorde's autobiography is a combative assertion of non-Western mythological sources that reflect her identity. She consequently goes back to African myths of the origin and recovers MawuLisa, the androgynous goddess, whom Geoffrey Parrinder describes:

Mawu is sometimes called male and sometimes female; Mawu has a partner called Lisa. . . . One myth says that these twins were born from a primordial mother, Nana Buluku, who created the world and then retired. Mawu was the moon and female, having control of the night and dwelling in the west. Lisa was male, the sun, and lived in the east. . . . Whenever there is an eclipse of the sun or moon it is said that Mawu and Lisa are making love.[36]

34. Newell S. Booth, Jr., "God and the Gods in West Africa," in *African Religions*, ed. Booth (New York: Nok Publishers, 1977), p. 162, says that for the eastern Ewe (Dahomey), Mawu is "the particular name of the deity associated with the moon."

35. For an analysis of the return of the goddess in contemporary arts, see Estelle Lauter, *Women as Myth-Makers: Poetry and Visual Art by Twentieth-Century Women* (Bloomington: Indiana University Press, 1984). Lauter's methodology is problematic when applied to a text by a black female writer. She refers to a history that is Western and European (the witch trials). The return of the goddess for Afro-American and Caribbean writers is necessarily inscribed in a different history.

36. Geoffrey Parrinder, *African Mythology* (London: Paul Hamlyn, 1967), p. 21. Booth, in "God and the Gods," also comments: "Among the Fon [Dahomey] each of the three main pantheons, sky (Mawulisa), earth-smallpox (Shapata), and water-thunder (Sogbo), has certain

The pounding of the spices for *souse* repeats the activity of African women pounding millet. To choose that act as the grounding experience of her female identity is both consistent with African culture and an inversion of African patriarchal mythology.[37] One African origin myth locates the alienation of the gods from human beings in an episode where a woman hits the sky god in the eye with her long pestle.[38]

While Kitty is Afrekete, she is also an incarnation of Lorde's mother. A certain thematic circularity, then, links Lorde's childhood to her adult years when Kitty brings her magical fruit from the West Indian markets: "'I got this under the bridge' was a saying from time immemorial, giving an adequate explanation that whatever it was had come from as far back and as close to home—that is to say, was as authentic—as was possible" (Z, p. 249). Kitty repeats Linda's search: "Little secret sparks of [home] were kept alive for years by my mother's search for tropical fruits 'under the bridge'" (Z, p. 10). By means of this evocation, Afrekete and Lorde's mother are brought together and blended into one woman. The stagnation, con/fusion, between lover and mother recall Luce Irigaray's words: "[Women] move almost without moving. They keep generating so that any distinction between, any clear re-tracing of, ascendance and descendance becomes difficult. The turn, the return, of genealogy is indefinitely repeated within them, between them, like an uninterrupted journey."[39] This regression ad infinitum along the matrilineal line, which is also a reflexive movement leading to the same, is attested to by the Ewe (Dahomey). As Melville J. Herskovits explains, "If I asked about the origin of Mawu, the answer might be that she was created by a pre-existent Mawu; there might have been many Mawus."[40] It is within this line of Mawus that Lorde defines herself. Daughter of the cosmic goddess MawuLisa, Afrekete is at the same time the mythic woman whom Lorde and all her sisters must become. She is the black woman of the future. Indeed, Lorde tells us that she owes her

---

characteristics. Each one . . . is headed by deities who are either androgynous or a pair of female and male twins. . . . The sky pantheon has come to have a certain precedence, with the heads of the other pantheons sometimes thought of as children of Mawu and Lisa" (p. 173). "In parts of central Dahomey and Togo the original creator is thought to have been Nana Buku (Bruku, Buluku), who is represented as female or androgynous. She is referred to as a 'sky god' but also as 'the oldest of the water gods'" (p. 162).

37. In a Dogon village (Sudan), the stone for oil crushing is a symbol of female genitalia. See Marcel Griaule, *Conversations with Ogotemmêli* (London: Oxford University Press, 1967), p. 95.

38. This myth is told in Parrinder's *African Mythology* to accompany the illustration of mortar and pestle (p. 29).

39. Irigaray, *Ethique,* p. 104.

40. Melville J. Herskovits, *Dahomey: An Ancient Western African Kingdom* (New York: J. J. Augustine, 1938), 2:162, quoted by Booth, "God and the Gods," p. 162.

identity "*to the journeywoman pieces of myself. / Becoming. / Afrekete.*" (*Z*, p. 5). The forward motion from fragmentation to wholeness should be added to this circular movement backward toward the origins, the mother, the native land, the female ancestors. The flowing back and forth between origin and destiny, between eden and utopia, eventually leads to a unified vision.

Wholeness means for Lorde a retelling of the myth of the androgyne: "*I have always wanted to be both man and woman, to incorporate the strongest and richest parts of my mother and my father within/into me*" (*Z*, p. 7). Recapturing the African myth of the primordial androgynous deity, Audre Lorde also opts for that "*other bisexuality*" proclaimed by Cixous, "on which every subject not enclosed in the false theater of phallocentric representationalism has founded his/her erotic universe. Bisexuality: that is, each one's location in self (*repérage en soi*) of the presence— variously manifest and insistent according to each person, male or female—of both sexes, non-exclusion either of the difference or of one sex, and, from this 'self-permission,' multiplication of the effects of the inscription of desire, over all parts of my body and the other body."[41] Lorde stresses bodily androgyny. She speaks of the inside ("*within/into me,*" "*the deep inside parts of me*") but she will also mention "*her pearl,*" "*a protruding part of [her], hard, sensitive in a different way*" (*Z*, p. 7). This physical bisexuality arises from African mythology, which states that human beings are born with two souls. The myth is a justification of circumcision and clitoral excision as Marcel Griaule explains: "In so far as the child retains the prepuce or the clitoris—characteristics of the sex opposite to its own apparent sex—its masculinity and femininity are equally potent."[42]

Woman's dual sexuality transforms itself into a varied landscape. Woman is earth. She is the earth goddess. Lorde dreams of merging with nature: "I have always wanted . . . to share valleys and mountains upon my body the way the earth does in hills and peaks" (*Z*, p. 7). Her vision is ultimately pantheistic, embracing "the mountains and valleys, trees, rocks. Sand and flowers and water and stone. Made in earth" (*Z*, p. 7). The eternity of woman fuses with the eternity of the natural world; we are back to the vision of "MawuLisa, thunder, sky, sun, the mother of us all" (*Z*, p. 255). This equation of woman and nature, which could seem to go along with patriarchal claims, stems in fact from African mythology. Though she uses Western sources for her mythical vision, Susan Griffin writes in similar vein: "We know our- selves to be made from this earth. We know this earth to be made from

41. Cixous, p. 254.
42. Griaule, p. 158.

our bodies. For we see ourselves and we are nature."[43] There are differences but no hierarchy. Ultimately, there is no other.[44]

In *Zami* the female autobiographer has the ability to turn the ordinariness of life into larger dreams. The utopian *élan* of the vision can become truly political only after the creation of a series of rituals. That is why Lorde insists upon the enactment of myth. The myth of creation, for instance, is echoed in a childhood episode when Lorde, using flour and vanilla extract, tries to bring to life the sister she did not have: the ideal other. She reenacts a cosmogonic myth; she creates life out of flour and vanilla, just like the first creator, who was female. The first human being she creates is also female.[45] Innocent child's play, personal memories, are endowed with mythic dimension. Remembering is not enough. The ordinary must be elevated to the level of the epic, the exemplary. It must make sense within a series of correspondences set by Lorde. Ordinary women are Amazon warriors; unsung prowess is reclaimed from the everyday life of poor black women. The reader is finally led to question and reexamine his/her own notions of the trivial, the banal, the utterly and desperately private.

Her quest for home, for Carriacou, for the reality and the quality of her link to her mother, her effort to find a tie, go hand in hand with an acknowledgment of difference. The black lesbian poet pictures herself as "the very house of difference" (*Z*, p. 206): "*Being women together was not enough. We were different. Being gay-girls together was not enough. We were different. Being Black together was not enough. We were different. Being Black women together was not enough. We were different. Being Black dykes together was not enough. We were different*" (*Z*, p. 226). Difference and sameness must be thought together in Lorde's epistemology.[46] With Afrekete she tells how hard it is to explain to "anyone who didn't already know it that soft and tough had to be one and the same for either to work at all" (*Z*, p. 250). In the epilogue, looking back on her life, she describes separation as creating the possibility of an encounter: "And in that growing, we came to separation, that place where work begins. Another meeting" (*Z*, p. 255). Breaking away is a meeting of the other in

43. Susan Griffin, *Woman and Nature: The Roaring Inside Her* (New York: Harper and Row, 1978), p. 226.

44. See Lauter, "Woman and Nature: Revisited Poetry by Women," in *Women as Myth-Makers*, pp. 172–203.

45. One can also find the theme of creation from earth, as well as a return to earth through death linked to the play of children, in Maya Angelou's *I Know Why the Caged Bird Sings* (New York: Bantam Books, 1969). Observing a corpse, the narrator remarks: "She had looked like a mud baby, lying on the white satin of her white coffin. A mud baby, molded into form by creative children on a rainy day, soon to run back into the loose earth" (p. 137).

46. Barbara Christian sees Lorde's assertion of difference as a powerful one within the growing body of black feminist thought. See "The Dynamics of Difference: Book Review of Audre Lorde's *Sister Outsider*," in *Black Feminist Criticism*, pp. 205–10.

the self, as separation from the mother is necessary to allow for a new return.

Lorde's refusal to privilege one difference, her insistence on placing herself at the crossroads of many differences, recalls Gloria Anzaldúa's self-definition as a balance among the different parts of her being: "The mixture of bloods and affinities, rather than confusing or unbalancing me, has forced me to achieve a kind of equilibrium. Both cultures deny me a place in *their* universe. Between them and among others, I build my own universe, *El Mundo Zurdo*. I belong to myself and not to any one people."[47] Rather than stress her uniqueness and her ultimate individualism, Lorde insists on mediation and on her indebtedness to other women. But recognition of difference should breed not strife but strength. As her self is finally a mosaic of other selves, integrated, welded into a powerful whole—"I live each of them as a piece of me" (*Z*, p. 256)—so the differences will yield more strength through union.[48] The radical otherness of the black lesbian poet does not bring her to visions of war, outright opposition, or isolation; instead, her otherness inspires her to elaborate a unified vision after the acknowledgment of difference.

Mythmaking is a political act, which Afro-American and Third World women writers describe as part of their agenda; patriarchal myths have to be broken, not merely reversed. Here, the personal, the autobiographical in its circumstantiality and idiosyncrasies give way to a collective vision. Yet it is precisely the embeddedness of the myth in the particulars of a woman's life (bio) which constitutes its power. In a way, Lorde seems to have answered Gloria Anzaldúa's warning: "The danger in writing is not fusing our personal experience and world view with the social reality we live in, with our inner life, our history, our economics, and our vision. What validates us as human beings validates us as writers."[49] Lorde has tried to fuse her personal life and her vision of an edenic lesbian community that extends itself into a feminist utopia yet to be lived. In a sense, she has created a myth that fits Mary Daly's definition of feminist mythmaking: "When I speak of gynocentric myth and feminist myth-making I do not refer to tales of reified gods and/or goddesses but to stories arising from the experience of the Crones— stories which convey primary and archetypal messages about our own Prehistory and about Female-identified power."[50] Yet, again, Lorde's is

47. Anzaldúa, "La prieta," in *This Bridge*, p. 209.

48. Farley, p. 238, remarks that diversity is a strength rather than a dividing force in *Les Guérillères*.

49. Anzaldúa, "Speaking in Tongues," p. 209.

50. Mary Daly, *Gyn/Ecology: The Metaethics of Radical Feminism* (Boston: Beacon Press, 1978), p. 47.

a myth with a difference. If the power of her myth is female, the prehistory is African. The material of the mythmaking is the cruelty of accumulated oppression, the feelings, the sad and joyous memories.[51] The means is poetry or, in the autobiographical instance, a broken-up poetic prose.

Lorde is Zami and Afrekete and Audre, the "mischievous linguist" (Z, p. 255) who "cannot be categorized."[52] Since self-definition is a source of liberation, she calls herself Zami, and she boldly names her own writing without waiting for other-imposed critical definitions: hers is a "biomythography."

51. One could trace an even more concrete trivial mythology of everyday life in the text. The ritual burial of the two cats, for instance, or the fact that when she burns herself the day Muriel leaves her, Lorde has to cut away the very ring Muriel had given her (p. 233).

52. Tate, p. 103.

12

Mothers, Displacement, and Language in the Autobiographies of Nathalie Sarraute and Christa Wolf

Bella Brodzki

To appropriate by means of the word has been a divine privilege rarely accorded women. Although every speaking and writing subject is in a sense a stranger in a strange land, the feeling of power derived from even provisional occupation of a certain linguistic or textual space (often confused with virtual possession) has been a characteristically masculinist delusion.[1] If in linguistic terms "I" is a shifter reflecting the figure of enunciation only in the instance of enunciating and carrying no transcendent status,[2] then staking out and negotiating the perilous terrain of autobiography not only challenge the notion "I am s/he who says I" but—more important still—constitute a veritable transgression of discursive as well as literary boundaries. Of course, transgression is in the eye of the transgressor as well as the beholder. To be susceptible to the power of transgression (while using it) means to be both within the space where the Law prevails and beyond the point at which it makes a difference.

Whether male or female, the autobiographer is always a displaced person: to speak and write from the space marked self-referential is to

1. The appropriation of meaning as a form of empowerment, says Peggy Kamuf, is an attempt to "contain an unlimited textual system, install a measure of protection between this boundlessness and one's own power to know, to be this power and to know that one is the power." Peggy Kamuf, "Writing Like a Woman," in *Women and Language in Literature and Society,* ed. Sally McConnell-Ginet, Ruth Borker, and Nelly Furman (New York: Praeger, 1980), p. 298.
2. Emile Benveniste, *Problems in General Linguistics,* trans. Mary Elizabeth Meek (Miami: University of Miami Press, 1971). For an analysis of the problematics of split subjectivity and split intentionality inherent in autobiography, see Louis Renza, "The Veto of the Imagination: A Theory of Autobiography," in *Autobiography: Essays Theoretical and Critical,* ed. James Olney (Princeton: Princeton University Press, 1980), pp. 268–95. For a discussion of the provocative connections between linguistic and specular subjectivity, see Elizabeth W. Bruss, "Eye for I: Making and Unmaking Autobiography in Film," in Olney, pp. 296–320; and Catherine Portuges, "Seeing Subjects: Women Directors and Cinematic Autobiography," this volume.

inhabit, in ontological, epistemological, and discursive terms, no place. Nothing but the rhetorical nature of literary language (and our desire to have all autobiographical acts be perforce performative utterances) guarantees the self-authenticating simpler mode of referentiality that autobiography is assumed at once to depend upon and to provide. Of all literary genres, autobiography is the most precariously poised between narrative and discourse or history and rhetoric. Invoking Nietzsche, Paul de Man makes the perverse point: "Death is a displaced name for a linguistic predicament, and the restoration of mortality by autobiography . . . deprives and disfigures to the precise extent that it restores."[3] Self-representation is the effect of a constructed similarity or equivalence between identity and language, an attempt to cast in fixed terms the self-reflexive, discontinuous shifts in modality and perspective, temporal and spatial, that are inherent in human experience—in a word, being— and to ground them in a single subjectivity. And to make this attempt is to confront the limitations of language head on.[4]

While the interrelated phenomenological and rhetorical aspects of alienated or displaced subjectivity interest me here, my particular considerations are the political and cultural implications of displacement and their bearing on diverse literary strategies in women's autobiographies. In the case of the female autobiographer who is compelled to strive for modes of expression and self-representation in a patriarchal world not generous enough to make room for her, "double displacement" is both a way of reading and writing and a way of life.[5] As Maxine Hong Kingston starkly renders the gender-specific prison house of language, "There is a Chinese word for the female I—which is slave. Break the women with their own tongues!"[6] Thus, to be a woman and to speak is already to submit to the phallocentric order while gloriously contradicting it, to serve as the very sign of transgression itself. Here we are only a step away from the Kristevan notion of woman as "eternal dissident,"[7] which has irresistible revolutionary appeal, even though the equation is both too simple and too self-congratulatory: it is as if every time "wom-

3. Paul de Man, "Autobiography as De-facement," *MLN* 94 (Dec. 1979): 930.
4. A lucid and succinct presentation of Nietzsche's philosophical critique of the subject can be found in the introduction to Paul Jay's *Being in the Text* (Ithaca: Cornell University Press, 1984), pp. 28–29.
5. See Gayatri Chakravorty Spivak, "Displacement and the Discourse of Woman," in *Displacement: Derrida and After,* ed. Mark Krupnick (Bloomington: Indiana University Press, 1983), pp. 169–95. See also Jonathan Culler, *On Deconstruction* (Ithaca: Cornell University Press, 1983), pp. 43–64; and Nancy K. Miller, "Writing Fictions: Women's Autobiography in France," this volume.
6. Maxine Hong Kingston, *The Woman Warrior: Memoirs of a Girlhood among Ghosts* (New York: Random House, 1977), p. 56.
7. Julia Kristeva, *Polylogue* (Paris: Seuil, 1977).

an" opens her mouth she (emblematically) speaks, as Josette Féral puts it, "this perpetual displacement which underlines her impossible choices . . . a displacement that stresses these multiples that constituted her and which by their co-existence assures this requestioning and this subversion of which she is the principle driving force."[8] There is an inherent danger in the kind of seductive thinking which allows a concept or a thematics of representation to be affixed to an identity already inscribed in/by the discourse of the dominant culture rather than to a linguistic (or historical) process, especially when what is explicitly at stake is the very concept of unrepresentability.

Modernists (in general) and postmodernists in (particular) have employed the metaphor of displacement to refer to the human condition (in general) and to diacritical and avant-garde practice (in particular); feminist theorists must take diacritical practice one step farther and continually displace "woman" as the metaphor for displacement or divest the movement of the energy that generates it and the context that specifically shapes it. Certainly it is the point at which rhetorical strategies and political practice converge wherein lies the greatest potential for transformations of the dominant structure, but it is also at that same point of convergence where self-deception and co-optation by that structure is most likely to be involved. Such a signifying act would displace signification itself: "It's no accident: women take after birds and robbers just as robbers take after women and birds. They go by, fly the coop, take pleasure in jumbling the order of space, in disorienting it, in changing around the furniture, dislocating things and values, breaking them all up, emptying structures, and turning propriety upside down."[9]

The autobiographies on which this essay will focus—Nathalie Sarraute's *Childhood* and Christa Wolf's *Patterns of Childhood*—struggle with the complicitous (and not always revolutionary) relationship between displacement and language. The struggle, represented by each narrator's/protagonist's linguistic disability or instability and cultural disorientation, pivots on one figure or object: her mother. Emblematic of the way language itself obscures and reveals, witholds and endows, prohibits and sanctions, the mother in each text hovers from within and without. Still powerful and now inaccessible (literally or figuratively), she is the pre-text for the daughter's autobiographical project. Indeed, these autobiographical narratives are generated out of a compelling need

8. Josette Féral, "Towards a Theory of Displacement," *Sub-Stance* 32 (1981): 52–64, Féral's discussion strongly echoes the work of Kristeva, as well as Hélène Cixous and Luce Irigaray, on strategies of displacement in women's writing and feminist theory.

9. Hélène Cixous, "The Laugh of the Medusa," trans. Keith Cohen and Paula Cohen, *Signs* 1 (1976): 875–93.

to enter into discourse with the absent or distant mother. As the child's first significant Other, the mother *engenders* subjectivity through language; she is the primary source of speech and love. And part of the maternal legacy is the conflation of the two. Thereafter, implicated in and overlaid with other modes of discourse, the maternal legacy of language becomes charged with ambiguity and fraught with ambivalence. In response (however deferred), the daughter's text, variously, seeks to reject, reconstruct, and reclaim—to locate and recontextualize—the mother's message.[10]

Classically, the autobiographical project symbolizes the search for origins, for women a search for maternal origins and that elusive part of the self that is coextensive with the birth of language. At this point in my discussion the reader might suspect that this narrative-strategy-become-intro/retrospective-journey has delivered her back to the familiar (if forgotten) intrauterine space called the womb, to that interior place where all conversations are fulfilling and speech is always adequate to the task it is called upon to perform. In this ontogenetic version of the creation story, speech is not necessary at all, because everything that passes between the symbiotic couple is osmotically communicated and understood: the matrix is there where there is no representation because there is no lack.

Mother lack, and all that it implies, comes later. In spite of her "best" critical defenses, the reader will recognize, mirrored in a projection of the autobiographer's "deepest" intentions, her own desire to return to the preexilic state of union with the mother. To be exiled from the maternal continent is to be forever subjected to the rules of a foreign economy for which one also serves as the medium of exchange. Women have devised many strategies for accomodating this loss which, in psychoanalytic terms, initiates the metonymic chain of substitute objects of desire, some more productive than others. As Luce Irigaray expresses it, "A woman, if she cannot in one way or another, recuperate her first object, that is the possibility of keeping her earliest libidinal attachments by displacing, is always exiled from herself."[11] Yet, however strong our need for maternal origins, it is important to keep in mind, in the words of Jean Laplanche, that "we never have at our disposal anything but what is patently observable. The constitutive is reconstructed from the constituted, or in any event from a constitutive process which is not

10. For an extensive and perceptive review of the theoretical and fictional literature on the mother-daughter relationship, see Marianne Hirsch, "Mothers and Daughters," *Signs* 7 (Autumn 1981): 200–22. See also *The (M)other Tongue: Essays in Feminist Psychoanalytic Interpretation,* ed. Shirley Nelson Garner, Claire Kahane, and Madelon Sprengnether (Ithaca: Cornell University Press, 1985).

11. Luce Irigaray, "Women's Exile," *Ideology and Consciousness* 1 (1977): 76.

primal, but derived; and that of course, is the definitive impasse in every quest for origins."[12] I am arguing against a thriving brand of feminist criticism (call it womb criticism) that seeks to replace or subvert phallic criticism—not only because a return to origins is impossible but because I think we should carefully consider the theoretical and political consequences of idealizing the maternal as a category even as each of us negotiates her way within a specific and complex mother-daughter configuration. What is at issue here is not the ideological justification for transforming the paradigm of paternity that exploits and represses the maternal or revoking patriarchal privilege in all its manifestations but rather the idea that in order to bring back the mother from Irigaray's "dark continent of the dark continent"[13] we must mythify her. Clearly, matriarchal myths serve very different real and symbolic functions from those served by patriarchal ones, for both women and men, but some of the inherent dangers of privileging principles are the same, and it is the ideology of the same that feminists need to subvert and work to transfigure.[14]

The narratives of Sarraute and Wolf, while matrocentric, are resolutely antinostalgic. They call into question the assumption of an unmediated presence embodied in/by the mother and an unproblematical relation to the maternal origin, while disclosing a genealogy of matronymic displacement and attempting to situate themselves within a genealogy as part of their overall strategy. They remind us that the autobiographical space is not to be taken for granted or assumed as a given; that "natural" is a cultural construct; and that motherhood is both an experience and an institution.[15]

The pervasive conflict between an overwhelming compulsion to address and an equally strong internal resistance against self-disclosure underscores what I have described as the transgressive nature of the autobiographical enterprise in general and women's autobiographies in particular. Engaged in a relentless self-interrogation (with all the political connotations of that word left intact) of the oft-times distressing, and oft-times exhilarating, indeterminacy of female psychic and moral boundaries, a matrocentric autobiography necessarily involves guilt and

12. Jean Laplanche, *Life and Death in Psychoanalysis,* trans. Jeffrey Mehlman (Baltimore: Johns Hopkins University Press, 1976), pp. 128–29.

13. Luce Irigaray, *Corps à corps avec la mère* (Paris: Editions de la Pleine Lune, 1981). I am quoting from an unpublished translation "Body-to-Body against the Mother," trans. and ed. Carole Sheaffer-Jones et al. (Manuscript, 1985), p. 34.

14. Domna Stanton also argues this point—in far more elaborate theoretical terms—in the third section of her excellent essay, "Difference on Trial: A Critique of the Maternal Metaphor in Cixous, Irigaray and Kristeva," in *The Poetics of Gender,* ed. Nancy K. Miller (New York: Columbia University Press, 1986), pp. 157–82.

15. Adrienne Rich, *Of Woman Born* (New York: Norton, 1976).

fear of (self)betrayal. By the very act of assuming the autobiographical stance the narrators perceive themselves to be "sinners" certainly, but they present themselves first and foremost as having been "sinned" against—by their mothers and, as Wolf's text suggests, by the patriarchal structures that have made her mother an unknowing collaborator with male authority. I shall pursue this point in greater detail later. Now let us look at how an act of textual transgression serves as the point of departure in the autobiographies under discussion.

Childhood assumes a split subjectivity to be the premise of writing autobiography, presents it within the sphere of privatized experience, and seeks to make no larger cultural statement. Structured like a psychotherapeutic dialogue or a very intimate conversation, this narrative of a personality caught in language, indeed caught between two languages, Russian and French, traverses the gaps and elisions of fragmented memory over seventy-one vignettes. It opens with the interlocutor/alter ego's question, "Then you really are going to do that?" Clearly the thematic and formal function of the alter ego, who addresses Sarraute in the familiar *tu,* is to probe and coax, doubt Sarraute's motives and credibility, make deductions, and provide commentary. Although it is occasionally difficult to distinguish one "I" from the other, especially in the opening pages, the splitting or doubling of the narrative voice can be said to fall into two gendered modes. The interlocutor represents the masculine (marked in French) and the analytic. Natasha/Tashok/Nathalie, the child-narrator shuttled between St. Petersburg and Paris, between her divorced parents, represents the expressive or experiential, moving between the past tense and the continuous, enduring present.

In the first few pages, as one voice picks up where the other leaves off, the alter ego offers an evocative description of "there," of the elusive childhood realm that the autobiographical act strives to reconstruct through language, before anticipating and challenging Sarraute's assertion of certitude:

> Is that true? Have you really *not* forgotten what it was like there? how everything there fluctuates, alters, escapes. . .you grope your way along, forever searching, straining. . . .towards what? what is it? it's like nothing else. . .no one talks about it. . .it evades you, you grasp it as best you can, you push it. . .where? no matter where, so long as it eventually finds some fertile ground where it can develop, where it can perhaps manage to live. . .My goodness, just thinking about it. . .[16]

16. Nathalie Sarraute, *Childhood,* trans. Barbara Wright (New York: George Braziller, 1983), p. 2 (my emphasis), hereafter cited in the text.

The associative method used by Sarraute quickly brings the narrative to a formative event that reveals her dominant sense of language, described by Roger Sturrock as both "essential and unbearable,"[17] suspended somewhere between the inchoate and the oracular. She remembers a childhood contest of wills between her and her German governess-tutor: "*Nein, das tust du nicht.* . . 'No, you're not to do that'. . .here they are again, these words, they have come to life again, just as living, just as potent as they were at that moment. . .they bear down with all their strength, with all their enormous weight. . .the words that come out of my mouth carry it, hammer it in. . . .*Doch, ich werde es tun.* 'Yes, I *am* going to do it'" (pp. 3–4). Childhood is that space where language arouses, materializes, and freezes the world in its own image(ry). For Sarraute what may be prior to language—the ineffable self—is that which is most desperately sought after, as is revealed in the narrator's stunning use of the ambiguous "it", but this text is testimony that the the very notion of subjectivity is absolutely contingent upon relation to (the language of) the other. All perceptions, all images, all sensations are indissolubly linguistic; through the process of reenacting the discourses of her past, Sarraute speaks a world of sensation into existence.

> The young woman had been engaged to look after me and to teach me German. . . I can't make her out very well, but I can distinctly see her work basket on her knees, and on top of it a pair of steel scissors. . . and me. . . I can't see myself, but I can feel it as if I were doing it now. . . I suddenly seize the scissors, I grip them in my hand. . . heavy closed scissors. . . I aim them, the point upwards, at the back of a settee covered in a delightful silk material. . . and I say in German. . . *Ich werde es zerreissen.* . . . "I'm going to slash it". . . the word *zerreissen* has a hissing, ferocious sound. . . . I'm going to slash, devastate, destroy. . . it will be an outrage. . . a criminal attack. . . I'm warning you, I'm going to take the plunge, leap out of this decent, inhabited, warm, gentle world, I'm going to wrench myself out of it, fall, sink into the uninhabited, into the void. . . *Nein, das tust du nicht.* . . "No you're not to do that". . . these words flow in a heavy massive tide, what it carries with it sinks into me in order to crush what is stirring in me. . .it braces itself. . .and violently projects out of me the words. . . "Yes, I'm going to do it." (Pp. 4–6)

The incantatory quality of this reverie, its dialogic rhythm of assertion and counterassertion, and the overwhelming corporeal tension between repression of the will and triumph over the terror of words by using

17. Roger Sturrock, "Life before Language," *New York Times Book Review,* 1 April 1984, pp. 1, 31.

them, dramatically shows how the power of (each) language to be a specific purveyor of truth is perceived by a child suffering linguistic vertigo. Before Natasha can commit the empowering violent and violating act of slashing the silk settee she must accede to the status of speaker: she must, in the discourse of the other (her German governess-tutor), dare to trespass the constricting boundaries of property and propriety. In this act of textual transgression the child-protagonist and not the autobiographer is the transgressor, but the established equivalence between the destructive act of slashing the silken cloth and writing her autobiography is made clear at the close of the vignette: "'No, you're not to do that'. . . these words surround me. . . I struggle. . . 'Yes, I'm going to do it'. . . There now, I'm freeing myself, excitement and exaltation impel my arm, I plunge the point of the scissors in with all my strength, the silk tears, I slash the back of the settee from top to bottom, and I look at what comes out of it. . . something flabby, greyish, is escaping from the slit. . ." (p. 6). The analogy between "disgorging" the contents of a beautiful object and spilling one's guts can not be lost on the reader; nor can the sense that this gesture is not as positively liberating as it was intended to be. What "escapes from the slit" is messy and ugly and unknowable. Staying within the bounds of prescribed convention—remaining silent—may be an untenable form of nonexistence, but assuming speech is fatal in its own way. Language is utter mystification for Natasha; divided into the sanctioned and the forbidden, the true and the treacherous, words have the singular capacity to forge and sever the social and natural relations between all things. Nothing in Natasha's world—love least of all—is unconditional, except as language makes it so. When her mother, before the first of many long voluntary separations from her child, makes her promise that she will always chew her food until it is "as liquid as soup," Natasha sacralizes these words in her absence, enduring physical pain and social ostracism rather than betray the "precious" legacy.

It is not, however, from the world's intervention that this maternal legacy is in constant danger of betrayal: it is threatened from within. If Natasha perceives language as that which binds her to her mother in her mother's absence, then it comes as no great surprise that the child ritualizes words, especially such words as *tragedy, happiness,* and *home* to an obsessive degree, and that she cathects the literality of language, indeed its materiality—"How many times since, have I not escaped, terrified, out of words which pounce on you and hold you captive"(p. 107)—for it could be argued that what she lacks is the referent that would ground her life's shifting and unstable signifiers: the maternal body/voice. But the kind of extreme linguistic disruption Sarraute represents here is an effect not of the way language mediates presence-in-absence but of the way language also mediates absence-in-plenitude: mother lack, Sarraute more than suggests, governs Natasha's phenomenological relationship to language through the various expressions of arbitrary maternal authority and affection (the embodiment of both Law and Love) that subvert the very ideal of body/voice itself. This Mama is the kind of elusive mother–object of desire who most witholds when she is physically present.

Sarraute's variations on the theme of language as oppression or estrangement hinge on widening the gap between the irreducible particular and the inaccessible universal, while she struggles to situate herself securely somewhere in between. She arranges occasions for Natasha to test her language-making powers against the depths or limits of her mother's love (and, we might say, indulgence), analyzes her own intentions (past and present) and imagines revisions of conversations. When Natasha says to her mother one day, after much premeditation and projection, that she thinks her doll is more beautiful than her Mama, her mother replies with displeasure that a "child who loves its mother thinks that no one is more beautiful than she" (p. 84). Strangely enough, in this fluid oscillation between retrospective analysis and continuing present, Sarraute does not insist upon the genuineness of her filial devotion; nor does she imply that her perhaps disingenuous observation was misinterpreted by an insensitive (or oversensitive) mother. Instead, she fastens on the exclusionary word *child* and its axiomatic implications: she must not be a "real" child if she can see her mother in comparative terms, but a "monster" or an "outlaw," one who deviates from or exceeds that which *child* means. Because on some level she fears her deduction to be true, she carries the solitary stigma of "a child who doesn't love its mother" and therefore should not expect to be loved in return. Providing countless examples of her mother's indifferent and deadly charm, Sarraute remarks that "no word, however powerfully uttered, has ever sunk into me with the same percussive force as some of hers" (p. 19).

In one of the last vignettes there is a mirror version of the doll scene when Nathalie asks her stepmother, Vera, "Do you hate me?". Vera responds not with a hoped-for reassurance—"What are you talking about? Quite the contrary, come on, how can you not feel that?"—but with a curt, peremptory "How can anyone hate a child?" (p. 241). Once again the fragile sense of identity of the daughter-in-quest is absorbed into an abstract "anyone" and obliterated by the exclusionary designation "child"—now referring to the class of beings not important enough to arouse such a serious emotion as hate. Through these cruel maternal initiations, Natasha realizes that one can only love or hate in the particular; language lays that bare. Although the generally nonlinear, scenic organization of this memoir, as well as a dialogical form that seems both to begin and to end in medias res, makes a totalized reading impossible, Sarraute's elliptical method reflects her concept of self as an ongoing process of alternately constructing and dismantling subjectivity in language, shoring up experiences deemed crucial to this process, and progressively yet provisionally shedding incapacities.

What I see as an emblematic moment in a series of such crystallized experiences is taken from a classic Russian winter scene: Natasha and her Mama are riding a train through the great white plains. In this attenuated departure scene, not "like the others," the mother figuratively delivers the girl to her father (a friend of both parents meets them in Berlin and accompanies Natasha the rest of the way to Paris). During those interludes when neither mother nor daughter is in tearful distress, Natasha amuses herself by chanting the French and Russian words for "sun"—*soleil* and *solntze*—curling them over her tongue. The poignant and striking image of the willful and precocious young girl caught between two maternal tongues is almost superimposed upon another vision—of the autobiographer still rolling strange and beautiful words over her tongue, but now using her displacement as the occasion for writing.

Patterns of Childhood, overtly concerned with the radical possibility of revising cultural and historical scripts of selfhood, interweaves self-reflective commentary with narrative description. This autobiographical project is multilayered, incorporating the period of writing into Wolf's account of a return one weekend in the summer of 1971 (accompanied by her husband, brother, and teenage daughter) to the German hometown she had not seen since 1945, now a part of Poland. The recent journey back serves as the catalyst for writing about her past experiences and as the theme for her text. Wolf dramatizes the lack of psychic and moral integrity which is masked by the generic use of the autobiographical "I" as well as the distance that separates the adult narrator from the child-protagonist, by referring to herself in the present in the second person (until the final pages where the "I" is finally authorized to emerge) and by referring to herself as child during and immediately after World War II in the third person, using the name Nelly.[18]

Fusion of the two persons is never achieved; Nelly recedes farther and farther into an unreachable distance, partly as a result of the narrator's own fear of meeting her and guilt about "exposing" her:

18. For a groundbreaking study of the use of the third person in autobiography, see Philippe Lejeune, "Autobiography in the Third Person," *New Literary History* 9 (1977): 27–49.

That's when you had to realize that you could never again be her ally, that you were an intruding stranger pursuing not a more or less well-marked trail but actually the child herself: her innermost secret that concerned no one else. . . . You'd have to stay on her trail, ruthlessly corner her, while your wish to turn your back on her, to disown her, would become ever stronger. The road you had taken was barred with taboos which no one may violate with impunity.[19]

Wolf is obsessed by the problem of memory, expressly because her own fractured memories of a childhood under the Third Reich are inextricably bound up with the cultivated, collective amnesia of postwar Germany (East and West), where "the absence of one category is acutely felt: moral memory" (p. 36). The narrator begins her first meditation on the nature of memory as an urgent but provisional attempt to forge a theoretical definition: "Memory according to today's interpretation: 'The preservation of previous experience, and the faculty to do so.' Not an organ then, but a process, and the capacity for carrying it out, expressed in one word. An unused memory gets lost, ceases to exist, dissolves into nothing—an alarming thought. Consequently, the faculty to preserve, to remember, must be developed" (p. 10). Then in the middle of the reflection the mode of discourse turns into something else: a dream narrative unfolds whose layers blur distinctions of space and time, deliberately betraying a declared intentionality and seemingly working at cross-purposes with the autobiographical enterprise but inevitably revealing on another level how productive a strategy of concealment can be. It begins as an invocation, a summons, a conjuring up of an image:

Before your inner eye, ghostly arms emerge, groping about in a dense fog, aimlessly. You have no way of penetrating all the layers systematically; you're wasting your energy, with no more result than fatigue; and you go and take a nap in broad daylight. Just then your mother comes in, even though she is dead, and sits down in the big room, something you had always secretly wanted. The whole family is gathered, the living and the dead. You alone are able to tell one from the other, but you have to go to the kitchen, to wash all those dishes. The sun is shining through the kitchen window, but you feel sad, and you lock the door so that no one can come in and help you. Suddenly, a shock that penetrates even the roots of your hair: in the big room on the table lies the manuscript with, on the first page, only one word, "MOTHER," in large letters. She'll read it, guess your purpose, and feel hurt. (P. 10)

19. Christa Wolf, *Patterns of Childhood* (formerly *A Model Childhood*), trans. Ursule Molinaro and Hedwig Rappolt (New York: Farrar, Straus and Giroux, 1980), pp. 119–20, hereafter cited in the text.

The rich, poignant, self-conscious ambiguity of this passage provides wonderful material for the analyst. Where to start? With the positioning of the narrator, who demonstrates how physically and psychologically exhausting it is to want to try to remember and forget at the same time. Does she go and take a nap in order to avoid eliciting unpleasant memories or does she seek sleep because only through dream can she conceive and articulate that which she both wants to confront and wishes to escape? What does she wish to escape—the memory "itself" or its inscription in the language of autobiography? By making the boundaries between writing and sleeping indistinct she can absent herself while still remaining present and absolve herself of a certain authorial responsibility; by contrast, having to leave the room to perform a domestic duty with which no one can "help" relieves her from sitting in judgment of family and nation though she feels herself singularly capable of judging: "You alone are able to tell one from the other."

She has now set the scene for the fantasy she both dreads and desires. Her dead mother comes back to life and sits in her adult living room; but the daughter is not there, so direct communication is impossible. As the director of this primal scene, the scene of originary writing, Wolf "sets her mother up" not to witness her daughter "in the act" of writing (which could be construed as another transgressive act) but to *read* her textual substitute, her autobiography. And her mother, "knowing" the complexity of Wolf's purpose, will understand that the word *mother* on the first page of the manuscript signifies not a tribute but an accusation. Haunting questions persist: what is the crime? who is the perpetrator and who is the victim? If the mother is the transmitter of cultural values in a culture that pretends it has no recent history, then what is the daughter's place in that continuum? To frame these questions in such a way, to break the silence, is, to say the least, to exceed acceptable cultural boundaries.

And as the imagery here and elsewhere indicates, overriding such powerful proscriptions comes at great psychic cost. Because the postwar narrator is so plagued by the shadowy intersections of the knowable and the unknowable, the concealed and the inaccessible, by the ruptured link between Nelly's acute suspicions and her own suspicious interpretations—the "limits of the expressible" become an issue of monstrous proportion, dominating her days of writing and her dream-filled nights. The ruptured links are "glitter words one couldn't ask about" (p. 57), because they referred to codes strictly protected and events defiantly ignored, forgotten, canceled, like the lives that were supposed to disappear with them. Wolf concludes over and over again, however, that despite this "age of universal loss of memory" (p. 153), "everyone knew" (p. 69). And yet, she also concludes that "memory's recall—which incidentally varies markedly in people who seem to have had the exact same experience—may not be a matter of biochemistry, and may not universally be a matter of choice. If this were not so, some people's assertions would be accurate: documents could not be surpassed; the narrator would therefore be superfluous" (p. 69). Such attempts at self-justification are purposeful; they save her from absolute despair and from the pride of ambition which inevitably accompanies a sense of purpose. They serve to reassure her that her autobiographical testimony is not superfluous; nor is it privileged, despite her remarkable interpretive intelligence and morbid self-irony. Because remembering and writing are one, ambivalence riddles the text; dream images of silence, mutation, amputation, and paralysis challenge the insistent will to write:

> The hand which shall wither or grow out of the grave if it is lifted against father or mother. Promptly you dream, exactly and in detail, all the stages of an operation in the course of which your right hand—the writing hand—is being expertly taken off . . . while you witness everything. What must happen must happen. You're not putting up any resistance. . . . What do you think when you wake up? In the semidarkness you lift your hand, you turn it this way and that, study it as if you were seeing it for the first time. It looks like a fit tool, but you could be wrong. (P. 30)

In another dream narrative she is accused by a blonde man with wavy hair of "having appropriated something that had been entrusted to [her] for safekeeping," while she affirms "that [she] deposited it "elsewhere." As in the kind of Kafkan universe where the guilty one is distinguished not by her simple and radical innocence but by her susceptibilty to feelings of guilt, the "appropriated" object, appropriately displaced, becomes a "beautiful. . . pale green, transparent, painfully pure and flawless" bottle. "That's it! You call out, infinitely relieved, although deep down you know that you'd been looking for something else. . . . You're happy to have an explanation for everything, one that exonerates you and with which you can agree" (p. 119). But Wolf never feels exonerated; the expression of relief at not being punished for a crime she didn't commit (embezzlement) is an act of bad faith and doesn't disguise the real issue, which is, of course, her own displacement. She could derive some psychological compensation from her horrifying excavatory efforts if she qualified as either victim or executioner, but identifying with the suffering of the hunted does not make her a survivor of the Holocaust; and neither does having been an impressionable though ambivalent member of the Hitler Youth make her a Nazi.

In still another dream narrative a small, deformed man with no mouth is being tortured on her bed. Paralyzed in the role of spectator and unable to help him, she thinks he should be given the means to write: "The poor creature uttered sounds that made the blood freeze in your veins. But the worst of it was that you understood him: he didn't know anything. They continued to torture him on your bed" (pp. 170–71).

Wolf's guilt derives from her precarious position as self-elected moral witness, a position that carries uneasy political implications. As she says almost simultaneously, "You thought your writing would make the bottom layer rise to the surface, but it may be impossible to be alive today without being implicated in the crime" and "Woe to our time, which forces the writer to exhibit the wound of his own crime before he is allowed to describe other people's wounds" (p. 171). In writing this autobiography she is a kind of parasite: she lives off the tragedies of others, not only the innocent dead who will never speak for themselves but, in a far more personally problematic way, those who are most intimately violated by her "laying bare of the innards" (p. 171). Her father's parting words to her before he is drafted into the German army,—"Stand by your mother!"—reverberate.

As obsessed as the narrator is with the ideological issues of collective repression, individual assent and complicity, and the attendant loss of sensation as well as memory, it is not until she prepares to describe "the beginning of the end"—the Allied victory and her family's subsequent evacuation—that the intersections of subjectivity and history appear most critical: "The lines—lifelines, work lines—will not cross at the point which used to be called 'truth.' You know only too well what you're permitted to find difficult, and what not. What you're permitted to know, and what not. What must be talked about, and in what tone. And what must be buried in silence forever" (pp. 275–76).

As she writes on 31 August 1974 about that fateful day in her childhood, 29 January 1945, she connects the never-ending parade of contemporary disasters and political "conflicts"—in Vietnam, Chile, the Middle East, Bangladesh—with the other point of the time triangle, 31 August 1939. On the day in question, "a girl, Nelly, stuffed and stiff in double and triple layers of clothes (stuffed with history, if these words mean anything), is dragged up on the truck, in order to leave her 'childhood abode,' so deeply anchored in German poetry and the German soul" (p. 284). This pseudoromantic scene reveals what is so striking about Wolf's autobiographical technique. Even as the narrator desperately attempts to recapture the feelings of the child, Nelly, as she is forced to leave her "abode" (an almost Heideggerian image of a dwelling place), she keeps an ironic and respectful distance: she will not permit Hitler(ism) to be redeemed by German poetry. And as she reaches the point in her narrative to which it seems she has been inevitably, though not continuously, moving, the reader's sense of dislocation mirrors the child's utter incomprehension of her mother's act: "Now it's time to leave, hurry up, quick, it's getting late. Nelly, already inside the truck, holds out her hand to help her mother climb in. But she suddenly steps back, shakes her head: I can't. I'm staying here. I just can't abandon everything" (p. 284).

What follows in the text is the continued intertwining of two unresolved questions, implicitly posed by the narrator, which remain connected thematically, though it would be difficult to argue that they are linked causally. The first is, of course, how could an entire generation participate in genocide and pretend to efface it from its past? Such monstrous and monumental gaps in consciousness and conscience can never in any way be accounted for. And although the magnitude of devastation is not to be compared, the second is, how could her mother be unable to "abandon everything" but yet abandon her child, knowing that they might never see each other again? The autobiographer-daughter does make several attempts to rewrite the scene of abandonment, from her mother's point of view as well as her own, but although these revisions poignantly and powerfully generate more narrative, no closure, no resolution is achieved, no consolation emerges. Her pointing to the word *Verfallen,* uniquely German in its multireferentiality, suggests something "irretrievably lost, because enslaved by one's own, deep-down consent" (p. 288).

And it is precisely from within this notion of *Verfallen* that the maternal subtext in the autobiography—so strongly interwoven from the very beginning with the thematics of memory, writing, personal politics, and national ideology—figures. Something in the narrative subtly but unmistakably changes after the traumatic abandonment scene: the mother's inconspicuous return is coolly reintegrated with barely a disrupting nod, and the narrator's compulsion to narrate at all costs seems her overriding consideration. The suspicious reader wonders about the cathartic effects of writing upon so self-analytic a writer as Wolf, who is always caught somewhere between "exhaustion and exhaustive." Is the theme of maternal abandonment overdetermined in this text, and if so, why? When the narrator of *Patterns of Childhood,* opening the autobiography with a meditation on the difficulty of beginning an autobiography, describes her problem as whether "to remain speechless, or else to live in the third person" and declares, "The first is impossible, the second strange" (p. 3), her double entendre situates the female autobiographer and lays the groundwork for her own project in the most specific terms. Fifty pages before what is a very inconclusive ending, Wolf says, "The final point would be reached when the second and the third person were to meet again in the first, or better still, were to meet with the first person. When it would no longer have to be 'you' and 'she' but a candid, unreserved 'I' " (p. 349).

Maternal abandonment is not overdetermined in this autobiography; it is *displaced*. Wolf's obsession with national and private guilt can be understood if we look again at the carefully constructed relationship between Charlotte (Wolf's mother) and Nelly (Wolf as a child) and Christa Wolf, the autobiographical narrator incapable of saying "I." Wolf's textual strategy for dealing with untenable psychic and moral separation—representing the split grammatically—is not derivative of this relationship. It is the condition that makes speaking/writing possible at all, for the mother who abandons her daughter in this text is *not* Charlotte, as we believe all along, but Wolf herself—Wolf as the mother of that part of herself that she was forced to disown and has lost irretrievably and for whose abandonment she feels inexplicably accountable. "Who are you? . . . What have you done? . . . What did they make me do?" (pp. 349, 350). Mother and daughter represent the aspects of Wolf's own estranged subjectivity, and the autobiographical project is her effort to bring back the dead within her.

> And the past, which can still split the first person into the second and the third—has its hegemony been broken? Will the voices be still? I don't know. At night I shall see—whether waking, whether dreaming—the outline of a human being who will change, through whom other persons, adults, children, will pass without hindrance. . . . Half-conscious, I shall experience the beautiful waking image drifting ever deeper into the dream, into ever new shapes, no longer accessible to words, shapes I believe I recognize. Sure of myself once again in the world of solid bodies upon awakening, I shall abandon myself to the experience of dreaming. I shall not revolt against the limits of the expressible. (Pp. 406–7).

But there is a forward projection, not because the narrator ever succumbs to the appeals of either pragmatism or idealism but because her actual daughter, Lenka, must be the touchstone of a future she can not deny. The concluding vision of the book might be seen as a kind of mystical retreat after the insistent (self)investigations that precede it. The reader senses Wolf's difficulty with ending, with "finally" confronting the open-endedness of a narrative so perturbed by origins and beginnings that it tends to begin again and again. Faintly oracular in tone, it reaches toward a transformed realm of experience, evoking with it aspects of all of Wolf's crucial dream work. Not a synthesis, it posits, like Wolf's technique itself, oppositions and lines of demarcation and tries to move beyond them. Not a viable political vision because it lacks the element of activism or resistance, it hovers in a state of almost serene suspension.

Whether what has been "irretrievably lost" can be recovered by the dialectic is of paramount importance to Christa Wolf as an East German socialist writer. This autobiography mourns the failure of human will and imagination, the indeterminacy of change, the undecidability of knowledge, and the ineffability of language, even as it seeks through writing to render a sense of originary and irrecuperable loss. The almost disembodied voice envisions another sphere where the trials and the joys of a displaced subject are no longer relevant.

13

Métissage, Emancipation, and Female Textuality in Two Francophone Writers

FRANÇOISE LIONNET

PROSPERO: . . . Miranda: But how is it
That this lives in thy mind? What seest thou else
In the dark backward and abysm of time?
William Shakespeare, *The Tempest*

. . . Mais je rêve, j'utopographe, je sais.
Annie Leclerc, *Parole de femme*

To read a narrative that depicts the journey of a female self striving to become the subject of her own discourse, the narrator of her own story, is to witness the unfolding of an autobiographical project. To raise the question of referentiality and ask whether the text points to an individual existence beyond the pages of the book is to distort the picture. As Picasso once said about his portrait of Gertrude Stein, although she was not exactly like it, she would eventually become so. The ability to "defamiliarize" ordinary experience, forcing us to notice what we live with but ignore, has long been considered an important characteristic of art. Such is the Russian formalists' notion of *ostraneniye,* or "making strange," the surrealists' dream of a heightened level of awareness, Nathalie Sarraute's "era of suspicion." New ways of seeing can indeed emancipate us. Literature, like all art, can show us new means of constructing the world, for it is by changing the images and structures through which we encode meaning that we can begin to develop new

I thank Ronnie Scharfman and Celeste Schenck for encouraging this project. I am also indebted to Michal Peled Ginsburg, Keala Jewell, John McCumber and Sylvie Romanowski for their incisive comments on an earlier version of this essay. Parts of the essay were read at the Third Colloquium on Twentieth-Century Literature in French, 6–8 March 1986, Louisiana State University.

scripts and assign new roles to the heroines of the stories we recount in order to explain and understand our lives.

The female writer who struggles to articulate a personal vision and to verbalize the vast areas of feminine experience which have remained unexpressed, if not repressed, is engaged in an attempt to excavate those elements of the female self which have been buried under the cultural and patriarchal myths of selfhood. She perceives these myths as alienating and radically *other* and her aim is often the retrieval of a more authentic image, one that may not be ostensibly "true" or "familiar" at first, since our ways of perceiving are so subtly conditioned by our social and historical circumstance and since our collective imagination is so overwhelmingly nonfemale. Having no literary tradition that empowers her to speak, she seeks to elaborate discursive patterns that will both reveal the "hidden face of Eve"[1] and displace the traditional distinctions of rigidly defined literary genres. Formulating a problematics of female authorship is thus an urgent task for feminist writers and one that they approach with much ambivalence.

Theorists of autobiography have traditionally assumed with Roy Pascal that we read autobiographies "not as factual truth, but as a wrestling with truth."[2] In their attempt at a selective grouping of first-person narratives, however, theorists have largely failed to "take hold of autobiography's protean forms," as Avrom Fleishman puts it.[3] And feminist critics in particular have been quick to suggest that, in the words of Nancy K. Miller, "any theoretical model *indifferent* to a problematics of genre as inflected by gender" must be regarded as suspect.[4] Since it is notoriously difficult for us as women to recognize ourselves in the images that literature and society (sometimes including our own mothers) traditionally project or uphold as models, it should not be surprising for an autobiographical narrative to proclaim itself as fiction: for the narrator's process of reflection, narration, and self-integration within language is bound to unveil patterns of self-definition (and self-dissimulation) which may seem new and strange and with which we are not always consciously familiar. The self engendered on the page allows a writer to subject ordinary experience to new scrutiny and to show that

1. I borrow the phrase from the book by Nawal El Saadawi, *The Hidden Face of Eve: Women in the Arab World* (London: Zed Press, 1980).

2. Roy Pascal, *Design and Truth in Autobiography* (London: Routledge and Kegan Paul, 1960), p. 75. But see also Elizabeth W. Bruss, *Autobiographical Acts: The Changing Situation of a Literary Genre* (Baltimore: Johns Hopkins University Press, 1976); James Olney, *Metaphors of Self: The Meaning of Autobiography* (Princeton: Princeton University Press, 1972); and Philippe Lejeune, *Le pacte autobiographique* (Paris: Seuil, 1975) and *Je est un autre* (Paris: Seuil, 1980).

3. Avrom Fleishman, *Figures of Autobiography: The Language of Self-Writing in Victorian and Modern England* (Berkeley: University of California Press, 1983), p. 37.

4. Nancy K. Miller, "Writing Fictions: Women's Autobiography in France," this volume.

the polarity fact/fiction does not establish and constitute absolute categories of feeling and perceiving reality. The narrative text epitomizes this duality in its splitting of the subject of discourse into a narrating self and an experiencing self, which can never coincide exactly. Addressing the problematics of authorship,[5] the female narrator gets caught in a duplicitous process: she exists in the text under circumstances of alienated communication because the text is the locus of her dialogue with a tradition she tacitly aims at subverting. Describing the events that have helped her assume a given heritage, she communicates with a narratee who figures in a particular kind of relationship both with her as narrator and with their shared cultural environment. By examining the narrative structure through these constitutive relational patterns, we can elicit from the text a model of reading which does not betray its complicated and duplicitous messages. For example, Marie Cardinal dedicates her novel to the "doctor who helped [her] be born," and he is the explicit listener of her life story.[6] As such, his role is clear. But as I will discuss later, the text encodes his presence as a catalyst whose function is not only to facilitate access to the narrator's effaced, forgotten, joyful "Algerian" self but also to mediate the reader's understanding of the story being told in the book, the "histoire racontée à du papier."[7]

Marie Cardinal and Marie-Thérèse Humbert are contemporary women writers who have lived and worked in France. They present us with new ways of reading the heroine's text, new ways that they perceive as emancipatory. Their cultural backgrounds and creative roots reach far beyond the confines of France's *hexagone;* they were both born and brought up in former colonies of France (Cardinal, in Algeria; Humbert, in Mauritius). Finding themselves at the confluence of different cultures, they must sort out their loyalties and affiliations on a personal as well as social and political level, and their predicament is analogous to that of any woman writer who tries to come to terms with her own sexual difference in a male-dominated society. They draw heavily on their personal colonial experience but publish their works as *romans,*

5. And its anxieties, as brilliantly analyzed by Sandra M. Gilbert and Susan Gubar in *The Madwoman in the Attic: The Woman Writer and the Nineteenth-Century Literary Imagination* (New Haven: Yale University Press, 1979), pp. 45–92.

6. "Au docteur qui m'a aidée à naître," in Marie Cardinal, *Les Mots pour le dire* (Paris: Grasset et Fasquelle, 1975). English translation by Pat Goodheart, *The Words to Say It* (Cambridge, Mass.: VanVactor and Goodheart, 1983), is cited hereafter in the text. Occasionally, I will modify the translation and indicate "tr.m." when I do so. When necessary, reference to the French edition will be given in the text or in the corresponding footnotes. Permission to cite from the French and English editions was granted by Editions Grasset, Paris, and VanVactor and Goodheart, Cambridge, Mass. I gratefully acknowledge this here.

7. *Les Mots pour le dire,* p. 266 ("the story as told to some paper"). The phrase recalls Montaigne's "mémoire de papier" and his well-known need to "parler au papier." See Michel de Montaigne, *Essais,* 3:1, in *Oeuvres complètes* (Paris: Gallimard/La Pléiade, 1962), p. 767.

first-person narratives of young women who are determined to make sense of their past and to inscribe themselves within and outside of the cultures that subtend that experience. They take their readers on a journey of personal discovery where the silent other of sex, language, and culture is allowed to emerge and is given a voice. This process of discovery thus becomes the source of rebirth and reconciliation, the mode of healing the narrating self.

Both Cardinal's and Humbert's tales center on the debilitating sexual and racial stereotypes of their colonial past and the degree to which their narrators have internalized them. Indoctrinated into a blind acceptance of these values (which at the time seem the only possible course for survival), the protagonists become progressively unable to cope with "reality" as presented and depicted in the master narratives of colonization.[8] They are thus alienated from something at once internal and external to the self. It is at that precise moment of disjunction that the narrative text articulates a dialogue between two instances of the self, the "I" and the "she," the "I" of the here and now, who reconstructs the absent, past "she," the emancipation of the "I" being triggered and actualized by the voice of the "she" taking shape on the page. These two instances of the self figuratively alternate roles as narrator and narratee in the context of different narrative segments.[9] The interaction between the narrator's self-image and her interlocutors (the reconstructed "she" as well as the various other protagonists of the story in their role as [virtual] narratees)—what she focuses on and what she omits—gives dynamism to the unfolding of the narrative and elicits a particular response from the reader. As Wolfgang Iser puts it: "Effect and response arise from a dialectical relationship between showing and concealing—in other words, from the difference between what is said and what is meant."[10] The topos created by this interaction is the privileged textual space where initially unquestioned assumptions about self and other, sex and language, belief and culture can be examined in a dramatic mode: this is where autobiography acquires a meaning and a function not unlike those of fiction with its mythmaking and myth-deflating power.

The novels have numerous formal and thematic similarities and offer a critique of colonialism from two different class perspectives. In *Les*

---

8. I use this term in the sense of Jean-Francois Lyotard's *"grand récits"* in *La Condition postmoderne: Rapport sur le savoir* (Paris: Minuit, 1979). It is translated as *The Postmodern Condition: A Report on Knowledge* (Minneapolis: University of Minnesota Press, 1984).

9. For a comprehensive approach to narratology, or general theory of narrative, see Seymour Chatman, *Story and Discourse: Narrative Structure in Fiction and Film* (Ithaca: Cornell University Press, 1978).

10. Wolfgang Iser, *The Act of Reading: A Theory of Esthetic Response* (Baltimore: Johns Hopkins University Press, 1978), p. 45.

Mots pour le dire the narrator belongs to the French landowning bourgeoisie, whose stance toward the Algerian Arabs is one of benevolent
paternalism laced with Catholic missionary zeal; in *A l'autre bout de moi*
the narrator's family lives on the margins of the rich white settlers'
world, which scorns them because their imperfect pedigree ("some Hindu great-grandmother who was all but forgotten since we carefully
avoided talking about her")[11] is not offset by any redeeming form of
financial success. Despite this important class distinction, the childhoods
of the protagonists benefit from a similar cultural diversity (a mothering
of sorts by the natural environment and the nonwhites who are part of
their daily lives, in the absence of a truly nurturing biological mother, in
the presence of a flamboyant and indifferent father). They both come to
identify with the non-European, Third World elements of their "alien"
cultures. For Cardinal's narrator, it is the acceptance of a privileged
difference that is a *métissage* of the heart and mind; for Humbert's, it is a
more telling trajectory back to her "mixed-blood" origins after a murderous confrontation with subjectivity in the guise of her twin sister, the
mirror image, the "monster" who steals her illusory individuality.

> J'appartiens à un pays que j'ai quitté. . . . il faut qu'une fois encore
> j'arrache, de mon pays, toutes mes racines qui saignent.
> Colette, "Jour gris," *Les Vrilles de la vigne*

The structure of *Les Mots pour le dire* parallels Cardinal's experience of
Freudian psychoanalysis. Having reached a point of dislocation and
madness after resettling in Paris with her family, she decides to enter
analysis. The combined influence of her church and class, along with the
traumas of a difficult relationship with her rejecting mother, have made
her completely *aliénée, folle* (insane—or alienated—mad). After years of
analysis, she succeeds in unlocking the source of the pain, and the process of writing becomes the process of rebirth: "I must think back to find
again the forgotten woman, more than forgotten, disintegrated. . . .
She and I. I am she. . . . I protect her; she lavishes freedom and invention on me. . . . I have to split myself in two" (p. 8). This is the most
complete and radical sort of rebirth: "self-engendering as a verbal body,"[12]

11. Marie-Thérèse Humbert, *A l'autre bout de moi* (Paris: Stock, 1979), p. 28, hereafter cited
in the text. All translations will be mine. Permission to quote the work of Humbert, granted
by Editions Stock, Paris, is gratefully acknowledged here.

12. Rodolphe Gasché, "Self-engendering as a Verbal Body," *MLN* 93 (May 1978):677–94.
This study of Antonin Artaud is relevant here for two reasons: madness, language and writing
are central to Cardinal's understanding of her access to the status of subject of discourse;
furthermore, the plague, Freud, Marseilles (Artaud's birthplace), and Algiers would figure as
the scenes of *dédoublement* for both writers: the plague being at once a *fléau* like Cardinal's
hemorrhaging and psychoanalysis, as Freud once put it.

the discovery of language and its infinite possibilities, the realization, the surfacing of an enormous creative potential: "I and the words were both on the surface and clearly visible" (p. 239); "words were boxes, they all contained living matter" (p. 239; tr. m.). Not so much the story of an analysis as an investigation of the analogies between the dialogical analytic process and the healing, self-directed exchange that allows the unmasking of the woman, the novel belies all attempts to label it as a social document about psychoanalysis.[13] It enacts a coherent staging of that process but, in so doing, subverts it.

At the beginning of the novel, the narrator is emotionally comatose, chemically tranquilized, silent, obedient and submissive; her body, however, is hysterically alive, constantly generating more blood, more fibroid tissue, anarchically feminine. She *is* her fibromatous uterus, and when her surgeon decides to cure her physical symptoms—constant hemorrhaging—by the "aggressive" method of hysterectomy, she knows that this would be a mutilation, an amputation of the madwoman who is a part of her and with whom she must learn to live: "I began to accept [the insane one], to love her even" (p. 10). She escapes into the dark office of the analyst, where for the next seven years, she will come at regular intervals to lie on the couch "curled up, like a fetus in the womb"; she feels herself to be a "huge embryo pregnant with myself" (p. 12, 13 tr. m.). The imagery she uses to describe the location of the office is particularly suited to the birthing metaphor; it is in an island of surprising calm and tranquility in the midst of Paris, at the end of a narrow cul-de-sac (p. 2), a "ruelle en impasse" (p. 7), just as her life is lived in an impasse, in limbo, while she undergoes analysis. She is only enduring until she can be strong enough to survive without the protection of the womblike room with its mirroring presence of the "little dark-skinned man" (p. 2), who never judges and will remain impersonal and masked till the end of the book. In this he is the opposite of the tall, dynamic surgeon, who wears white and examines his patient in a glaringly lit room with a ceiling "white as a lie" (p. 7).

How are we to understand this contrast between the surgeon and the analyst? Clearly, the surgeon stands for a patriarchal society intent on annihilating the disturbing signs of a feminine difference flowing out of control. But more important, in the textual context of the narrative situation he is an antimodel for the critic, whereas the analyst figures as

---

13. See in particular Bruno Bettelheim's Preface and Afterword to the English translation by Pat Goodheart; Marilyn Yalom, *Maternity, Mortality, and the Literature of Madness* (University Park: Pennsylvania State University Press, 1985), chap. 5; Elaine A. Martin, "Mothers, Madness and the Middle Class in *The Bell Jar* and *Les Mots pour le dire,*" *French-American Review* 5 (Spring 1981): 24–47; and the following reviews: Diane McWhorter, "Recovering from Insanity," *New York Times Book Review,* 1 Jan. 1984, p. 15; and Fernande Schulmann, "Marie Cardinal: *Les Mots pour le dire,*" *Esprit* 452 (Dec. 1975): 942–43.

an ideal other. The analyst's silent, invisible (she cannot see him from the couch), but very attentive presence casts him in the role of a midwife who helps the narrator pregnant with her effaced self. The text constructs him as an ideal listener-reader, one without preconceived and Procrustean notions of literary or autobiographical canon. It is in this implicit contrast between the two doctors that the narrative signals itself as a "communicational act," as Ross Chambers formulates it, and provides us with the model of reading most appropriate to the "point" it is trying to make.[14]

This is a model, needless to say, that would neither amputate the text of meaning nor fit it into a preexisting theoretical framework: here, the text figures as the female body of the writer and the critic, as the midwife of its meaning. What is being advocated is a female reappropriation of the best form of ancient Socratic *maieusis*, not surprising for a feminist author who was trained as professor of philosophy. The metaphor of "physician of the soul" is, of course, well known to readers of Augustine's *Confessions* (10.3: "medice meus intime"), in which God, the transcendental addressee, is the model of Augustine's ideal reader, the one who can help the narrator transcend his own corporeality, so that his soul may be reborn. In a reversal of this mind/body dichotomy and of the traditional quest of spiritual autobiographers for a transcendent self, Cardinal aims at rediscovering the body in its female specificity as the source of her own discursive practice.

The specular relationship created between writer and reader (or critic) in the analytical situation suggests that for the writer as well, there is an antimodel of creativity; her inability to write without constant reference to a rigid code and pious reverence for the great masters stifles her completely:

> That's what writing was for me: to put correctly into words, in accordance with the strict rules of grammar, references and information that had been given to me. In this area improvement consisted in expanding vocabulary in so far as it was possible, and learning Grevisse almost by heart. I was attached to this book, whose old-fashioned title, *Good Usage,* seemed to me to guarantee the seriousness and suitability of my passion for it. In the same way I loved saying that I read *Les Petites Filles modèles* when I was little. In Grevisse, there are many doors open to freedom and fantasy, many good-natured winks, like little signs of collusion, meant for those who do not wish to be confirmed in the orthodoxy of a dead language and a tightly corseted grammar. I felt that these evasions were, nevertheless, not for me,

---

14. Cf. Ross Chambers, *Story and Situation: Narrative Seduction and the Power of Fiction* (Minneapolis: University of Minnesota Press, 1984), pp. 3–15. My own critical method in this paper owes much to Ross Chambers's seminar on narrative at the University of Michigan.

but were reserved for writers. I had too much respect, even veneration, for books to imagine that I could write one. . . . Writing itself seemed to be an important act of which I was unworthy. (Pp. 215, 216; tr. m.)

Such a thorough internalization of the repressive rules of the symbolic order puts the writer in the role of a surgeon operating a ruthless censorship on her own text, asphyxiating any free-play of subjectivity.[15] It is not surprising that when she does start finding her own "mots pour le dire," she hides herself to write and then hides her notebooks under her mattress as though this transgression of the symbolic order can only be effective if it is not subjected to the judging eye of the literary law.

This eye is also the one she sees in her hallucination (chap. 8), which terrorizes her: it is the eye behind the camera of her father, who had attempted to photograph her as a toddler while she was urinating on the ground. This experience, lived by the child as a violation of her secret desires, unleashed a formidable anger against this peeping father: "I strike him with all my strength. . . . I want to kill him!" (p. 152). Her hatred is then promptly repressed by the shame she is made to feel for her violent impulses: "You musn't hit mama, you mustn't hit papa! It's very wicked, it's shameful! Punished, crazy! Very ugly, very naughty, crazy!" (p. 152; tr. m.). Once the "eye" of the hallucination is exorcised, she can begin to deal with her fear of being "a genuine monster" (p. 165). This is the combined fear, as Barbara Johnson puts it, of "effecting the death of [her] own parents" and of being creatively different, free, and successful.[16] To overcome this fear, which paralyzes her writing, she has to learn to let the words flow freely, without regard for grammatical rules or objective reality: the flow of words must mimic the anarchic flow of blood and eventually replace it. Describing her apprenticeship at self-portrayal, she explains: "With pencil and paper, I let my mind wander. Not like on the couch in the cul-de-sac. The divagations in the notebooks were made up of the elements of my life which were arranged according to my fancy: going where I pleased, living out moments I had only imagined. *I was not in the yoke of truth, as in analysis.* I was conscious of being more free than I had ever been" (p. 215; my emphasis).

15. The rules are the *règles*, the female menstrual cycle, which "may provide a near-perfect metaphor for Cardinal's dialectic . . . of subversion and conformity," according to Carolyn A. Durham in her excellent study of another work by Cardinal: "Feminism and Formalism: Dialectical Structures in Marie Cardinal's *Une Vie pour deux*" *Tulsa Studies in Women's Literature* 4 (Spring 1985): 84.

16. See Barbara Johnson, "My Monster/My Self," *Diacritics* 12 (Summer 1982): 9. In this review of Mary Shelley's *Frankenstein*, Nancy Friday's *My Mother/My Self*, and Dorothy Dinnerstein's *Mermaid and the Minotaur*, Johnson suggests that these "three books deploy a *theory* of autobiography as monstrosity" (p. 10).

The distinction between the analysis and the book we are reading is clearly established. Later on, allowing her husband to read her manuscript she confesses with some trepidation: "I should have thought of it before; I should have stopped to consider that I was writing, that I was telling a story if only to the paper [*que je racontais une histoire à du papier* (p. 266)]; I should have spoken about it to the doctor" (p. 226). The freedom to write, and to write secretly, is yet another transgression, a transgression of the rules of psychoanalytic practice. But the risk she takes of being judged by Jean-Pierre, her husband, the *agrégé de grammaire*, is not a gratuitous one: the book exists in a homologous relationship to her analytic discourse, and just as analysis has changed her perception of herself, so reading her text will change Jean-Pierre's perception of his wife: "How you've changed. You intimidate me. Who are you?" (p. 228). The invitation to read/know her anew is thus an invitation to love again after the long estrangement caused by her "illness." Sharing in the power of language to redefine reality, to name the woman who had become effaced under her social role as wife and mother, "model young wife and mother, worthy of my own mother" (p. 219), Jean-Pierre now sees the new/old face of the narrator, the one that conveys a harmonious relationship to Mediterranean nature, where the sea, the sand, the sun, the sky are one continuous whole, interacting in their difference to allow the free-play of meaning. The female is again the equal partner of the male, who needs her to assume her difference so he can become capable of a genuine act of love, an act of loving/reading. The staging of Jean-Pierre as the receptive reader par excellence can be interpreted as a *mise en abyme* of the reading process and of its effect as it is encoded in the narrative structure.[17] The power to be read on her own terms is thus inseparable, for the female writer, from a genuine "suspension of disbelief" on the part of her audience, whereas her right to be a narrator is acquired through an arduous effort at self-emancipation from the laws of preexisting and distorting master discourses (such as the literary tradition and psychoanalytic practice).

Not surprisingly, this newfound freedom results from her understanding and acceptance of the specificity of her female experience, a specificity that stretches her beyond the personal to the political and historical context of Algeria. Along with the discovery of what it means to be a woman and a victim comes the realization that her victimization as daughter coexisted with her mother's inability to assume and legitimize her own lack of sexual and maternal love and to face her own fear of sexual difference. This fear caused the mother's complicity with the repressive, paternalistic colonial order, despite her qualities of intelli-

17. See Lucien Dällenbach, *Le Récit spéculaire* (Paris: Seuil, 1977); Chambers, pp. 18–49.

gence, sensuality, and integrity (cf. chap. 16). Although the narrator rejects her as mother, she can see the woman and relate to her as victim. Like Algeria during the war of independence, the mother's agony is the scene of a civil war between conflicting ideologies. Rather than reexamine all the values she lives by, the mother prefers to let herself go completely, to give in to the profound distress that had inhabited her psyche all along. She loses all self-respect, is drunk and incontinent, and subsequently dies. Her daughter finds her, "on the floor. She had been dead for ten or twelve hours already. She was curled up in a ball. Rigor mortis had fixed horror on her face and body" (p. 289). It is the mother now who is the monster, the fetuslike creature whose posture mirrors that of the fetus-daughter she has unsuccessfully tried to abort; that daughter, now safely beyond her nefarious influence, can at last say, "I love you" (p. 292), and make her peace with the past.

It is during a visit to her mother's grave that the daughter is able to recall with poetic tenderness the moments of genuine joy she had experienced when walking on the beach or gazing at the stars with her mother. Looking for shells washed ashore by the waves, looking at the stars in the warmth of the Mediterranean night, together, they had been "in contact with the cosmos" (p. 202). Her mother knew the names of all the shells—"the mother-of-pearl shells, cowries, pointed sea snails, ear shells and the pink razor clam shells" (p. 291)—and of all the stars— "the shepherd's star . . . the Big Dipper . . . the Charioteer . . . the Little Dipper . . . Vega . . . the Milky Way" (p. 202; tr. m.). This naming of the universe is her most precious maternal legacy and the daughter is able to insert herself, her book, her words into that universe. The daughter thereby erases the narrative of hatred and unsuccessful abortion which her mother had divulged to her when she was twelve. They were both standing on a sidewalk of Algiers, "the same sidewalk on which later would run the blood of enmity" (p. 132). The recounting of these secrets had been the mother's *saloperie* (p. 131), her villainy (p. 105), to her daughter, and the words fell on the young daughter "like so many mutilating swords" (p. 135). This information about the girl's gestation (that prehistoric time of her life) thwarts her feminine development. She does not start menstruating before the age of twenty. The doubly archaic revelation—reproduction as a "female problem" and excavation of her prediscursive past—is lived by the narrator as the murder of her femininity. Indeed, a story can kill, it can be what Peter Brooks calls "un acte d'agression,"[18] and to counter it, another story, more powerful in its enabling, nurturing, or life-affirming characteris-

18. Peter Brooks, "Constructions psychanalytiques et narratives," *Poétique* 61 (Feb. 1985): 64.

tics, is needed. Such are the tales and legends that the old Algerian woman Daïba tells to the children on the farm while feeding them "pastry dripping with honey" (p. 98) and unleavened bread. Hers are mythic tales with a powerful, positive, imaginary content, "sudden flights on winged horses prancing all the way to Allah's Paradise . . . adventures of black giants who shook mountains, fountains springing up in the desert, and genies inside bottles" (p. 98). Such was the magic of those days on the farm: contact with an archaic civilization, games with the Arab children, freedom from French reason and religion. The richness and diversity of her early experiences give the girl a strength to draw from when she is forced to leave Algeria and to cope with the psychic wounds that both her mother and the war inflicted upon her.

Talking to her dead mother in the cemetery, she recalls trips to another cemetery in Algeria, where her dead sister lies and where her mother, inconsolable over the loss of that "exceptional" child, the absent daughter who can never be replaced, used to take her. This loss is the original cause of the mother's profound and murderous contempt for the second daughter. The death of the mother, then, frees this daughter, who can simultaneously terminate her analysis and end her narrative: writing *is* symbolic matricide. Writing is the act of self-emancipation which allows the narrator to reach autonomy, despite her painful bleeding, much as Algeria won independence through its own bloodbath.

The novel contains two parallel chapters (6 and 16), which describe the Algerian tragedy and the mother's demise in much the same terms: "French Algeria lived out its agony" (p. 87) and "During this last year of my analysis, my mother was living through her final agony" (p. 270); "While lacerated Algeria showed her infected wounds in the full light of day, I revived a country of love and tenderness where the earth smelled of jasmine and fried food" (p. 88) and "On the contrary, she [the mother] didn't give a damn, she exhibited herself as if she took pleasure in exposing her wounds" (p. 280). Colonialism, like sexism, is thus degrading and abject: it is their combined forces that kill "the mother and the motherland"[19] and give the narrator the opportunity to discover what femininity really means in that context. The role of women is to be mothers of future soldiers, who will fight wars and perpetuate inequality and injustice. The only way to break the cycle is to start sharing in the power of men to make decisions that affect all of our lives, to

19. See Marguerite Le Clézio, "Mother and Motherland: The Daughter's Quest for Origins," *Stanford French Review* 5 (Winter 1981): 381–89. This is a study of Marie Cardinal and Jeanne Hyvrard.

become an active participant in society. In fact, it is her feeling of impotence in affairs of the state that provokes the narrator's major attacks of anxiety: "It seems to me that the Thing took root in me permanently when I understood that we were about to assassinate Algeria. For Algeria was my real mother" (p. 88). The way out of the impasse is a heightened political awareness of the complicated structures of domination that amputate freedom and self-determination from people and countries.

In a direct confession of the apolitical nature of her life before she started to write, the narrator admits that she never even used to read the newspapers. She had first seen the Algerian war as a sentimental family affair of fraternal enmity. Her life had been "thirty-seven years of absolute submission. Thirty-seven years of accepting the inequality and the injustice, without flinching, without even being aware of it!" (p. 264). But with self-integration comes a raised consciousness. The book ends on the historical marker: "Quelques jours plus tard, c'était mai 68."[20] We have come full circle; the personal and the political are inseparable.

> If I'd been black that would at least have given the information I was from Africa. . . . But nobody could see me, there, for what I am back where I come from. Nobody in Paris.
> Nadine Gordimer, *Burger's Daughter*

> Mi patria en el recuerdo
> y yo en París clavado
> como un blando murciélago
> Nicolás Guillén, "Exilio," *Man-Making Words*

The year 1968 was also an important one in the history of Mauritius. It marked the island's independence from Britain, its access to the rank of country. Independence was achieved with little or no bloodshed, because none of the diverse ethnic groups could really claim original ownership of the place. The island had been uninhabited until European

---

20. The last chapter of the book, which consists of this single line, "A few days later it was May 68," is inexplicably missing from the English version. I take this textual "mutilation" as an ironic and unfortunate instance of the kinds of distortion that reductionist theories—psychoanalytic or otherwise—can perform on historical context. The irony, of course, lies in the fact that the narrator of *Les Mots pour le dire* sees herself as narrowly escaping a similar amputation at the hands of her surgeon, but it is also clear that just as the narrator's mother tries to abort her, certain Western theoretical traditions would rather deny (abort?) the historical realities that subtend the experiences of marginal (women) writers. Thus Bruno Bettelheim in his Preface and Afterword does not once mention the word *Algeria* and effectively succeeds in silencing that geopolitical dimension of the text.

settlers began visiting it in the seventeenth and eighteenth centuries, and today it is peopled with the descendants of the French settlers, their black slaves, the Indian laborers who came to work the sugarcane fields when slavery was abolished in 1835, the Chinese and Muslim shop-keepers, and the métis whose status varies greatly depending on the relative darkness of their skin and the size of their fortune.

Marie-Thérèse Humbert's novel *A l'autre bout de moi* is the story of these "apatrides de la race" (p. 22) ("racially homeless people"), the coloreds or mixed-bloods, whose marginality is partly the result of their own inability to assume their nonwhite heritage because they have inter-nalized the ideals of the racist colonial society. Twin sisters, Anne and Nadège, live in a house on the outskirts of the vast colonial domains of the white bourgeoisie and a short distance from the Hindu quarter. This "house on the margins, on the limits, without ties and without parent-age" (p. 17) is a metaphor for their racial and cultural contexts. Coming of age in the 1950s, the decade preceding independence, the sisters are set on a collision course, for they choose to be loyal to different tradi-tions; Nadège gleefully accepts her *métissage:* she is chameleonlike, ad-venturous, imaginative, interested in Hindu culture and religion as well as popular superstitions; she is a free spirit, at once the Ariel and the Caliban of this "enchant'd isle," full of humor, impossible to define and constantly changing. She is the favored daughter of the family and she has an affair with a young Indian politician. For both reasons, she incurs the wrath of Anne, the controlled, reasonable, calculating one, whose rigid need for respectability, like that of the heroines of the romances she reads, includes romantic hopes of a bourgeois marriage. These hopes are thwarted by Nadège's pregnancy, for in Anne's world of almost-white-but-not-quite, any wrong step can be the first on the road back to further ostracism by the whites. When Nadège proudly announces her condition, Anne's murderous hatred is unleashed. She tells Nadège why she had always resented her; she shouts her contempt and her fury, disclosing her own profound distress. In an act of love for Anne, Nadège decides to obtain an (illegal) abortion and dies hemorrhaging. Her death and the police investigations that follow rob Anne of her pretensions to a purely Western life-style, revealing the "air d'étrangeté" (p. 398), the *Unheimlichkeit,* the uncanniness, of her own home and coun-try. At the end, the impossible fusion with her twin is realized in Anne's appropriation of Nadège's place as the lover of the Indian, Aunauth Gopaul. It is interesting to note that the names of the twins, Anne-Nadège, spoken quickly with the Mauritian Creole accent, sound much like "*anamnèse,*" since consonants are softened and the -*ège* ending is always pronounced like -*èse.* Thus Anne literally figures as the "one who returns" (*ana-*) and Nadège as her "memory" (*-mnesis*), or previous self.[21]

Anne's autobiographical narrative is an attempt to return Nadège's love, Nadège's loving offer to immolate her (pro)creation. It engages Anne, the narrator, in a dialogue with Nadège and with the repressed (sister) in herself. She can begin to tell her their story after she has allowed Nadège's voice to emerge: "But the voice which used to be Nadège's is now mine; I know it, I am certain of it" (p. 12). The narrative is framed by a Prologue, which situates Anne and Aunauth as exiles in Paris, where they are studying at the Sorbonne. This seemingly self-imposed exile creates sufficient distance from the recent past to be the revealer of Anne's narrative impulse, the Archimedean point she needed to lift the veil of silence on that past and on her country.[22] The present reality of Paris silences her too: it is lived as a jarring hiatus from the past, and her impulse to write is a defensive one, spurred on by the desire to recreate that past and reintegrate it into a new present, to shout "Mauritius [Nadège] exists!" to people who have never paid any attention to it, been indifferent to its fate. Like her island, she feels "abolie" (p. 12) (negated) by the ignorance of others, especially since France is a spiritual motherland for the Francophones of Mauritius. Her situation as Mauritian in Paris thus triggers the memory—enacts the repetition—of an earlier trauma: her parents' inability to see her as different from Nadège. She still resents their mother's legacy of shame, hatred, bitterness, and silence: "Mother-Silence, Mother-Gloom, our marine silence" (p. 43). And now in France, she also resents the sea of ignorance in which Mauritius floats. Like her parents' indifference, the ignorance of the *métropole* makes her feel painfully nonexistent.

Anne the protagonist can become Anne the narrator only after she has decided to return to her privileged "place of origin" and let the island tell itself through the voices of its inhabitants—all of whom have their own different stories, "life/lines," to tell her, in the form of direct or indirect discourses of which, as we shall see later, she is both the narratee and relayer. In this return to the "origins," Anne is like Augustine's narrator in the *Confessions,* who is finally whole after he has reached his resting place in God, who can then speak through him and whose words are translated textually by the weaving of scriptural verses into the narrative. Anne's autobiographical gesture is implicitly similar to the Au-

21. I develop this point in a chapter of my forthcoming book *Autobiographical Voices.*
22. I purposely use this image—as Myra Jehlen has in "Archimedes and the Paradox of Feminist Criticism," reprinted in *The Signs Reader: Women, Gender and Scholarship* (Chicago: University of Chicago Press, 1983), pp. 69–95—in order to propose that exile and marginality are perhaps the necessary preconditions for "our seeing the old world from a genuinely new perspective" (p. 94).

gustinian project but covertly aims at subverting it. The narrative is divided into thirteen parts (like the *Confessions*), and as it unfolds, Anne confesses her "sins" to her sister. These are the sins of Western metaphysics: to wish desperately to *be* a unique individual, "être à tout prix" (p. 419) (to be at any cost), and to capture one essential truth about oneself—whereas life is flux, theater, dream. Striving to occult in her the elements of a different race, her Hindu ancestry, and the qualities embodied by Nadège, she is a victim of the Western obsession with being, an obsession that shows nothing but contempt for its unassimilable opposites. Nadège, who is remarkably free of this totalizing goal, is self-assured in her difference. She has no distance, no duality: inner and outer are the same for her. Her life is lived in harmony with the passing of time, the mysteries of life. "Strangely intimate with the earth's profane mysteries and long seasonal gestations, with the winds' and the clouds' infinite wanderings" (p. 312), she projects a persona that needs no mirror to reassure itself of its own existence:

Nadège never cared about being. . . . Never, but never, did she try to see herself elsewhere than in *the eyes of others.* She would amuse herself with these fortuitous mirrors as a child would with the changing colors of a prism, perpetually enjoying her ability to create new shades, becoming by turns intrigued, charmed, shocked or seduced by these external reflections, and thus deviating constantly from herself. There is nothing less imaginative and less true than a mirror! she used to declare contemptuously. But while she played, I would contemplate with despair my own dull shadow, lusterless compared to the shimmer of her multiple reflections; my wretched face, never quite mine because it was always too similar or too different from her own. (P. 419, my emphasis)

Nadège is interested in Christian mysticism as well as Hindu rites. She participates every year in the Hindu festival of lights, the *Divali*, adorning their house with a small brass lantern, and the Hindu gods with colorful flowers. She is like a joyful Zarathustra; she does not need origins. Her very name also connotes nirvana, emptiness, nothingness, *nada*, Nadège. Anne, on the other hand, cannot surrender to polysemy and experiences it as a threat to her ego. She is always narcissistically searching for approval in the form of a reflection that would give her substance, ground her firmly somewhere: "Where is the place where I should live?" (p. 122) she asks. But the reflection she finds always turns out to be illusory and elusive: "When I look in the mirror, it is you I see, you who need no mirror, you who *are* without a mirror. The image of myself that I try to capture deceives me, escapes me; it's you who are there in the mirror, only the expression of the eyes differs and the reflection that I see, my own image, looks like a bad photograph" (p. 121).

The place where she can, and should live, of course, is on the page, in the book that embodies these tensions in its own narrative structure, combining the self-portraits of all the characters, these *autres* who are Nadège's mirrors, her infinite dispersion. The words "my own image looks like a bad photograph" connote the scriptural phrase, "per speculum in aenigmate" (I Cor. 13:12),[23] which Augustine repeatedly uses to signify his state of imperfection, which will be reversed when he reaches the "intellectual heaven." In Book 12:13 of the *Confessions,* Augustine articulates his project of self-knowledge as the search for completeness and perfection. Augustine the sinner is now converted and the book is a reflection of the man as a creature in the image of God, ready to enter "the intellectual heaven, where the intellect is privileged to know all at once, not in part only, not as if it were *looking at as a confused reflection in a mirror [non in aenigmate, non per speculum],* but as a whole, clearly, *face to face [facie ad faciem].*"[24]

Humbert's text never makes explicit reference to Augustine's *Confessions* as it does to Shakespeare's *Tempest,* for example; but it embodies in its structure an undeniable reflection of that *architexte*[25] of Western auto-biographical discourse, while also reversing its messages. Humbert's text points to a negative view of mirroring, in the Western sense, as usurpation, occultation of difference. As Roland Barthes has said: "In the West, the mirror is essentially a narcissistic object: man thinks about the mirror only so as to look at himself; but it would seem that in the Orient the mirror is void; it is a symbol of the very emptiness of symbols. . . . The mirror only reflects other mirrors and this infinite reflecting is the void. . . ."[26]

It is in Chapter 12 of *A l'autre bout de moi,* during the police interrogation, that Anne recalls (privately, not publicly) her confrontation with Nadège: "I had slapped her face with all my strength and rage. She took another step with her arms spread out. Then she slowly lowered them, as if in a daze. And before me, there was only her strangely distorted face, like a mask. No, I felt no pity, but once again this hideous joy, so keen that it seemed closer to pain than to pleasure; *before this unexpressive mask, at last, I had a face!*" (p. 427, my emphasis). Anne's insults literally

23. This phrase is traditionally translated as "through a glass, darkly." I prefer to follow R. S. Pine-Coffin's rendering of it: "like a confused reflection in a mirror."

24. Saint Augustine, *Confessions,* trans. R. S. Pine-Coffin (New York: Penguin Books, 1961), p. 289.

25. To use Gérard Genette's term. See his *Introduction à l'architexte* (Paris: Seuil, 1979).

26. Roland Barthes, *L'Empire des signes,* Les Sentiers de la création series (Geneva: Skira, 1970), p. 104, my translation.

deface Nadège, steal her face, effecting her death as surely as the botched abortion will on the following day. It is not just the abortionist who is on trial; Anne too must account—on the page, by writing—for her inability to tolerate Nadège's polysemic difference and for her secret desire to assimilate it. She recalls how, during their altercation, Nadège had fallen down in the sand and had lain there, curled in a fetal position; she, Anne, had shouted "Fetus! Hideous fetus! Die!" (p. 428), aiming the insult at her sister but thereby amputating herself, depriviliging otherness as radically *other* in order to co-opt it, to abort it.

I would like to suggest that what is implied (and at stake) here is the immolation of the métis, the Creole, as symbol, product, and (pro)creation of Western colonialism, on the altars of Western belief in the One and the Same, in a humanism that subsumes all heterogeneity. Anne the narrator sees herself as the product of this indoctrination, which resulted in a damaging self-image. In that, her predicament is analogous to that of all individuals who have internalized their society's negative view, or ignorance, of their specificity. These individuals include women in any patriarchial system, and women writers in particular, as they face the dilemmas inherent in recapturing what has been effaced or diminished. Anne's journey back to the past aims at deconstructing that indoctrination, peeling off the layers of a damaging belief in the importance of origins and rootedness.

Her journey, then, is that of her island itself at the time of its political independence from Britain. Its multiracial society was burdened by two centuries of colonization, first by the French, then by the English, whereas its survival had been ensured by the labor of the Indian and black populations who were not native either. All these diverse ethnic groups had to devise a mode of pacific coexistence that would allow the free play of influences and exchanges among different cultures. The issue, therefore, was not to define the national identity of the island (since it did not have any) but to use this geographical space, this topos, this "house without ties and without parentage" as the place where a mosaic of forms, styles, and languages could interact and survive.

Viewed from that angle, the political problematic of the island becomes the personal problematic of the woman writer. She has no specifically female tradition to build on but, in order to survive, must quilt together from the pieces of her legacy a viable whole—viable in that it embraces a multiplicity of elements that can allow the writer to assume the past (the literary tradition) as past and therefore to reintegrate it into a radically different present,[27] making it the implicit or explicit intertext

27. I am paraphrasing Peter Brooks's discussion (p. 65) of transference in Balzac's *Le Colonel Chabert*.

of her text, adding that past to the texture of her voice so she may begin to transform and reinterpret history. This problematic would point to a notion of the female text as *mé-tissage,* that is, the weaving of different strands of raw material and threads of various colors into one piece of fabric; female textuality as *métissage.* It would emancipate the writer from any internal or external coercion to use any one literary style or form, freeing her to enlarge, redefine, or explode the canons of our discursive practices.

Humbert's text encodes heterogeneity through this use of intertextual references to various generic and ideological models or antimodels—to Augustine and Shakespeare but also to Corneille, Racine, Baudelaire, Nietzsche, Conrad, Faulkner, Sylvia Plath, Michel Tournier, and others. Intratextually, she encodes diversity by giving her text over to a polyphonic chorus of voices who relate their own stories to us by means of her narrative. The purpose of these stories is twofold: to give a voice to the silenced ones of history and to allow Anne to become the heroine of her own tale by choosing a script for the way she will live her life from the various life stories that are recounted to her. Her situation as listener and interpreter of these stories is homologous to ours before her text, suggesting that she encodes certain models of reading appropriate to her own discourse. Without going into a detailed analysis of the many instances of situational self-reflexivity which would illustrate my point here, I would like to focus on two embedded stories ("narrational embedding") which are both narratives of abandonment.[28] Anne retells these stories in order to deal with and break away from that age-old script of female passivity. They are the stories of her own mother and of Sassita, the young Indian maid. Both women are quiet, submissive, "dead to desire as well as to revolt" (p. 352), as Nadège will become when she too is all but abandoned by her lover, who wants to protect his political image.

Sassita was married at the age of fourteen to a fifty-six-year-old man who promptly repudiated her on their wedding night because the bedsheets had failed to become stained with blood. Dumbfounded at her bad luck and at the man's obstinate attempts to draw blood, she had rejoined her family and resigned herself to their daylong beatings as punishment for tarnishing the family's honor. She fatalistically accepted the guilt imposed on her by external circumstances. Listening to her story, Anne is filled with shame at the troubling unfairness of life and at the fatalism of the Indian woman.

The mother's story is disclosed when the sisters discover her diary

28. On situational self-reflexivity and "narrational embedding," see Chambers, pp. 18–49, 33.

after her death; they learn how disappointed she had been at their birth because they were "of a golden terracotta color" (p. 130), not pink and blond and safely beyond their nonwhite ancestry. Also, her fear of sex and her disappointment in her husband's infidelities added to the debilitation of her young daughters. The discovery of their mother's secrets further accentuates the sisters' alienation from each other: Anne is progressively absorbed by her hopes to live a normal/respectable life, whereas Nadège gives free rein to her "blaze of vital energy" (p. 120).

These pictures of effaced, obliterated femininity are the only paradigms or frames of reference Anne and Nadège have, their only lifelines to the status of female persons. In a reversal typical of the deployment and resolution of Humbert's narrative text, it is Nadège who is abandoned when her father threatens her lover with a political scandal (Nadège is still a minor at the time of her affair). She resigns herself to her fate as Sassita had, becoming a "tragic heroine," whereas Anne learns to dissimulate, to swerve, and to survive, thus gradually distancing herself from her role as "romantic heroine." Anne deviates from the traditional script and thereby frees herself to say her own lines, on her own stage, the island, to which she decides to return.[29]

When her father reveals to her his own view of married life, Anne writes: "I think that the most embarrassing thing for me was not just the content of these confidences, but the mere fact of listening. The habit of silence is a hard one to give up, and I sensed all too clearly that this kind of thing was never meant to be a one-way street. Wasn't I too committing myself to speak in turn, to emerge from the opportune shadow where I stood?" (p. 134). Paradoxically, then, these (negative) stories do have a positive effect, for they contribute to Anne's impulse to break the code of silence that had been the mother's legacy to her daughters. Listening to "confidences" (reading autobiographical novels) propels the hearer into a dialogical encounter, one that can only empower her to speak, to write.

29. This decision to return after having first left for Paris is set in implicit contrast to the move planned by her Uncle André, who decides to emigrate to South Africa with his family, thus getting an official seal of approval that he safely "passes" for one of pure European descent, since there is indeed "no whiter white than the South African white man" (cf. p. 449).

PART IV

DE-LIMITING GENRE:
OTHER AUTOBIOGRAPHICAL
ACTS

14

All of a Piece:
Women's Poetry and Autobiography

CELESTE SCHENCK

Adding yet another textile metaphor to feminist criticism's homespun lexicon of quilts, webs, and tapestries, I shall begin by invoking as an idiom and floating as a figure the first half of my title. "All of a Piece" suggests, as idiom, that two pieces of cloth are cut from the same bolt, and it figures, as chiasmus, the exchange between or interchangeability of two terms. Certain forms of women's poetry and autobiography can be read coextensively, in a manner that profitably destabilizes theory of mainstream autobiography and calls into question the patriarchal determination of genre theory more generally.

Toward a Feminist Theory of Genre: The Autobiographical Paradigm

The law of genre, the enforcement of generic purity, the policing of borders, has remained since the classical period a preoccupation of *homo* (properly understood man) *taxonomicus*. The *locus classicus* of "literature as system," is, of course, Aristotle's *Poetics*, that text which made taxonomy the very praxis of poetics, system its very theory, authorizing the hypostasizing of literary genre in its opening sentence: "I propose to treat of poetry in itself and of its various kinds, noting the essential quality of each."[1] Even the hierarchizing of genres—behind which rears

A skeletal version of this essay was first prepared for a Modern Language Association special session (New York, 1986) organized by Julia Watson: "Destabilizing the Theory of Autobiography: The Challenge of Gender." I thank Susan Stanford Friedman, Louise Yelin, and the anonymous readers called upon by Cornell University Press for their generous commentary on later drafts of this essay.

1. Aristotle, *Aristotle's Theory of Poetry and Fine Art, With . . . The Poetics*, ed. and trans. S. H. Butcher (London: Macmillan, 1932), p. 7.

a "benignly conservationist influence,"[2] if not a correspondent conservative politics—has its origin in classical polemics over the proper ordering of drama and epic. K. K. Ruthven, for example, finds a "displacement of class-bias into literary forms" in classical taxonomies based on the criterion of decorum; Alastair Fowler has noted that the *rota Virgilii* correlates style with the divisions of feudal society; Northrop Frye detects an ideological bias in Matthew Arnold's demotion of Chaucer and Burns to class 2 in his touchstone scheme; and Shari Benstock exposes the hierarchical values implicit in gender distinctions as they manifest themselves in the epistolary mode.[3] Critical distinctions between "low" and "high" cultural products, between rough pastoral and polished epic, between the eighteenth-century novel and the higher, more refined Augustan mode, between pop art and the Great Books—all partake of what I will call the politics of genre.[4]

As these few examples indicate, beginning with classical theory the ordering of genres has rested upon much more than aesthetic judgment. Traditionally viewed as purely aesthetic markers, genres have been highly politicized (not only gendered but also class biased and racially biased) in the long history of Western literary criticism, a phenomenon that has had enormous implications for the banishment of women writers (and other marginalized groups) from the canon. Genres—the sonnet and the epic, the realistic novel and autobiography, as well as the history of genre theory accompanying them—are fairly drenched in ideologies. In fact, given that, in Fredric Jameson's words, "genres are so clearly implicated in the literary history and formal production they were traditionally supposed to classify and neutrally to describe,"[5] given that genres are, after all, cultural constructions themselves, they might be more usefully conceived as overdetermined loci of contention and conflict than as ideal types that transcendentally precede and predetermine a literary work. Although contemporary theory has all but effaced

2. Alastair Fowler, *Kinds of Literature: An Introduction to the Theory of Genres and Modes* (Oxford: Clarendon Press, 1982), p. 36.

3. K. K. Ruthven, *Feminist Literary Studies: An Introduction* (Cambridge: Cambridge University Press, 1984), p. 116; Fowler, p. 35; Northrop Frye, *The Anatomy of Criticism: Four Essays* (Princeton: Princeton University Press, 1957), p. 22; Shari Benstock, "From Letters to Literature: *La Carte postale* in the Epistolary Mode," *Genre* 18 (Fall 1985): 257–95.

4. A more elaborate discussion of the politics of genre is included in the first chapter of my book, *Corinna Sings: Women Poets and the Politics of Genre* (Ithaca: Cornell University Press, forthcoming).

5. Fredric Jameson, *The Political Unconscious: Narrative as a Socially Symbolic Act* (Ithaca: Cornell University Press, 1981), p. 107. For a discussion of these issues in the context of female poetic modernism, see my "Exiled by Genre: Modernism, Canonicity and the Politics of Exile," forthcoming in the first volume of *Alien and Critical: Women Writers in Exile,* ed. Mary Lynn Broe and Angela Ingram (Chapel Hill: University of North Carolina Press, 1989).

genre as a category of literary interest in favor of a borderless *écriture*, if we are to believe Jameson generic perspectives are *nonetheless* living something like a "return of the repressed," probably because they serve the critic as markers of social and historical experience where it intersects with the ideology of form.

While generic hierarchies may not have pursued us with equal zeal into the twentieth century, the celebrated modernist death of genre has not prevented the proliferation of literary critical classification. Indeed, taxonomy—with its ranks and files, its implicit politics of inclusion and exclusion—can be said to be the obsessive, and continuing, concern of Western genre theory. Since the time of the Greeks generic bird watching has led a long and vital history in the works of rhetoricians, Renaissance codifiers such as Minturno and Scaliger, Sidney and Dryden, the more lenient Puttenham and Jonson.[6] Even after Croce's strong reservations about genre—"All books dealing with classifications and systems of the arts could be burned without any loss whatsoever"—and the romantics' call to "emancipate ourselves of a false association from misapplied names"[7]—twentieth-century literary theory has continued to invest in taxonomic schemes: Stephen's classificatory meditation on Aristotle in *Portrait of the Artist as a Young Man,* Renato Poggioli's system of "Poetics and Metrics," neo-Aristotelean categories of the so-called Chicago School, New Critical schemata for explicating the varieties of poetic experience, Russian formalist maps of folklore motifs, structural studies of myth, linguistic distinctions between deep and surface structures, raw and cooked cultures, even semiotic readings of the codes beneath narrative fiction and sign systems, and finally, constitution of the fantastic as genre by Todorov, a coherent verbal universe by Northrop Frye, literature as system by Claudio Guillén, the resources of kind by Rosalie Colie.[8]

Moreover, beneath the Western will to taxonomize lies not only a defensive history of exclusions that constitute a political ideology but also a fetishizing of aesthetic purity—not unlike that which this culture maintains of virginity—which has distinctly gendered overtones. Pure

6. For a survey of genre theory, see Heather Dubrow, *Genre* (London: Methuen, 1982), chaps. 3 and 4.

7. Benedetto Croce, *Aesthetic as a Science of Expression and General Linguistic,* trans. Douglas Ainslie (London: Macmillan, 1922), p. 188, quoted in Adena Rosmarin, *The Power of Genre* (Minneapolis: University of Minnesota Press, 1985), p. 6; S. T. Coleridge, *Coleridge's Miscellaneous Criticism,* ed. Thomas Middleton Raysor (Cambridge: Harvard University Press, 1936), p. 138.

8. Tzvetan Todorov, *The Fantastic,* trans. Richard Howard (Cleveland: Case Western Reserve Press, 1973); Frye, *The Anatomy of Criticism;* Claudio Guillén, *Literature as System* (Princeton: Princeton University Press, 1971); Rosalie Colie, *The Resources of Kind,* ed. Barbara Lewalski (Berkeley: University of California Press, 1973).

genres, like biological genders, had best remain discrete and intact.[9] Mixed, unclassifiable, blurred, or hybrid genres, like impure, anomalous, or monstrous genders, have traditionally offered up problems to their diagnosticians. Implicit in these sexual metaphors as thoroughly as in genre theory itself is also a binary opposition between norm and departure, between convention and confusion, Platonic idea and deceiving appearance, pure form and polluted copy, which bears a subtext of not only gender but also racial oppression. The imperialist language of Marcelin Pleynet's "La poésie doit avoir pour but," italics below *his* own, underlines the need for an originating master genre that might subdue the text's complexities, manage the difficulty of the reading process, uphold its own law and order: "It is indeed this word (novel, poem) placed on the cover of the book which (by convention) genetically produces, programmes, or 'originates' our reading. We have here (with the genre 'novel,' 'poem') a *master word* which from the outset reduces complexity, reduces the textual encounter, by making it a function of the type of reading already implicit in the law of this word."[10] In fact, as Jacques Derrida reminds us, "*the* genre has always in all genres been able to play the role of order's principle: resemblance, analogy, identity and difference, taxonomic classification, organization and genealogical tree, order of reason, order of reasons, sense of sense, truth of truth, natural light and sense of history."[11] When he begins his meditation on "The Law of Genre" with the soon-to-be-deconstructed proposition that "genres are not to be mixed," he reminds us that the "law of 'do' or 'do not' . . . , as everyone knows, occupies the concept or constitutes the value of genre" (p. 203). Even when critics gesture toward a theory of genre beyond taxonomy, they still emphasize the recuperative, naturalizing, motivating, *vraisemblablisation* of genre. Jonathan Culler, for example, glossing Todorov and, more generally, the structural approach to genre, falls back upon a domesticating vocabulary of his own:

"Recuperation" stresses the notion of recovery, of putting to use. It may be defined as the desire to leave no chaff, to make everything wheat, to let nothing escape the process of assimilation; it is thus a central component of studies which assert the organic unity of the text and the contribution of all its parts to its meanings or effects. "Naturalization" emphasizes the fact that the strange or deviant is brought within a discursive order and thus

9. Benstock, pp. 259–60.

10. Marcelin Pleynet, *Théorie d'ensemble* (Paris: Seuil, 1968), pp. 95–96, quoted by Jonathan Culler, *Structuralist Poetics* (Ithaca: Cornell University Press, 1975), pp. 136–37.

11. Jacques Derrida, "La Loi du Genre/The Law of Genre," trans. Avital Ronnell, *Glyph* 7 (1980): 228, hereafter cited in the text.

made to seem natural. "Motivation," which was the Russian formalists' term, is the process of justifying items within the work itself by showing that they are not arbitrary or incoherent but quite comprehensible in terms of functions which we can name. *Vraisemblablisation* stresses the importance of cultural models of the *vraisemblable* as sources of meaning and coherence.[12]

Western genre theory thus remains for the most part prescriptive, legislative, even metaphysical: its traditional preoccupations have been the establishment of limits, the drawing of exclusionary lines, the fierce protection of idealized generic (and implicitly sexual and racial) purity. Although Derrida reminds us that in French the word *genre* includes and even connotes gender (p. 221), the history of genre, seemingly, has not only failed to address its own politics adequately; it has also been blind to its own gender inflection, an elision that feminist critics have sought variously to redress. Feminist attention to "gender generics"[13] first focused on the ways in which women were edged into marginalized, noncanonical genres as a result of their exclusion from central cultural concerns. Women became "custodians of the ballad tradition,"[14] and they also found a more hospitable home in the novel than in the Augustan modes of the eighteenth century.[15] A second strain has critiqued the masculinist bias of some genres, accounting for differences between male and female appropriations of the same genre by invoking the distinct psychosexual development of each gender: epic is organized around martial conflict, gynophobia, and aggressivity, for example, and elegy may depend upon a male psychosocial model of separation based on competition and succession.[16] Comedy and tragedy, in the classical period as in the Renaissance, reflect the cultural imagery of sexual difference.[17] Still another project of feminist genre theory has been the study

12. Jonathan Culler, *Structuralist Poetics*, pp. 136–37. See also Nancy Miller's discussion of plausibility and *vraisemblance* in her "Emphasis Added: Plots and Plausibilities in Women's Fiction," in *The New Feminist Criticism: Essays on Women, Literature, Theory*, ed. Elaine Showalter (New York: Pantheon, 1985), pp. 239–60.

13. Kathleen Blake, "Pure Tess: Hardy on Knowing a Woman," *Studies in English Literature* 22 (1982): 705.

14. Ruthven, p. 117.

15. Virginia Woolf, *A Room of One's Own* (New York: Harcourt Brace, 1929), p. 115: "Less concentration is required" for the writing of prose.

16. Susan Stanford Friedman, "Gender and Genre Anxiety: Elizabeth Barrett Browning and H.D. as Epic Poets," *Tulsa Studies in Women's Literature* 5 (Fall 1986): 203–28; and Schenck, "Feminism and Deconstruction: Re-Constructing the Elegy," *Tulsa Studies in Women's Literature* 5 (Spring 1986): 13–28.

17. Froma Zeitlin, "Travesties of Gender and Genre in Aristophanes' *Thesmophoriazousae*," *Critical Inquiry* 8 (Winter 1981): 301–28; and Linda Bamber, *Comic Women, Tragic Men: A Study of Gender and Genre in Shakespeare* (Stanford: Stanford University Press, 1982).

of women authors' use of genres traditionally dominated by men, such as the epithalamium, or, alternatively, the domination by women writers of some genres of their own, such as the gothic.[18] Finally, feminist attention to genre has determined that forms previously thought to be gender free are in fact gender specific, that certain forms could even *be* interestingly gendered by asking what a text would look like if it were written, if it were read, by a woman. The critical goal in all these operations has been to deconstruct the normative (masculine) criteria of genre, which consign feminine practice to inferior, idiosyncratic, or debased use of forms.

A remaining task for feminist genre theory is to question the hypostasizing of genre and its consequences for diagnosing women's writing as shapeless and indeterminate: that is, the limiting of genre to a designation of *form* or *norm*. In partial response to this question, I propose that reading certain kinds of women's poetry with autobiography as continuous and related discourses bound by their parallel concern with subject formation hastens the undoing of a Western generic practice based on exclusion, limit, hierarchy, and taxonomy, and formal norms, and sets up a fluid, dialogical relationship between two of the not-so-discrete literary forms that female self-inscription takes; that is, I suggest that we think of genres in terms less of transcendental shapes than of often-complementary discourses, particularly when we look at women's writing and the history and politics of its exclusion from dominant generic hierarchies.

If, in fact, as many of the essays in this collection document, the poetics of women's autobiography issues from its concern with constituting a female subject—a precarious operation, which, as I have described it elsewhere, requires working on two fronts at once, *both* occupying a kind of center, assuming a subjectivity long denied, *and* maintaining the vigilant, disruptive stance that speaking from the postmodern margin provides—the autobiographical genre may be paradigmatic of all women's writing. It may also overlap or indeed exist coextensively with other genres used by women writers. For example, within the corpus of a woman writer, autobiography may have functioned differently from the way it has functioned in male careers: it may not bear resemblance to the *"dark Africa of the genres"* (my emphasis) which male critics such as Olney and Steven Shapiro have sought to "map."[19] Not a summing up of a lived life, written at the end of a

18. Claire Kahane, "The Gothic Mirror," in *The (M)other Tongue: Essays in Feminist Psychoanalytic Interpretation,* ed. Shirley Nelson Garner, Claire Kahane, and Madelon Sprengnether (Ithaca: Cornell University Press, 1985), pp. 334–51.

19. Steven Shapiro, "The Dark Continent of Literature: Autobiography," *Comparative Literature Studies* 5 (Dec. 1968): 421–54.

career,[20] and consequently a literary monument difficult to place in the corpus, autobiography can be a way of coming *to* writing for a woman (as in the case of Maya Angelou, for example), or it can function as her only or most important mode of self-expression (as it did for Violette Leduc, among many other lesbian writers). Women's poetry has often been assigned similar "autobiographical" status, which has relegated it as well to the unsorted pile of sanitized generic laundry. Often modern and contemporary women's poetry and autobiography—as texts recording the negotiation of the female self-in-process between the historical fact of displacement and the possibility of textual self-presence—may be fruitfully conceived of as cut from the same bolt.

Autobiography and Poetry

Ample precedent exists for the pairing of poetry and autobiography, a history I shall rehearse here in order to locate this gendered discussion of genre. James Olney, the "father" of autobiographical criticism, was the first to use what he calls the "poetic-autobiographic metaphor" in his contention that "art, both autobiographic and poetic, mediates between the transient world of sensation and feeling, of event and emotion, and a constant, stable realm of pattern and significance." He continues: "Poetry, like psychology and philosophy, is about life, not about part of it but potentially about all of it. The truth that poetry embodies . . . is a whole truth."[21] But Olney stresses the identity between poetry and autobiography principally as a way of legitimizing, by elevating to the status of "art," the heretofore marginal genre of autobiography. William Spengemann extends the analogy further, holding up poetic autobiography as the apex of the genre's post-Augustinian development because it displaces into literature and the verbal structures of the text any previous belief in an "absolute, unconditioned self or soul that transcends and hence justifies all conditioned experience." The author who can no longer know his "true being, his true society, and his true immortality" can, according to Spengemann, recapture that unitary self in his own poetic output, as Hawthorne was able to recover him/self in *The Scarlett Letter*.[22]

20. See William Howarth, "Some Principles of Autobiography," in *Autobiography: Essays Theoretical and Critical,* ed. James Olney (Princeton: Princeton University Press, 1980), p. 86: "An autobiography is equally a work of art and life, for no one writes such a book until he has lived out the requisite years." Hereafter citations follow in the text.

21. James Olney, *Metaphors of Self: The Meaning of Autobiography* (Princeton: Princeton University Press, 1972), pp. 45, 260–61.

22. William C. Spengemann, *The Forms of Autobiography: Episodes in the History of a Literary Genre* (New Haven: Yale University Press, 1980), pp. 120, 165.

Candace Lang decries the romanticism implicit in both of these attempts to conflate poetry and autobiography. Seemingly the analogy with poetry does seem to be based on a shared metaphysics of transcendental selfhood and truth rather than any similarities of form or function. But Lang's argument is ultimately deconstructionist: she inevitably "calls into question," given the ungraspability of postmodern selfhood, "the very possibility of writing an autobiography in the traditional sense, that is, a work, discursive or 'poetic,' 'about' oneself." What she does offer the project of rethinking genre theory is the articulation of a possible continuum between metacritical discourse and self-conscious autobiography as twin "discourses of language on—'about'—language," that is, a model for thinking of generic categories as extended along a spectrum. Lang closes by calling for an end to obsession with the accuracy of self-portraiture and envisions autobiographical analysis of "those moments in which the self-critical act begins to expose its status as an act of self-writing," an act that, productively for my purposes, transcends generic borders.[23]

Here, however, feminist and deconstructionist must part ways. The deconstructionist would have autobiography "problematize" itself by calling into question the authority and source of any utterance, any coherent experience, any attempt at self-location, as Stendhal's *Brulard* fails, so instructively for Lang, in its own outsetting terms. If the "transcendent subject is an illusion," writes Lang, "then not only is autobiography in the Augustinian sense no longer possible, *it never was*."[24] A feminist reading of women's writing would argue, by contrast, that women, never having achieved the self-possession of post-Cartesian subjects, do not have the luxury of "flirting with the escape from identity," which the deconstructed subject may enjoy.[25] Nancy Miller's and Teresa de Lauretis's vitally necessary theorizing of the female self out of the materiality of her writing, the historicity of her experience, underwrite my assertions here.[26] Women's autobiographical writing, whether narrative or poetic, can thus occupy, in the political sense, a literary space in which issues about representing the self have been traditionally fought out; by occupying territory in a genre so shapeless and un(rule)y

23. Candace Lang, "Autobiography in the Aftermath of Romanticism," *Diacritics* 12 (Winter 1982): 10, 11, 12.

24. Ibid., p. 5.

25. Nancy K. Miller, "Arachnologies," in *The Poetics of Gender*, ed. Nancy K. Miller (New York: Columbia University Press, 1986), p. 274. See also Bella Brodzki, "'She Was Unable Not To Think': Borges' *Emma Zunz* and the Female Subject," *MLN* (March 1985): 330–47, for a demonstration of the inextricability of identity and gender.

26. Miller, pp. 273–75; and Teresa de Lauretis, *Alice Doesn't: Feminism, Semiotics, Cinema* (Bloomington: Indiana University Press, 1982), esp. chap. 6.

as to have needed colonizing by male critics, women autobiographers (in all the modal forms autobiography takes in women's writing) have found some shelter from the pervasive law of genre; such positioning tenders the possibility for women of writing out an enabling subjectivity, however un-unitary, swiftly changing, even inconsistent that selfhood may be as experienced; and herein might lie the tie that binds women's poetry to autobiography and beyond that to the continuous bolt of female textual production.

Poetry as Autobiography

This section of my essay attempts the first half of the reciprocal exchange I envisioned at the start, pressing a feminist analysis of autobiography (as a "sexual/textual" site of subject formation) into the service of reading certain kinds of women's poetry. Not only feminist critics have remarked upon the "personal" and "autobiographical" dimensions of much women's poetry; in fact, male disparagements of women's poetry usually begin with some mention of the incessant "spinning-out," "the embroidering of trivial themes." I quote here from Roethke's "defense" of Louise Bogan's oeuvre as against the "caterwauling" of most women's poetry.[27] Carolyn Heilbrun more sympathetically notes that "the most remarkable autobiographical accounts" of women writers have been "tucked away into other forms, other genres (poetry, interviews, essays, social or literary criticism)." For her, it is precisely the "confessional" aspect of autobiography and poetry, which Heilbrun does not read as indictingly as Roethke, which links these two forms of writing by women. In the coextensive, unbounded genres she lists, Heilbrun finds a record of women's struggles to believe in the authority of their own experience, and she suggests that generic boundaries were first stretched in poetry to include women's life experience. "It is chiefly in [Adrienne] Rich's generation of women poets—Sylvia Plath, Anne Sexton, Maxine Kumin, Carolyn Kizer, Denise Levertov— that the T. S. Eliot ban upon the personal fell."[28] Clearly, however, as early as Anne Bradstreet, if not as far back as Sappho, and certainly in the case of Emily Dickinson, the female poetic corpus has been read as her autobiography.[29]

27. Theodore Roethke, "The Poetry of Louise Bogan," *Selected Prose of Theodore Roethke*, ed. Ralph J. Mills, Jr. (Seattle: University of Washington Press, 1965), pp. 133–34.

28. Carolyn Heilbrun, "Women's Autobiographical Writings: New Forms," *Prose Studies* 8 (Sept. 1985): 20, 26.

29. Susan Stanford Friedman, "Theories of Autobiography and Fictions of the Self in H.D.'s Canon," forthcoming in *Self-Representations: Autobiographical Writing in the Nineteenth*

I would like to press beyond the thematic similarities that link the two genres I am considering—Robert Penn Warren, for example, has already written that "poetry . . . is the deepest part of autobiography, a hazardous attempt at self-understanding"[30]—and move to another level of comparison. What interests me more than autobiographical form or even content in the poetic corpus of a Bradstreet or a Dickinson, a Kumin, Sexton, Plath, or a Rich, is the functional identity between the two genres: the serial effort at sketching a self in time and over time is the poetic equivalent of snapshots recording a process of personal becoming during a period of historical change. Rich, for one, uses this metaphor outright in her aptly titled "Snapshots of a Daughter-in-Law." The resulting corpus is not a deliberate disruption of a bounded and unified, belatedly perceived, autobiographical self, a programmatic pastiche of contradictory speaking positions, as Barthes might see his *Roland Barthes by Roland Barthes*, but something I would like to describe as multiplicity of self-representation in a necessarily discontinuous because serial and temporally elaborated form. Given the dearth of autobiographical information about women before the eighteenth century, the poetic corpus of many women poets, beginning with Sappho, has been read precisely as autobiography ("Writing poetry in fragments," as Woolf and Rich both knew, was all that leisure allowed),[31] but that generic label here has nothing in common with the after-the-fact, unified, masculine re-creation of the "image of one's own method"[32] or late-career justification of one's own life as representative of the lives of others, which characterize mainstream masculine autobiography. Women poets, like women autobiographers, have often begun from the other direction, intent upon writing the self but daunted by Enid Bagnold's dilemma—"Myself has no outline"—or Dickinson's—"I'm nobody."[33] Often the female poetic corpus, like many but by no means all

---

and *Twentieth Centuries*, ed. Thomas R. Smith, concentrates on H.D.'s prose memoirs, tributes, and autobiographical fictions, noting that H.D. comes to the personal poetry of *Trilogy* and *Hermetic Definition* by breaking boundaries in gendered prose. Even though the "personal" poetry of Dickinson and Rich should be placed in historical context—Dickinson's does have much in common with lyric poetry of the American romantics and Rich charts her own reaction against Eliot's doctrine of impersonality—even poets whose historical location did not promote autobiographical output have written works that read this way. H.D.'s *Collected Poems*, for all the impersonality of certain of the poems, might still be read retroactively as an autobiography of a female subject in the provisional sense I have been exploring.

30. Robert Penn Warren, "Poetry Is a Kind of Unconscious Autobiography," *New York Times Book Review*, 12 May 1985, pp. 9–10.

31. Adrienne Rich, "When We Dead Awaken: Writing as Re-Vision," in *On Lies, Secrets, and Silence: Selected Prose, 1966–1978* (New York: Norton, 1979), p. 44, hereafter cited in the text.

32. Erik Erikson, quoted in Heilbrun, p. 21.

33. Enid Bagnold, *Autobiography* (Boston: Little, Brown, 1969), p. 3; Emily Dickinson, *The Complete Poems of Emily Dickinson*, ed. Thomas H. Johnson (1890; rpt., Boston: Little, Brown,

women's autobiographies, serves simultaneously as a historical record of women's absence from literary culture and as evidence of one woman's presence to herself within contiguous modes of life writing, an often programmatically fragmentary, yet nonetheless inclusive record of self-inscription.

I do not mean to suggest that all autobiographies written by men manifest organic form or that Robert Lowell's *Life Studies* is not fragmentary and even autobiographical. Male authors too have contributed to and will benefit from a lifting of generic prohibition. William Howarth speaks briefly of male "poetic autobiographers," for example, in "Some Principles of Autobiography," which, although it does not include women, bears directly on the aesthetics I am trying to name. "Poetic autobiographies" are "tentative," "inconclusive," "experimental," and "uncertain," "paradoxical," "difficult," "unpremeditated." In extreme cases, like Rousseau's, they are "paranoid." Howarth links this "negative capability" of "poetic autobiographies" to a peculiarly modern poetics of "anxiety and dislocation," noting, however, that its fundamental undecidability "operates at cross purposes with the genre" as codified. "We must," warns Howarth, "puzzle over how well these accounts record 'the truth.'"[34]

There is an implicit identification here of identity and truth with formal integrity, which upholds our Western prejudice in favor of generic purity and perhaps even a transcendental metaphysics of genre, even as it leaves women out of the picture. If we gender this description and remove from it the trace of aesthetic judgment founded on male valuations of autobiography as genre, we might approach an understanding of women's poetic corpuses as autobiography in the sense we have been exploring, an understanding that will not seek to define them formally, to impose order and give shape, but rather see reflected in the particularity of each corpus the lineaments of some particular woman's life experience as dialectically constructed both by cultural imposition and by her own countering agency. The simultaneous experience of historical alienation and of the consoling possibility of present, albeit intermittent, self-presence is one that women share with other minority groups. As Gordon Taylor describes the function of autobiography for the black writer, "Autobiographical scrutiny of a self poised between

1960), no. 288, p. 133, hereafter cited by poem number in the text. See Domna Stanton, "Autogynography: Is the Subject Different?" in *The Female Autograph* (New York: New York Literary Forum, 1984), p. 13, for a deconstruction of the simple binary opposition between male autobiographical narrative ("linear, chronological, coherent") and female ("discontinuous, digressive, fragmented"). See also Germaine Brée, "Autogynographies," *Southern Review* 22 (Spring 1986): 244.

34. Howarth, p. 110.

actuality and extinction rescues it from the incompletion which is part of its experience."[35] I would argue, following Taylor's lead here, that the indeterminacy of some poetic autobiographies written by women is a deliberate strategy; the discontinuity enforced by nonlinearity, the accretion of subjective moments in the form of a series of poems, the emphatically vocal signaled by the presence of the first-person lyric speaker are the signs of more than aesthetic rebellion. Poetry as autobiography constitutes a potential space in which a subject may be repeatedly and repeat*ably* present to herself during the act of utterance, in a genre that, Audre Lorde reminds us, is economical; having been the refuge of women and the poor in this century, she argues, poetry has been an underprivileged genre itself.[36]

The poetic corpuses of Emily Dickinson and Adrienne Rich are the inevitable examples of such self/life/writing, and reconsideration of each tantalizingly blurs the generic border between poetry and autobiography. Poetry, especially that recording a life serially, yet discontinuously, if we are to believe Emily Dickinson, is *piecework,* the radical travail of a "Spider sewing at night" (no. 1138); it is also, to borrow a second instructive metaphor from Dickinson, "as full as opera" (no. 326), ventriloquistic experiments in self-articulation—as she would have it, the lyric vocalizings of a "supposed person."[37] First-person poetry, then, in its supposition of personhood has provided women writers of lyric with infinitely more immediate access to subjectivity than the novel or other literary genres allows.[38] At the very least, a linguistic convention for writing the self as subject generically underwrites poetic as well as autobiographical writing. Sandra Gilbert and Susan Gubar have documented at length how Dickinson, like Christina Rossetti and Elizabeth Barrett Browning, experimented with identity in her extended, wonderfully self-contradictory corpus. She was her own "multiple heroine," each pose—

35. Gordon O. Taylor, "Voices from the Veil: Black American Autobiography," *Georgia Review* 35 (Summer 1981): 342, quoted by Friedman, "Theories of Autobiography and Fictions of the Self in H.D.'s Canon," ms. p. 11.

36. Audre Lorde, "Poetry Is Not a Luxury," in *Sister Outsider: Essays and Speeches* (Trumansburg, N.Y.: Crossing Press, 1984), p. 36. The second quotation is from "Age, Race, Class and Sex: Women Redefining Difference," p. 116.

37. Emily Dickinson, letter to T. W. Higginson, July 1862, in *The Letters of Emily Dickinson,* ed. Thomas Johnson, 2:412; quoted in Sandra M. Gilbert and Susan Gubar, *The Madwoman in the Attic: The Woman Writer and the Nineteenth-Century Literary Imagination* (New Haven: Yale University Press, 1979), p. 548.

38. See Gilbert and Gubar's comparison of novel writing and verse writing; according to them, generic history consigns nineteenth-century women writers to the novel as a more "selfless occupation," pp. 545–48. I would argue that twentieth-century women writers may in fact be drawn to poetry and autobiography, precisely as a means of saying "I" more resonantly.

child, bride, gnome, poet, queen, empress, white elect—"representing alternative possibilities of selfhood."[39] But the process of coming to subjectivity for Dickinson is more complex, in my view, than the accretion of positive identities or roles. Dickinson inscribes female selfhood dialectically, both by imagining herself into a full range of subjective positions in what amount to poetic power fantasies—the memorable "Loaded Gun" and "Empress of Calvary" are notable examples—and also by documenting the historicity of female exile in the poems that invoke (often for ironic purposes) female lack of presence. If the host of poems in which she figures herself as "mouse," "daisy," "little girl" (nos. 61, 70, 106) are paired with the those in which she exalts the "woman—white" (no. 271), evanescence appears to interest her as much as immortality, and the very business of oscillation, favoring process, prevents stasis at either pole.[40]

Sharon Cameron, using Dickinson to exemplify certain lyric processes in general, misreads the reciprocal strategies I have sketched, even as she correctly identifies the correspondent movement of thought: "Dialectical knowledge in which experience is put in touch with its antithesis involves the mind's ability to construct, through memory, a connection between that which is not present at a given moment in time and that which is." But in her reading of individual poems Cameron often names Dickinson's doubling as "failure" "revelatory of narrative breakdown, not of controlled narrative transformation:" "The speaker is not in possession of her story, or rather she is in possession of two stories, the bringing together of which points to a fundamental ambivalence and an attendant obfuscation of meaning. As a consequence of the ambivalence, meaning becomes symptomatic, breaks out into gesture where it cannot be fully comprehended and where it often expresses feelings that seem antithetical to the earlier intention of the speaker or author."[41] Dickinson is in possession of her two stories, although Cameron is not prepared to read them as one. "Half Child—Half Heroine," wearing "A Bonnet like a Duke— / And yet a Wren's Peruke," Dickinson refuses to

---

39. Gilbert and Gubar, p. 564.

40. For a deconstructionist reading of Dickinson's doubling, see Margaret Homans, *Women Writers and Poetic Identity: Dorothy Wordsworth, Emily Brontë, and Emily Dickinson* (Princeton: Princeton University Press, 1980), chap. 4. See also, for a discussion of Dickinson and identity, Paula Bennett, *My Life a Loaded Gun: Female Creativity and Feminist Poetics* (Boston: Beacon, 1983); and *Feminist Critics Read Emily Dickinson*, ed. Suzanne Juhasz (Bloomingon: Indiana University Press, 1983), esp. essays by Sandra M. Gilbert, Barbara Mossberg, Margaret Homans, and Christanne Miller.

41. Sharon Cameron, *Lyric Time: Dickinson and the Limits of Genre* (Baltimore: Johns Hopkins University Press, 1979), pp. 60–61.

get her singular story straight, encoding in poem after poem the contradictory valences of her own experience (no. 283).

The poetic-autobiographical oeuvre of Adrienne Rich—because her corpus defies any less complicated generic definition—alternately entertains like that of Dickinson, the imagining and the deflating of an essential selfhood as a strategy for achieving a subjectivity that remains alert to woman's absence from history. Speaking in "Writing as Re-Vision" of her own "fragments and scraps" stolen at naptimes (*Lies*, p. 44), Rich tells how she learned her political strategy from Dickinson—"your hoard of dazzling scraps a battlefield." From this predecessor Rich absorbed how *not* to perjure herself by using the "spoiled language" and ideologically burdened genres of the oppressor.[42] Rich's and Dickinson's most important shared stance is the refusal of a totalized, unitary selfhood, although they do not flaunt, as might Roland Barthes, the impossibility of subjectivity; that assertion remains too dangerously annihilating to the as-yet-inadequately-reconstructed female subject. Rich's "In the Woods," for example, exults in the momentary integration of soul with body, in a powerful move reminiscent of Dickinson's exuberant exercise of her own subjective and occasionally unified voice: "my soul wheeled back / and burst into my body. / Found! Ready, or not" (p. 58). "Snapshots" itself had ended with a similar vision of the integrated helicopter soul, "poised, still coming, / her fine blades making the air wince" (p. 38). A still later poem, "The Phenomenology of Anger," describes the transformative power of mobilized subjectivity experienced as physical power: "white acetylene / ripples from my body / effortlessly released / perfectly trained / on the true enemy" (pp. 166–67). Might not these images in their hyper-self-assertion, like that of Dickinson's "Soul *at the White Heat*" (no. 365), be "the scream / of an illegitimate voice," that of the historically illegitimate female subject? ("Cartographies of Silence," p. 234).

With *Snapshots*, not coincidentally, Rich had begun, as David Kalstone notes, "dating each of her poems by year," as "a way of limiting their claims, of signaling that they spoke only for their moment. The poems were seen as instruments of passage, of self-scrutiny and resolve in the present."[43] More than one reader has noted that Rich's poems become less shapely, more journallike and autobiographical after *Neces-*

---

42. Adrienne Rich, *The Fact of a Doorframe: Poems Selected and New, 1950–1984* (1984; rpt., New York: Norton, 1975), p. 70, hereafter cited in the text.

43. David Kalstone, *Five Temperaments* (New York: Oxford, 1977), p. 148. I am indebted to Kalstone's discussion of Rich's self-making and unmaking, and his analysis of her interest in the photographic metaphor in chap. 4. However, Kalstone reads Rich's autobiographical impulse differently from me, placing hers alongside James Merrill's and Robert Lowell's, pp. 131–32.

sities of Life,[44] and she herself speaks of her early poetic formalism as a "strategy—like asbestos gloves, it allowed me to handle materials I couldn't pick up bare-handed" (*Lies,* p. 40). In *Leaflets* (1969) and *The Will to Change* (1971), for example, she includes dated entries, such as "The Blue Ghazals," "Pieces," and "The Photograph of the Unmade Bed," with no illusions about the eternity of artifice. Rich is as attracted by the tentative, inessential quality of serial, poetic snapshots as a means of portraying the self, as she is dismayed by the dangerous distance imposed by the decontextualized photograph. Accordingly, she both evokes the "camera-flash" of a woman anthropologists's "quiet/ eye" ("The Observer," p. 98) or envisions the poet "at the movies / dreaming the film-maker's dream" in "Images for Godard," *and* plays the metaphor oppositely in "Pierrot Le Fou": "Suppose you stood facing / a wall / of photographs / from your unlived life" and "Yourself against a wall / curiously stuccoed / Yourself in unfamiliar clothes / with the same eyes. / On a screen as wide as this, I grope for the titles" (p. 123). In poems of this period, selfhood itself is called into question as a stable entity of any kind—the group of poems based on leaflets, pieces, takes, snapshots reflects Rich's conviction that the self can only be perceived fragmentarily; in poems beginning with *The Dream of a Common Language,* however, Rich pushes beyond her foremother Dickinson to envision a new kind of subjectivity which she recovers in poetic dialogue with "Heroines" and "Grandmothers," with climber Elvira Shatayev and Julie in Nebraska, with the lover to whom the "Twenty-One Love Poems" were addressed, and with a utopian separatist community of women she pictured as speaking her "common language."

But in the large, elaborated middle section of Rich's poetic autobiography, as in the long, self-contradictory corpus of Dickinson's, subjectivity is grasped as an alternation between fantasies of self-presence and the personal *and* the more broadly cultural fact of women's historical absence. Dickinson's and Rich's piecework, then, differs from Barthes's "patchwork"[45] because they defiantly reclaim their displacement in order to have both sides of it. Dickinson, for example, manages to convey both self-division and sturdy identity in verbal formulations like "Ourself behind ourself" or "Itself—it's Sovreign—of itself." Dickinson and Rich, in what I view as a crucial political gesture for the female self-in-process, prefer to reclaim both halves of our difficult

44. William Logan, reviewing Rich's *Your Native Land, Your Life,* for the *New York Times Book Review,* 18 Jan. 1987, p. 13, chastises her for "descent into a verse diary full of contradiction."

45. Roland Barthes, *Roland Barthes by Roland Barthes,* trans. Richard Howard (New York: Hill and Wang, 1977), p. 142.

"Double Estate," where Roland Barthes can luxuriantly disperse what has been all too capitalized upon in philosophical discourse of the masculine unified subject.

Autobiography as Poetry

Of all the critical conflations of poetry and autobiography, only one rests upon sexual difference, theorizing a continuum of generic interest along lines arising from a distinctly female psychosexual experience. In a chapter on Kathleen Raine's autobiography in her *L'Ecriture-femme*, Béatrice Didier argues that it is artificial to erect barriers between poetry and autobiography since they both refer to what she names as a characteristically feminine writing: the work of "translating the fundamental rhythms, of finding once again the mother's face." In Didier's view, both poetry and autobiography have as their goal the reachievement of symbiotic forgetfulness, plenitude, identity, not by means of the militant, bounded separation that psychoanalytic culture prescribes for us but by means of the blurring of subject/object dualism. The poetic and autobiographical acts collide as a means of access to language, maternal and primitive; both are orphic acts that might empower the female artist, according to Didier, although "it is not Eurydice who must be brought back, but the mother."[46] Kathleen Raine's autobiography, founded like poetry upon a myth of return, according to Didier, is thus a "long poem" of resuscitation in which the mother, the earthly paradise of early union with her, and the mother tongue are equally reclaimed in what amounts to an act of the deepest identity for the woman poet. For men, Didier argues, the return would be to an Other, whereas for women it is to the Same. Sexual difference, in this instance, has important bearings upon the construction of female identity, particularly in the continuity with the maternal, which manifests itself at the level of identity as well as textuality; that is, the "homosexual-maternal facet," as Kristeva terms it, specific (it seems in this case) to female experience, is suprageneric, and it affects the continuity of women's writing in textual even more than thematic ways.[47] In Audre Lorde's autobiography, as Claudine Raynaud demonstrates in this volume (adapting Didier's notion of poetic autobiography as a writing of maternal/self re-

46. Béatrice Didier, *L'Ecriture-femme* (Paris: Presses Universitaires de France, 1981), pp. 257, 264, my translation.

47. Julia Kristeva, "Motherhood According to Bellini," *Desire in Language: A Semiotic Approach to Literature and Art* (New York: Columbia University Press, 1980), p. 239.

cuperation), the mother's "secret poetry" is the intertext, manifesting itself at the level of linguistic signs as well as actual words, typographical interruption of the page, visual as well as auditory rhythms.[48] The effect of its dialogical presence in the daughter's autobiography is the diminishment of exile, ultimately of both textual and psychological consequence for the female subject.

But a second theory of autobiography-as-poetry might be advanced on the heels of the foregoing, a theory having its roots in a more complex and increasingly, as I have arranged my texts, ambivalent maternal recuperation. If contemporary women's autobiography shares with poetry a preoccupation with the constitution of subjectivity, then the dependence of poetry upon voice or enunciation—that mark of female subjectivity present to itself in the act of first-person lyric utterance—might also lie beneath modern and contemporary autobiographical acts. *Vocation* thus resonates doubly in, for example, the work of Colette, among other modern autobiographers, in whose acknowledgment of wholly unambivalent umbilical indebtedness—"I learn it from you, to whom I turn without ceasing"[49]—we retrieve an alternate "daughteronomy."[50] The models for female coming-to-voice which Colette's *Break of Day*, Zora Neale Hurston's *Dust Tracks*, Maxine Hong Kingston's *Woman Warrior*, and Claribel Alegría's *Luisa in Realityland* propose depart substantially from that which Sandra Gilbert finds in the culturally constructed "female myth of origin" or from that which Jacques Lacan envisions for the postmodern split subject, initiated into language at the price of exile, or even from that which Harold Bloom diagnoses in the psycholiterary struggles of the sons of patriarchy—as Adrienne Rich would later say in a not-so-different context: "A whole new poetry beginning here" ("Transcendental Etude," p. 268).

Colette's fictional-autobiographical *Break of Day* begins and ends with the "embryo word," the benedictory voice of her mother, folded into Colette's own text in the form of inset letters. The book is prefaced by a letter reproduced in its entirety, but her mother's final, nonnarrative letter, a "pencilled sheet" of images and isolated words, is worked into

48. Didier would call this return to the mother a recovery of plenitude, whereas Bella Brodzki and Françoise Lionnet, this volume, question the idealization of the maternal.

49. Colette, *Break of Day*, trans. Enid McLeod (New York: Ballantine, 1961), pp. 116–17. I am indebted to my student Beth McGroarty for drawing my attention to this passage. All citations are from these pages.

50. Sandra Gilbert, "Life's Empty Pack: Notes toward a Literary Daughteronomy," *Critical Inquiry* 11 (March 1985): 355–84. The following reference is also to this article, in which Gilbert describes a "female myth of origin narrated by a severe literary mother who uses the vehicle of a half-allegorical family romance to urge acquiescence in the Law of the Father" (p. 359).

Colette's own narrative and presented to us by indirect discourse. The maternal legacy in this closing instance of Colette's book marks a retreat from phallocentrically ordered language. Instead, it is a gift of "joyful signs": the animated "yes, yes" and "she danced" the sole inscriptions on a page of lively pencil marks, a virtual maternal caress in the vocative "my treasure," which term of endearment her mother would use "when our separations had lasted a long time and she was longing to see me again." Colette recognizes in this text, she tells us, not the "confused delirium" of a dying "head half vanquished" but a familiar, readable verbal landscape, "messages from a hand that was trying to transmit to me a new alphabet." One is thus tempted to read in this maternal postscript not postverbal ramblings of a mind unhinged—Colette herself resists the "image I don't want to see" of the dying mother—but preverbal encoding of a joy only this daughter can decipher. Like a palimpsest, the mother's language, coded as parts of a loved body, must be read: "I see in that letter one of those haunted landscapes where, to puzzle you, a face lies hidden among the leaves, an arm in the fork of a tree, a body under a cluster of rock." Colette even describes this language by its rhythms—it "has a place among strokes, swallow-like interweavings, plant-like convolutions."

In short, the mother tongue is all that subverts logical narrative: associated with metaphor, with signs, with primitive rhythms, it counterposes the poetic against the narrative, the fictional, the autobiographical. Salutarily for Colette in this instance, it asserts the imperative of the prior. In an essay on Samuel Beckett, Julia Kristeva makes a generic distinction between poetry and narrative by suggesting that had Beckett had access to the transgressively *jouissant* semiotic rhythm of the occluded mother, he would have written poetry rather than the narrative of the paternal symbolic.[51] Colette's text, as it merges with her mother's, abandons narrative syntax for poetic. Her text and her mother's become indistinguishable in her closing repetition of the maternal rhythm, in what Didier might call a reconstitutive effort to diminish exile: the passage actually comes to rest upon the word *oasis.* Her own "open and unending book," to the extent that it "ends" at all, does so in the poetry of a fragmenting text that eschews narrative syntax, closure, the classical structure of *peroratio:* "The ambiguous friend who leapt through the window is still wandering about. He did not put off his shape as he touched the ground. He has not had time enough to perfect himself. But I only have to help him and lo! he will turn into a quickset hedge, spindrift, meteors, an open and unending book, a cluster of

51. Julia Kristeva, "The Father, Love, and Banishment," in *Desire in Language*, p. 157.

grapes, a ship, an oasis" (p. 117). Striking in Colette's autobiographical close are the writing daughter's empowered control over the masculine (the "ambiguous friend" is transfigured by means of language alone into the culminating "oasis"; he who cannot "perfect himself" is perfected instead by the beholder, the poet-in-process who makes the text), her transformative access *to* and not banishment *from* the language that can accomplish this, her exultant exercise of mother-begotten voice as narrative breaks down or through into a series of generative poetic metaphors.

Another maternal deathbed scene inscribed in an autobiographical text demands equally to be read as a Scene of Writing or, more accurately, an explicit Scene of Female Coming-to-Voice, punctuated by what I'd like to call the maternal-poetic intertext. In the chapter of Hurston's *Dust Tracks* titled "Wandering," the nine-year-old Zora Neale is called upon by her mother's early death to "set my will against my father, the village dames and village custom."[52] At nine, she has been assigned the task of carrying out her mother's wishes, of making sure that certain rituals are not performed until her mother is dead. In short, as the narrator tells us, "she depended upon me for a voice" (p. 88). The poignancy of this remembered scene is that "no nine-year-old's voice was going to thwart them" (p. 89); to her unending guilt, "they" precipitously carry out the offending ceremonies. But the grieving daughter finds another voice at "the foot of mama's bed," a voice, incantatory and poetic, which enables the daughter, by telling her mother's death, to virtually reproduce the maternal voice within her own text. "She depended upon me for a voice," introducing the following passage, carries special weight: "The Master-Maker in His making had made Old Death. Made him with big, soft feet and square toes. Made him with a face that reflects the face of all things, but neither changes itself, nor is mirrored anywhere. Made the body of Death out of infinite hunger. Made a weapon for his hand to satisfy his needs. This was the morning of the day of the beginning of things" (p. 87). This is a creation story, embedded in the daughter's own self-creation story and *invented* to console at the hour of death; it is projected in a voice that might be a mother's, reassuringly pedagogical, domesticating terrors for a quaking child. In these lines, the speaker becomes, in fact, not only her mother's mother, whose passing she maternally ushers in the rhythms of this comforting anaphora, but her own mother as well, both taking on her mother's voice and locating, for the first palpable time in the auto-

---

52. Zora Neale Hurston, *Dust Tracks on a Road*, ed. Robert Hemenway (Urbana: Illinois University Press, 1984), p. 86, hereafter cited in the text.

biography, her own coextensive one. Maternal loss is real as experienced—"Mama died at sundown and changed a world"—but writing in the mother's voice becomes a means of effectively deferring resolution until Zora is ready to "accept my bereavement."[53] Colette's and Hurston's texts suggest that it is not loss or exile, as Lacanians would have it, that predicates writing; it is continuity with the presence of the *re-created* maternal voice that makes writing at all possible for these daughters who would write.

Perhaps no other contemporary autobiography is more obsessed with the ideas of voice, vocation, and the vocative—once again defined for the writing daughter in relation to the mother—than Maxine Hong Kingston's *Woman Warrior*. But unlike Colette and Hurston, Kingston views the mother's language, not to mention the entire concept of cultural origins, with deep ambivalence, and the chiasmus of poetry and autobiography thus works to very different ends in this fictionalized memoir. Colette's text concludes with a return to the unambivalently loved maternal rhythm, as it manifests itself in language. Despite Colette's "scruple in claiming for myself so burning a word" [as the mother's], speaking in the mother's voice is a way of making alienation and displacement work for her. In Kingston's text, however, there is more than room in the final duet for two distinct voices: the daughter's must continue but also correct the mother's own.

Kingston's memoir is the story of a Chinese-American woman raised in Stockton under the inexorable rule of a mother fighting to stay alive as a displaced person in an alien and discriminatory culture. It is also the daughter's story of her own calling, her own election to writing, achieved by coming to terms with the psychic burdens and riches she receives from her mother, most notably the richly colored, mythic intensity of her mother's own oral narrative mode: "talk-story." The text begins with a clear assertion of maternal authority, the confiding of a secret, the injunction not to tell: "You must not tell anyone."[54] The mother's first role is thus that of silence enforcer, the child's voice stopper. But as Leslie Rabine has brilliantly demonstrated, in a text that takes as its project the disruption of all oppositions, categories, logics, codes, even the mother's first prohibition against speaking contains a counterauthorization: the mother, emblematically it turns out for the daughter, breaks silence productively even as she does so to transmit the patriarchal legacy

---

53. "Daughters-in-Texts: Maternal Elegies in Women's Poetry," a chapter in my own *Corinna Sings*, is a demonstration of how women poets maintain a dialogue in a kind of continuous present with the lost loved one.

54. Maxine Hong Kingston, *The Woman Warrior: Memoirs of a Girlhood among Ghosts* (New York: Random House, 1975), p. 3, hereafter cited in the text.

of woman's silence.[55] Kingston's first, perhaps resultant, gesture at independence is her attempt to give voice to "No Name Woman" by reinscribing the story erased from family memory, the opening story her mother forbids her to tell. But the adult narrator of this autobiography will bypass the injunction by translating, as she tells us in the last story, her mother's song into a new key, by tuning "talk-story" to the barbarian reed pipe intelligible to Kingston's own American audience. Whereas the text begins with a speaking mother and a silent/silenced daughter, the act of writing the memoir enfranchises the daughter, initiating her into the subtleties of her mother's poetic "talk-story" but, more important, enabling her to talk her own story differently and otherwise.

"The Song for a Barbarian Reed Pipe" which concludes the book, is in the fullest sense a collaboration between mother and daughter, a parable in itself of female artistry and achievement of voice that begins and ends in productive, neither annihilating nor symbiotic continuity with the maternal rhythm: "Here is a story my mother told me, not when I was young, but recently, when I told her I also talk-story. The beginning is hers, the ending, mine" (p. 240). But the "resolve" of this ending differs from the unison celebrated in Colette's and Hurston's texts, in which either the daughter or the mother *depends* upon the other for a voice; instead, the duet performed by mother and daughter at the end of Kingston's text retains all the tension implicit in their differences and all the daughter's ambivalence at the contradictions of the maternal legacy—strikingly rich poiesis paired with voicelessness in the public arena, the potential for expansive, even operatic sound silenced by the Chinese woman's historically enclosed femininity, the possibilities for oral elaboration as against written language. The last section of the book vividly evokes, by means of the dramatic, self-directed attack on the girl who refuses to speak, the life-threatening dangers of not speaking. Silence, ultimately odious to Kingston, has been experienced as dangerous, imprisoning, both personally and culturally; it is the imperative to speak which finally prompts a kind of reconciliation—with a difference—with the mother, both collaborative silencer and yet simultaneous bestower of voice. The evolution of the writing daughter's own voice can be traced within the memoir through a series of telling images, from the disturbing high-pitched "quack" of her childhood (p. 224) to the inarticulateness of the young bride prospect, from the empowering, full-throated ease of the opera singer (p. 224) and the girl of the freed

55. Leslie Rabine, "No Lost Paradise: Social Gender and Symbolic Gender in the Writings of Maxine Hong Kingston," *Signs* 12 (Spring 1987): 483.

tongue to the flute, singular and clear, of the close.[56] The last pages of the book signal an election to vocation which can originate only in the daughter's acceptance of the maternal linguistic legacy, but in a manner that acknowledges difference, ambivalence, the simultaneous need for closeness and recognition of separateness. This different solution to mother/daughter conflict is accomplished, once again, by means of the interpenetration of generic discourses, poetic and autobiographical.

Indeed her mother reappears in the last tale of the memoir transfigured as a poetess. Framed within her mother's story of how much her grandmother loved the theater, is Kingston's own maternal tribute: she imagines that at "some of those performances, they heard the songs of Ts'ai Yen, a poetess born in A.D. 175" (pp. 242–43). As the history of the poetess unfolds, it becomes recognizably that of Kingston's own mother: her twelve years in the land of the barbarians, her two children who did not speak Chinese. Ts'ai Yen cannot speak the language of the barbarians, nor can she understand their music—"its sharpness and cold made her ache." Yet one evening, barbarian flute players, striving for the "high note" that throughout the text has symbolized achievement of voice, reach that operatic high, that "icicle in the desert," that mix of contrasts, Chinese and barbarian, and hold it. For during the course of this narrative, Ts'ai Yen, the exiled poetess who has represented the mother, comes to represent the daughter as well. Far from overcoming exile, however, the double image captures the poignancy of exile for them both: "The tribe rode like the haunted from one oasis to the next," condemned by cultural and linguistic displacement to wander between evanescent and provisional achievements of relief and plenitude (and how differently "oasis" signifies in this text). The figure of the poetess thus comes to stand both for a potentially redeemed Brave Orchid whose children would no longer laugh at her, whose "song so high and clear" might now be understood by the barbarians, whose poetry of "sadness and anger" at last "translated well," and for the daughter-translator, in whose version of the song of the Chinese ancestors the barbarians "thought they could catch barbarian phrases about forever wandering." But if the legend of Ts'ai Yen marks sameness, it also enforces difference.[57] As the warrior ancestry of the poetess unfolds, we recall the mythic swordswoman of "White Tigers," whose masculinized demeanor allows both verbal agency and real power in the world. As

56. Loren Rusk, "Her Self in Relation to the Reader: Maxine Hong Kingston's *The Women Warrior*" (Paper given at Stanford Conference on Autobiography and Biography: Gender, Text, and Context, Stanford Center for Research on Women, 12 April 1986).

57. Rabine writes, although her argument goes in a different direction from mine, that "they can both fit the figure, but not at the same time" (p. 486).

the poetess thus comes to stand for the writing daughter, she catches up the contradictions of the narrator's split inheritance: the semiotic orality of her mother's poetic "talk-story" is only one component of Kingston's legacy. She herself, who wishes to be understood by the barbarians, must translate that learned rhythm into the prose of the cultural symbolic, a shift that requires of her an identification with the masculine as well. By means of the daughter's translation of "Eighteen Stanzas for a Barbarian Reed Pipe," Kingston aligns her mother-begotten Chinese heritage with her American vocation of writing. *Woman Warrior* closes with the song of Ts'ai Yen, that doubled "woman's voice singing," which simultaneously represents the return to the exiled mother as the source of poetry and the difference between mother and daughter which allows this female subject to find her own writing voice.

The maternal-poetic intertext in these autobiographies, in dialogic relationship to narrative autobiography, functions to blur boundaries—at the level of genre as well as psychology. In spite of the differences among the texts I have discussed, what is created within each text is a position from which the writing daughter can speak as a subject, in metonymic relationship to an other she experiences as same, in a process that thereby circumvents inscription into anything like singular autobiographical representative selfhood. The alterity many critics have noted as characteristic of women's autobiography takes on new meaning when the other is a mother, a locus of identity but also difficult sameness.[58] Candace Lang has said of Barthes's own self-deconstructing autobiographical text that writing "must be understood as a process of collaboration between an individual consciousness and that Other which permeates it."[59] The question to ask at the end of our reading here is whether that formulation requires gendering. In the texts of ColetteSido, ZoraMama, and more problematically, the mother/daughter poetess Ts'ai Yen, a complex politics/poetics of Same might very well replace the masculine economy of Otherness. Experiencing the excessively bounded *autos* of traditional autobiography as a more fluid, actively negotiable subjectivity, writing daughters may speak from an autobiographical place we have not yet learned to name.

Claribel Alegría's *Luisa in Realityland,* a self-proclaimed "autobiographical prose/verse novel," serves as my concluding text not only

58. Mary G. Mason and Doris Sommer, this volume; see also Susan Stanford Friedman, "Women's Autobiographical Selves: Theory and Practice," in *The Private Self: Theory and Practice in Women's Autobiographical Writings*, ed. Shari Benstock (Chapel Hill: University of North Carolina Press, 1989). Friedman is concerned with how "women as a group can develop an alternative way of seeing themselves by constructing a group identity based on their historical experience."

59. Lang, p. 16.

because it politicizes the generic modulations and admixtures I note throughout in women's writing, but also because it provocatively reverses the order of genres that often seems to structure women's poetic autobiographies.[60] Alegría's text works fragments of story, autobiographical narrative, poems of various densities and genres, and historical sketch into a mosaic of brilliant colors. Whereas at the outset this book appears to invert the categories of poetry and prose within autobiography that I have sketched, assigning childhood myth and memory, imagery of home and diminished exile to the prose passages, and "childhood lost" in the increasingly intrusive flashes of Central American political conflict to the stark poetic sequences, it remains as preoccupied, although differently, with issues of voice, and vocation as the autobiographies of Colette, Hurston, and Kingston. In this book, however, poetry is not the mode that leads back to the mother as the source of language but rather the genre in which the contemporary poet bears witness to the facts, the politics, and the terrible costs of present exile. Early in *Luisa,* the prose fragments celebrate the safety of the child's world, while the interleaved poems baldly, unemotionally, and often impotently describe current events: political torture and war. As the text unfolds, however, a generic chiasmus occurs. Salvadoran conflict increasingly occupies the prose sections, diminishing the hold of childhood security upon Luisa's/Claribel's adult experience, and the poems take on first apocalyptic, then transcendental dimension, becoming the genre in which Alegría rises to poetic vocation. The prose passages also shrink to paragraphs, while the poems swell in length, dominating the book generically. The concluding poem bears a title uncannily close to Adrienne Rich's "Cartographies of Silence." Called "The Cartography of Memory," it is, like Rich's, written in psychic (and in Alegría's case also geopolitical) exile; it locates, like Rich's, the source of political vision and "common language" in material conditions.[61] Like Colette's, Hurston's, and Kingston's, Alegría's book ends with an imagined return to the mother country even though "my parents won't be there," even though she has never seen her "mother's tomb"—"my childhood / next to her / my first seedbed / of memories" (p. 151)—but not to the beatitude and idyllic regression Didier finds characteristic of this maternal recuperation. Instead, the book ends with the word *future,* a word that stakes out a new domain for poetry as a kind of politics, redefining the genre's role altogether as it works against prose within a particular woman writer's autobiography. In *Luisa,* the genre that ultimately re-

60. Claribel Alegría, *Luisa in Realityland,* trans. Darwin Flakoll (Willimantic, Conn.: Curbstone Press, 1987), inside cover, hereafter cited in the text.
61. Rich, *The Fact of a Doorframe,* pp. 232–36.

quires the poet's acceptance of "realityland"—the politics of real mothers' absence in Salvador—demands also that she bear witness to the impotence of mothering under these specific contemporary conditions: "it is easy to distract yourself / with a mother's role / and shrink the world / to a household" (p. 139). The plenitude of Alegría's close, predicated on the politicized rather than psychoanalytic absence of the mother, is owed to a poetry that locates agency, subjectivity, voice, and a future in political vocation.

Conclusion

The reading of women's poetry and autobiographies I attempt above rests above all upon what I would call the supplemental nature of all women's *writing:* its work of giving priority and presence to an all-too-historically absent *life,* a process that has been seen to lie beneath both autobiographical and poetic utterances. It is precisely in their parallel reliance upon voice, that vital evidence of the female subject at the heart of her own discourse, that women's autobiography and poetry are profitably seen as coextensive, recuperative, not necessarily unified discourses of female subjectivity, rather than as ideal, pure, coherent, and discrete formal constructs. We do not need to read Derrida to know that the disruptive underside of *la loi du genre*—"Genres are not to be mixed"[62]—is declined in the feminine. We have only to read women's texts of self-inscription as continuous, as life/lines even to our own recoverable subjectivity: that is, to read them both as records of historical marginality and, increasingly, as vocative evidence of potential self-presence. To read women's autobiography and poetry as *of a piece* is thus both to approach a female poetics that transcends genre and to call into question the gender specificity of any genre system that pretends to rest completely upon aesthetic criteria.

62. Derrida, p. 203.

15

Elisabeth to Meta: Epistolary Autobiography and the Postulation of the Self

KATHERINE R. GOODMAN

Doubts that are currently circulating concerning the authenticity of the subject were actually articulated quite clearly nearly two centuries ago. Indeed, the task of reimagining the self can be be aided considerably by examining texts written in Germany around 1800, however unlikely this assertion might at first appear. In Germany at least that period was a kind of golden age of autobiography, representing the consolidation of a strong sense of self, of individuality, indeed of bourgeois culture in general. It is precisely the period that Barthes and Foucault would cite as falsely hypostasizing individual "identity." This age culminated, so most scholars assert, in Goethe's *Dichtung und Wahrheit*— that work which most perfectly embodies the ideal of a harmonious and naturally unfolding individual.

And yet it was precisely in Goethe's shadow that epistolary autobiography emerged. In the eighteenth century readers took epistolary novels as truth, or at least they pretended to. Most of these novels told the story of a woman's life; and around 1800 a few German women took this tradition seriously enough to write their own "real" life stories in the epistolary form, eschewing what was rapidly becoming standard autobiographical narration. Selecting from a variety of such texts, I would like to focus here on Elisabeth von Stägemann's autobiography, *Erinnerungen für edle Frauen* ("Reminiscences for noble women").

Elisabeth von Stägemann (1761–1835) was at the center of one of the

This article contains material reworked from the introduction and second chapter of my book *Dis/Closures: Women's Autobiography in Germany, 1790–1914* (Bern: Peter Lang, 1986). Research for that project was supported in part by a fellowship from the Alexander-von-Humboldt Stiftung. I would like to thank Susan Lanser for her comments on an early version of this article.

famous intellectual salons in Berlin at the turn of the eighteenth and nineteenth centuries. Although her reminiscences were completed in 1804, they were not published until 1846, eleven years after Stägemann's death.[1] (As a point of reference it might be noted that Goethe began his autobiography, *Dichtung und Wahrheit*, in 1809.) Stägemann had contemplated publishing her autobiography in 1810 and for that purpose had written a false introduction in the manner of many epistolary novels of the time. In this introduction a fictional editor claims to have received the correspondence from a dear friend (Stägemann) on her deathbed. The letters narrate a major portion of the life of one of the correspondents, but the unified, teleological perspective of most autobiographers is shattered by the piecemeal narration of the epistolary form. But there is more. The friend (Stägemann) had also written an introduction, in which she freely admits that the letters are not authentic in the sense of actually having been sent between two real persons. Rather they are letters she, the author, had written in a period of semiisolation to clarify for herself the direction of her life. It was good pietist form to carry on dialogues in the soul to resolve inner dilemmas or doubts, and Stägemann's autobiography is a secular version of that pietist practice. For our purposes, this narrative technique is nothing less than a manifestation of the fragmented and sometimes contradictory nature of the author's "self".

Before examining this unique document in more detail I must make a theoretical digression. Contemporary literary theories deny authorshhip in a traditional sense. When Roland Barthes asks of a Balzac text, "Who is speaking thus?" he determines—as Nietzsche had for God—that the author is dead.[2] He further postulates that authorial interiority is "pure superstition" (pp. 142, 144). In the "humanist" tradition "the *explanation* of a work is always sought in the man or woman who produced it, as if it were always in the end, through the more or less transparent allegory of the fiction, the voice of a single person, the *author* 'confiding' in us" (p. 143). Indeed, he ventures to assert that "linguistically, the author is never more than the instance writing, just as *I* is nothing other than the instance saying *I*: language knows a 'subject', not a 'person', and this subject, empty outside of the very enunciation which defines it, suffices to make language 'hold together', suffices, that is to say, to exhaust it" (p. 145). Just what the "instance" represents remains something of a

---

1. Elisabeth von Stägemann, *Erinnerungen für edle Frauen: Nebst Lebensnachrichten über die Verfasserin und einem Anhange von Briefen* (Leipzig: Hinrichs, 1846). All quotations are from this edition, and unless otherwise noted, all translations in this essay are my own.

2. Roland Barthes, "The Death of the Author," in *Image-Music-Text,* ed. Stephen Heath (New York: Hill and Wang, 1977), pp. 142–48, hereafter cited in the text.

mystery, but Barthes further asserts: "Did [an author] wish to *express himself*, he ought at least to know that the inner 'thing' he thinks to 'translate' is itself only a ready-formed dictionary, its words only explainable through other words, and so on indefinitely." (p. 146).

If Barthes pronounced the author dead, Foucault sought to bury "him."[3] He notes that despite Barthes's pronouncement, the mystique surrounding the concepts of a "work" or of "writing" (*écriture*) continually resuscitate the notion of author. For Foucault, writing is an "interplay of signs, regulated less by the content it signifies than by the very nature of the signifier. . . . the writing subject endlessly disappears" (p. 116). Implicitly the meaning and value society has attached to a text depend on the identification of the author, especially, of course, for autobiography. Foucault claims to undermine this identification. He distinguishes author from writer from first-person narrator. For autobiography, such a theory implies the absence of any connection between the autobiographer and the life described. A writer—and on this point Foucault explicitly includes not only texts of recognized literary value but also functional texts, such as reports of scientific experiments—creates "a second self." An autobiographer becomes a linguistic construct severed from authentic experience. In the end Foucault answers the question of who is speaking with a question originally posed by Samuel Beckett: "What matter who's speaking?" (p. 138).

It is difficult to imagine a concept of writing and expression more antithetical to traditional definitions of autobiography or to recent feminist concerns with women's experience. Barthes's and Foucault's analyses dissolve the very interiority of the autobiographical subject into a pose or, at best, a role and nothing more. An author/autobiographer neither exists nor possesses a history outside the presence of the text. Every text necessarily participates in the prevailing discourse, the origins of which remain unidentified and unlocalized.

Feminists, however, know that it makes a great deal of difference who is speaking. The discourse of authority, of patriarchy, of morality can be spoken very differently from various vantage points. The discourse may be the same, but it affects people differently, and people affected differently are likely to think, act, and feel differently. Prisoners in a detention center, under the gaze of someone in a panopticon, "know" that system in a way a guard could not. Similarly women have known things about themselves (from experience) which men have never known when they articulated a discourse on the family or women.

---

3. Michel Foucault, "What Is an Author?" in *Language, Counter-Memory, Practice: Selected Essays and Interviews,* ed. Donald F. Bouchard (Ithaca: Cornell University Press, 1977), pp. 116–38, hereafter cited in the text.

But such a statement already carries a conviction of the concreteness of women's (and men's) existence and of some subjectivity in experience. It also carries the implication that it is possible to express at least something of originary experience.

The explanatory force of these theories fails in the face of difference and particularity of experience. They cannot explain why a woman would feel imprisoned by marriage (and express it) when society tells her it is her destiny. They cannot explain the unorthodox desire of a woman to paint or go to sea rather than care for a family. They may account, to some extent, for the form in which that sentiment or this desire is expressed but not for the sentiment or desire itself. They cannot account for originality and innovation. Whence arise new combinations of old discourses?

In the end Foucault's "subversive" critical thought yields a brand of positivism, collecting artifacts of civilization and arranging them in chronological order. It is a rational arrangement. It studies discursive manifestations of power relationships and claims that is all there is. There is no allowance for individuals and their passions. Feminists (and others) should ask just whose power *this* discourse of power relationships subverts.

To question the radical deconstruction of the subject, however, is not to ignore the valuable critique of traditional conceptions of the "self" supplied by these theories. Their authors may have been reacting to mid-twentieth-century revolutionary dogmatism centered on modern versions of a "humanistic" discourse, but feminists have also found that discourse antithetical to a recognition of women's traditional concerns, indeed, to a qualitatively different reorganization of social structures. Feminists may, therefore, share a certain portion of these critical perspectives.

To the extent that the critique of "humanism" concerns the way in which we conceptualize the self, the issues are particularly apparent in and inextricably linked to traditional conceptions of autobiography. On this score the case of Georg Misch is quite instructive. Misch's comprehensive pioneering study of autobiography in Western civilization (1904) was a bold attempt to historicize awareness of individuality, or "the evolution of the human spirit in European culture," as Misch put it.[4] "The history of autobiography," he claimed, "is in a certain sense the evolution of human consciousness" (1:11). In his idealist and teleological view of history, human consciousness resides in the works of

---

4. Georg Misch, *Geschichte der Autobiographie* (Frankfurt am Main: G. Schulte, 1969), 1:6, hereafter cited in the text.

"significant personalities" of any age, for these are the ones able to cap-
ure its truth. He traced "humanity in the art of great individuals" as it
progressed toward its completion in Goethe's *Dichtung und Wahrheit* (1:15).
Above all, he admired Goethe's comprehensive and unified view of himself, the way in which he was able to demonstrate the workings of all
historical and intellectual currents in the evolution of his personality.
The virtual identity of that historical moment with Goethe's personal
evolution represented for Misch the epitome of the genre and of history.
For those unable to demonstrate this harmony it would be impossible to
write successful autobiographies. Therefore, while *in theory* Misch's
"humanistic" approach did not exclude women's autobiographies, it
obviously did so *in practice,* and variants of this theory survive in a
healthy state today.[5]

Nevertheless, feminists will find it necessary to employ aspects of
Misch's analysis in any search for traces of female subjectivity. For
despite efforts to harmonize and universalize individual and collective
history and despite his (and Foucault's) tendency to discredit different
experience, Misch does accord central importance to the concept of
experience (*Erlebnis*) in general. And it is precisely this concept that
remains essential for understanding women's autobiography.

For his concept of experience, as for much else, Misch drew on the work
of his mentor (and father-in-law) Wilhelm Dilthey (1833–1911), the
originator of the German school of *Geistesgeschichte* (frequently translated as "history of ideas"). In reaction to the prevailing interest in positivism in the latter part of the nineteenth century it was Dilthey who sought
to understand and formulate originary experience as *Erlebnis*. On the
one hand, his philosophy represented an effort to recapture something
of the richness of German idealism (from the period around 1800), and
to that end he emphasized areas of human life ignored by the positivists:
sentiment and imagination, for instance. On the other hand, he also
aimed to ground idealism in something concrete, rather than abstractly
rational—namely, personal experience, that which (according to him)
we best know. In this difficult mediatory effort, Dilthey in turn drew
heavily on the German pietist tradition of searching the soul for authen-

5. Though some scholars have historicized Misch's categories and assigned them to the
bourgeoisie, most accept his understanding of human identity. For examples of recent scholar-
ship in this vein, see Roy Pascal, *Design and Truth in Autobiography* (London: Routledge and
Kegan Paul, 1960); Wayne Schumaker, *English Autobiography: Its Emergence, Materials and Form*
(Berkeley: University of California Press, 1954); Bernd Neumann, *Identität und Rollenzwang:
Zur Theorie der Autobiographie* (Frankfurt am Main: Athenäum, 1970); Klaus-Detlef Müller,
Autobiographie der Goethezeit (Tübingen: Niemeyer, 1976); Günter Niggl, *Geschichte der de-
utschen Autobiographie im 18. Jahrhundert: Theoretische und literarische Entfaltung* (Stuttgart: J. B.
Metzler, 1977); Georges May, *L'Autobiographie* (Paris: Presses Universitaires de France, 1979).

tic experiences of God, especially as it had been formulated in the late eighteenth century by the theologian Friedrich Schleiermacher. It may not be a coincidence that this is a tradition—and perhaps an art—that shows its secular side plainly in the autobiography of Elisabeth Stäge-mann (completed 1804).

Although by Dilthey's time pietism had lost its social resonance, it possessed such a bountiful history of interior investigation that it was a logical source from which to posit interiority and subjectivity. It was indeed a realm of human life untapped by positivists, whose concern for experience was restricted to the reactions of the senses and to that which could be measured by external observers and was therefore "scientific." For Dilthey—as for Schleiermacher, Stägemann, and others—experience included the realm in which feelings were located: imagination, emotion, and intuition. As a means to knowledge, of course, this method of inquiry was unacceptable to positivists because the subject and the object of investigation were identical. "Unscientific" it was, and so it remains for Foucault, who affirms "pure" devotion to the object and who asserts that truth and being lie in "the exteriority of accidents."[6] It is not Dilthey's conceptualizing of experience but rather his notion of a unified and harmonized truth that has proven so inimical to the inclusion of women's truths.

In the quest for a concept of the "self" which both credits individual experience and avoids harmonizing and unifying the subject, I turn to the autobiography of Elisabeth Stägemann, one of the many auto-biographies omitted from the canon. This particular work has been ignored, no doubt at least in part, because historians of autobiography have unnecessarily limited the scope of texts they choose to examine. It is an epistolary autobiography and therefore falls outside traditional distinctions made between autobiography (narrated retrospectively by one voice) and a correspondence (narrated in medias res by more than one voice). By focusing exclusively on the evolution of a self-identical narrator in autobiography, critics of the genre have overlooked experiments based on other constructions of experience. In this case the auto-biography is narrated by two voices but probably (despite the epistolary form) in large measure retrospectively. And Stägemann was not alone in her experimentation with this form. The erroneous assumption about the nature of a subject has produced a history of the genre which is ignorant of major diversions from the prescribed form and is, therefore, incorrect.

This autobiography can be called fragmentary both insofar as letters

6. Michel Foucault, "Nietzsche, Genealogy, History," in *Language, Counter-Memory, Practice*, p. 146.

are, virtually by definition, a fragmentary form (not a continuously or objectively narrated text) and insofar as the work covers a limited period of Stägemann's life: her arrival in Berlin to live with her father, his pressure for her to marry well, the misfortune of her first marriage, the death of that husband, her attempt to remain single and become an artist, and her decision finally to remarry. Her childhood and adolescence, thought of as formative years for most "traditional" autobiographers, is only alluded to in a flashback. In contrast to what we now perceive as proper autobiographical form—in which teleological perspectives emphasize the importance of childhood fragments of life—Stägemann pinpoints the critical period of her life at marriage.

The opposition of interior voices lends this narrative startling modernity. In the autobiographer's introduction she states that her imagination created the friend she had never had, the friend to whom she could communicate her innermost feelings and thoughts. The correspondent, who gives herself over totally "to the outpourings of (her) heart," is given the author's own first name, Elisabeth (p. 8). Since she expresses Stägemann's yearnings, sensitivity, and imagination, it is most likely this character that would be identified as the "true" self by most critics of autobiography; certainly it is she who represents Dilthey's concept of interior experience. But we must try to see her as only a portion of Stägemann's projection of her experience.

The other correspondent is called "the voice of reason" (p. 8). What name should that friend have, but Meta? She is the Meta-Elisabeth, a kind of prudent, yet supportive guide, and as such she represents another facet of Stägemann's own personality. The author's conflicts with her family, her husband, and society are worked out through the imagined correspondence between these two inner voices. Her autobiography, then, is narrated as a dialogue between Meta, whom Elisabeth calls her mentor and the voice of reason, and Elisabeth, whom the prefatory narrator identifies with the soundings of her heart.

Meta advises sensibly, urging Elisabeth to accept the social role accorded women, i.e., to marry and have children. And Elisabeth seeks Meta's advice and frequently follows it. Indeed, it was Meta who had long foreseen that Gerson would be the appropriate second husband for Elisabeth. Her first husband had belittled Elisabeth's artistic talents, even opposed her artistic work. When he died, Elisabeth, wishing to fulfill her individual promise, complained that a husband would not permit her to do that, but Meta suggests that Elisabeth would not be happy as a social outcast. Her voice is effective because she unquestionably cares for Elisabeth's well-being; Meta is no confrontational outsider. Yet Elisabeth and Meta agree that Meta, portrayed as happily married with several children, has lost something valuable by giving up painting to care for her family. Her domestic bliss is not the perfect answer for either of them, and Elisabeth apears as Meta's more profound understanding and imagination. Elisabeth dreams of playing a role in a larger social entity than a family and of pursuing her own ideal.

The silences in this correspondence further reflect the nature of the relationship between soul and reason. Meta fails to write when Elisabeth is happy and not in need of a conscience. Nor does Elisabeth consult Meta while she is enjoying unclouded freedom at no one's expense in the period between her marriages. Such lapses suggest, in part at least, Meta's role as social conscience. Elisabeth also fails to write after the shattering death of her daughter, implying that her soul can brook no contact with even compassionate reassurances. Stägemann presents her soul (read imagination, creativity, passion) as dead. But Meta (read voice of reason, social conscience) writes that she cannot bear living without hearing from Elisabeth. She appears to require Elisabeth's voice, her heart, ideals, and desires, which had suffered in the experience of the daughter's death. Though Meta loves her family, she claims she cannot live solely for them; she, too, needs broader concerns and stimulation. Reason and social conscience require desire and creativity.

Elisabeth's final letter to Meta, after her marriage to Meta's cousin, acknowledges that neither has written in a while. Since the failing is mutual and neither is unhappy, we can only conclude that their need for each other has subsided. Elisabeth now fulfills society's expectations in a happy marriage, and her desires and conscience are presumably reconciled. Nor is it probably an accident that Elisabeth has married someone related to Meta, who could occupy Meta's position to some extent. Elisabeth seems to require their calm reasoning as much as Gerson and Meta require her heart and imagination. Indeed, Elisabeth goes so far as to say that she found her true independence only in an ordered life (2:103). By projecting such a harmonious ending, Stägemann reveals herself as at least partially influenced by various classicizing tendencies.

Fictional techniques of the eighteenth-century epistolary novel are plainly apparent in this autobiography, and some would find in these techniques indications of Stägemann's absorption of dominant literary modes to express her own life. Naturally, neither Stägemann nor the other German epistolary autobiographers could have been oblivious to this tradition. What remains to be explored is Stägemann's manipulation of conventions, for her "self" manifests itself not only in those conventions but also in her innovations, her creativity and imagination.

Two texts in particular yield fruitful comparisons, and it is likely that Stägemann was influenced by both of them. Goethe's *Sorrows of Young*

Werther (1774)—one of the relatively few examples of a male hero in epistolary fiction—is one of these. Stägemann's concern with painting and her critique of paintings is reminiscent of Werther's, and the considered inclusion of parallel histories suggests a structural reliance on Goethe's earlier novel. Elisabeth had married her first husband at her father's strenuous exhortation and been mortally unhappy. In the autobiography she narrates possible alternative scenarios for women, as Goethe has Werther relate life stories with some relevance to his own. Elisabeth includes the story of one woman who rebels against her father's wishes to follow the desires of her heart and is then nearly carried to her grave by remorse. Another parallel story concerns a woman whose marriage of convenience is a miserable failure but who manages to play the hypocritical social role expected of her. Through these tales, Stägemann's personal dilemma—the conflict of social reason and individual desire—is both modulated and given broader significance.

Even more striking are the parallels with Rousseau's *Nouvelle Héloise* (Gerson, Elisabeth's second husband, had given her Rousseau's complete works). General similarities are to be found in thematic elements: the sentimental appreciation of nature and corresponding distaste for urban, mercantilist life; the premise of a historical/personal idyllic past; conflict between desire and renunciation; and anguish over the immutable laws of social hierarchy (after her husband's death Elisabeth falls in love with Count Werdenberg, whose family unalterably opposes his marriage to a nonaristocrat). But more precise similarities extend to the very structure of the epistolary voices, for the relationship of Elisabeth to Meta recalls that of Julie to Claire (indeed, also recalls that of Werther to Wilhelm). In each case an emotional voice filled with desire for and insistence on personal happiness communicates with the voice of social reason. But Goethe's hero and Rousseau's heroine ostensibly correspond with other individuals, who are only implicit alter egos; in Stägemann's autobiography, by contrast, the characters are identified from the outset as two aspects of the same person. Stägemann has explicitly interiorized what Goethe and Rousseau had exteriorized. She presents her core, her personality as divided. There can be no doubt that Elisabeth does not represent Stägemann's whole self, whereas the tendency when reading *Werther,* say, is to assume the author's identification with that hero. (It is a misreading about which Goethe later complained.) Differences represented by these male authors as differences between discrete individuals are portrayed by Stägemann as occurring within the soul itself. There is no Elisabeth against the world but rather an interior Elisabeth in conflict and dialogue with her own interior Meta.

At least as important as Stägemann's full realization of a discordant self in epistolary voices is the difference in resolution of this conflict/correspondence. Rousseau's Julie dies, apparently because she cannot totally repress her desires for a personal happiness antagonistic to the wishes of the patriarchal order. The tyrannical and patriarchal society of Rousseau's novel is "punished" by the "crime" of Julie's death: "If there is some unhappy region in the world where a cruel authority may break these innocent bonds [of mutual attachment], it is punished, no doubt, by the crimes that this coercion engenders."[7] The obligation to live by society's standards ultimately kills her.

In Goethe's *Werther*, perhaps brecause the hero is male, a more active solution is found: suicide. The soul (or portion of the soul) that desires personal happiness and fulfillment in a rationalized world is doomed to suffer. Rather than wait for any exterior person or object to kill him, Werther undertakes the task himself. While one reading of the text might suggest that an individual must kill that portion of his/her soul which possesses those desires, such a reading is not the usual one. Usually Werther is taken as a discrete individual. In either case, however, there is little distinction to be made between the subtle murder of Julie and the suicide of Werther. Both are victims of the social order.

Stägemann finds a different, far less violent and drastic solution. Instead of the murder or suicide of any portion of herself, she proposes the possibility of a true harmony of interests, a reconciliation of desire and reason. She declares the possibility of integrating the self.

From this perspective Stägemann's ending would seem to be less radical than Goethe's and Rousseau's or even one that her own structuring of internal voices might lead us to expect. And to be sure she supports the existing social order, at least to some extent. She upholds the class structure by having Elisabeth relinquish her claims on the count, thereby renouncing flaming passion for gentler love and bourgeois morality for aristocratic tradition. And she upholds the sexual order by having Elisabeth abandon her desire to pursue her individual artistic ideal, her goal of fame and worldly recognition, for the exercise of art among a circle of friends.

Despite these overtones of conservatism, however, Stägemann's is not an unequivocally reactionary, recalcitrant, and closed solution. She rejects a radical, "humanistic" revolution in the same way she rejects personal subjugation and self-destruction. Class boundaries are broken, for her, by a new salonlike sociability. The count and his admirable wife become the intimate friends of Elisabeth and Gerson, sharing a relationship founded on the kinship of souls rather than social hierarchy. And

7. Jean-Jacques Rousseau, *Julie; or, The New Eloise [La Nouvelle Héloïse]*, trans. Judith H. McDowell (University Park: Pennsylvania State University Press, 1968), p. 69.

the patriarchal order is broken in similarly subtle ways. Elisabeth's second husband is not a rationalistic mercantilist like her first husband. In fact, Gerson appears somewhat feminine insofar as he can express his emotions, cry occasionally, lie down at least once because of a headache, and defer to his female guardian. Not only does Elisabeth find a more androgynous husband, but the salonlike society in which they live centers on women's art and domesticity, rather than the mercantilist world of Elisabeth's first husband. The final scene Elisabeth describes for Meta is a gathering of the four adults (the count and countess, Elisabeth and Gerson) with their children in the countess's inner sanctum. Elisabeth's drawing hangs on the wall; the countess plays the piano, and all join hands and embrace. Moonlight shines through the window. Neither the masked murder-suicide of Julie nor the overt murder-suicide of Werther is the necessary outcome of this less absolute and less integrated autobiographer's epistolary struggles with a rationalized social order.

What should be stressed as Stägemann's innovation is in fact her vision of a nonviolent restructuring of society to center on artistic values and feminine sensibilities as a solution to the antagonistic contradictions facing Elisabeth. Indeed, this is the necessary precondition for her assumption of that ultimately utopian harmony of self. In such a society she need not kill or repress a part of herself. It was in the salon culture in which Stägemann formed one nucleus, Varnhagen and von Arnim others, that these women recorded in semipublic, epistolary form their opinions and experiences.

In the interest of candor it should be mentioned that there are serious biographical distortions in this work. Stägemann's first husband did not die; she divorced him. And she did not lose the only daughter born to that marriage; two children survived it (although perhaps they are embodied, after all, in Meta's children). On the side of autobiographical intent, however, it should also be noted that Stägemann herself deciphered the disguising initials and names in her introduction and even appended authentic correspondence with the real Gerson and Count Werdenberg for the convenience of the reader who sought to compare her work with reality. Titling the work *Reminiscences* and naming the central figure after herself was not a capricious gesture, but the distortions do highlight the very tenuous distinctions to be made between fiction and autobiography, particularly at that time, but now once again.

Just this tenuousness, however, and the need to fictionalize may be relevant here and partially responsible for the choice of narrative form. It was highly unusual at the beginning of the nineteenth century to make such sensitive information public. Not that *fiction* had not dealt with problems of marital discord and even divorce, but for an autobiogra-

pher, especially a woman, to identify herself with unhappiness in domestic affairs and to name relatives upon whom she was emotionally
and financially dependent as the source of unbearable pain was virtually
unheard of—and very threatening.

It is precisely that tension between social expectations and genuine
feelings, however, which is given voice in Stägemann's particular use of
epistolary narration, indeed, which required it. Only by explicitly positing both a voice of social reason (Meta) and a voice of personal experience (Elisabeth)—imagination, emotion, and intuition—was she able to
give a fair representation of her personal history and struggle. In her
own introduction Stägemann writes, "I attempted, to the best of my
ability to merge truth and fiction in my conversation with [this imaginary friend] and found a strange satisfaction in being able to express my
feelings without speaking of myself" (p. 7). Only by attributing unacceptable feelings to a character with whom she only partially identified
was she able to express them at all. Another part of her could provide
the rational, socially acceptable responses to impermissible sentiments.
It was necessary to posit a self in conflict in order *not* to identify totally
either with an alienated, conventional self or with an uncomplicated
vision of a single repressed self. For her it was essential *not* to portray
these voices as discrete individuals. As Stägemann has shaped her work,
neither an Elisabeth nor a Meta would have been adequate alone to
portray her experience. She knew both and struggled with both; and she
constructed both to express portions of her experience.

The concept of a nonidentical self was a precondition for the epistolary forms of women's autobiography, but it is not necessary that such
works suggest eventual integration. Even the harmonious scene Stägemann projects at the end is illuminated by such an unreal moonlight that
it seems more like a utopian fantasy than actual life, more like a goal
than reality. In any case, both of Stägemann's friends are alive and
happy and may pick up the pen at any moment to continue the dialogue.
Other women who have portrayed their lives through letters have not
represented the possibility of harmony for nonidentical aspects of the
experience. The works of Bettina von Arnim and Rahel Varnhagen, for
example, remain absolutely open-ended. For them the subject is continually engaging itself and emerging through inner dialogue projected
into correspondence with real people.

As far as I am aware, epistolary autobiography is unique to women.
Heinrich von Kleist, an acquaintance of Elisabeth Stägemann's, had
considered such a work (to be called *Geschichte meiner Seele* ("History of
my soul")), but any portion of it he may have completed is lost. None
of the other examples of the genre I have found is quite like Stägemann's in

the implications of its narrative technique; none other, for instance, imagines a rational and an emotional self. Isabella von Wallenrodt narrates her life in a series of letters to a man who eventually wishes to publish them. Elisa von der Recke allegedly writes letters to her woman friend revealing her true feelings about her marriage. Bettina von Arnim does not narrate so much as demonstrate the story of her life in letters to various friends corresponding to various aspects of her soul. Rahel Varnhagen, who never published her letters herself, apparently had something similar in mind.[8] But like Stägemann, all implicitly question the universality of the traditionally intepreted Goethean notion of a self-identical and autonomous self fulfilling its telos in harmony with the external world. Such an apotheosis was an impossibility for a woman. Epistolary autobiography permitted formal expression of that fundamental lack of harmonious identity.

The demise of epistolary autobiography is intimately connected to the demise of epistolary fiction and the emerging critical importance attached to "objective" narrators, like the one who narrates Goethe's autobiography. Even before Stägemann and the others wrote their life stories in letters, the earliest German theorist of the novel, Friedrich von Blanckenburg, attempted to discredit the epistolary form. In his highly influential late eighteenth-century discussion of the novel (appearing simultaneously with *Werther* in 1774), Blanckenburg scornfully observed the pervasive and detrimental influence of contemporary popular novels. He desired to raise the genre "to a very pleasant and very edifying vehicle for passing time . . . not something for idle women, but also for the thinking mind."[9] He maintained that contemporary novels lacked an all-encompassing, objective perspective that could lend meaning to the trivial events narrated in them. Because the epistolary form was narrated by persons in the midst of an action, he argued, it could not plausibly develop such a broad and objective narrative perspective. He wanted a legitimating voice, and in the following century he got it, with the triumph of the single, authoritative autobiographical voice.

Today we would undo that nineteenth-century tradition. We seek a concept of the "self" which fully recognizes both the inevitable role of

8. Isabella von Wallenrodt, *Das Leben der Frau von Wallenrodt in Briefen an einen Freund: Ein Beitrag zur Seelenkunde und Weltkenntniss* (Leipzig: Stiller, 1797); Elisa von der Recke, *Aufzeichnungen und Briefe aus ihren Jugendtagen,* ed. Paul Rachel (Leipzig: Dietrich, 1900); Bettina von Arnim, *Clemens Brentanos Frühlingskranz, Die Günderode,* and *Goethes Briefwechsel mit einem Kinde,* in *Sämtliche Werke,* ed. Waldemar Oehlke (Berlin: Propyläen, 1920); Rahel Varnhagen, *Rahel: Ein Buch des Andenkens für ihre Freunde,* ed. Karl August Varnhagen von Ense (1834; rpt., Bern: Herbert Lange, 1972).

9. Friedrich von Blanckenburg, *Versuch über den Roman* (1774; rpt., Stuttgart: J. B. Metzler, 1965), p. vii.

social discourse in our self-imagining and the authenticity of individual interior experience. If we do not reconcile differences into a unitary concept of "identity," we will be able to perceive what Foucault calls the "unstable assemblages of faults, fissures, and heterogeneous layers" of the self[10] and still assert the authenticity of experience. We need to break open the self-identical subject in order to achieve a more complex understanding of identity and history, one that allows women and women's history a place. We need to dis-close the subject, but without discrediting experience.

10. Foucault, "Nietzsche, Genealogy, History", p. 146.

16

Taking Her Life/History: The Autobiography of Charlotte Salomon

Autobiographies as we know them look nothing like this one—but then neither do most lives as we know them. Charlotte Salomon bore in mind a childhood in a motherless family, an adolescence in Nazi Germany, a young adulthood in exile. She also harbored a presentiment that family disorder or European disaster would destroy her. At age twenty-three, Charlotte Salomon found a way to portray both her past and her presentiment. She invented an art form.

The autobiography of Charlotte Salomon stands alone, without antecedents and so far without descendants. It unfolds in 1,325 notebook-size gouache paintings of astonishing force, accompanied by textual narration and musical cues, arranged into acts and scenes, titled *Life or Theater?* and subtitled *An Operetta.* Its sequential vignettes move over a painting as through a theatrical scene. Even the autobiographical "I" becomes a fictional "she"—a principal character named Charlotte Kann interpreted by an unseen narrator called simply The Author. *Life or Theater?* deals in dialogues and soliloquies, in recitatives and arias, all written into the paintings or onto transparent sheets taped over them. The work is at once a diary and a drama; it turns events into episodes, people into personae; it tells a true story and treats it like a script. It is artwork that defines autobiography anew.

Life or Theater? took form in 1941 and 1942, when Charlotte Salomon was living as a German Jewish refugee on the French Riviera, one corner

I thank Katja Reichenfeld and Judith Belinfante of the Joods Historisch Museum in Amsterdam for the use of the Charlotte Salomon Collection and for permission to reproduce paintings; Paula Salomon-Lindberg of Amsterdam for information and kindness; the Center for Research on Women of Stanford University for the Autobiography and Biography Conference (1986), where I presented part of this essay; and finally Bella Brodzki, John Felstiner, and Joan Weimer for generous discussion of the whole.

of Europe not occupied by Nazis, one place safe enough so she could paint. The autobiography she painted there recalls Nazism encroaching on an untried life and finally wrenching it into exile. Like other personal accounts of the time, her work registers destruction, but it stands virtually alone in exposing self-destruction too—the end point of personal despair, female futility, and political trauma.

Charlotte was twenty-three and a refugee when she learned that the women in her family—her mother's sister, her mother's aunt, her mother's cousin, and her mother—had killed themselves. From 1926, when Charlotte's mother took her life, till 1939, when her mother's mother tried to take hers too, the family kept its suicides secret for fear of perpetuating them. Chances were that whatever struck her relatives would take Charlotte too, and unawares. So the recovery of a silenced past became her project, her protection.

Life or Theater? was a monumental work of retrieval. Without the paintings, the family's history would have been lost. Without the painter's foresight, the paintings would have been lost as well. After the war, her father and stepmother found what Charlotte had hidden and brought the work from France to Amsterdam, where it now resides in the Joods Historisch Museum. From the museum, exhibits of selected paintings travel throughout the world. The majority have been beautifully reproduced and informatively prefaced in *Charlotte: Life or Theater?* (1981); in addition, an English and Dutch film (1981), an Israeli and American play (1984–1985), and a German exhibition catalogue and documentary (1986–1987) have expanded Charlotte Salomon's reputation; all these enterprises make available considerable information about her.[1] But concerning Charlotte Salomon's life and her *Life or Theater?* no sustained analysis has yet appeared. My own starts with what struck me first about *Life or Theater?*— that as autobiography and as artwork there is simply nothing like it.

1. Charlotte Salomon's paintings can be seen in Charlotte Salomon, *Leben oder Theater? Ein autobiographisches Singspiel in 769 Bildern* (Cologne: Kiepenheuer & Witsch, 1981). The English translation is *Charlotte: Life or Theater? An Autobiographical Play by Charlotte Salomon*, trans. Leila Vennewitz (New York: Viking Press in association with Gary Schwartz, 1981). The page numbers in my text refer to the German edition (the English edition has the same page numbers). Translations from Charlotte Salomon's texts are my own. An earlier selection of eighty reproductions was published as Charlotte Salomon, *Ein Tagebuch in Bildern, 1917–1943* (Hamburg: Rowohlt, 1963), and in English as *Charlotte: A Diary in Pictures*, trans. Ralph Manheim (New York: Harcourt, 1963). Information about Charlotte Salomon has been published in the prefaces to *Charlotte: Life or Theater?* by Judith Herzberg, Judith Belinfante, and Gary Schwartz; in the introduction to *Charlotte: A Diary in Pictures* by Emil Straus; in the film *Charlotte* by Judith Herzberg and Frans Weisz (1981); and in the exhibition catalogue compiled by Christine Fischer-Defroy, published as *Charlotte Salomon—Leben oder Theater?* (Berlin: Das Arsenal, 1986).

Charlotte Salomon's style might have conformed to convention had she not learned her craft under Nazi aesthetic strictures, had she not been the only "full Jew" (to use the label Nazis gave her) in the famous Berlin Fine Arts Academy, had she not lost her right to study art though her work excelled, had she not been sent away for safety from everything she cared about, had she not looked for a link with her severed past. Her means of expression developed against her conventional training, finding affinities with avant-garde theater, caricature, cartoon—with art forms the Nazis were working to suppress. But this artistic context does not fully explain Charlotte Salomon's innovations in the genre of autobiography.

To what extent, I ask in what follows, does the unprecedented form of *Life or Theater?* emerge from one condition of the author—her sex—and one precondition of the work—suicide? That is to say: How do its genre, her gender, and its genesis intersect?

Feminist scholars are beginning to assert the primacy of female self-consciousness as an incentive to autobiography.[2] Yet for Charlotte Salomon and many other autobiographers, femaleness was not what affected them most or what impelled them to recollect their lives. In her case, it was the context of race (or what the Nazis called race) that enforced the state of exile that prompted the work of memory that generated the work of art. The historical preconditions of *Life or Theater?* complicate what the work tells us of female experience. It is one of those women's autobiographies that does not specify gender as the crucial mark on a life. But examining what it does instead may help illuminate the ways women present their pasts.

Women's autobiographies serve best as sources on private life, on autobiographical process, on common history, if we perceive them as meaningful layerings. On the surface, a particular woman explicitly describes her past and implicitly discloses her present condition; on another level, an autobiography reveals how a particular woman and a particular context assessed gender; on yet another, it manifests the preconditions (of gender and other factors) that make for self-disclosure. If all these combinations of individual psyche and historical situation entered analyses of autobiography, as they ought to, each autobiographical text would appear fastened to its own context, disallowing most gener-

2. See, for example, Estelle Jelinek, "Introduction: Women's Autobiography and the Male Tradition," in *Women's Autobiography: Essays in Criticism,* ed. Estelle Jelinek (Bloomington: Indiana University Press, 1980), pp. 1–20; Mary G. Mason, "The Other Voice: Autobiographies of Women Writers," this volume; Domna Stanton, "Autogynography: Is the Subject Different?" in *The Female Autograph* (New York: New York Literary Forum, 1984), pp. 5–22.

alities about the genre. *Life or Theater?* in particular would seem too extreme to exemplify women's autobiographies: think of its threatening content and theatrical construction; think of the aberrations in its context—a suicidal family, a genocidal enemy. But in fact its very extremity sets standards for interpretation. To place a work like *Life or Theater?* within the newly named genre of female autobiography, our analyses have to situate gender where it belongs—in a matrix of historical contingencies.

The uniqueness of *Life or Theater?* derives, at least in part, from the historical meanings of gender within it. Otherness (to use Simone de Beauvoir's term for the female condition) certainly determined the lot of Charlotte Salomon, but more because she was Jewish and exiled than female. Relative to those conditions, a female identity—usually considered the least variable of features—was not forced upon her. To some extent, she could *choose* female affiliations; she could try out variants of female behavior through her characters. So female identity surfaces in *Life or Theater?* not because Charlotte Salomon was born woman but because woman was one part she could still play. The features of gender, taken in context, framed the work's dramatic form.

Charlotte Salomon's case demonstrates that gender can emerge most interestingly precisely where it does not wholly condition experience. The ways gender delimits behavior form a subtext in this autobiography, as in many lives. *Life or Theater?* uses female experience for perspective, especially when it accounts for suicide. It presents contrasting approaches to reality by distinguishing male from female behavior. It fashions its very origins from an affinity with women. And it does all this without identifying femaleness as a primary category. Interpreting *Life or Theater?* requires disclosing deep signs of female experience, affiliation, and perception.

The beginning of an autobiography announces an autobiographer's notion of origins. This autobiography begins, as it ends, with a character named Charlotte facing suicide. In 1913 "Charlotte"—the autobiographer, in a sense, but actually the aunt she was named after—"left her parents' home and threw herself into the water" (p. 7). In the sympathetic painting of this scene, the woman's face dissolves peacefully. But the woman's sister, Charlotte's future mother, is shown tormented by the suicide: "Am I to blame for her death?" (pp. 125–26).

This could be Charlotte's transposed question about herself and the mother she later lost: she had to know if she was to blame for her mother's death. Suicide (not influenza, as Charlotte was told) had taken her mother from her at age eight, but she learned the truth long after anyone could provide concrete details. The absence of explanation forced Charlotte to formulate a concept of cause. Perhaps to preclude thinking that her own character had failed to keep her mother's intact, she found an explanation that unburdened her. She chose to link suicide to the misappropriation of a woman's life.

The adult Charlotte designed a drama for what the child Charlotte could not make sense of. A sequence of seventeen early scenes, then nineteen later ones (pp. 15–32, 121–41) stage a story of maternal loss. Charlotte's mother, Franziska, happily married to a surgeon named Albert Salomon, settles in Berlin and gives birth on 16 April 1917 to a daughter, called Charlotte "in memory of her younger sister." Franziska vibrates with motherliness: she feeds the baby, takes the growing child on vacations, invites the child's friends to a birthday party, plays piano for the gym group. The bright colors and continuous action of these early scenes show a mother in love with her life. But a few years later, "for incomprehensible reasons Franziska can find no more joy in anything" (p. 27).

Of course, autobiographers always impose their own explanations after the fact. But Charlotte's work, designed as a play, distributes interpretations among its characters. For Franziska herself, daily living has dissolved into "yearning and dreaming" (p. 138). To Charlotte the child it is "incomprehensible" that "Franziska can find no more joy in anything." To Franziska's own mother the reasons are all too comprehensible: she thinks Franziska "could not be happy with that kind of husband, with that kind of child" (p. 132). This commentary appears on a transparent paper taped over a picture of little Charlotte with her parents: she and Franziska tangle their arms round each other, while the father looks down lovingly. But one could also notice the gap between mother/child and father, the stiffness of his arm as against their fluid embrace; one could notice the distrustful text contradicting the image of shared joy. This autobiography plays text against image and substitutes multiple perspectives for what might otherwise be a single devastating vision: Charlotte responsible for her mother's despair.

At the source of suicide, this story fails to find an event or influence, a personal flaw or family failing; rather it suggests an entire structure of female futility. In one scene, for instance, when the family goes out for a promenade, the mother reaches out, one hand unable to break into her husband's grip, the other hand just failing to hold Charlotte, a lively girl venturing out of the picture (p. 134). In another scene, Franziska turns to her husband for consolation; he jerks his head from his books, then back again, covering his ears. His lines read: "And I will be a professor. Don't disturb me, please don't disturb me" (p. 136). In yet another, Charlotte's father turns to his books, head in his hands, face obscured;

on a lower tier in the painting, three figures of Franziska stare out expectantly, day after day, charming dress after dress, *her* face overexposed (p. 131). The border between man and wife is sealed. The scene is a brilliant visual portrayal of gender segregation, the source of which is voiced bitterly by Franziska's mother: "The only thing he ever thought about was his career" (p. 129). In the script of *Life or Theater?* Franziska's existence looks fruitless. She tells herself, "I will be a professor's wife," but her husband does not want her in his study; her own mother says, "I would love to have had a son"; her child pulls away from her; so she ends up "yearning and dreaming," staring through windows as if through borders of a closed domestic domain (pp. 129, 136, 145, 134, 138–39).

Charlotte's portrayal of this female dilemma was a gift of insight to the mother who left her behind. In the artist's empathic re-creation, Franziska finally resorts to raiding her husband's medical bag for a lethal dose of opium (p. 27). Suddenly Franziska's husband and father push their way into the frame—"But what kind of business are you acting out for us? How could anybody poison herself?"—swooping down while she defends her face with her arm (p. 28). As Charlotte scripts this event, three men—psychiatrist, husband, father—judge the suicide attempt as "temporary emotionalism." They treat a woman who takes her husband's drugs as if she could not be abandoning life, only leaving messages of need. In the spatial arrangement of this and other scenes, men break into women's domains, but women are not permitted to break into men's. Men are entitled to avoid the painful issues: Charlotte's father covers his ears against his wife's recitals of melancholy. But the women keep asking themselves terrifying questions: "Am I to blame for her death?" and "For what am I staying alive?"

This was Franziska's last question in *Life or Theater?* inscribed in her imagined suicide note: "And my husband—who does not love me. And my child—who does not need me. For what, for what am I staying alive?" (p. 137). Beneath the mother's words the image catches her with her husband's and daughter's faces projecting from her head. One surface and color grounds all three faces, so that the boundaries between them look painted on, like makeup. Franziska's mouth locks open for speech but no space extends behind it for forming thoughts, no room for anything except the husband and child—as if there were no Franziska untenanted by them, no Franziska possible if they should leave. To be occupied and vacated at the same time, to be separate from others and undifferentiated at the same time: this, as Charlotte imagined it, is suicidal sentience.

I cannot help taking this painting as a portrait of the artist, projecting

"And my husband—who does not love me. And my child—who does not need me. For what, for what am I staying alive?"

upon her mother mentalities she came to know herself. For the content and construction of the paintings affiliate Charlotte with her mother's state of mind. Whereas not one painting explores the father's inner life, many record Franziska's words, center her in the frame, catch her private moments. The autobiographer, as heir to the family misfortune, allowed herself no safe distance from Franziska's fate.

Charlotte's visualization of her mother's mind amounts to an analysis of suicide, one that emphasizes the solitude in a woman's life, the absence of tangible purpose, the alienation from those she was meant to love. If this interpretation simply reflected ideas common in Charlotte's time, then it needn't be linked to the particularity of female autobiography. But in fact Charlotte's vision of suicide ran counter to the understanding of suicide prevalent in her day.

Influential contemporary studies adopted a dismissive bias toward female suicide, rationalized by means of contemporary German statistics: between World War I and the mid-1920s, when Charlotte's family suffered most of its suicides, only half as many women committed suicide as men. The problem is that the statistics themselves incorporated a bias, for they usually failed to consider suicide *attempts* along with suicides. Almost everywhere in Europe, women attempted suicide at least as often as men. Women survived more often, probably because men used more effective means, such as ropes and firearms, the tools of male trades.[3]

The absence of focus on female suicide exemplifies exactly that inattention to women's experience which made so many women feel abnormal. In Charlotte's day, studies analyzed suicide in terms of inheritance, insanity, nationality, occupation, or religion—rarely in terms of gender. Influential accounts that did examine gender refused to consider women's social condition as anything but a privilege. For instance, Thomas Masaryk's famous 1881 study of suicide envied women their protection against it. "Women in most countries remain at a distance from the agitating activities of politics" (as if by choice); "they aim less at the acquisition of property" (as if by preference) "and therefore are less troubled by ruinous financial conditions, poverty, and need than men" (as if by miracle). In the same vein, Emile Durkheim's *Suicide* (1897) asserted: "Woman kills herself less . . . because she does not participate in collective life in the same way" that man does (as if the family cannot

3. [Reich Statistical Bureau], *Statistisches Jahrbuch für das deutsche Reich* (Berlin: Verlag für Politik und Wirtschaft, 1922–25, Verlag von Reimar Hobbing, 1926); Sigismund Peller, "Zur Statistik der Selbstmordhandlung," *Allgemeines statistisches Archiv* 22 (1932): 343; *Statistisches Jahrbuch der Stadt Berlin, 1915–1919* (Berlin: Stankiewicz, 1920) p. 147; Frederick Hoffman, *Suicide Problems* (Newark, N.J.: Prudential, 1927) p. 387.

count as collective life). "We have long known that women kill them-selves less often than do men," concluded Maurice Halbwachs in his monumental 1930 study *The Causes of Suicide*, and his assumptions implied that whatever women do, even not committing suicide, falls short of normal behavior.[4]

What would a gender-sensitive interpretation of suicide (so seldom ventured then or now) look like?[5] It might show how gender bifurcates human aspirations, as Charlotte did in contrasting her mother with her father; it might show how gender constrains some people beyond repair; it might counter the charge of mental disorder leveled against women. In those days at least half the female suicides in Germany were officially attributed to madness, as against less than a third of the male suicides.[6] But clearly Charlotte did not see it that way. She never represented a woman's suicide as insane or senseless; she never blamed women who committed it. Such an account broke through long-held assumptions that those who contend with the cruel world (men) have good reason for suicide; that women are inoculated against it by domesticity; that if the inoculation fails, they must be mad. Here is a work that sees suicide as one response to social circumstance, not as a singular female failing. A gender-sensitive interpretation of suicide might look like Charlotte Salomon's autobiography.

What underlies *Life or Theater?* is an engagement with other women's suicides almost to the point of reiterating them. Its visual images suggest such affiliation more starkly than most verbal accounts would dare. For example, the painter shows her susceptibility to her subject in one of the autobiography's climactic scenes, the scene in which Franziska admits "I cannot put up with it. I am so alone" (p. 30). Suicide in mind, she approaches a window whose frame, bordering the whole scene, is contiguous with the painting's frame. Outside the frame, in front of the window and the painting both, *in Charlotte's plane*—Franziska falls to her death. By design this image contradicts the invisible placement of artists within a painting's scene, a placement we read easily as a sign of their safe distance from it. Here the event is transported to the artist,

4. Thomas G. Masaryk, *Suicide and the Meaning of Civilization* (Chicago: University of Chicago Press, 1970), p. 27; Emile Durkheim, *Suicide: A Study in Sociology* (Glencoe: Free Press, 1951), p. 341; Maurice Halbwachs, *The Causes of Suicide* (1930; rpt., London: Routledge and Kegan Paul, 1978), p. 45.

5. There are still very few studies of suicide that reflect the concerns of women's history. In feminist social science and literary criticism, respectively, see Phyllis Chesler, *Women and Madness* (New York: Avon, 1973); and Margaret Higonnet, "Speaking Silences: Women's Suicide," in *The Female Body in Western Culture: Contemporary Perspectives*, ed. Susan Suleiman (Cambridge: Harvard University Press, 1986), pp. 68–83.

6. Halbwachs, p. 248; Hoffman, p. 46; Ruth Shonle Cavan, *Suicide* (Chicago: University of Chicago Press, 1928), p. 114.

who steps back only enough to give her mother room to fall. It is hard to look at this painting without sensing Charlotte accommodating her mother's death.

In *Life or Theater?* the autobiographer willingly makes herself vulnerable to an inheritance from women, even though it could be fatal. While sons often honor their maternal legacies, only a daughter sees herself as the designated heir—at least in Charlotte's milieu, and probably in most environments where women live.

A susceptibility to maternal legacies may make women different from men at the deepest psychological level. Some theorists see female identity formed by a daughter's linkage with the mother, in contrast to male identity, formed by severance from her.[7] So women's autobiographies, if studied in numbers, might show how readily daughters reproduce maternal patterns. But they might also show, more interestingly, what conditions—and not of gender alone—lead women to *acknowledge* a female legacy. What made Charlotte attest to an affinity between mother and daughter? I think it came about when she experienced the helplessness of a refugee, when she saw the structures of dependency encircling them both. Her autobiography embraced the female condition when historical circumstances recapitulated it.

Exile began for Charlotte in 1939, when she had to leave her family, her lover, and her country, to join her grandparents in Villefranche, a village near Nice in southern France, where they had settled for safety soon after Hitler came to power in 1933. Displaced from their homeland, men like Charlotte's grandfather found it much harder to carry out their responsiblities as providers, and women theirs as social connecters. When Charlotte's grandparents arrived in France, 90 percent of the refugees from Nazism were men.[8] Charlotte and her grandmother were living in a male world of exiles within the foreign world of France.

In Charlotte's interpretation, the grandmother's vulnerability as an exiled Jewish woman intensified her previous guilt as a mother of two daughters taken by suicide: "The heavy pain that pursued her life, till now somewhat submerged in her depths, seems called up by the raging war, till it appears fully in her recollection, and she feels her sharp intelligence and her self-control—what made her life worth living— breaking to pieces against something of greater force" (p. 693). The greater force was Germany's. When the Nazis started to seize Europe in September 1939, Charlotte's grandmother tried to kill herself.

7. See Nancy Chodorow, *The Reproduction of Mothering: Psychoanalysis and the Sociology of Gender* (Berkeley: University of California Press, 1978); Dorothy Dinnerstein, *The Mermaid and the Minotaur: Sexual Arrangement and Human Malaise* (New York: Harper, 1977).

8. Statistics from Gilbert Badia, "L'Emigration en France: Ses conditions et ses problèmes," in *Les Barbelés de l'exil: Etudes sur l'émigration allemande et autrichienne, 1938–1940*, ed. Gilbert Badia et al. (Grenoble: Presses Universitaires, 1979), pp. 15, 17, 21.

What rescued her was empathy. Charlotte, instead of protecting herself from her grandmother's breakup, made a conscious choice "to go wholly out of herself and be engaged only with her grandmother" (p. 697). Knowing that nothing could redeem losses from suicide and exile, Charlotte chose to transcend them. We see her singing Beethoven's "Ode to Joy," till her rising voice draws the grandmother right up from her bed. "Joy, thou spark from flame immortal, Daughter of Elysium. We shall enter, drunk with fire, Holy One, Your sacred realm." The grandfather asks, "What's all that junk supposed to mean?" (pp. 702–5). Exhausted and incapable of caring more, he finally reveals the secret kept from Charlotte for thirteen years: that the women in her family, all but her grandmother and herself, have taken their lives. As her grandfather recites his grievances toward such women, Charlotte reduces herself to two colors and an outline, as deprived of features as she had been of facts: "I KNEW NOTHING ABOUT ALL THAT" (p. 713). Now she knew. Now she set herself to save the two women who still survived.

The forty-odd paintings of Charlotte's attempts to rescue her grandmother (pp. 697–748) unsettle our presumption that individualism is proper to autobiography. This autobiography doubles its central figure with another woman. It assumes the access women have to each other's bodies and minds. Outlines cross and colors liquefy between Charlotte and her grandmother; the same circulation runs through both their bodies. The figures lose their separateness so that a shared therapy can emerge, culminating in a "proposition" that the younger woman makes to the older one: "Instead of taking your life in such a dreadful way, apply the same powers to describing your life. . . . As you write down whatever oppresses you, you free yourself and maybe even render a service to the world" (pp. 722–23).

What she charted for her grandmother eventually led Charlotte herself to autobiography. She shows us that the autobiographical process can start with the capacity to join another's journey. Charlotte tested her affiliation with women—what she called "going wholly out of herself"—on the most precarious ground, where her relatives found reason for suicide. Her image overturns our idea (drawn from the accounts of men) that autobiography sets its course by self-differentiation. In Charlotte's language identity gets discovered by "learning to walk all paths" of one's female ancestors, knowing what the end might be.[9]

Being "engaged only with her grandmother," encouraging her to set down her memoirs, Charlotte arrives at the central "proposition" of the

---

9. Unnumbered sheet, Box 81 N7. (Aside from the paintings Charlotte Salomon chose and numbered for *Life or Theater?* she saved hundreds of painted studies, cited hereafter as unnumbered sheets with the box number in Amsterdam's Joods Historisch Museum archives).

play: take your life history not your life. But the proposition fails to reach the older woman, saturated by guilt for the suicides of her two daughters. Finally, her mind turns along well-worn synapses to her husband, who prefers (in Charlotte's portrayal) to bear no guilt at all. In the most terrifying of the paintings, the grandmother frantically tries to recruit Charlotte: "You go strangle him. . . . If you don't want to, I'll do it myself right now." (pp. 733–34).

This is the sort of mad occurrence that could have been suppressed in autobiography. But Charlotte must have sensed in it a revelation of her grandmother's subconscious, and perhaps of her own. The grandmother's murderous impulses terrified Charlotte (as the lurid frenzy of the painting makes clear) but they also made self-destruction plausible, an example of the popular idea that "no one kills himself who has never wanted to kill another."[10] In fact, the next day the grandmother turns her murderous intent inward and hurls herself from a window, like her daughter before her. Charlotte arrives a moment too late to stop her (pp. 746–48).

The grandfather, returning from his morning walk, says abruptly, "She has done it after all. . . . That is the fate of this family. They are all so unnatural. . . . Most likely I will live to see the woman in the next room lay hands upon *herself* too." In the next room, Charlotte cries out, "DEAR GOD, JUST DO NOT LET ME GO MAD" (pp. 749, 753, 755).

She did not go mad. She painted. In her own view, what she painted originated in life-threatening affinities with women: "My life commenced when my grandmother wanted to take her life, when I found out that my mother had taken hers,"[11] and "I was my mother my grandmother, yes I was all the people in my play. Learning to walk all paths, I became MY SELF."[12] If such sympathetic fusions jeopardized Charlotte, they also led to the summoning of identity indispensable for autobiography.

The self composed of "my mother my grandmother" found representation in what Charlotte called "an opera in three colors," in the actions of people she called "the performers." Transforming persons into dramatis personae lent them an allegorical significance in which gender played a critical part. The autobiography's moral framework set exemption against engagement, and the contrast revealed itself in divergent traits allotted to male and female characters. Charlotte's father plays a

10. Wilhelm Stekel, in discussions of the Vienna Psychoanalytic Society [1910], published as *On Suicide*, ed. Paul Friedman (New York: International University Press, 1967), p. 87.

11. *Charlotte: Life or Theater?* p. vii.

12. Unnumbered sheet, Box 81 N7.

"You go strangle him."

man who shuts out his wife and retreats to his work; that he was a self-sacrificing surgeon does not figure in the drama. Her grandfather is cast to represent unconscious egoism, the obsession with one's immediate needs. He responds to the suicides in his wife's family—"*They* are all so unnatural"—by exculpating himself (p. 753). In Charlotte's paintings, the grandfather often commands the space that could belong to others. Sometimes the top of the painting simply decapitates him (pp. 113, 145). By casting men this way, she holds them partly responsible for the wasting of women's lives.

Context is crucial here. Charlotte assigned men this role at a moment when exile was demeaning her as a person *and* as a woman. The grandfather's condition as a helpless and widowed refugee was reducing Charlotte from artist to domestic. She had always kept clear of woman's work, by class and by choice. Now exile forced *her* to cook and keep house for *him*. Privately she wrote: "Living with my grandfather makes me sick. . . . To have had such insights and now back to this buffoon—to look after him. . . . Everything I did for my grandfather made the blood rush to my face. I was ill, my face always red with dull rage and grief."[13]

It was not Charlotte's purpose to show the generic incapacities of men. What concerned her was a difference in mentality between the women who extended themselves into others and the men who never, thanks to the women, had to take that risk. "My grandfather," she wrote, "was a symbol to me of the people I had to fight."[14] *Kämpfen*, fight, do battle, is strong language. The "symbol . . . to fight" was that of "never feeling true fervor for anything in the world" except oneself, of always "accepting things the way things are, and not trying to search for hidden meanings or reasons," especially in regard to suicide.[15] In reaction, Charlotte trained herself against exoneration and toward empathy. Above all, she taught herself to avoid "the mistake that people make all the time—seeing things only from their own point of view."[16]

In contrast to her father and grandfather, the autobiographer has her mother and grandmother represent the ability to step from one's own vantage point onto another's. The mother's mind (as Charlotte depicts it) absorbs the minds of her sister and husband and child. The grandmother (as Charlotte represents her) incorporates the pain of her daughters and of a war-torn world. Charlotte's self-portrayals emphasize the

---

13. Unnumbered sheet, ibid.
14. Unnumbered sheet, Box 81 N4.
15. Unnumbered sheet, ibid.
16. Unnumbered sheet, Box 81 N5.

"family resemblance—anyone can see it" between these women and herself (p. 546).

Precisely what Charlotte chose to inherit from women—the capacity for association—gives her autobiography its extraordinary pattern and purpose. An effort "to go wholly out of herself" thrusts her work toward theatricality, as the prologue to *Life or Theater?* suggests: "The author has taken pains to go out of herself entirely and let the characters sing or speak in their own voices" (p. 6). No first-person protagonist monopolizes the perspective in this work. Whereas the (rare) third-person principals of other autobiographies are represented as superior or exemplary personages,[17] Charlotte's motive was to present a composite personality. All of *Life or Theater?* dedicates itself to dislodging the self-enclosed stance that her male characters project. A fluid outlook is its final aspiration.

Does such a model perpetuate female dilemmas? A fluid outlook seems to exhibit the unsealed ego so often attributed to women. A composite personality seems too penetrable for its own good. But Charlotte's autobiography manages to move beyond its own evidence of female futility and finality. Because it never names self-destruction feminine or expects solutions by means of gender redress, it is free to frame femaleness in a symbolic dimension. The unique form of *Life or Theater?* models itself on women—as emblems of empathy.

Here is autobiography construed as the assumption of others' losses. "Letting the characters sing or speak" through one's own story restores the voices of all those who forfeited theirs by suicide or exile. In the last dialogue of *Life or Theater?* Charlotte tries to explain to her grandfather the act of restoration she sees as her task:

> (Charlotte): "Grandfather, I have come to feel that one has to piece
>   the whole world back together again."
> (Grandfather): "Oh just do away with yourself too so your
>   nonsense will stop." (P. 774)

This fateful exchange brings the narrative to its crux, to what Charlotte called "the question of whether to take her life or undertake something unheard of and mad" (p. 777).

Life or Theater? owed its existence to this question—and its uniqueness to Charlotte's inability to answer it definitively. The suicidal infection she contracted by caring for her grandmother worsened in the

17. See Philippe Lejeune, *Le Pacte autobiographique* (Paris: Seuil, 1975), pp. 16–17.

(Charlotte): "Grandfather, I have come to feel that one has to piece the whole world back together again." (Grandfather): "Oh just do away with yourself too so your nonsense will stop."

environment of exile. The autobiography recorded her "sense of the great helplessness of all people who try to catch at straws in the most terrible inundations" (p. 776). And privately she wrote: "The world has really been disintegrating more and more."[18] Conditions in Nazi Europe pressed her to collect the past in an unexampled manner. Looking at the scenes of Charlotte in exile, one may feel the artist's technique breaking down under the strain. The paintings revert to flat swatches of color, brief outlines without features, simple tones—orange on brown or blue on blue—a predominance of words over images, evacuated backgrounds. Nothing seems situated, nothing rests on anything else. To my eye this shows not disintegration of technique but a technique designed to convey disintegration. Privately Charlotte confessed: "I felt so hopeless." "My happiness was at an end." "I was in despair." "My old despair . . . threw me back into a slow death-like lethargy: if I can't find any joy in my life and in my work I will kill myself."[19]

And yet: averting the future served alike for inscribing the past. At a time when she was "desperately unhappy"—"at that time, I began to work on the drawings in hand."[20] The more exile and suicide bore down on her, the harder they pressed her to paint.

"She was facing the question of whether to take her life or undertake something unheard of and mad." *Life or Theater?* culminates with Charlotte's turn toward something unheard of and mad, an anomaly in art, a detour through her destiny. Marking the decision to begin her autobiography, the last scenes point us back to the start of the story, to the suicide of a woman named Charlotte. The end comes full circle with the beginning, the potential for suicide full circle with the potential for autobiography. *Life or Theater?* asserts the artist's power to close off her drama *and* her duration, to take her own life/history.

When Charlotte, at age twenty-six, brought her work to this conclusion, she placed it with French friends.[21] "Keep this safe," she said to them: "It is my whole life." Did she mean that living her life was the same as painting it? Was portraying it the same as prolonging it?

The Germans occupied the Riviera in September 1943. They put Charlotte on a transport. They pulled her out at Auschwitz. *They* took her life.

18. Unnumbered sheet, Box 81 N4.
19. Unnumbered sheet, Box 81 N6, N7.
20. Unnumbered sheet, Box 81 N6.
21. Dr. and Mme Moridis safeguarded the paintings; she remembered what Charlotte said when delivering them; quoted by Judith Herzberg in her Foreword to *Charlotte: Life or Theater?* pp. vii, xii. Auschwitz was the death camp in Poland where most of the seventy-five thousand Jews deported from France lost their lives.

17

Seeing Subjects: Women Directors and Cinematic Autobiography

CATHERINE PORTUGES

The history of motion pictures is also the history of autobiography. Among the very first films, the "home movies" of the Lumière brothers showed their own family members at table, at home, feeding the baby—images that, seen today, appear both comfortably familiar and strangely surprising in their straightforward recording of personal, domestic life. Films that take as their subject aspects, however disguised, of the filmmaker's own life have in fact long been attractive to audiences. Some more recent examples—those of Ingmar Bergman and Federico Fellini, François Truffaut and Woody Allen—evoke one popular tendency of the autobiographical impulse enacted through the camera, which has been described with typical voyeuristic pleasure by Fellini: "I am a film / I am my own still-life / Everything and nothing in my work is autobiographical."[1]

These directors and many others—primarily male, it should be noted—have often featured themselves in the films they have scripted; *Annie Hall, Scenes from a Marriage, 8-1/2,* and others like them have become emblematic of the cinematic use of first-person narrative. Each also contains memorable representations of female sexuality by actresses whose role as signifier has become synonymous with masculine desire, fantasy, and longing. Jeanne Moreau, Liv Ullmann, Anouk Aimée, Claudia Cardinale, and Diane Keaton portray with classic empathy and complexity the phantasmagorical creatures that issue forth from the directors' unconscious; in these and other works by the same auteurs, they reenact the repertoire of sexual reminiscence, the repressed that never fails to return.

1. Federico Fellini, *Fellini on Fellini,* ed. Anna Keel and Christian Strick (New York: Delta, 1977), Preface.

Such films embody motifs traditionally associated with the auto-biographical genre: a desire to set the record straight, the wish to restore a creativity presumed lost or attenuated, the need to tell one's family story, the longing for reconciliation with persons loved or feared from the past. Not unexpectedly, scenes of childhood and adolescence figure prominently in these works, as they do in literary autobiography. As Bergman notes: "I take up the images from my childhood, put them into the 'projector,' run them into myself, and have an entirely new way of evaluating them."[2] Roy Schafer has addressed this need for reworking one's internal relationship to primary persons from one's past by proposing that in psychic reality "the object is immortal." Assuming that from the subject's standpoint, "there can be no thoroughgoing object loss," he suggests that:

> the object loses or gains importance; it takes on new hostile or loving significance or becomes more neutral; it is expelled, though it may intrude again; it disappears and reappears; it is broken apart and put together again; it gets sick and recovers; it is replaced by a substitute and may later replace its replacement; it is either swallowed up by or swallows up the subjective self, or both, object relation thereby being transformed into a unity which, however, remains a unity of two-in-one and not one-unto-itself—hence, the subjective bliss and terror it occasions. . . . it appears to retain a fundamental sameness; this sameness reflects the subject's unchanging fundamental wishful tie to the object.[3]

While a verbal narrative of one's past is always subject to the vicissitudes of distortion, the filtering of endless recastings and transformations, images partake more directly of the internal experiential world, as Bergman suggests. As every analyst and analysand knows only too well, words, in Foucault's phrase, are "insuperably inadequate" to the task of expressing visual memory: the image is eroded by the effort to translate it verbally.[4] What Roland Barthes termed the "photographic para-dox"—the impossibility of communicating through language the meaning of a photograph—defines the challenge to the filmmaker engaged in translating a screen memory into visual text.[5] In constructing a retro-spective reality the filmmaker reverses the activity of the analysand who by free association translates visual and other sensory material into

2. Ingmar Bergman, *Bergman on Bergman* (New York: Simon and Schuster, 1973), p. 147.

3. Roy Schafer, "The Fates of the Immortal Object," in *Aspects of Internalization* (New York: International Universities Press, 1968).

4. Michel Foucault, *The Order of Things* (New York: Vintage, 1973), p. 57.

5. Roland Barthes, *Camera Lucida: Reflections on Photography* (New York: Hill and Wang, 1981), p. 12.

words. Whereas the analysand, perpetually tempted to abandon the truer image in favor of the more available verbalization, faces unconscious conflict between that which is true of her or his experience and that which is describable, the filmmaker does not have the luxury of the seduction of language, itself a form of resistance. Recovery of primary images in the autobiographical film, and the placement of the subject within that framework, is the fundamental task of the director motivated, however unconsciously, by the desire to reincarnate past experiences or to reanimate an "immortal object."

Elizabeth Bruss tackles one aspect of this question in her provocative essay "Eye for I: Making and Unmaking Autobiography in Film" by asserting that the technical specificity of the cinematic apparatus undermines its potential for finding a true equivalent for the autobiographical mode. Her objections concern the putative shattering of the unity of subjectivity and subject matter—the "implied identity of author, narrator, and protagonist on which classical autobiography depends"—inherent in the dynamics of the motion picture.[6] It is perhaps undeniable that in view of the divergent specificities of the two forms, no exact equivalent of autobiography is possible in film. Nevertheless, we can, I think, reconsider this vexing issue from the perspective of gender-based autobiographical theory. For the proliferation of feature films by women directors since the time of Bruss's essay bears witness to a stage in the evolution of this admittedly hybrid genre that derives from the combined determinants of feminist theory, psychoanalysis, and recent history. In the first place, the mother-daughter relationship has become a central focus of experimental filmmaking, primarily among Anglo-American filmmakers. Informed by feminist theory and a critical stance toward classical psychoanalysis and working within the tradition of documentary and avant-garde film, they have emphasized a revision of oedipal dynamics and shifted the locus of vision from the paternal to the maternal. Michelle Citron's *Daughter Rite,* for example, concerns the central problem of making a film about a woman's relations with her family, without at the same time producing a first-person "confessional" film or a fictional family portrait. Yvonne Rainer's *Film about a Woman Who . . . ,* Jackie Raynal's *Deux Fois,* and Laura Mulvey's *Riddles of the Sphinx* all reconstruct and juxtapose different narrative forms within the dynamics of locating female subjectivity and desire; these forms include cinéma vérité, soap opera, melodrama, home video, and journals—all of which challenge the notion of identity itself, the "hu-

6. Elizabeth W. Bruss, "Eye for I: Making and Unmaking Autobiography in Film," in *Autobiography: Essays Theoretical and Critical,* ed. James Olney (Princeton: Princeton University Press, 1980), pp. 296–320.

manistic" assumption of a centered, unified subject. At the same time, these directors deconstruct the spectator's relationship to the illusion of unity and truth associated with mainstream, "illusionist," or "dominant," cinema. Another major intervention in the discourse of gender-conscious cinema seeking to implicate the viewer's gaze is *Sigmund Freud's Dora: A Case of Mistaken Identity,* by Andrew Tyndall and others, a collective endeavor using advertising, pornography, and psychoanalytic theory in the service of reclaiming the feminine subject.[7] While these films contain autobiographical elements, they are not, strictly speaking, autobiographical in intent or content. Yet this formalistic and theoretical investigation by feminist filmmakers of the late 1970s, while still flourishing in new works by Yvonne Rainer, Sally Potter, Laura Mulvey, and others, can be said to have engendered a return to narrative film, albeit with a new awareness of its potential to address audiences presumably now cognizant of the lure of dominant cinema. Several of the directors working in the narrative mode have previously been engaged in the feminist revision of classical Hollywood codes of production and distribution and were hence prepared to reappropriate aspects of the feature narrative film, using innovative as well as traditional cinematic strategies. Their work combines familiar forms borrowed from conventional motion pictures with an urgent personal agenda, informed by an awareness of cinema as an ideological entity, the product of culture, economics, and history.

Fellini's *8-1/2,* unapologetically autobiographical, shifts between flashback and fantasy within the diegetic space of the narrative to explore the humorous and tragic conflicts of the artist's life and work, centering on women, who are indispensable to his creativity and self-esteem. That film has remained a prototype of the genre, to which other directors pay homage in their own cinematic search for lost lovers and wives, their own reckonings with guilt and rejection. Its blurring of the boundaries between the delusional and the real still provokes the argument about the director's technique, his personal history, and his creative life. Subsequent films whose formal and psychological preoccupations are derived from those of Fellini are inevitably indebted to his: we have only to recall Woody Allen's *Stardust Memories, Manhattan,* and *Annie Hall* or, to a lesser extent, Bob Fosse's *All That Jazz* to be reminded of the link between them, to realize that in each case the protagonist is portrayed as a man with strongly narcissistic characteristics. In describing the narcis-

7. For a discussion of these and related films, see E. Ann Kaplan, *Women & Film: Both Sides of the Camera* (New York: Methuen, 1983); and *Re-Vision: Essays in Feminist Film Criticism,* ed. Mary Ann Doane, Patricia Mellencamp, and Linda Williams (Los Angeles: American Film Institute Monograph Series, vol. 3, 1984).

sistic personality, Otto Kernberg emphasizes a configuration of distur-
bances in the sphere of intimate relationships, accompanied by a sense of
grandiosity.[8] This syndrome is seen as coexistent with a sense of emptiness, inferiority, and dependency on the admiration of others as a reg-
ulator of self-esteem. Although the films of Bergman, Fellini, Truffaut,
and Allen should not be considered simply as illustrations of case studies
in narcissism, they do seem to exemplify Kernberg's theoretical model
in uncannily tragic fashion. Their protagonists, from Marcello Mas-
troianni's tormented Guido to Woody Allen's self-portrayal, are driven
by a nearly uncontrollable need to ward off the inevitable decline of
aging and death. These characters, along with those of Bergman and
Truffaut, are shown to be anxiously in quest of youth and potency, re-
quiring the admiration of younger, beautiful partners to gratify their
quest. Theirs is a psychoanalytic drama whose terms Melanie Klein would
have seen as involving a manic relationship to objects deriving from
three affective components: control, triumph, and contempt. In her
view, these affects come into play to defend against the overwhelming
fear of loss, guilt, and the mourning that accompanies loss, whether it
be of a cherished love object or one's own youth and unfulfilled promise.

That women directors of autobiographical films inescapably share
such narcissistic impulses seems indisputable, given the qualities of self-
disclosure inherent in autobiography. They too seem, in some cases, to
seek from the judging audience exculpation, exoneration, the imprimatur of acceptance of the stuff of their own lives. They too make
drama out of marriage and birth, sex, aging, infidelity, and the quest for
self-fulfillment. Nadine Trintignant's *Next Summer,* for instance, shot
with her husband, Jean-Louis Trintignant, in the lead role of the husband and her own daughter in the daughter's role, demonstrates all too
clearly the genderlessness of narcissism. The film's subject is the several
generations of Nadine Trintignant's own family. Still, there are differences, and they are important. The women's films, by their very insistence on a multigenerational rendering of autobiographical material and
by their tendency to situate the female protagonists in a scenario that
highlights links among people rather than the isolated heroine surveying
her world suggest a sensibility at once more attuned to and more embedded within a social world than those of their male counterparts.

These films share as a common gesture, whether acknowledged directly in the narrative, in the credits, or in published interviews with the
director, the desire to create an intergenerational testimonial for the benefit of parents or children and to recount a story formerly repressed,

8. Otto Kernberg, *Borderline Conditions and Pathological Narcissism* (New York: Jason Aron-
son Press, 1974).

silenced, or distorted. The Hungarian director Márta Mészáros, the Belgian Chantal Akerman, the French Diane Kurys and Marguerite Duras, and the German Jutta Bruckner have all made films in which one or both parents figure prominently as recipients of the reparative motif that both Schafer and Klein emphasize in their psychoanalytic work. And in view of their ages—generally from forty to fifty—it is equally understandable that a number of these directors' films begin during World War II, at or just before the time of their own birth. We might well imagine why European filmmakers who have experienced, to whatever degree, the dislocations and trauma of that war might, at midlife, feel both ready and compelled to examine the conditions of their childhood, their parents' lives, and their national identity. Among these, Márta Mészáros's *Diary for My Children* offers a particularly instructive and eloquent example, originating as it does in an East European context that speaks directly, as the title indicates, to a new generation.[9] Most frankly autobiographical of all, Mészáros's film waited fifteen years to come into being, doubly censored by ideological repression and the director's own internal conflicts. Her search for parents swallowed up by the massive horrors of war operates both on the biographical level and as a metaphor of separation and the longing for fusion with primary love objects. Its unsentimental adolescent protagonist undertakes a quest for reparation and reconciliation with lost family and national identity. This same reparative motif, while not exclusively the province of female directors, nevertheless constitutes a major impulse in their autobiographical work. It is the desire to make restitution for pain inflicted, real or imagined, and to see the other as a whole individual with a separate identity that infuses these films, rather than the "manic defense" more typical of the work of male autobiographical filmmakers.

Diary is set in postwar Hungary, and its point of view is carried by Juli, a teenage representation of the director, who, like the protagonist, returned to Hungary in 1947 after a decade in the Soviet Union. Juli's politically committed Stalinist Aunt Magda, the former revolutionary who had withstood the rigors of prison and torture, surviving to see the victory of the revolution, emerges as perhaps the most complex female character. Sorrowful and even elegiac in tone, *Diary* uses substantial newsreel footage from the period, intercut with semiautobiographical and fictionalized material, to create a richly textured portrayal of Hungarian cultural, social, political, and domestic life in the late 1940s. It is

9. For discussion of the historical and cultural context of Hungarian cinema, see Graham Petrie, *History Must Answer to Man: The Contemporary Hungarian Cinema* (Budapest: Corvina Books, 1978); and Istvan Nemeskürty, *Word and Image: History of the Hungarian Cinema* (Budapest: Corvina Books, 1974).

photographed by Miklos Jancso, Jr., the son of Mészáros and her former husband, the renowned film director Miklos Jancso. The direction stresses subtleties in relationships while allowing full play to political content. A prolific and widely respected filmmaker, Mészáros concentrates in her later feature work on women who are struggling to achieve both autonomy and intimacy, often compelled by a desire to choose a daughter. Yet the most insistent motif of *Diary for My Children* is not, as in the experimental films of the 1970s, a desire for a good mother but the longing for a father. "At the time when my country's new society was in its childhood, I was a child too," says the director.[10] Juli's father, a sculptor, had emigrated to Russia in the late 1930s, only to be obliterated in the Stalinist terror. Her mother, we learn, also died there during the war. Her orphaned status does not, however, suffice to make the sullen fifteen-year-old accept Magda, although she is deeply drawn to Magda's comrade Janos, a factory engineer whose wife and daughter died during the war.

Concurrently with the unfolding of this narrative, Juli's childhood memories are visualized in lyrical, heroicized iconography, eternally arrested at the developmental stage of a five-year-old. Juli's mother, portrayed with unearthly blonde beauty, is represented as the fertile peasant mother, while her father, pictured in soft focus and beardless (in contrast to the bearded Janos, both played by Jan Nowicki, Mészáros's real-life partner), is the soul of nobility as he works in a monumental stone quarry in the Ural mountains. After an unsuccessful attempt to seek her father's family in the countryside, Juli eventually moves in with Janos and his son, concluding the circle of the film's narrative.

In a frightening scene of a totalitarian nightmare, Juli awakens from a dream of her father as the police seize Janos. The scene is intercut with a flashback to her father's arrest as the young child looks on, mute with rage and humiliation. "Forgetting is a form of death ever-present in life," says Milan Kundera in the afterword of his *Book of Laughter and Forgetting:* "But forgetting is also the great problem of politics. When a big power wants to deprive a small country of its national consciousness it uses the method of organized forgetting."[11] Márta Mészáros was not allowed to make this film, the story of her own life, for a decade and a half; its suppression by Hungarian censors is mirrored by her own internal repression. *Diary for My Children* uncovers both and, hence,

10. Márta Mészáros, interview with Annette Insdorf, "Childhood Loss Shapes a Director's Life and Art," *New York Times,* 28 Oct. 1984, sec. 2, p. 20.

11. Kundera quoted in J. Hoberman, "Family Feud," review of *Diary for My Children, Village Voice,* 6 Nov. 1984, p. 50.

constitutes an act of mourning and restoration. For the longing for a father is doubled by the longing to own her own past. Mészáros acknowledges that "totalitarianism is not only hell, but also the dream of paradise . . . and the whole period of Stalinist terror was a period of collective lyrical delirium."[12]

Such motifs of violent oppression and fear are echoed in Diane Kurys's *Entre nous,* the third in a series of autobiographical films retracing the director's youth, adolescence, and young adulthood. Like *Diary for My Children,* it too begins with the war, in a concentration camp. The young Jewish protagonist attracts the sympathy of a man who rescues her and later becomes her husband. Only after the final frame, by means of an afterword dedicating the film to the director's parents, does the viewer learn that the film has been told from the point of view of a child, the daughter of that woman. This autobiographical appendix necessitates an immediate retrospective revision by the spectator, who thus becomes a more than usually active participant in the autobiographical process.

Entre nous is informed throughout by a spirit of tolerant compassion, despite scenes of domestic and psychic violence and wrenching moments of familial and interpersonal alienation. Each of its characters is afforded respect and integrity in the director's reconstruction of an intimate erotic relationship between her mother and her mother's closest female friend, a passion that wreaks havoc between and within two families. Although her project lacks the political and historical sweep of Mészáros's film, Kurys shares with her Hungarian colleague an intense desire to repay a debt to her parents, this time in the form of forgiveness toward a mother whose actions might well have been experienced as rejecting or painful. Its underlying reparative motif again recalls Melanie Klein's elaboration of that concept to describe efforts to restore damaged aspects of the self and of the mother, who is perceived as harmed by the infant's primitive aggression.[13]

A more recent example of intergenerational autobiographical films played out against the background of World War II is Vera Belmont's *Rouge baiser,* publicized as a "remembrance of what it was like to be young, beautiful, rebellious, and Jewish in post-war Paris."[14] Despite its rather crude cinematography and mise-en-scène, this film, whose title plays on the red of communism and the name of a favorite lipstick of the

12. Mészáros quoted in Hoberman, p. 51.

13. Melanie Klein and Joan Rivière, *Love, Hate, and Reparation* (New York: W. W. Norton, 1964). See also Hanna Segal, *Melanie Klein* (New York: Penguin, 1979).

14. J. Hoberman, Review of *Rouge baiser, Village Voice,* 4 Nov. 1986, p. 67.

period, provides a Western European counterpart to Mészáros's Hungarian Communist childhood. The family in *Rouge baiser* is part of the Communist Jewish resistance in France. Dedicated, like *Entre nous,* to the director's mother, *Rouge baiser* is a nostalgic quest for reconciliation of her adolescent self with the youthful lovers who were her true parents. Nadia's belated realization that she was the issue of her mother's love affair with a young revolutionary, Moishe, rather than her mother's marriage to the stern Herschel who raised her, affirms the mother's faith in the love that caused her such suffering and loss and establishes the parallel destinies of mother and daughter. At the center of the young heroine's fantasy is a film clip of Rita Hayworth singing "Put the Blame on Mame," in a celebrated sequence from the 1945 film *Gilda.* This highly erotic, glamorous moment serves as the linchpin for Nadia's desire for sensual fulfillment and power, echoing her mother's earlier passionate attachment to Moishe. As Nadia repeats her mother's story by falling in love with the photographer who rescues her from a violent anti-American demonstration, she too endures the anguish of betrayed love. In a moment of shared intimacy, mother and daughter lie in bed together, and Nadia urges Bronka to speak of her love for Moishe: "I thought his departure the worst thing that could happen to me, but what horrors we have lived through since."[15] Nadia, too, loses her forbidden first lover, a man considerably older than she, at the same age her mother fell in love with and lost Moishe in the cataclysm of war. Together they acknowledge they have each followed the dictates of the heart, convinced that love alone makes change possible.

From Kurys to Duras a recognition that individual autobiography exists within a historicized universe unfolds. And the desire, conscious or otherwise, to make reparation for the pain one has caused one's actual parents or imagined, unnamed others finds its most eloquent—and least conventional—cinematic form in the films of Marguerite Duras. Since her screenwriting debut in 1959 with *Hiroshima mon amour,* directed by Alain Resnais, Duras has been in search of traces of the past, signs along the road to a continuously renewed construction of her own history and that of her time. On the question of the interconnections between fiction and autobiography, Duras has written: "I wanted to tell you that if I were young, if I were 18, if I knew nothing yet of the separation between people and the nearly mathematical certitude of this separation between people, I would do the same thing as I am now doing, I would write the same books, make the same movies. . . . If I had died yesterday I would have died at 18. If I die in ten years I would also have died at

---

15. From screening notes, translation mine.

18."[16] Just as Kurys, Mészáros, and Belmont are haunted to the point of obsession by a certain moment of the past, one that must be visually represented as if to restore equilibrium to the filmmaker, Duras, too, returns to the adolescent self that reappears so insistently in her texts. The filmmaker's own face is both sign and signifier of her destiny, transmuted through word and image:

> Now I see that when I was very young, 18, 15, I already had a face that foretold the one I acquired through drink in middle age. Drink accomplished what God did not. It also served to kill me; to kill. I acquired that drinker's face before I drank. Drink only confirmed it. The space for it existed in me. I knew it the same as other people but, strangely, in advance. Just as the space existed in me for desire. At the age of 15 I had the face of pleasure, and yet I had no knowledge of pleasure. Even my mother must have seen it. My brother did. That was how everything started for me— with that flagrant, exhausted face, those rings around the eyes, in advance of time and experience.[17]

Throughout *The Lover,* such portraits of the self are offered repeatedly, reworked in multiple variants as they are throughout her fiction and films. This longing to see one's life as destiny is further corroborated by the original title Duras had proposed for the book, "La Photographie absolue," which conveys a fantasy of permanence in the face of the transitory, a desire for transcendence in the face of immance, an instant fixed forever from which all else unfolds and to which all returns. The scene of this occurrence in *The Lover* is perhaps equally valid for *Hiroshima mon amour* and the films directed by Duras. Here, however, its setting was to have been the ferry crossing a branch of the Mekong River. The adolescent protagonist is returning on that ferry to boarding school in Saigon, wearing outrageous gold lamé shoes, a transparent silk dress, and a sepia hat, a man's fedora with broad black ribbons:

> I think it was during this journey that the image became detached, removed from all the rest. It might have existed, a photograph might have been taken, just like any other, somewhere else, in other circumstances. But it wasn't. The subject was too slight. Who would have thought of such a thing? The photograph could only have been taken if someone could have known in advance how important it was to be in my life, that event, that crossing of the river. But while it was happening, no one even knew of its

16. Marguerite Duras, "Les Yeux verts" *Cahiers du Cinéma,* 312–13 (June 1980): my translation.

17. Marguerite Duras, *The Lover,* trans. Barbara Bray (New York: Pantheon Books, 1985), p. 8, first published as *L'Amant* (Paris: Minuit, 1984).

existence. Except God. And that's why—it couldn't have been otherwise—that image doesn't exist. It was omitted. Forgotten. It never was
detached or removed from all the rest. And it's to this, this failure to have
been created, that the image owes its virtue: the virtue of representing, of
being the creator of, an absolute.[18]

This obsession with the longing for an absolute, fixed temporally and
visually as a reference point for the future self, is not, as I have noted,
solely the province of one writer or filmmaker, nor does it belong
uniquely to women autobiographers. Taken together with the reparative impulse, it does, however, reappear in each of the cinematic texts I
have examined. In one of Duras's most formalistically experimental
films, *Aurelia Steiner-Melbourne* (1979), the desire for reparation with a
lost love is meshed with the phantasm of holocaust, implicating the
spectator as both voyeur and eavesdropper by means of the director's
sustained use of a woman's speaking voice.[19] An encounter between
word and image (joining to the same incantatory and hypnotic effect
initiated by *Hiroshima mon amour*), *Aurelia Steiner* takes place—if indeed
one can speak of it in such narrative terms—on and around a river, just
as *Hiroshima mon amour* is both linked and divided by the temporal
crossings of the Loire River in France and the Otra Estuaries in Japan,
and *The Lover* is marked by the young girl's passage on the delta ferry.
A woman's voice (Duras's own, in the original French version) reads
letters to her imaginary (or lost) lover, object of her impossible desire,
while the camera records the varying moods of the Seine as a boat makes
its way under vaulted bridges and changing skies. This disembodied
voice speaks from that nameless place where image, voice, text, and
memory converge:

> I write you all the time, always, you see, nothing but that, nothing. Maybe
> I will write you a thousand letters, give you letters . . . about my life now.
> And you will do with them what I expect you to do with them, by that I
> mean exactly as you please. That's the way I want it. That it should be
> meant for you. Where are you? How can I reach you? How can the two of
> us draw ourselves nearer to that love and erase the illusory fragments of
> time that separate us from each other?[20]

In this zone of visual and auditory pleasure and pain, that privileged
terrain which is also the space of autobiography, both subject and read-

18. Ibid., p. 10.

19. Marguerite Duras, *Aurelia Steiner-Melbourne* (1979), 16 mm. Film courtesy of French-
American Cultural Services and Educational Aid, New York City.

20. Ibid., my transcription of film text.

er/spectator may experience what Lacan has called "correct distance," and Winnicott "potential space," the safety of apprehending the desired object without fear either of the suffocation of excessive closeness or the detachment of too wide a separation.[21] To experience pleasure, the viewer of women's autobiographical films must establish in relation to the visual text a locus of receptivity which encourages the integrity of her own identificatory process. Duras enables this dynamic to take place not, as more conventional directors might, by drawing in the viewer through illusionistic cinematic strategies but by offering a primary material that appears formless, aimless, without closure or coherent narrative order. Such technique—for it is highly crafted and conscious—she attributes to a feminine quality of seeing and experiencing: "It is as a woman that I cause things to be seen in this way."[22] What Marie Cardinal has called "the words to say it" are, in Duras's autobiographical representation, owned by the speaking subject whose story is told in her own voice, a voice accorded primacy because the visual can only intensify its meaning, not alter it.[23] "I think there is no hiatus," writes Duras, "no blank between the voice and what she speaks. . . . In a sense, when I am speaking, I am Aurelia Steiner. What I pay attention to is less, not more. It is not to convey the text but rather to be careful not to distance myself from her, from Aurelia, who is speaking. It demands extreme attention, every second, not to lose Aurelia, to stay with her, not to speak in my own name. To respect Aurelia, even if she comes from me."[24]

As I have suggested, the loss of a loved object, through death, disappearance, or separation, confronts the autobiographer with the necessity of mourning. Immortalized in turn by the cinematic apparatus, the "immortal object" is rescued from the finality of total loss, recovered from the oblivion of repression, only to live again for the benefit of others. While the self-exploration of literary autobiography may also serve to restore lost or damaged parts of internal objects by which the writing subject is haunted, more pertinent still in the realm of cinematic

21. Jacques Lacan, *The Four Fundamental Concepts of Psychoanalysis* (New York: Norton, 1978). See also D. W. Winnicott, *Through Paediatrics to Psychoanalysis* (London: International Psychoanalytical Library, 1973), *The Maturational Processes and the Facilitating Environment* (London: International Psychoanalytical Library, 1963), and *Playing and Reality* (London: Tavistock, 1971).

22. Marguerite Duras, "Le Malheur merveilleux: Pourquoi mes films?" *Cahiers du Cinéma*, June 1980, pp. 79–86.

23. Marie Cardinal, *The Words to Say It: An Autobiographical Novel*, trans. Pat Goodheart, preface and afterword by Bruno Bettelheim; originally published in French as *Les Mots pour le dire* (Paris: Grasset et Fasquelle, 1975).

24. Interview with Marguerite Duras on *Apostrophes*, Bernard Pivot, interviewer, Radio-Télévision française, Station 2, translation mine.

autobiography are the entwined themes of loss, mourning, and reparation. And while neither tendency is, properly speaking, strictly gender-
specific—both male and female autobiographers in literature and film
partake of both—it is clear nonetheless that recent films by women
directors gravitate markedly toward the latter. Rather than reveal themselves as a mere refuge, an escape from reality, "the pool of another
Narcissus,"[25] these works embrace history while they locate the filmmaker as a speaking, seeing subject.

In the examples I have examined there are, obviously, a variety of
styles, ideological concerns, and narrative structures. Yet within that
diversity a hierarchy is discernible, which can be read as guiding the
order in which the filmmakers were discussed. For to whatever extent
the reparative wish informs each of the directors' work, in Duras's
hands it is both historically situated and profoundly individual. Her
achievement allows us to summarize the others from a slightly different
angle, formally speaking, by virtue of her minimalist, avant-garde, and
resolutely independent stance toward cinema. By "hierarchy" I mean to
suggest not a competition for most revelatory autobiographical text but
the extent to which an autobiographical endeavor is capable of stimulat-
ing wider reflection, of engaging the viewer's projections in the service
of critical thought. Because Duras embodies the practice of her contemporaries, she stands within an identifiable tradition while taking it beyond familiar boundaries, permitting the viewer a major role as participant in the autobiographical cinematic project. This she accomplishes,
however paradoxical it may appear, by writing and speaking from the
phantasmal place of her own desire, by insisting upon the obsessional
and deceptively simple questions that continue to torment human
beings, despite efforts to gain distance from them: why do we love,
suffer, die? what do we want from the indescribably and eternally lost
object—man, woman, child? how is anything possible without absolute
love, absolute desire? In this sense Duras and Mészáros, Kurys and
Belmont suggest that the greater purpose of cinematic autobiography
may finally be not that of guarantor of the subject's narcissistic equilibrium but rather that of agent provocateur to the very "implied unity"
of subjectivity and subject matter so presciently anticipated by Elizabeth
Bruss.

25. Letter from Henry Miller to Anaïs Nin, in *Henry and June: Journals of Anaïs Nin,* nos. 32–
36, Oct. 1931–Oct. 1932 (New York: Harcourt Brace Jovanovich, 1986), p. 263.

Contributors

Leila Ahmed, Assistant Professor in Women's Studies at the University of Massachusetts, has just completed *A Common Past: Women in Middle Eastern History* while on leave at the Bunting Institute. She is author of *E. W. Lane: A Study of His Life and Works and of British Ideas of the Middle East in the Nineteenth Century* and of many articles on women in the Middle East.

Germaine Brée is Professor Emeritus at Wake Forest University and at the Institute for Research in the Humanities at the University of Wisconsin at Madison. She is currently working on the emergence in French literature of the "imaginaire," a genre having affinity with certain aspects of surrealism. Among her works are *Women Writers in France* (1973); an essay on Leiris for James Olney's collection on autobiography; "Autogynography," which appeared in the *Southern Review* special issue on autobiography; and many articles on French women's writing.

Bella Brodzki is on the faculty at Sarah Lawrence College, where she teaches autobiography, literary theory, and modern fiction. She was the recipient of an NEH Summer Seminar Fellowship, "Autobiography and Fiction." She has published articles on deconstruction and feminist theory and is currently working on a study of the politics of subjectivity.

Helen Carr has taught at the University of London, University of Essex, and Thames Polytechnic. For the last two years she has been coeditor of the British arts and literary magazine *Women's Review*.

351

MARY LOWENTHAL FELSTINER, Professor of History at San Francisco State University, has published articles on the history of women and of Latin America; she is writing a book about Charlotte Salomon.

KATHERINE R. GOODMAN is in the German Department at Brown University. She is interested in motherhood in turn-of-the-century literature and has published papers on "Weibliche Autobiographien" and late nineteenth-century German women's autobiographies. Her book *Dis/Closures: Women's Autobiography in Germany, 1790-1914* has just been published in the Ottendorfer Series of Peter Lang Verlag.

MARY JEAN GREEN is Professor of French at Dartmouth College, where she also teaches Women's Studies. She is author of *Louis Guilloux: An Artisan of Language* (1981) and *Fiction in the Historical Present: French Writers and the Thirties* (1986). She is writing on women's fiction in Quebec and is editor of the journal *Quebec Studies*.

CAROLYN G. HEILBRUN is Avalon Foundation Professor in the Humanities at Columbia University. She is author of *The Garnett Family*, *Christopher Isherwood*, *Toward a Recognition of Androgyny*, and *Reinventing Womanhood*, as well as many articles on women in culture. She is working on a book on women's biographies.

FRANÇOISE LIONNET teaches French and Comparative Literature at Northwestern University. She is the author of *Autobiographical Voices: Race, Gender, Self-Portraiture* (forthcoming from Cornell University Press), written while she was on leave at the Society for the Humanities, Cornell University. She was born in Mauritius.

NELLIE Y. MCKAY teaches at the University of Wisconsin at Madison, and was a Research Fellow last year at the Harvard Divinity School. She has published widely on black women writers.

BIDDY MARTIN is Assistant Professor of German Literature and Women's Studies at Cornell University. Her essays on contemporary German women's literature, feminist theory, and Lou Andreas-Salomé have been published in *Studies in Twentieth-Century Literature, New German Critique,* and several collections of essays. She is completing a book on Lou Andreas-Salomé.

MARY G. MASON teaches at Emmanuel College. She has published articles and reviews on nineteenth-century literature, on women writers, and on feminist pedagogy. She coedited, with Carol Hurd Green, *Jour-*

neys: Autobiographical Writings by Women (G. K. Hall, 1979) and published the only essay on women's autobiography in the James Olney anthology, *Autobiography: Essays Theoretical and Critical* (Princeton, 1980). She is working on a book-length study of women's autobiography.

NANCY K. MILLER is Distinguished Professor of English at Lehman College and the Graduate Center, City University of New York. She is the author of *The Heroine's Text: Readings in the French and English Novel, 1722–1782* and *Subject to Change: Reading Feminist Writing,* and editor of *The Poetics of Gender.*

CATHERINE PORTUGES is Director of the Women's Studies Program at the University of Massachusetts, Amherst, where she teaches film in the Department of Comparative Literature. She has been a Mellon Fellow at the Wellesley Center for Research on Women, has published articles, reviews and interviews on the intersections of psychoanalysis, feminism, and cinema, and is at work on a book on the representations of gender in avant-garde European film.

CLAUDINE RAYNAUD teaches literature at University of Paris at Nanterre and the Collège Picasso. She received her doctorate last year in Women's Studies from the University of Michigan. She has published on Joyce and has given papers on black women writers, the subject of her dissertation.

GAIL TWERSKY REIMER teaches Victorian literature and women's fiction at Wellesley College. She is working on a book on the shape of George Eliot's artistic career.

CELESTE SCHENCK is the Ann Whitney Olin Junior Fellow at Barnard College. She is cofounder of "Women Poets at Barnard," a series of readings and publications featuring the work of new women poets, and coeditor of "Reading Women Writing," a series in feminist criticism published by Cornell University Press. She is author of *Mourning and Panegyric: The Poetics of Pastoral Ceremony* (Pennsylvania State University Press, 1988) and *Corinna Sings: Women Poets and the Politics of Genre* (forthcoming).

DORIS SOMMER has taught courses on the Americas in the Spanish Department at Amherst College. Her book, *One Master for Another: Populism and Patriarchal Rhetoric in Dominican Novels* is in preparation. She has published articles on nationalism and identity in the Americas.

Index

Library of Congress Cataloging-in-Publication Data

Life lines.

   Includes bibliographies and index.
   1. Women's studies—Biographical methods. I. Brodzki, Bella. II. Schenck, Celeste
   Marguerite.
HQ1185.L54   1988   305.4′092′4   88-47718
ISBN 0-8014-2208-6 (alk. paper)
ISBN 0-8014-9520-2 (pbk. : alk. paper)